Chinese Women's Cinema

FILM AND CULTURE

JOHN BELTON, EDITOR

Edited by Lingzhen Wang

Chinese Women's Cinema

TRANSNATIONAL CONTEXTS

COLUMBIA UNIVERSITY PRESS / NEW YORK

Columbia University Press
Publishers Since 1893
New York   Chichester, West Sussex
cup.columbia.edu
Copyright © 2011 Columbia University Press
All rights reserved

Library of Congress Cataloging-in-Publication Data

Chinese women's cinema : transnational contexts /
    edited by Lingzhen Wang.
        p. cm.—(Film and culture)
    Includes bibliographical references and index.
    Includes filmography.
    ISBN 978-0-231-15674-5 (cloth : alk. paper)—
    ISBN 978-0-231-15675-2 (pbk. : alk. paper)—
    ISBN 978-0-231-52744-6 (ebook)
    1. Motion pictures–China–History–20th century. 2. Motion
pictures–Taiwan–History–20th century. 3. Motion
pictures–China–Hong Kong–History–20th century. 4. Women motion
picture producers and directors–China. 5. Feminist films–History
and criticism. 6. Women in motion pictures. I. Wang, Lingzhen.
    PN1993.5.C4C4635 2011
    791.43082–dc22

                                                        2011011872

Columbia University Press books are printed on permanent
    and durable acid-free paper.
This book is printed on paper with recycled content.
Printed in the United States of America

c 10 9 8 7 6 5 4 3 2 1
p 10 9 8 7 6 5 4 3 2 1

References to Internet Web sites (URLs) were accurate at the time of writing.
Neither the author nor Columbia University Press is responsible for URLs
that may have expired or changed since the manuscript was prepared.

Contents

Acknowledgments

THIS VOLUME is made possible by the concerted effort of numerous academic and administrative units at Brown and Nanjing universities. First and foremost, since its establishment in 2008, the Nanjing-Brown Joint Program in Gender Studies and the Humanities* has offered international scholars a rigorous, critical platform for issues related to globalization, higher education, gender, and contemporary China. Much of the Program's research and teaching has focused on gender and Chinese cinema in particular. Together with the Department of Drama and Movie Arts and the National Center for Modern Chinese Literature at Nanjing University, the Nanjing-Brown Joint Program co-organized the first international conference on gender and Chinese cinema in June 2008, providing the springboard for this collection's formation. The School of Liberal Arts in Chinese at Nanjing University generously sponsored the

* The Nanjing-Brown Joint Program in Gender Studies and the Humanities is a major transnational collaboration between the Institute for Advanced Studies in the Humanities and Social Sciences at Nanjing University and three academic units at Brown, namely: the Pembroke Center for Teaching and Research on Women, the East Asian Studies Department, and the Cogut Center for the Humanities.

conference, hosting up to 150 international scholars, filmmakers, and graduate students for the four-day event. Brown University's Office of the Provost also provided an internationalization seed fund for the Program in 2008, paving the way for translations and editing of two critical anthologies on Chinese female filmmakers and gender issues in Chinese cinema, respectively.

In different ways and at different stages, many individuals were integral to the production of this anthology. Special thanks to Director Huang Shuqin from Shanghai Film Studio, Professor Dong Jian of Nanjing University, and Professor Mary Ann Doane at Brown University for their enthusiastic support of research on gender and Chinese cinema and their inspiring keynote speeches at the international conference. I am deeply grateful to Nanjing University Professors Lü Xiaoping, Yang Yishu, Zhang Jianqin, and Li Xingyang as well, for their tireless efforts in managing all logistical details for the event.

Over one-third of the essays in this collection are not from the conference. I also thank these contributors for their quick and enthusiastic responses to my soliciting letters and subsequent commitment to the project. Thomas Moran, Robin Visser, and Chris Tong are much appreciated for their excellent translations of three Chinese essays in the volume.

The critical vision and detailed suggestions of Jennifer Crewe, Associate Director and Editorial Director at Columbia University Press, were indispensable to the final version of this book. In addition, two anonymous readers from Columbia University Press offered most constructive revisions and great encouragement. Finally, I thank my friends, colleagues, and students, who have given invaluable advice and assistance in the process of editing and producing this volume: Christopher Lupke, Thomas Moran, Julia Perkins, Susan Solomon, Melina Packer, and Cui Han.

Chinese Women's Cinema

Introduction

TRANSNATIONAL FEMINIST RECONFIGURATION
OF FILM DISCOURSE AND WOMEN'S CINEMA

LINGZHEN WANG

THIS ANTHOLOGY centers on Chinese women filmmakers from mainland China, Hong Kong, Taiwan, and the Chinese diaspora from the 1920s to 2007. It studies twenty-five women filmmakers, while offering critical comments on many others. The sixteen contributors provide critical insights and interdisciplinary dialogues to this volume, which is the first dedicated to Chinese female filmmakers and their films. Foregrounding Chinese women's complex negotiations with global and local politics, cinematic representation, and issues related to gender and sexuality, the anthology aims to reassess and revise theoretical, political, and academic frameworks for transnational feminist research on women and cinema.

Three issues are the central concerns of this anthology. First, despite their large number and historical significance, few English-language studies have been devoted to Chinese women filmmakers or their films. This is particularly disconcerting considering the rapid development of Chinese film studies and the increased establishment of feminist film studies in Western academia. This volume interrogates the gendered nature of Chinese film studies, its long-term focus on national cinema, and its recent trend in global media. Second, classical feminist film theories have undergone crises since the mid-1980s. The advent of poststructuralism and the theories of semiotics and psychoanalysis have restrained conceptions of female authorship and agency. Furthermore, exclusive reference to Hollywood productions and Western avant-garde cinema rendered classical feminist film theory blind to its complicity in perpetuating racial, heterosexual, and cultural hegemony. This anthology joins recent feminist endeavors within and outside film studies to reevaluate established film theories, remap feminist film discourse, and engage neglected but diverse practices of women filmmakers around the world.

Finally, American studies of "non-Western" women and feminist practice have been relegated to area studies, which is predicated on the framework of the nation-state. The women who are objects of these studies have been marked as the other, isolated from the "center" with a fictive cultural essence.[1] Today's accelerated global circulation of capital, people, commodities, information, and media (including Hollywood films) has led to questions of the suitability of area studies as the site for, and the nation-state as the organizing principle of, studies on transnational gender and cinema. Challenges from different economic and political positions can, however, lead research in different directions and produce radically different meanings. Instead of viewing globalization as a means of erasing existing borders and differences for the sake of a future cosmopolitan utopia, this anthology engages with transnational feminist practice, which views globalization processes as inherently gendered, sexualized, and racialized, as erecting new borders even while erasing old ones,[2] and as continuously generating uneven relationships. Today, feminist film studies must step outside the restrictive framework of the nation-state and critically resituate gender and cinema in a transnational feminist configuration that enables the examination of relationships of power and knowledge among and within cultures and nation-states.

In the following, I first provide a critical overview of the history and limitations of established feminist film theory, particularly in relation to female cinematic authorship and agency. I move next to existing critiques of established feminist film theory and of feminist theory generally, before turning to recent developments in feminist practice to remap feminist film discourse in transnational and interdisciplinary contexts. Finally, I redefine women's cinema and offer a brief history of women's diverse cinematic practices in modern China.

FEMALE AUTHORSHIP AND FEMINIST FILM THEORY

Female cinematic authorship—and its controversial history—occupies a central place in the development of feminist film theory. Judith Mayne states, "Virtually all feminist critics who argue in defense of female authorship as a useful and necessary category assume the political necessity for doing so."[3] This statement indicates that the political significance of female authorship makes it a central concern in feminist film studies and that the study of female authorship requires defending. But against what forces must feminist critics defend female authorship, and what discourses are available for such a battle? Since several important reviews of feminist film theory exist already,[4] I will not provide another detailed study here, but will survey the most critical issues concerning female film authorship in feminist film theory's development.

The concept of the film *auteur* is usually traced to a group of young French critics and film directors who contributed to the magazine *Cahiers* in the 1950s. They sought to elevate film to the status of art, and called for a cinema distinguished by visual artistry that would express the director's individual personality, in contrast to traditional script-based French films adapted from works by established writers.[5] Holding that only geniuses could produce the new art cinema, they adopted the traditional romantic and literary conception of the artist. This contradiction, according to some, led to productive debates that eventually shifted the analysis of auteurism from a critical policy of the 1950s and 1960s to a theory of authorship in the 1970s.[6] During the late 1960s and 1970s, influenced by the structural linguistics of Ferdinand de Saussure and structural anthropology of Claude Lévi-Strauss, the study of film authorship transformed into "auteur-structuralism." The attraction of structuralism for film criticism lay in its "scientificness," which allowed "critics to practice a descriptive mode of analysis that moved them beyond the impressionistic declarations of value that characterized Romantic auteurism."[7] The intervention of semiotics and psychoanalysis in the field of film theory in the 1970s moved this structuralist endeavor in the direction of poststructuralism, calling into question the unity of the author exterior to or prior to the text.

Feminist film theory developed during the 1970s' and 1980s' heyday of structuralism and poststructuralism. Semiotics, which concentrated on the structures, systems, and conventions by which cultural texts signify, helped feminist film theory "shift its focus from the critique of the ideological content of films to the analysis of the mechanisms and devices for the production of meaning in films."[8] It transformed the perception of film as a reflection of reality to an active, systematic reproduction of dominant patriarchal cultural values, especially through its construction of subject positions for viewers' identification. Concerned with the gendered effects of the dominant mode of film production typified by Hollywood, feminist scholars appropriated Lacanian psychoanalysis to account for the internal logic of sexual difference coded in dominant cinema. Structuralism, semiotics, and psychoanalysis helped feminist scholars break with the previous empirical and sociological study of films as realist texts. Furthermore, they led to the critical revelation of film as a coded cinematic reproduction of a phallocentric system representing woman either as nonexistent and nonmale[9] or as the object of the male gaze and desire[10] without desire of her own.[11] But in the process, feminist scholars faced the danger of collapsing overdetermined structures, or structuralist specificities, into a universal, ahistorical homogeneity[12] that overlooked the contradictions and interplay among different structures and subjects and inadvertently reinforced the coded condition of woman as a nonsubject. This is evident in feminist scholars' original theorization of Hollywood cinematic spectatorship as a relation involving one-way identifications with the central male subject positions,[13] leaving little space for resistance and difference, and none for female subjects.

4

Feminist film theory of the 1970s and 1980s became especially vulnerable when coming to terms with female authorship, historical agency, and socially embedded subjectivity. Psychoanalysis, although providing a way to discuss sexual difference, bases its system on male desire and subjectivity, allowing little room for assessing female desire, sexuality, and subjectivity in the symbolic and cinematic narrative structure. As some feminist critics have argued, sexual difference in psychoanalysis is fundamentally a pseudodifference, because it centers exclusively on the male and reduces the female to its symmetrical other.[14] French feminists have responded with the concept of radical feminine difference, which, according to Lacan, can be perceived only as something already repressed and thus unrepresentable in the symbolic order. Though it might erupt or disturb the order, the feminine never positively appears in the symbolic and linguistic order.

The more significant challenge to the study of female authorship in any field came from poststructuralist theory and practice. The 1970s antihumanist structuralist and poststructuralist claim of the death of the author in literary and cultural studies has paradigmatically reconfigured the critical focus from "the concept of artist as a self-expressive personality to the concept of subject positions within the text"[15] occupied mostly by readers. Poststructuralism invalidated any consideration of authorial intent or of the external author's relation to the text's production of meaning. Despite the need to foreground women's and other minorities' cultural practices as well as their agencies and voices, feminist scholars have encountered difficulty bridging the gap between the author outside the text together with specific social, cultural, and political positions and experiences in history, and the author within the text, who can only be traced or re-imagined through circumvented means, like recurring styles, images, and other textual evidence. In addition, antiessentialism has questioned the stability of individual identity and the uniqueness of female representation,[16] further dissolving the significance of the woman author's relation to the text.

Since the 1970s, feminist scholar filmmakers and critics have attempted to address the political issue concerning feminist cinema and women's historical and social agency. For Laura Mulvey, a feminist film should promote experimental and avant-garde film practice to imagine radical alternatives and shun classic Hollywood narrative technique, which centers exclusively on male voyeuristic and fetishist desire and pleasure. While the iconoclastic style and film language of avant-garde cinema departed from that of traditional commercially oriented films, it introduced new problematic implications for the feminist political agenda. For instance, avant-garde cinema had been practiced mainly by male elites for a small, exclusive audience. Its individualistic style and association with high culture drew on the model of authorship associated with male-centered arts.[17] Additionally, as some feminist critics point out, given "the institutionalized ways in which cinema functions, and how individuals are acculturated to respond to it, it is difficult to know to what extent a truly alternative cinematic practice is possible."[18]

Feminist critics since the late 1980s have attempted to retheorize cinematic female authorship within the general frame of semiotics, psychoanalysis, and poststructuralism. Most significantly, they have reconceived cinema as a discourse and not a fixed structure, reformulated female desire within the symbolic order, and regarded Hollywood cinema as diverse rather than monolithic. According to John Caughie, the introduction of semiotics to the analysis of film generally took two forms. The first, typified by Christian Melz's early work and found largely in English-language scholarship, centers on the structure, form, and codes of narrative. The second, influenced by Emile Benveniste's work and concerned with signifying practice and film as discourse,[19] addresses the problem with the formalism of the first approach by reconceptualizing film "not simply as a statement (something already formulated, 'given'), but also as an enunciating practice, an 'utterance' (something in process at the moment of projection)."[20] This analysis privileges the enunciating subject who speaks or provides visual representation from her or his particular perspective. Feminist psychoanalysis also shifted its focus from the critique of the patriarchal apparatus in dominant cinema and the question of spectatorship to the exploration of female desire, fantasy, expression, and authorship.[21]

Kaja Silverman's *The Acoustic Mirror: The Female Voice in Psychoanalysis and Cinema* combines the reformulation of female desire and identification in psychoanalysis with the discursive turn in film studies described above.[22] Returning to Freud, she stresses maternal loss as the original loss for boys and girls and reconfigures female desire and identification through the concept of the negative Oedipus complex (a girl desires and identifies with the mother). Silverman concentrates not on the male gaze and visual image but on female and maternal voice in her critique of male dominance in classic Hollywood cinema, bringing issues of subjectivity to the discussion of female authorship. In discussing the female authorial voice, she extends her attention from the constructed subject and the spectator "to consider the ways in which the Benvenistian model might help us to rethink authorship, as well."[23] Her reformulation of authorship relies on the idea of an enunciating subject and of film as an enunciation process. But situating her project in poststructuralism, especially in linguistically based semiotics and psychoanalysis, Silverman must argue that the author is constructed in and through discourse and can only be inferred, traced, or imagined through textual and libidinal enunciations and inscriptions in the text: "an author 'outside' the text who would come into existence as a dreaming, desiring, self-affirming subject *only* through the inscription of an author 'inside' the text"[24] (my emphasis). Accordingly, authorial inscription assumes several textual forms: through voice-over and points of view, namely through the subject of speech in the film, through formal expression of the more general "libidinal coherence" or desire circulating in a single author's films, through "second identification" with a fictional character that stands for the film's director, or through a "nodal point"—a sound, image, or scene to which the film or films repeatedly return.[25] Her re-theorization of female desire, identification, and unconscious fantasy in the pre-Oedipal realm helps her launch, to a certain extent, (one type of) sexual difference into the discussion of enunciating subjects and authorial inscription at the textual and formal level; it furthermore aids in projecting a bridge that gestures toward the extratextual gendered speaking subject.

Silverman's work has advanced theories of female authorship within feminist film theory. But her achievement has also revealed the historical incapacity of semiotic and psychoanalytic theory to address women as historical, social, and cultural subjects outside or in relation to the text. Although Silverman demonstrates her awareness of the political signifi-cance of the biographical author when she states: "the libidinal mascu-linity or femininity [in the text] must be read in relation to the biological gender of the biographical author, since it is clearly not the same thing, socially or politically, for a woman to speak with a female voice as it is for a man to do so, and vice versa,"[26] the model she provides for "conceptual-izing the relation between the author 'inside' the text and . . . the author 'outside' the text"[27] is, as some critics have pointed out, based on a vague assertion.[28] Though she attends to the authorial inscription and enuncia-tions within the libidinal economy of the film text, it remains unclear to what extent "the fact of female authorship gives a particular or distinct inflection to the representation of female desire."[29]

In "Female Authorship Reconsidered," Judith Mayne is preoccupied by precisely these questions of female authorship and the representation of female desire. She continues the work Claire Johnston began in her study of the director Dorothy Arzner, who made eighteen films in the Hollywood studio system during the late 1920s, 1930s, and 1940s. One of the first feminist critics to shift the sociological and realistic focus in feminist film criticism to structuralist (semiotics and psychoanalysis) and ideological (ideology defined as the system of representation via Louis Althusser) film studies,[30] Johnston has left a controversial legacy over the concept of female political agency in film production. She rejects the concepts of artistic creativity and authorial intent by embracing the structuralist approach to auteurism, which took an individual director's preoccupations (generated by her or his psychoanalytic history) in the text to decode the unconscious structure of the film and its unintended meanings.[31] At the same time, however, as a feminist and Marxist critic, she promotes the development of political and subversive strategies in female filmmaking. The contradiction—between textual and unconscious structure and political agency—embodied in Johnston's position is both

7

emblematic and symptomatic of feminist film theory. She reasons that disruptions, dislocations, and demystifications of patriarchal ideology at the textual level were the only forms of subversion women's cinema of the early 1970s could take: "New meanings have to be created by disrupting the fabric of the male bourgeois cinema within the text of the film."[32] A genuinely revolutionary conception of counter-cinema for women's struggle, she held, was not realizable under the then-historical conditions, but a future practice.[33] Yet Johnston does not say how women's disruptive cinema could develop into women's counter-cinema. This unresolved methodological tension led decades later to renewed discussions of women's historical roles in filmmaking.

Several of Johnston's early arguments helped advance feminist film theory during the late 1980s and 1990s. Questioning several stances of early 1970s feminist film criticism, she insisted on the usefulness of the theory of auteurism (albeit with a structuralist bent), and pointed out that European avant-garde cinema was prone to reproducing patriarchal myth[34] and that women's cinema should combine politics with entertainment.[35] Her studies of Arzner illustrate how while patriarchal discourse dominated Hollywood cinema, it contained complex internal heterogeneity through which other discourses could appear.[36] "The discourse of the woman," according to Johnston, "is the principal structuring element which rewrites the dominant discourse of the film together with the patriarchal ideology into which it locks."[37]

Mayne attempts to readdress issues raised by Johnston and other feminist film scholars. Most importantly, she develops Johnston's work on the existence of female discourse in Hollywood cinema and advances the discussion of the author outside the cinematic text. Johnston defines woman's discourse as a disruption and dislocation of male discourse from within; Mayne tries to turn deconstructive and negative strategies into constructive and positive policies. Drawing on Donna Haraway's understanding that "irony is about contradictions that do not resolve into larger wholes, even dialectically, about the tension of holding incompatible things together because both or all are necessary and true,"[38] Mayne argues that woman's discourse in Arzner's *Dance, Girl, Dance* (1940) (female friendship and community) and the dominant discourse (heterosexual romance) should be understood as two compelling and incompatible truths that coexist with equal visibility in the cinematic text.[39] In other words, female discourse is not merely a disruption that is subsequently absorbed into the dominant narrative, but helps construct a different relationship or self-representation that coexists and competes with the dominant discourse.

Furthermore, Mayne has linked the persona of Arzner the director, especially her public identity as a lesbian, to more radical readings of her films. She notes that despite the attention given to Arzner's work, "one striking aspect of her persona . . . has been largely ignored." While photos accompanying feminist research on Arzner imply a lesbian identity, virtually none of the critics who analyze Arzner's work have discussed it. Mayne reveals how the relationship between women's historical social and sexual roles and the films they produce is marginalized within feminist film discourse: "discussions of her work always stop short of any recognition that sexual identity might have something to do with how her films function, particularly concerning the 'discourse of the woman' and female communities, or that the contours of female authorship in her films might be defined in lesbian terms."[40] She illustrates, in contrast, how Arzner's sexual identity sheds light on the secondary female figures in Arzner's films, "who do not evaporate into the margins,"[41] because they are mirror reflections of Arzner herself.[42] The components of self-reflection and female community so central to female authorship in Arzner's work are not identical, according to Mayne, yet the lesbian gesture, so incompatible with the heterosexual assumptions of psychoanalytic language, uncovers a desire for *another* representation of desire.[43]

To be sure, Mayne's article does not draw any historical connections between Rainer's biography and her films. Rather, she uses Arzner's photos as an artistic *text* to render her critical intervention of female authorship at the *intertextual* level. Though Mayne claims that challenging the implicit homophobia in feminist film theory would be reason enough to read the marks of lesbian authorship in Arzner's work, she eschews discussion of Arzner's life and biography to avoid charges of essentialism from the poststructuralist position. The title of Catherine Grant's article, "Secret Agents,"[44] captures the complex situation of female film authorship theorized over the last thirty years. Despite recognition of the political necessity of engaging women's social and historical roles in studies of women's cinema, and despite the implicit yet persistent arguments made by feminist film critics that films directed by (some) women directors contain—however limited—the power to disrupt, subvert, and reshape, it has proven difficult to break from the "pure" poststructuralist and psychoanalytic stance to a more productive framework embracing textual-contextual and representational-historical interactions.

9

The seemingly antiessentialist feminist film theory on authorship has locked itself into an essentialist and antihistorical logic. First, its very restraint from discussing the author or director in its analysis of her/his text presumes the author's essential existence. If authorship is understood, via Michel Foucault, as a historical and institutional function,[45] and if the identity of the individual author is regarded as socially, economically, and culturally formed, the author and the text should be understood as interconnected. Put differently, unless the author is understood as an essential entity completely outside discourse, she/he should not be barred from the discussion of her/his text. Situated historically, Roland Barthes's proclamation of the death of the author does not renounce all connections between the author and the text; instead it pronounces the end of the patriarchal, individualist, and Western definition of authorship dominant at the time.[46]

Second, confined within textual structure and psychoanalysis, feminist film theory adopts a textual essentialism and a universal model of sexual difference. Though Mayne's intertextual strategy has brought her research closer to Arzner, it has nevertheless flattened and fixed the historical subject into mere performative images. These images may strongly suggest an alternative sexual desire and identity, but they are deprived of specific historical and social significations. What did it mean to be a lesbian in 1930s' and 1940s' Hollywood? What do these images suggest about lesbian status in the United States at the time? Did Arzner express opinions about being a lesbian and a woman director? Ironically and unexpectedly, Mayne's antiessentialist stance reinforces a textual essentialism that reduces complex social, historical, and sexual issues to imagery texts and that assumes a universal and ahistorical truth or essence about lesbian desire and identity. Bracketing the female author together with her social and historical background when discussing her cinematic text could, therefore, lead to a universal essentialism deprived of specific socioeconomic and historical experiences of women in the world.

These problems have been addressed but also perpetuated more recently by Geetha Ramanathan. Turning to feminist discourse to break down the wall between text and context in previous discussions of women's cinema,[47] she argues, "[f]eminist auteurship entails the impression of feminist authority, not necessarily that of the auteur herself, on screen. What is at stake here is the films' larger acknowledgement of an informing discourse that is ideological in both form and content."[48] The author might be the facilitator, but not a key element in constituting feminist

authority. Ramanathan focuses instead on aesthetic formats or representation strategies in women's films that contest or refuse the dominant
patriarchal mode of representation and that enhance the conditions of
representability for women. In other words, if a *contextually recognized*
feminist discourse (counter-hegemonic and patriarchal ways of representation) is clearly conveyed in *the diegesis of a film text*, the film is impressed
with a feminist authority;[49] but this authority does not necessarily origi-
nate with female authors/directors—it is, in her words, "not necessarily or exclusively their own."[50] Whereas she claims, "I do want to hold
out for an articulated existence of women outside the discursive frame
of representation, and would maintain that unrecorded experience does
not necessarily mean absence,"[51] her focus on visual strategies and narrative aesthetics in her discussion of feminist authorship nonetheless elides
women's diverse experiences and their roles as participating historical
subjects.

11

TRANSNATIONAL FEMINISM AND THE REMAPPING
OF FEMINIST FILM DISCOURSE

Since its inception, feminist film theory has received criticism on a number of counts. In a 1976 essay,[52] E. Ann Kaplan points out that the abstraction and esotericism of Claire Johnston and Pam Cook's mode of
feminism are "at odds with the early notion that women's studies should
be accessible to a broad spectrum of women."[53] This early feminist theory
often reduced all women to a single position in a monolithic, patriarchal
system, a tendency that "leaves no room for discussing and clarifying
specific class differences among women." Kaplan shows that, because semiotic and structuralist theories are "applied to any work without specific
reference to time, place or historical period,"[54] they are limited by their
ahistorical, universalized, and implicitly elitist nature.

Lesbian and queer scholars have argued that because of its psychoanalytic foundation early feminist film theory fails to address homosexual desire and pleasure without reference to binary heterosexuality.[55]
Scholars of race and ethnicity fault textual and spectator theories based
on the psychoanalytic concept of sexual difference for being "unequipped
to deal with a film which is about racial difference and sexuality,"[56] and
actively "suppress[ing] recognition of race."[57] Alternatively, as Jane Gaines
suggests, "history seems to be the key to understanding black female

sexuality."[58] Theories of women's sexuality universalized from a particular experience of white women have dismissed and failed to conceive of differently configured female sexuality in, for example, the history of black slavery. The sexual violence, repression, and displacement in black history have a stronger formative force than the Oedipal myth.

In the 1980s and 1990s, new interdisciplinary modes of criticism began addressing the hierarchy, hegemony, and exclusivity regarding class, race, and sexuality implicit in feminist theories and practices based on the experiences of Western, white, middle-class, heterosexual women. In 1989, the term "intersectionality" was coined by the legal scholar Kimberlé Crenshaw to underscore the multidimensionality of marginalized groups' lived experiences and to denote how race and gender interact to shape the dimensions of black women's employment experience.[59] By ignoring women's experiences unaccounted for by categories of race or gender discrimination, feminist and antiracist discourses failed to address the intersections of racism and patriarchy. The result, Crenshaw writes, is "that the resistance strategies of feminism will often replicate and reinforce the subordination of people of color."[60] According to intersectional feminism, cultural patterns of oppression are influenced and bound together by intersecting systems of society, especially race, gender, class, and ethnicity.[61] Although racism and sexism intersect in the lives of people, they seldom do in feminist and antiracist practices: "The problem with identity politics is not that it fails to transcend difference, as some critics [liberal feminists] charge, but rather the opposite—that it frequently conflates or ignores intra group differences."[62]

Having also emerged in the late 1980s, third-world (women of color) feminism likewise critiqued the middle-class and white hegemony in feminism's conceptualization and homogenization of women's experience. Together with postcolonial theory, it has shed light on globalized histories of gender and power and revealed the role Western imperialism plays in the productions of knowledge and identity in the colonial and postcolonial world.[63] If intersectionality theory has helped transform feminist discourse from a universal, single-axis framework to a dynamic, interconnected multiaxis movement within the United States, third-world feminism has emphasized cultural specificity and historical differences in feminist research in a global context and repositioned the center of feminist discourse beyond the Western-oriented paradigm.

Transnational feminism's political and intellectual roots grew out of a confluence of critical discourses and activities like intersectionality theory, third-world feminism, postmodernist discourse, and postcolonial studies in the early 1990s, but at the same time it critically revised these positions, committing itself to the critique of modernity, capitalism, different forms of patriarchy, and Western imperialism. Whereas conventional postmodernism celebrates hybridity and cultural difference as something cosmopolitan, Western, and an apolitical matter of style, and popular neoliberalism endorses the development of so-called global civil society, transnational feminist practice, like postcolonialism, endeavors to uncover the unequal and political power relationships among different subjects and spaces. It pays attention to imperial processes in colonial and neo-colonial societies, and examines the strategies to subvert the material and discursive effects of those processes. According to Inderpal Grewal and Caren Kaplan, patriarchal hegemonies take many forms with different geopolitical centers and exist in a scattered, sometimes overlapping manner. Transnational feminist practice intends to "articulate the relationship of gender to scattered hegemonies such as global economic structures, patriarchal nationalisms, 'authentic' forms of tradition, religious fundamentalism, local structures of domination, and legal-juridical oppression on multiple levels."[64]

It differentiates itself from earlier "international" and "global" feminism or sisterhood based on existing configurations of nation-states as discrete and sovereign entities. Though international feminism dates from the late nineteenth century, most of its international organizations and endeavors have centered on Western European and North American nations. Global feminism, on the other hand, has upheld a universalized Western model of women's liberation celebrating individuality and modernity. Eliding the diversity of women's agency in world history, it perpetuates Western cultural imperialism. The discourses of "international" and "global" feminism therefore "rely on political and economic as well as cultural concepts of discrete nations who can be placed into comparative or relational status, always maintaining the West as the center."[65]

As a consequence, choosing the term "transnational" over "international," according to Grewal and Kaplan, reflects the need to "destabilize rather than maintain boundaries of nation, race, and gender."[66] Yet transnational feminism also considers the historical formation and effect of those boundaries, which have produced specific, diverse, and unequal relationships among different regions and groups of people. "Through such critical recognition, the links between patriarchies, colonialisms, racisms, and other forms of domination become more apparent and

13

available for critique or appropriation."[67] This way of thinking about scattered hegemonies and the "shared or common context of struggle due to common exploration and domination across the north-south divide," Chandra Talpade Mohanty argues, forms "political links" and thus "a political rather than biological or cultural base for alliance" and solidarity.[68]

As a historically situated practice, transnational feminism has limitations:[69] its indebtedness to postcolonial, postmodernist, intersectional, and third-world feminist discourses situated in Western academia reveals its privileged geopolitical position and accounts for its neglect of economic issues and of still other parts of the world, such as socialist and postsocialist nations and areas. But no critical and political discourse is free of historical conditions. While fully aware of its historical position as having originated from the U.S., transnational feminist practice targets transnational issues as its subject and commits itself to critiquing Western imperialism and modernity. Since "[T]here IS NO SUCH THING as a feminism free of asymmetrical power relations," transnational feminist practice "involves forms of alliance, subversion, and complicity within which asymmetries and inequalities can be critiqued."[70]

The most significant contribution of transnational feminism is its remapping of feminist practice in a politically reassessed global and globalized context without losing sight of the importance of specific feminist practice at any given time and place. It offers the most effective approach to interdisciplinary studies of women and representation in diverse parts of the world. In other words, transnational feminism helps to chart both the linked historical analogies and the different perspectives of disempowered and marginalized groups. Though transnational feminist practice arose in the early 1990s as a specific response to globalization and the expanding transnational flow of capital, technology, and people, its critical findings and insights nonetheless have direct relevance to the study of gender in the entire modern period. Globalization "is not a new development; it must be seen as part of the much longer history of colonialism in which Europe attempted to submit the world to a single 'universal' regime of truth and global institutional power."[71] The significance of transnational feminism for film and media studies continues to grow,[72] because it offers the possibility of addressing issues related to women and cinema in the world at multiple and diverse levels.

First, transnational feminism helps resituate established feminist film theory in the global and neocolonial context, by not just revealing the universal and ahistorical model assumed in Western feminist film theory, but by also linking the model to colonial and neocolonial histories that facilitated and disseminated that theory. Even in the current era of globalization, when the European unitary subject has indeed become scattered by the effects of mobile capital and multiple competing subjectivities, transnational feminism cautions that "the historical thread or inertia of First World domination remains a powerful presence."[73] The geopolitical recontextualization of established feminist film theory helps to trace the asymmetrical power relationship in the production and circulation of discourse and knowledge in a global context and to better reassess the complex roles Western feminist film theory has played in different parts of the world. Instead of dismissing universalized Western feminist theory as irrelevant to studies of women and representation in other parts of the world, transnational feminist practice directs attention to the diverse historical effects produced by the colonial and neocolonial transmissions of power and knowledge. It is, therefore, critical to both discover the uneven power relationship that sets in motion Western feminist discourse across different parts of the world and examine the specific historical significations Western feminist film theory has made in a particular local setting.

15

In Chinese context, feminist discourse was originally bound together with Western imperialism and then took different routes and transformations. After China's defeat in its war against Western imperialist countries toward the end of the nineteenth century, Western feminist discourse began appearing in China together with discourses of the modern nation-state, modernity, and Marxism. Socialist state feminism was influenced by Marxism and class revolution. In mainland China, except for socialist state feminism, which was for a period part of the political system, the effects of other Western feminisms (anarchical, liberal, or psychoanalytic) were confined to an elite Westernized circle. On the other hand, Western feminisms have been received differently depending on context and have very often been appropriated for varied local agendas. Liberal and psychoanalytic feminisms, for example, were completely rejected in socialist China as individualistic and bourgeois practices. But in the postsocialist 1980s, they were adopted piecemeal by Chinese cultural critics to address gender issues in presocialist modern China.[74] The applications of Western feminist film theory and criticism to 1980s and 1990s film production have encountered different receptions in mainland China, Hong Kong, and Taiwan, due to their different geopolitical locations and historical demands. In this volume Yu-Shan

Huang and Chun-Chi Wang illustrate how Western feminist film practice and criticism played a significant role in the development of Taiwan women's cinema in a film industry still dominated by men in the early 1990s. But in postsocialist, mainland China, after over thirty years of state-socialist feminism, Western cinefeminism has never played a major role in the development of women's cinema. Scholars like Louisa Wei, well-versed in Western feminist film theory, have sought out films by Chinese women directors to validate points made by Western feminist film critics (the gesture itself is indicative of both the uneven power relationship between Chinese women's cinematic practice and Western feminist film theory and of a reflection on the relationship), but have come to an unexpected conclusion. In her chapter in this volume, Wei reveals that the theoretical frameworks of psychoanalysis, Marxism, and other feminist film theories are not readily applicable to the Chinese context of the 1980s and 1990s, although some specific concepts are useful for textual analysis. In her chapter on Mabel Cheung Yuen-Ting, Staci Ford discusses the mixed features of Hong Kong–style feminism (among middle-class women). She argues that traditional Chinese gender culture and Western neoliberal values as well as Western third-wave feminism have contributed most to the formation of Hong Kong–style feminism, which seeks harmony rather than confrontation with men or patriarchal gender roles. Ford compares this feminism with second- and third-wave feminism in the United States, and advocates cross-Pacific conversations on women and cultural values. Transnational feminism calls our attention to global but uneven and dissimilar circuits of culture and capital, and also allows us to zoom in on a specific temporospatial and geopolitical frame to examine effects produced by interactions among multiple and diverse historical forces.

Second, transnational feminism helps explore the historical effects of the modern nation-state and nationalism, which first-world feminism usually dismisses.[75] Transnational feminism recognizes the importance of nationalism in the rise of women's movements and feminism in third-world countries and has helped bring "nation" as an important category, together with race and sexuality, into its counter-Western-universal research on feminism and women. Third-world women first articulated their critical voices through anticolonialism and nationalism, a departure from Western women's rights-oriented movements. But transnational feminism does not homogenize third-world nationalist or feminist practices. It reveals diverse and contradictory situations in third-world countries and questions the (hetero)masculine patriarchy that emerged with modern nationalism and collaborated with patriarchal forces in local regions. Transnational feminism refuses to romanticize transnational globalism as a form of neutral universalism or third-world nationalism as a final means of salvation. Transnational feminism addresses the Eurocentric assumptions of Western feminism as well as various patriarchal cultures of nationalist movements in history. Furthermore, it interrogates women's internalization of nationalism in their transnational encounters. Although first-world women and feminism have seemed to transcend nationalist concerns, they are in fact tied to the projection of their national power. While women's movements in the third world have exhibited an explicit relationship to anticolonial nationalism, Western women, according to some transnational feminists, are invisibly complicit with their national power.[76] This explains why, for instance, many working class women in labor struggles in Britain still supported British colonialism.[77] Contrary to the belief that feminism exists in an antagonistic relation to nationalism, transnational feminism reveals how feminism and nationalism often constitute and depend on each other[78] with both positive and negative effects.

17

This perspective on nationalism and feminism provides an effective and flexible approach to the complicated, historically specific situations regarding women and nationalism in different parts of the world. Discussing women's cinema in socialist China, for example, requires examining the role of socialist nation-states and socialist feminism. Neither the Western feminist view of dominant cinema as phallocentric and repressive, which leaves no space for female subjectivity, nor its call for a counter-cinema in commercial society has much relevance to socialist China. In my chapter on socialist female director Dong Kena, I demonstrate a historically nuanced relationship between the socialist nation-state, its feminist policy, and the Chinese women who participated in socialist national formations. After taking power in mainland China in 1949, the socialist state empowered women by promoting and institutionalizing their political, social, and economic roles; nevertheless, it demanded women's self-sacrifice and identification with an implicitly masculine model. Most Chinese women, like Dong Kena, embraced socialist views and ideals, but their involvement in socialist filmmaking also exposed discrepancies in socialist gender ideology, articulated an implicit critique of its masculine nature, and enunciated a displaced and alternative vision of life and the female self. The relationship between women

and the Chinese socialist nation is neither purely conformist nor oppositional. Ching Yau, on the other hand, reveals how in the 1970s Hong Kong
director Tang Shu Shuen was caught in a set of contradictory discourses
of orientalism, colonialism, and nationalism. Westerners criticized Tang's
award-winning film *Dong furen* (The Arch, 1969) as lacking authentic and
original Chinese-ness, while the local press, following Hong Kong's colonial policy to import Anglo-American culture and to delegitimize residual
Chinese culture, celebrated Tang's supposed Western image. Meanwhile,
local, cultural-nationalist discourse split between expecting Tang's film to
be "Westernized" enough to gain recognition for Chinese cinema abroad
and blaming it for selling out to Westerners. Contemporary public receptions of Tang's film dismissed both her representation of female subjectivity and her resistance to colonialism and nationalism. The question
regarding the modern nation and nationalism therefore demands critical
engagement in the study of gender and cinema.

    Third, transnational feminism can provide a political perspective for
the study of transnational cinema. In film studies, the concept of transnational cinema has emerged in response to increasing economic and
media globalization and the acceleration of technological development.
As a relatively new conceptual category, transnational cinema is mobilized to address the significance of transnational financing, production,
distribution, and reception of films, to express the need to go beyond the
limitations of national cinema, to draw attention to films made by filmmakers living in cosmopolitan centers or in the diaspora, and to denote
a transnational and hybrid cinematic aesthetics and emotional identification. Some scholars of transnational media have projected an apolitical
and utopian vision of transnationalism by arguing that it unfolds as an
essentially self-motivated, and apparently amoral, cultural force[79] and that
the real world is no longer defined by its colonial past (or its neocolonial
present), but by its technological future, in which people will gain greater
access to the means of global representation.[80] Transnational feminism,
on the other hand, argues the opposite by directing our attention to dis-
proportioned movements across borders, and by exposing the underbelly
of "the global village": racism, illegal border crossing, forced economic
migration, political exile, and xenophobia.[81] Transnational flows of capital
and people, according to transnational feminism, are not neutral. Not
all crossings are equal, and the flows of capital run upstream as well as
down. As some critics of films on transnational migration have pointed
out, "when privileged first worlders venture abroad," for example, "border

crossing is a matter of 'cosmopolitan' choice; and their trauma can be alleviated by the international apparatus of embassies and rescue helicopters. When the third worlders cross borders. . . , however, there is no aid, only the risk of severe punishment."[82] Staci Ford echoes this view in her contribution to this volume: "When Americans come to Hong Kong many experience a status increase while for the Hong Kong person who has grown up with a relative amount of privilege, a move to the United States is often accompanied by—at least initially—some status decline." In addition to the uneven relationships between nation-states or regions, gender, race, and religion also contribute to the dramatically different effects of border crossings.

Many chapters in this volume discuss transnational and transregional migration and issues related to the diaspora. Especially foregrounding the transnational feature are essays on Hong Kong cinema, since, as a British colony and world commercial center before 1997, Hong Kong served as both a destination for migrants from around the world, including mainland China, and as a port for Chinese migration to the West. Consequently, the content and form of its cinema has long exhibited transnational characteristics. As some critics have argued, the notion of transnational cinema should not act as a mere corollary of contemporary globalization; transnational cinematic productions of earlier periods can be conceptualized within the schema.[83] Given the history of colonization and globalization and the transnational nature of cinema, the concept of transnational cinema can offer a critically revisionist perspective to the study of world film history. Colonization not only gave rise to regional nationalism, but also produced different forms of diaspora due to transnational flows of capital, people, knowledge, and technology. As the chapters on Hong Kong cinema in this volume illustrate, the processes of colonization and globalization, nationalism, the existence of diaspora, and individual senses of self are mutually implicated. Kar Law researches in his chapter the life and career of Esther Eng, Hong Kong's first female director and the first Chinese American director in Hollywood, who made more than ten films in her lifetime, during which she moved back and forth between the United States and Hong Kong. Whereas Ching Yau reveals a feminist message that is critical of both nationalism and colonialism in her reading of Tang Shu Shuen's *The Arch*, Kar Law details how Esther Eng's patriotism, as a second-generation Chinese American growing up in San Francisco, was key to jumpstarting her filmmaking career during the outbreak of the Sino-Japanese war in the early 1930s,

19

and how her early films featuring patriotic Chinese heroes and heroines (with a certain commercial formula) helped establish her in Hong Kong. Tang and Eng embodied and articulated different concerns over nationalism, imperialism/colonialism, and the diaspora in their cinematic practice, but their experience as Chinese women straddling different national and cultural identities assigned both to the margins of film history. In the United States, Eng's racial profile as a Chinese American accounts for her exclusion from Hollywood film history; in Hong Kong, Eng's and Tang's gender and hybrid identities (Tang's ambivalent Chinese-ness and Eng's Chinese American status), as Yau and Law have argued, contributed to their erasure from the history of Hong Kong film. The collaboration of regional patriarchal culture and colonialism or racism is evident in their obliterating Tang and Eng from "His-(s)tory."

In the 1980s and 1990s, due to anxieties about Hong Kong's return to the PRC in 1997, Hong Kong migration to Canada and the United States surged; likewise as open-door economic reform continued in mainland China, migration to Western countries increased. Mable Cheung Yuen-Ting and Clara Law, prominent Hong Kong women directors who studied filmmaking in the United States, both rose to fame with early films on Chinese migration to the U.S. and its relation to gender, cultural identity, and politics. Their careers diverged in the late 1990s when Law chose to migrate to Australia, and Cheung chose to stay in Hong Kong. Staci Ford's study of Cheung in this collection situates her films in a broad transnational and cultural framework and reveals diverse national and transnational influences on her filmmaking. Attending to the asymmetrical situations involved in migrations, Ford also relates Cheung's films to discourses related to nationalism, feminism, and the history of the diaspora. The Chinese-ness Cheung explores, according to Ford, is not only tied to an implicit pan-Chinese cultural solidarity, but is linked more crucially to the political uncertainties of contemporary Hong Kong, the economic development of mainland China, the universalized American dream, as well as American racism and Western hegemonic standards of lifestyle and beauty. Shiao-ying Shen, in her chapter on Clara Law, on the other hand, zooms in on Law's individual and emotional migration to Australia by reading her Australia films as metaphorically autobiographical. Shen locates Law's films squarely in the realm of the diaspora and compares them with migration films by other Australian filmmakers. Turning inward and concentrating on the psychic space of diaspora, Shen's chapter explores emotional and identity issues concerning modern-day, transnational migration, issues once again tied to class, race, gender, and culture. As an independent woman (economically, professionally, and politically), Law's struggle and transformation in the process of her migration appears, Shen seems to suggest, to be culturally oriented. She uses films to express melancholy and loss; and most recently, to enact a new sense of home(lessness) and identity in the diaspora.

Last but not least, transnational feminist practice challenges the existing disciplinary boundaries and trends in fields like gender studies or area studies. Gender studies considers Western feminist theory and studies of Western women to be normative; whereas feminism and studies of women outside of "Western" spaces are often "demoted" to area studies. "There the experts of the day, it is assumed, will tell us about the plight of women; each outlandish geographical zone will be matched with an abused bodily part."[84] In her discussion of the structure of American academia, Ella Shohat has shown that institutional hierarchies have long existed, and women's studies programs have reproduced these hierarchies through a division "whereby required courses focus on 'pure' issues of gender and sexuality, while optional courses focus on women of color and Third World women as 'special topics.' Within this approach, Third World women are seen as if living on another planet, in another time."[85] Shohat has cautioned us against this cultural essentialism, which implicitly relegates women from other parts of the world to fundamentally different and thus inferior or victimized positions.[86]

Despite changes and the emergence of different perspectives in the domain of area studies (such as Chinese studies), residual cold-war mentalities, traditional sinology, nation-state-oriented research, and recent cosmopolitan approaches have joined hands to marginalize, whether explicitly or implicitly, the role of women's studies and feminist research. The glaring absence of scholarly interest in women's work can surely be found in the study of Chinese cinema as well. Scholarship on Taiwan cinema, for example, has conspicuously excluded women filmmakers. Zhen Zhang demonstrates in her chapter how despite Sylvia Chang's unprecedented achievements in acting, screenwriting, and directing in Taiwan and Hong Kong, she has never been seriously studied. Despite the large number of Chinese women filmmakers and the major roles they have played in mainstream film production and experimental cinema alike, few have been studied in published scholarship.[87] While some recent anthologies include one or, in rare cases, two chapters on women filmmakers, they function as a token, isolated from the contextual history of women's varied engagements with cinematic representation and their contributions to Chinese film production. Auteurism and auteur criticism, which have been dismantled or challenged by poststructuralism and feminist film theory, have made, as Zhen Zhang argues, an unapologetic comeback in Chinese area studies' interest in national cinema and modernist, international, art-house cinema. Women directors have, however, been exiled from this masculine style of cinematic studies. The accelerated globalization of capital and media has recently led to research trends that question the suitability of the nation-state category in area studies. Instead of seeing transnational or globalization processes as inherently gendered, sexualized, and racialized, these growing movements endorse depoliticization, aesthetic transcendence, and an indifferent cosmopolitan style,[88] and dismiss the significance of gender and alternative histories. As a consequence of the hierarchical trend in both gender and area studies, Chinese women's studies and cinema remain on the margins of American academia.

Transnational feminist critiques of cultural essentialism, cold-war politics, nationalism, the apolitical view of globalization, and academic hierarchy help address issues in gender studies and area studies and foster critical dialogues and mutual illuminations between them. The study of women from non-Western parts of the world requires a substantial reconfiguration of current feminist theories and American institutional structure to foreground these women as historical subjects and to highlight the concrete and multilevel engagements they have made with diverse global and local historical forces. This must take place without reducing them to any single, fixed position, whether as cultural or political victim, the symbol or token of masculine modernity, or a fundamentally different "other" from a cultural relativist perspective. It is, therefore, critical for projects on Chinese women's cinema to focus on women's active involvements in Chinese film production, to examine their historical and subjective negotiations with various forces in a multi-axis context, to reveal their diverse manners and styles in the process, and to assess the different significations of their cinematic practices. Going beyond purely text-and-form-based criticism, the study of Chinese women's cinematic authorship, which is affected by and affects sociohistorical discourses, provides the most compelling site to address Chinese women as negotiating historical subjects.

22

WOMEN'S CINEMA AND HISTORY OF CHINESE
WOMEN'S FILMMAKING

Compared with female cinematic authorship, the concept of women's cinema has not, despite its complicated history, encountered the deadlock
situation concerning historical subjects outside the text. But women's
cinema needs first of all to be differentiated from the woman's film, a
Hollywood genre of emotional melodrama targeting a female audience
popular throughout the 1930s, 1940s, and 1950s. Also known as weep-
ies, this genre is, according to Molly Haskell, "founded on a mock-Ar-
istotelian and politically conservative aesthetic whereby women spectators are moved, not by pity and fear but by self-pity and tears, to accept,
rather than reject, their lot."[89] For Mary Ann Doane, the woman's film
identifies female pleasure in cinema as being complicit with masochistic
constructions of femininity.[90] Women's cinema on the other hand generally denotes, despite certain disputes, films made and mostly directed by
women.[91] Some critics may argue that only those films addressed to or
concerned with women should be called women's cinema, but few critics
question whether women's cinema must have female authorship.

The idea of women's cinema emerged in film theory in the late 1960s
and had, by the early 1970s, developed into a political counter-cinema
challenging mainstream and patriarchal cinema by resisting its language.
In her 1973 essay, "Women's Cinema as Counter-cinema," Claire Johnston
maintains that woman's discourse can grow from within the ideological
contradictions and heterogeneous discourses of mainstream Hollywood
cinema. She describes the function of women's cinema in Hollywood
from the 1920s to the 1940s as primarily disruptive and revisionary: "its
very survival in the form of irony is in itself a kind of triumph, a victory
against being expelled or erased."[92] Laura Mulvey dismisses the possibility of feminist work emerging from within mainstream narrative film.
In "Film, Feminism and the Avant-Garde," Mulvey envisages women's
counter-cinema in the tradition of political modernism[93] and perceives
avant-garde cinema—with its storehouse of feminist aesthetic strategies
of defamiliarisation, rupture, and reflexivity—as a model for feminist
film.[94]

Women's cinema has been further contested and developed since the
1980s. Teresa de Lauretis has argued that women function both in the cinema as representation, and outside the cinema as subjects of practice, and
that for feminists to pose critique from within and without patriarchal

culture, the tension between "woman" (e.g., constituted by Hollywood and psychoanalytic narrative) and "women" (historical subjects) should be maintained.[95] She defines women's cinema as one that "crosses the boundaries between avant-garde and narrative cinema, independent and mainstream, but which is rigorously exclusive on political grounds."[96] Other feminist critics have also viewed women's cinema to be in intertextual relation with hegemonic cinematic traditions.[97] In her 2002 book on women's cinema, Alison Butler notices that unlike the feminist film theory that emerged in the 1970s, when few films were made by women, the diverse forms and contents of contemporary women's cinema of the new millennium exceed the most flexible definition of counter-cinema.[98] She proposes redefining women's cinema as "minor" cinema, a term adapted from Gilles Deleuze and Felix Guattari's concept of minor literature, the literature of a minority or marginalized group written in a major language. Butler moreover shows that the defining features of minor literature—displacement or deterritorialization, the sense of everything as political, and the tendency for everything to take on collective value—characterize women's cinema. Just as minor literature involves a community's projection rather than its expression, it is useful to perceive women's cinema as premised on ways of imagining future communities instead of an essentialist understanding of women.

Butler's reformulation of women's cinema distances itself from the narrow, politically signified women's cinema of earlier discussions to include the diversity of women's cinema in the world. But in tracing its history in Anglophone feminist film theory, Butler also naturalizes the concept's development. She perceives 1970s feminist film theory as the source of minor cinema and understands its growth as the automatic consequence of the globalized expansion of women's film production.[99] The concept of minor cinema, as a result, runs the risk of being ahistorical, abstract, and unable to account for historical complicity or collaboration between feminist practices and the major language.

Two major issues need to be addressed before we can move to a more historically defined women's cinema. First of all, until the 1990s, women's cinema was understood as a feminist and political concept—a counter-cinema offering feminist insights and modes of opposing or disrupting mainstream and patriarchal film production. Feminist critics did not dispute whether feminist counter-cinema must be practiced by women. The political necessity that women make counter-patriarchal-cinema is, however, inconsistent with the semiotic and psychoanalytic approach to women's films, which, in discussing the meaning of the female author's films, always defers or brackets her along with her intentions and interventions, her background and experience, and her social and historical positions. This discrepancy cannot be attended to without discussing its underlying cause: the early feminist expectation of a homogeneous group of women involved in the production and discussion of women's cinema. As discussed above, semiotic and psychoanalytic approaches to film texts have contributed to textual and sexual essentialism relying on a white and Western-centric universal model. The counter-cinema early feminist scholars promoted presumed the makers of women's cinema to be white, elite Western women. Consequently, the need to consider their social and cultural positions in discussions of their films was much less significant. The only difference among them lay in their sexual identity, which explains why the lesbian identity of an author (as in Arzner's case) and the role of lesbian relationships in films were among the first issues feminist film critics dealt with in both Hollywood and psychoanalytic narratives. The political goal of early women's counter-cinema, which appears to contradict textual and (post)structural analysis, has in fact reinforced the exclusion of other historical contexts and different social and cultural positions of the director from consideration.

Claire Johnston's insight that mainstream and dominant cinema is not monolithic and contains alternative and marginalized discourses is significant, but it must be further argued that dominant discourses and mainstream cinemas exist in plural forms, and that any given patriarchal discourse is historically conditioned, coded along sexual, racial, social, geopolitical, and cultural axes, and needs to be analyzed on multiple levels. Only through transnational feminist understandings of patriarchy as scattered, overlapping, and multileveled, can we understand that women's cinema is not practiced against one dimension of a universal mainstream discourse (psychoanalytic interpretation of Hollywood cinema), nor does it constitute a uniform discourse (counter-Hollywood-cinema) in itself. To historicize women's cinema and bring authorial subjects into discussions will not invoke the traditional patriarchal concept of authorial control over meaning production, because it is not the essentialized or unified identity, but the historically conditioned relationship (a form of continuity) and performative interactions between the author outside the text and the textual significations that need to be studied.[100] The agency of women filmmakers has long existed, but it is historically conditioned and diverse. It is situated in women's concrete and various negotiations with differently established dominant discourses and in their socially and politically conditioned cinematic practice or performance.

Chinese women have made mainstream, commercial, independent, and experimental films. Some are in line with dominant discourses, some oppose; most, however, negotiate existing worldviews and ideological assumptions.[101] Rather than perceiving women's cinema as containing fixed intrinsic and generic values—whether aesthetic, sexual, or political—contributors of this anthology demonstrate the necessity of approaching women's cinema as historically constituted. Attending to the historical and discursive conditions of women's filmmaking, they assess women filmmakers' lives and experiences in relation to their cinematic practices and conduct analyses of women filmmaker's cinematic texts and language. In this book, Chinese women's cinema generally refers to Chinese-language (dialects included) films directed and sometimes written by Chinese women in Greater China, including mainland China, Hong Kong, Taiwan, and the Chinese diaspora.[102] The screenplay is an essential part of filmmaking, and since the 1920s, Chinese women have produced screen scripts for numerous influential films. Many directors discussed in this anthology are also screenwriters. This volume in part explores the roles women have played through writing, performing, and directing for a modern mass media and commercial industry. The diversity of geopolitical locations and the regional differences within those locations challenge any understanding of *Chinese* women's cinema as a unified practice. Moreover, the turbulent and dynamic history of modern China disables any view of Chinese women's cinema as a linear development. With these caveats, I will offer a brief history of Chinese women's filmmaking in the mainland, Taiwan, Hong Kong, and the diaspora;[103] I will also situate and introduce chapters of this volume in their respective historical contexts.

Chinese women's filmmaking, which includes directing and screenwriting, began in Shanghai, when in 1925, Xie Caizhen directed the family melodrama, *Guchu beisheng* (An Orphan's Cry, 1925), and Pu Shunqing's screenplay *Aiqing de wanou* (Cupid's Puppets, 1925) was adapted to film. In 1928, Yang Naimei wrote *Qi nüzi* (A Wondrous Woman, 1928) with the film version released in the same year; in 1929, Wang Hanlun helped direct and edit *Nüling fuchouji* (Revenge of an Actress, 1929). Women's relationships to filmmaking at this stage appeared accidental because of the lack of institutional and social support. Early female filmmakers' initial careers as star actresses played a significant role in their transition to film directing and screenwriting. In addition, their relationships with men also accounted for their success in the 1920s Shanghai film industry.[104] The highly contingent character of their participation in early filmmaking in China aside, the first wave of Chinese women filmmakers produced a wide variety of films, illustrating the complexity of women's negotiations with Shanghai's semi-colonial conditions, the film industry, mainstream discourses, and commercial and popular cultures. While *An Orphan's Cry* followed a popular genre of the time, Wang Hanlun's family melodrama, *Revenge of an Actress,* continues the late Qing Mandarin ducks-and-butterflies tradition, a popular urban literary genre of sentimental love and forbidden romance that privileges the entertainment. Pu Shunqing's *Cupid's Puppets,* on the other hand, turned to the Westernized and nationalist May Fourth movement, which critiqued the traditional family and advocated freedom in love and marriage. Yang Naimei's *A Wondrous Woman* portrays a decadent Westernized modern woman with a distinctive autobiographical feature, promoting Yang's own unconventional sense of self and wish for self-creation. She thereby depicted a complicated negotiation of the female self with the Westernized new woman, the commercial film industry, and cinematic representation.

27

With the advancement of modern women's writing and the rise of left-wing drama and literary movements in the 1930s, some talented women emerged as writer-stars. In her chapter on Shanghai actress-writers from the 1920s and 1930s, Yiman Wang traces an intricate social and historical condition within which women with public careers mediated their lives. She situates Yang Naimei and Ai Xia (who wrote and acted in *Xiandai yi nüxing,* A Woman of Today, 1933) in a discursive framework of multifarious and even contradictory historical forces that include Ibsen's Nora of *A Doll's House* and her transformations in China, the May Fourth cultural movement, the Western modern-girl phenomenon, left-wing ideology, the National Party's New Life Movement, commercialism, and Chinese cultural traditions. Her general argument is that attached to domestic space, writing helps to discipline and not merely express female selves, and that acting, by displaying intractable somatic materiality on and off the screen, can challenge sublimation. Her insight that writing cannot be automatically conflated with female agency is significant, because, as Wang notes, the social functions of women's reading, writing, and acting vary according to specific contexts and thus need to be specifically examined.

While Ai Xia committed suicide as a result of these diverse historical forces, Chen Boer, another star-writer in the 1930s, succeeded as the first screenwriter and director in the Communist base of Yan'an (with *Bianqu laodong yingxiong*, Working Hero in the Communist Base, 1946), after persuading the Communist government to establish the studio in 1946.[105] Chen was the first woman screenwriter and director fully supported and endorsed by the Communist government.

In the 1930s and 1940s, the first professional Chinese American woman director, Esther Eng, a second-generation Chinese American, developed her filmmaking career in Hong Kong and made more than ten Cantonese films. Pro-feminist and patriotic, Eng was forgotten by both Hong Kong and Hollywood film history. Kar Law, one of the first critics to rediscover Eng in the mid-1990s, provides a historically rich and critically provocative account of Eng's life, career, and films.

The end of the Chinese Civil War (1946 to 1949) led to the formation of three distinctive yet related Chinese systems and geographical areas: socialist mainland China, Taiwan under the Nationalist Party's rule, and colonial Hong Kong under British governance. Since the three areas enjoyed relatively stable political situations, their film production increased in the 1950s, marking a new beginning for Chinese women's filmmaking. The policy and development of the film industry in the three regions, however, also began to diverge into different cinematic trajectories and traditions. The first generation of professional women directors in each Chinese community was closely tied to its historical situation, geopolitical context, and personal backgrounds. Though their cinematic practices exhibit different social, cultural, and market influences and demands, each first group of directors participated in its communities' mainstream film production.

After the establishment of the People's Republic of China in 1949, mainland China underwent unprecedented political, social, and economic transformation: Chinese women's emancipation reached its highest level in history, and the Chinese film industry adjusted itself to the socialist economy and party-state leadership. The implementation of socialist state feminism, which claimed absolute equality between men and women, played a tremendous role in Chinese women's filmmaking. Wang Ping, Wang Shaoyan, and Dong Kena, the three best-known woman directors of the 1950s and 1960s, received institutional endorsement from state film studios. The relationship of Chinese women directors with the nation-state and its socialist feminism demands more scholarly attention. Obviously, socialist mainstream cinema contains a feminist discourse that makes us rethink the function and role of feminist practice to dominant, mainstream discourse.

Wang Ping is the most well-known woman director of socialist China. In almost all of her popular revolutionary films, like *Liubao de gushi* (The Story of Liubao Village, 1957), *Yongbu xiaoshi de dianbo* (The Everlasting Radio Signals, 1958), *Huaishu zhuang* (Locust Tree Village, 1961), and *Nihongdeng xia de shaobing* (Sentinels under the Neon Lights, 1964), she endorses both class revolution and socialist feminism. One could conclude that Wang subjected herself to the "mainstream" socialist discourse, or that socialist ideology left no space for personal expression, but Wang's early personal struggles and her trajectory from a Chinese "Nora" in the 1930s to a left-wing activist in the 1940s, and finally to a Communist film director in the 1950s,[106] provides an alternative understanding of Wang's personal and emotional commitment to socialist ideals. In my study of a socialist director Dong Kena's *Kunlunshan shang yikecao* (Small Grass Grows on the Kunlun Mountain, 1962), I locate her subject in the state ideology and mainstream cinema of socialist China. I reveal that socialist cinema is not monolithic, and that socialist female authorship is contingent on a dynamic interaction of different and sometimes contradictory historical forces surrounding a particular film's production.

In the 1950s Hong Kong film industry, Shanghai film culture continued to have influence, especially during the early postwar period, despite competition from the local, Cantonese film tradition. Among the many Shanghai filmmakers to move to Hong Kong after 1949 were the actresses-turned-directors Chen Juanjuan and Ren Yizhi (Yam Yi-Ji). Eileen Chang connected Hong Kong's cinema in the 1950s and 1960s to Shanghai culture and the aesthetic she developed there. Yingjin Zhang's chapter on Chang's screenplays from the 1940s to 1960s contributes to the study of Eileen Chang more generally. Pertinent to this discussion is Zhang's persuasive argument that despite their general dismissal, Chang's 1950s and 1960s screenplays exhibit a discernable continuity, in their treatment of gender and aesthetic style, with her Shanghai literary writing. This chapter exposes academic prejudices against the commercial intent of Chang's screenplays and the comic and popular film genres of the time. Zhang also examines how certain film genres constrain women writers and how Chang's strategy of repetitive performance negotiates a space for her female characters and for her aesthetic preference for equivalent contrast and harmony.

The 1950s and 1960s Taiwan film industry differed dramatically from that of Hong Kong. Without its own heritage, Taiwan film production began developing only after the Nationalist government moved there in the 1950s.[107] Due to political censorship, inconsistent cultural policy, and the development of the local and rural economies, the number of privately produced Taiwanese-dialect films increased. Ch'en Wen-min, a small businesswoman of peasant origin, accidentally became Taiwan's first woman screenwriter and director. Her first screenplay, *Nüxing de chouren* (The Enemy of Women, 1957) was immediately filmed in 1957, and her second, *Xue Rengui yu Liu Jinhua* (Xue Rengui and Liu Jinhua, 1957) was finished in 1957 with Shao Luohui directing. During their second collaboration on *Xue Rengui zhengdong* (Xue Rengui's Eastern Campaign, 1957), however, a dispute led to Shao Luohui dropping out of the project, which made Ch'en Wen-min the first woman director in Taiwan. In her direction of seven more Taiwanese-dialect films between 1958 and 1959, Chen focused on stories of underprivileged women and their troubled family relationships.[108] The success of Taiwan's local, private business model granted inexperienced but talented people such as Chen access to resources. Chen also demonstrated how much a woman could achieve despite a socio-economic environment largely inhospitable to women, especially those with working-class origins.

In 1960s socialist China, a younger generation of women began receiving professional training in Beijing and Shanghai film schools, but the Cultural Revolution brought feature film production in mainland China to a virtual halt from 1966 to 1972. Although Wang Ping and Dong Kena resumed in 1974, the younger generation of women directors did not independently direct films until the late 1970s. In 1970s Hong Kong, two women directors were well known: Kao Pao-shu, an actress-turned-director who made seven conventional films in that decade, and Tang Shu-shuen, an independent filmmaker, whose first film, *The Arch,* gained her international recognition. Tang Shu-shuen was the first Chinese woman to study film in the United States. Her privileged family background and the geopolitical and cultural contexts of colonial Hong Kong in the 1960s and 1970s made it possible for her to return to make films in Hong Kong. Ching Yau published a detailed study of Tang Shu-shuen in 2004,[109] and in this volume, Yau provides a feminist reading of *The Arch* and a discussion of its colonialist, nationalist, and orientalist receptions.

In 1960s and 1970s Taiwan, the film industry experienced drastic changes. Influences from government, folktales and theater, modern literature, and Hong Kong film culture were evident during the years when Mandarin films came to dominate the Taiwan market. More woman directors emerged to produce a diverse body of films. From 1958 to 1979, actress-turned-director Chang Fang-Shia directed about twenty films, becoming the most prolific Taiwan woman director to date. In the mid-1960s, government-promoted "Healthy Realism" became the new trend, but was soon replaced by romantic melodrama, a genre created by the popular romance writer Chiung Yao. Liu Li-Li became the best-known and most prolific woman director of Chiung Yao's films. In the mid- and late-1970s, when government film studios responded to Taiwan's declining political status in international affairs by encouraging and supporting patriotic propaganda films, Wang Ying, who had studied film in the United States and returned to Taiwan in 1968, directed *Nübing riji* (Diaries of a Female Soldier, 1975) based on Xie Bingying's diaries written during the Northern Expedition and published in 1928.[110]

The late 1970s and early 1980s witnessed innovations in all three Chinese cinemas, which for different reasons broke from their immediate film and cultural traditions to usher in unprecedented opportunities for a variety of cinematic practices. The new wave movements redefined regional and national cinema in relation to international art and commercial cinema, but their relationship to women's cinema remains complicated and demands critical attention. In all three regions, women such as Zhang Nuanxin, Anne Hui, and Chu T'ien-wen played key roles in the initial development of new waves, but they were either subdued or consciously retreated as the Chinese new waves drew a group of male auteur filmmakers into the world spotlight. The impact of new wave cinema on women's cinema varied by region; while it stimulated younger generations of filmmakers in 1980s and early 1990s mainland China and Hong Kong, its male dominance directly and indirectly prompted a reactive, feminist cinema in Taiwan. In all cases, the number of woman directors rose and remained high during this period, totaling around one hundred. More films were directed by women in China at this time than in any other country in the world.

In mainland China, the economic reforms initiated in 1978 heralded an era of social, cultural, and economic change. Several generations of woman directors with diverse backgrounds had assumed directing positions in state studios by the end of the 1970s. The most influential group included Zhang Nuanxin, Huang Shuqin, Wang Haowei, Shi Shujun, Shi Xiaohua, Ji Wenyan, Xiao Guiyun, Ling Zi, Wang Junzheng, and Siqi Gaowa, who, having graduated from film academies and institutes in the 1960s, helped diversify mainstream films in the 1980s and pioneered new cinematic practices. When the new wave cinema rose in mainland China to counter socialist realism and melodrama, it drew its first inspiration from French New Wave, Italian neo-realism, and Andre Bazin's theory of the long take, before climaxing in the practice of Fifth-Generation male filmmakers such as Chen Kaige and Zhang Yimou. In 1979 Zhang Nuanxin was among the first to introduce the new wave documentary style to China and to call for reform in Chinese cinematic language.[111] But her personal documentary style and gendered self-consciousness in the early 1980s set her films apart from works by the Fifth Generation male directors, who renewed national cinema by connecting it to international masculine art-house filmmaking. Zhang's subjective and personal mode of cinema is among the most significant achievements of mainland Chinese women's cinema's to date and has been continued by directors such as Hu Mei and Ma Liwen/Ma Xiaoying. The subjective mode, while rare, is not absent from pre-1980s women's cinema, but it was never linked to personal narrative until Zhang Nuanxin's first film, *Sha'ou* (The Drive to Win, 1981). The personal narrative refers to the construction of emotional and historical experiences directly or indirectly related to the filmmaker her/himself. In other words, women's cinema turned self-expressive and self-conscious in the mainland during this period.[112] This personal filmmaking, together with an increase in Chinese women's autobiographical literature, decentralized socialist realism and articulated subjective gendered perspectives. Yet this personal mode of representation should not be understood according to an individualistic or liberal feminist framework; it remains embedded in socialist history and early postsocialist conditions. While Western influences are noticeable, for example, in Zhang's documentary style, she reorganizes them in her films to enunciate historically constituted personal voices from the early postsocialist era.[113]

32

After making several mainstream films, Huang Shuqin rose to fame with *Ren, gui, qing* (Woman, Demon, Human, 1987), an exploration of the predicament of a woman who embraces unconventional visions and desires that Chinese cultural and feminist critic, Dai Jinhua, hails as the first feminist film in China.[114] In this anthology, Xingyang Li situates Huang Shuqin's representative films—*Qingchun wansui* (Forever Young, 1983), *Woman, Demon, Human,* and *Hua hun* (The Soul of the Painter, 1994)—in relation to the mainstream discourses of the time in which each is set: the socialist political discourse of the 1950s, the open-door cultural discourse of the 1980s, and the popular and commercial discourses of the 1990s. Historicizing women's consciousness in each film, he argues that the significance of women's cinema must be situated in a polyphonic context and understood as a consequence of dialogues between women and mainstream discourses. Although *Woman, Demon, Human* has mostly been praised as a women's film, Li attributes the film's success to its polyphonic nature.

In 1982, the first film students graduated from Beijing Film Academy since the Cultural Revolution. Female directors of this so-called Fifth Generation, most of whom grew up during the Cultural Revolution, proved to be the most innovative in the 1980s and 1990s. The films of Hu Mei, Li Shaohong, Ning Ying, Peng Xiaolian, and Liu Miaomiao exhibit different aesthetic styles and thematic concerns. In her chapter on Hu Mei, Liu Miaomiao, Li Shaohong, and Peng Xiaolian, Louisa Wei argues for the existence of a female counter-cinema in 1980s and 1990s China, which functioned to (re)write women's history/story, (re)construct women's speeches/voice, and/or (re)map women's space/place. Wei bases her discussions on textual analysis, but her knowledge of these directors from interviews brings their historically situated "intentions" and "actions" into the discussion of the meaning and effect of their films. Women directors' intentions are linked to their films' cinematic significations. Wei situates her project in dialogue with Western cinefeminism, revealing, however, the limitation of the latter in analyzing Chinese women's cinema. By focusing on Ning Ying's 2005 *Wu qiong dong* (Perpetual Motion, 2005) in her chapter, Gina Marchetti shifts the discussion to contemporary China, where a globalized market economy, neoliberal policies, postmodern fragmentation of subjectivity, and post-feminist popular culture reinforce each other and provide little hope for any effective feminist re-interventions. Marchetti connects Ning's film with an array of different Western and Chinese film traditions, genres, and cultures to indicate its highly historical and transnational nature and to reveal the film's, as well as the elite female characters', inconsistent and, at times contradictory, moves between Maoism and global capitalism, traditional patriarchy and consumerism, and Chinese culture and Western style. Though Marchetti's chapter ends on a tentatively positive note, it questions globalization's gendered effects and its potential for positive change.

After the penetration of China's market economy into film starting in the early 1990s, the state retreated from its previous full sponsorship of film production and support of women, and the late 1990s saw a significant reduction in films made by women, and many established women

33

directors faded from view. At the same time, market-oriented cultural production also granted women directors of younger generations space to explore independent and commercial filmmaking. Significant among this group are Ma Liwen, Li Hong, Xiao Jiang, Xu Jinglei, Li Yu, and Liu Jiaying. In her chapter, Kaplan compares the representation of emotion in Hu Mei's *Nüer lou* (Army Nurse, 1985) and Xu Jinglei's *Yige mosheng nüren de laixin* (Letter from an Unknown Woman, 2004) to assess the transformations of different conceptions of female subjectivity from 1985 to 2004, when China changed from a nation-state to a transnational-state with a market economy. Basing her analysis on Brian Massumi's distinction between affect and emotion, Kaplan finds that although Hu's film was made under the strong control of a nation-state that granted less agency to women, Hu paradoxically establishes a less "normative" heroine with her unconventional style (comparable to neo-New Wave) and expressive representation of feeling. On the other hand, because it was produced in market-oriented China, Xu's remake of Ophüls's 1948 film resembles commercial Hollywood-style melodrama. Although its heroine demonstrates control and agency over her fate, she is represented as a normative and individualist woman with fixed emotions. In her chapter, Jingyuan Zhang first studies Xu Jinglei as a multitalented cinematic force: a film director, screenwriter (her first two films), and lead actress in *Wo he baba* (My Father and I, 2003), *Letter from an Unknown Woman,* and *Mengxiang zhaojin xianshi* (Dreams May Come, 2006). Second, Zhang reveals that while the films' styles range from realistic and commercial to avant-garde, Xu's authorship can be traced through the thematic similarities of gender and emotions. Zhang draws our attention to the commercial function of Xu Jinglei's public persona, which lends another unity to her films in a highly commercialized society. Finally, Zhang explores the extent to which Xu's films can be called feminist.

In her chapter, Shuqin Cui concentrates on sexuality and feminism in the films by Li Yu, from her independent film on female homosexuality, *Jinnian xiatian* (Fish and Elephant, 2001), to *Hongyan* (Dam Street, 2005), her mainstream film on the female body and male voyeurism, and to her recent commercial film, *Pingguo* (Lost in Beijing, 2007), on the commodification of women and their bodies. Cui argues that although the first two films contain promising feminist elements, the confinement of homosexual experience within heterosexual discourse in the first inhibits a potentially queer discourse capable of going beyond homo/hetero-binary conventions, and that the representation of women's bodies as spectacle in the second film induces sociocultural norms. Although Li Yu's films produce a certain resistance to mainstream cinema, they are full of contradictions and uncertainties. Cui questions the possibility of feminist interventions in a globalized market economy and the validity of one global, pure feminist cinema.

The year 1979 marked the beginning of Hong Kong new wave cinema, which for many critics and filmmakers was a historical "coincidence," whose significance lay not in its challenge to, but its diverse influences on, Hong Kong cinema. Ann Hui's *Feng jie* (The Secret, 1979), based on a real-life murder case, together with Tsui Hark's *Die bian* (The Butterfly Murders, 1979), was regarded as the germination of the Hong Kong new wave. Hui was known for her "Vietnamese trilogy"—*Lai ke* (The Boy from Vietnam, 1978), *Hu Yue de gushi* (The Story of Woo Viet, 1981), and *Touben nuhai* (Boat People, 1982)—films examining the transnational social and political issues related to the experiences of Vietnamese refugees. In 1990, she made the semiautobiographical *Ketu qiuhen* (Song of the Exile, 1990), which interweaves subjective memory, political history, and the mother–daughter relationship, foregrounding the role of transnational landscapes and cultures (mainland China, Macau, Hong Kong, Britain, and Japan) in constituting personal identities and intersubjective relationships. Whereas the women's subjective cinema Zhang Nuanxin and Hu Mei practiced during the 1980s in the mainland shows the political dimension of the personal within national boundaries, Hui's *Song of the Exile* illustrates a compelling aspect of the transnational in its negotiation of the personal from different diasporas. With twenty-five art-house and commercial films to her credit by 2009, Hui has become the most versatile new wave film director in Hong Kong and the most prolific Chinese woman director in the world.

Perhaps because the majority of its directors studied or lived abroad, women's cinema in Hong Kong is distinguished by its transnational, transcultural, and border-crossing characteristics. Unlike mainland Chinese woman directors, whose professional rise had until the late 1990s relied on institutional support from within the nation-state boundary, Hong Kong directors have long negotiated a commercial market in a transnational context. Compared with their male counterparts, Hong Kong woman directors have demonstrated a pronounced preoccupation with migration, diaspora, and Chinese identity in a global setting. As Staci Ford and Shiao-Ying Shen show in their chapters, Cheung's and Law's personal and historical backgrounds shed light on their cinematic practice, especially their persistent attention to migration and the question of being Chinese and Hong Kong Chinese in political and transnational contexts. Since the mid 1990s, the Hong Kong film industry has declined in the face of financial, political, and commercial uncertainties, but a small group of young independent women filmmakers has emerged in Hong Kong. Among them are Barbara Wong, Carol Lai, Ching Yau, and Yan Yan Mak, who have made successful independent and/or award-winning mainstream films.[115] Although the number of women's films on migration has decreased in Hong Kong cinema in the new century, the transcultural character of Hong Kong women's cinema continues.

The development of Taiwan women's cinema in the 1980s and 1990s is connected to several important historical and cultural movements, particularly the new Taiwan cinema movement of the early 1980s, the women's visual arts festival of the early 1990s, and women's documentary filmmaking since the mid-1990s. After Chiang Kai-shek's death in 1975, Taiwan began a series of economic, cultural, and political reforms under the leadership of Chiang Ching-kuo. New Taiwan cinema, initiated by male directors such as Edward Yang, Hou Hsiao-hsien, and Chang Yi in the late 1970s and early 1980s, promotes social realism, local/native culture, and cinematic innovation (semidocumentary style) to respond to the political melodramas and commercial genre films (romance and martial arts) of the 1970s. No women filmmakers directly participated in the new Taiwan cinema movement, but women writers contributed to it. As Yu-Shan Huang and Chun-Chi Wang show in their chapter, new Taiwan cinema was influenced by Taiwan women's and native-soil literature.

As one of the leading figures of the new Taiwan cinema, Hou Hsiao-hsien has been hailed as an auteur and the single engine of the "Hou Hsiao-hsien aesthetic." In his chapter, Christopher Lupke offers a study of the long-term collaboration between Hou Hsiao-hsien and Chu T'ien-wen, an award-winning female writer and the screenwriter of the films in which Hou's "aesthetic" emerges and matures. According to Lupke, Hou discovered his artistic cornerstone after Chu introduced him to Shen Congwen's autobiography. Lupke reveals how Chu co-authored with Hou the cinematic themes, stories, styles, and the multi-vocal effect of his films. Lupke further argues, in his analysis of Hou's *Dongdong de jiaqi* (Summer at Grandfather's, 1984), that Chu T'ien-wen's scriptwriting, which shifts between male and female characters and between gender-specific experiences, exhibits the capacity to lay out an ostensibly patriarchal framework and perspective, while undercutting it with the subversive sotto voce of the female voice, however attenuated it may be.

Only a few women directed in Taiwan in the mid and late 1980s. Sylvia Chang, a well-known actress, turned to directing in 1986 with *Zui ai* (Passion, 1986), which explores female bonding, heterosexual love and marriage, and extramarital affairs, topics also dealt with in her later films. Wang Hsiao-ti, who studied drama and film in the United States and returned to Taiwan in 1979, designed and co-directed with Sylvia Chang and Jin Kuo-Zhao the three-part anthology *Huangse gushi* (The Game They Call Sex, 1987), focusing on women's awakened consciousness of their sexuality and constructed gendered roles. Centering on issues of gender and family, Chang's later films lie closer to mainstream melodrama. Wang has explored different types of films, including children's, martial arts, and cartoon drama films.

Confronting the blindness of English scholarship to Sylvia Chang's success as an actress, screenwriter, and film director, Zhen Zhang probes academic prejudices to gender, genre, and transnational and regional identities in her chapter. She situates Chang and her works within the contexts of the Sinophone film culture and transcultural melodrama studies, and offers analysis of *Passion, Xin dong* (Tempting Heart, 1999), and *20 30 40* (2004). Set in Taiwan, Hong Kong, Japan, and New York, the films' characters are transnational subjects with diverse cultural backgrounds, class standings, and sexual orientations. Zhang illustrates how Chang's everyday feminism repositions the family-home motif of Chinese melodrama outside the allegorical space of nation, organizing it not around the father-son relationship but around relationships among women within the context of globalization.

Yu-Shan Huang and Chun-Chi Wang' s chapter, in addition to considering directors Sylvia Chang, Huang Yu-Shan, and Zero Zhou, provides the most comprehensive study yet of post-1980s Taiwan women's cinema. They locate women's films and directors in the political and economic history of Taiwan and trace the cultural movements and events that contributed to the development of Taiwan women's cinema. In 1993, Taiwan's first women's film festival was held in Taipei. Since the establishment, five years later, of the Taipei Women's Film Association (the precursor to the Taiwan Women's Film Association), an international women's film festival has been held annually in Taiwan, which has stimulated the development of local feminist cinema and women's independent filmmaking. In 1995, the biannual International Documentary Film Festival and

37

documentary channels on public television were formed, which contributed to a new tide of Taiwan documentary filmmaking. These movements and festivals have helped produce generations of women filmmakers concerned with representing feminist issues and the local cultures, customs, and history of Taiwan. Some filmmakers who appeared at the turn of the new century, such as Alice Wang and D. J. Chen, have directly addressed market demands; others, such as Singing Chen, Lisa Chen, and Zero Chou, have made art films with social and feminist concerns.

The most salient characteristic of Taiwan women's cinema since the 1980s is the exploration of the body and sexuality. Attending to women's bodies and their sexual desires has registered in new Taiwan cinema as part of its general concern for marginalized groups under political oppression. When women directors like Wang Hsiao-ti and Huang Yu-Shan represented these themes in their films in the late 1980s, they shifted the focus to women's awakening consciousness of their bodies and sexualities. This helped mark gender and sexuality as distinctive categories and called for critical examinations of patriarchal repression and the compulsive heterosexual paradigm. Taiwan women's cinema became self-conscious when it transformed new Taiwan cinema's general exploration of female sexuality into the specific examination and self-expression of gender. While such feminist representations of the female body have persisted in women's films, new significations of the female body appeared in the 1990s after several international Taiwan women's film festivals centering on the body and sexuality took place.[116] Some documentary and experimental films treat the female body as an object for exploring unconventional sexual desires and identities. For instance, Chien Wei-ssu's short experimental film, *Dengdai yueshi de nüren* (A Woman Waiting for Her Period, 1993), depicts a woman's experience of her body and the relationship of such experience to her ambiguous desire and her social relationships. Zero Chou's docudrama, *Shenti dianying* (A Film about the Body, 1996), and documentary, *Si jiaoluo* (Corner's, 2001), also turn to the body to re-examine and re-imagine marginalized or repressed desires and homosexual relationships. The cinematic representation of homosexuality by Taiwan woman directors traces to 1982, if not earlier, when Li Mei-Mi's *Nüzi xuexiao* (Girl's School, 1982) was released. Huang Yu-Shan's *Shuang zhuo* (Twin Bracelets, 1990) focuses on a Fujian local tradition of sisterhood and explores the political and sexual implications of female bonding. Not until the late 1990s did cinematic representations of (homo)sexual relationship become conventionalized. Mainstream and commercial

38

filmmakers such as Sylvia Chang, Alice Wang, and D. J. Chen have drawn on the cultural as well as commercial values of homosexual representations. Several independent directors, especially lesbian filmmaker Zero Chou, have recently made a critical breakthrough in the representation of the body and homosexual intersubjective relationships. While Chou's *Ciqing* (Spider Lilies, 2007) incorporated a mainstream formula and became a commercial success, her *Yanguang sishe gewutuan* (Splendid Float, 2004) and *Piaolang qingchun* (Drifting Flowers, 2008) go beyond conventional portraits of homosexual relationships and link the representation of sexuality to explorations of life, death, and local customs and cultures. Compared with other Chinese-language homosexual and lesbian films, which are usually set in urban landscapes and have transnational and transregional appeal, Chou's films reconfigure the body and homosexual relationships in the local history and cultures of Taiwan, articulating an embedded and concrete aesthetic of Taiwan queer cinema.

The history of Chinese women's cinema illustrates how women's participation in filmmaking is geopolitically and historically contingent, and how women's films' meanings resist uniform interpretation. Gender matters in understanding Chinese women's cinema but is itself a historically and geopolitically specific concept always in need of close examination. Since the 1990s, Chinese women directors across geopolitical divides have confronted similar demands from the market but have responded differently. It is in and through a diverse cinematic engagement with historical forces, whether of the market, politics, or patriarchal traditions at national, transnational, or diasporic levels, that Chinese women filmmakers, as historical and authorial subjects, have exhibited their agency, reorienting gender configurations and articulating different meanings and aesthetics in history.

39

NOTES

1. Ella Shohat, "Area Studies, Gender Studies, and the Cartographies of Knowledge."
2. Katarzyna Marchiniak et al., eds., *Transnational Feminism in Film and Media*, 4.
3. Judith Mayne, *The Woman at the Keyhole*, 97.
4. I will discuss and refer to these reviews over the course of this chapter.
5. Virginia Wright Wexman, ed., *Film and Authorship*, 2–3.
6. John Caughie, ed., *Theories of Authorship*, 11–15.
7. Wexman, *Film and Authorship*, 5.
8. Anneke Smelik, *And the Mirror Cracked*, 9.

9. Claire Johnston, "Women's Cinema as Counter-Cinema," 25.
10. Laura Mulvey, "Visual Pleasure and Narrative Cinema."
11. Mary Ann Doane, *The Desire to Desire.*
12. Caughie, *Theories of Authorship*, 126.
13. Mulvey, "Visual Pleasure and Narrative Cinema."
14. Luce Irigaray, *Speculum of the Other Woman.*
15. Caughie, *Theories of Authorship*, 200.
16. Judith Mayne, "Female Authorship Reconsidered," 93.
17. Wexman, *Film and Authorship*, 11.
18. Mayne, *The Woman at the Keyhole*, 4.
19. Caughie, *Theories of Authorship*, 201.
20. Ibid.
21. Janet McCabe, "Conceiving Subjectivity, Sexual Difference and Fantasy Differently."
22. Kaja Silverman, "The Female Authorial Voice."
23. Ibid., 202.
24. Ibid.
25. Ibid., 212–218. See also Smelik, *And the Mirror Cracked*, 45–48.
26. Silverman, "The Female Authorial Voice," 217.
27. Ibid., 193.
28. Catherine Grant, "Secret Agents," 119.
29. Mayne, "Female Authorship Reconsidered," 100. See also Grant, "Secret Agents," 119.
30. For an early, insightful analysis of Claire Johnston's works, see E. Ann Kaplan, "Feminist Criticism of Claire Johnston and Pam Cook."
31. Johnston, "Women's Cinema as Countercinema," 28.
32. Ibid., 29.
33. Ibid., 32–33.
34. Ibid., 32.
35. Ibid., 32–33.
36. Johnston, "Women's Cinema as Countercinema." See also Alison Butler, *Women's Cinema.*
37. Butler, *Women's Cinema*, 8.
38. Donna Haraway, "A Manifesto for Cyborgs," 65.
39. Mayne, "Female Authorship Reconsidered," 102.
40. Ibid., 104.
41. Ibid., 113.
42. Ibid., 112.
43. Ibid., 122.
44. Grant, "Secret Agents."
45. Michel Foucault, "What is an Author?"
46. Roland Barthes, "The Death of the Author."
47. Geetha Ramanathan, *Feminist Auteurs.*
48. Ibid., 3–4.
49. Ibid., 6.
50. Ibid., 4.

51. Ibid., 4–5.

52. Kaplan, "Feminist Criticism of Claire Johnston and Pam Cook."

53. Ibid., 52.

54. Ibid., 53–54.

55. Teresa de Lauretis, "Sexual Indifference and Lesbian Representation," 155–77; Jane Gaines, "White Privilege and Looking Relations," 340.

56. Gaines, "White Privilege and Looking Relations," 336.

57. bell hooks, "The Oppositional Gaze."

58. Gaines, "White Privilege and Looking Relations," 347.

59. Kimberlé Crenshaw, "Demarginalizing the Intersection of Race and Sex," 139.

60. Kimberlé Crenshaw, "Mapping the Margins," 1241.

61. Patricia Hill Collins, "Gender, Black Feminism and Black Political Economy," 42.

62. Crenshaw, "Mapping the Margins," 1241.

63. Chandra Talpade Mohanty, "Under Western Eyes."

64. Inderpal Grewal and Caren Kaplan, *Scattered Hegemonies*, 17.

65. Caren Kaplan, et al., eds., *Between Woman and Nation*, 12.

66. Inderpal Grewal and Caren Kaplan, "Postcolonial Studies and Transnational Feminist Practices."

67. Ibid.

68. Chandra Talpade Mohanty, "Cartographies of Struggle," 4.

69. For a constructive critique of transnational feminism, see Breny Mendoza, "Transnational Feminisms in Question."

70. Grewal and Kaplan, "Postcolonial Studies and Transnational Feminist Practices" (original emphasis).

71. Ella Shohat, ed., introduction to her *Talking Visions*, 46.

72. Publications on transnational feminism in relation to visual culture and film studies include: Shohat, *Talking Visions*; special issue on "New Feminist Theories of Visual Culture"; Shohat, "Post-Third-Worldist Culture"; and Marchiniak, et al., *Transnational Feminism in Film and Media*.

73. Shohat, introduction to her *Talking Visions*, 46.

74. Meng Yue and Dai Jinhua's book on modern Chinese women's literature is one of the best examples. See Meng Yue and Dai Jinhua, *Fuchu lishi dibiao* (Emerging from the Historical Horizon).

75. For a focused study on women and nation from a transnational feminist perspective, see Kaplan, et al., *Between Woman and Nation*.

76. For related arguments, see Grewal and Kaplan, "Postcolonial Studies and Transnational Feminist Practices"; Kaplan, et al., *Between Woman and Nation*; and Shohat, "Post-Third-Worldist Culture," 40–41.

77. Grewal and Kaplan, "Postcolonial Studies and Transnational Feminist Practices."

78. Ibid.

79. Elizabeth Ezra and Terry Rowden, "General Introduction," 9.

80. Ibid., 5.

81. Marchiniak, et al., "Introduction," 3.

82. Ibid., 2.

83. Vijay Devadas, "Rethinking Transnational Cinema."

84. Shohat, "Area Studies," 67.

85. Shohat, introduction to her *Talking Visions,* 38–39.

86. Shohat, "Area Studies," 73–74.

87. For the limited publications on Chinese women filmmakers, see Zhen Zhang's chapter in this collection.

88. For an in-depth discussion of the trajectory of area studies, especially Chinese studies, see Ban Wang, "The Cold War, Imperial Aesthetics and Area Studies."

89. Molly Haskell, *From Reverence to Rape,* 155.

90. Mary Ann Doane, "The Moving Image."

91. Mayne, *The Woman at the Keyhole,* 2.

92. Claire Johnston, "Dorothy Arzner," 7.

93. Laura Mulvey, "Film, Feminism and the Avant-Garde." See also Butler, *Women's Cinema,* 6.

94. Butler, *Women's Cinema,* 6.

95. Teresa de Lauretis, *Alice Doesn't,* 15.

96. Butler, *Women's Cinema,* 16–17.

97. Ibid., 18–19.

98. Ibid., 1–24; 119–123.

99. Butler, *Women's Cinema,* 119.

100. For a related discussion, see Hamid Naficy, *An Accented Cinema,* 4.

101. I consider Stuart Hall's discussion of modes of reading mainstream texts useful in understanding women's negotiations with mainstream culture and discourse. He describes the three types of analysis as dominant, negotiated, and oppositional reading. See Stuart Hall, "Encoding/Decoding."

102. An exceptional case in this volume is Clara Law's English films. Shiao-Ying Shen's chapter focuses on Law's emotional and artistic transformation from a Hong Kong film director to a migrant director in Australia. The piece is not only tied to Law's past Chinese-language films, but also indicates a direction for Chinese women's transnational cinema.

103. For full-length articles on the history of Chinese women's filmmaking, see Lingzhen Wang, "Chinese Women's Cinema," and Louisa S. Wei, "Women's Trajectories in Chinese and Japanese Cinemas."

104. Pu Shunqing collaborated with her well-known director husband, Hou Yao, who filmed her screenplays. Yang Naimei, on the other hand, was said to rely on a warlord general in the North to back her film company financially.

105. Liu Shouhua "Zhanhuofengyanzhong de yan'an dianying shiye" (Yan'an Film Industry during the War).

106. For a detailed account of Wang Ping's life, see Song Zhao, *Mama de yisheng* (The Life of My Mother).

107. Zhang Yingjin, *Chinese National Cinema,* 113.

108. For a detailed account of Chen Wenmin's life and films, see Chen Yansheng, *Taiwan de nüer* (The Daughter of Taiwan).

109. Ching Yau, *Filming Margins.*

110. For detailed information regarding Taiwan women directors, see Wang, "Chinese Women's Cinema."

111. See Zhang Nuanxin and Li Tuo, "*Tan dianying yuyan de xiandai hua*" (On the Modernization of Film Language).

112. For a related discussion, see Chris Berry, "China's New 'Women's Cinema,'" and "Interviews with Zhang Nuanxin."

113. This personal mode was later developed into an autobiographical mode of cinematic representation by several directors across different generations. For detailed studies on this topic, see Lingzhen Wang, "*Nüxing de jingjie*" (Female Cinematic Imaginary).

114. Dai Jinhua, *Cinema and Desire*, 153.

115. For detailed information regarding the films and achievements made by this group, see Wang, "Chinese Women's Cinema."

116. See Huang and Wang's chapter in this volume.

Part I

FEMALE AUTHORSHIP NEGOTIATED IN
DIFFERENT TIMES, SPACES, AND GENRES

1

Socialist Cinema and Female Authorship

OVERDETERMINATION AND SUBJECTIVE REVISIONS IN
DONG KENA'S *SMALL GRASS GROWS ON THE KUNLUN
MOUNTAIN* (1962)

LINGZHEN WANG

DESPITE THEIR lack of experience in directing films, Wang Ping, Wang Shaoyan, and Dong Kena, the three best-known female directors in 1950s' and 1960s' mainland China, all became film directors with the institutional endorsement of state film studios such as August First Film Studio and Beijing Film Studio. Given the extremely limited alternatives in the early socialist film industry, state sponsorship—as well as the institutional and moral support these women received after the Chinese Communist Party assumed power—was critical to their success as the first group of female directors in modern China. The entrance of Chinese women into film production resulted to a large extent from the new government's official discourse and practice, which claimed absolute equality between men and women. The inadequate number of experienced filmmakers with revolutionary backgrounds in the early years of socialist China also accounted for the incorporation of women into the industry—all three directors, for example, were revolutionary cultural workers and/or left-wing film actresses before the party came to power. Of course their experiences, artistic talents, visions, and determinations are also important factors in understanding their roles in socialist filmmaking. As a result, female authorship of Chinese socialist films from this period must be examined among multiple social, political, institutional, and personal forces.

Recent scholars in Chinese studies have reevaluated socialist literature and film from different critical and comparative perspectives instead of highlighting their propagandistic nature and conformist tendency as previous English-language scholarship on socialist literature and art has done.[1] By examining specific ideological, aesthetic, imaginary, and formal characteristics of socialist art, these scholars have revealed both the dominant mode of artistic production, as well as its variations, and the different mechanisms by which socialist art functioned effectively to move, bring pleasure to, entertain, educate, and construct a socialist mass audience. While didacticism is assumed to be the fundamental goal of socialist artistic practice, it is nonetheless achieved through overdetermining structures and in tension with other subordinated themes and elements. This chapter joins that revisionist approach as it attempts to illustrate a more complex picture of socialist art and literature by exploring the concept of female authorship and Chinese women's roles in socialist cinema through a particular focus on the female director Dong Kena.

Given the historical and political circumstances that had enabled Chinese women to assume directing positions, it is not surprising that films made by first-generation female directors in the 1950s and 1960s conformed to contemporary mainstream political and artistic ideologies. While conformity itself may signify different meanings in different contexts, and thus demands more critical analysis and historical examination than mere dismissal, what I intend to argue is that conformity does not exhaust the meaning and significance of films directed by women of that period. Through closely analyzing Dong's most influential film, *Kunlunshan shang yikecao* (Small grass grows on the Kunlun Mountain, 1962; hereafter *Small Grass*), and its production, I will reveal a multifaceted picture of women's roles in representing revolutionary ethics, socialist construction, and the gendered self. Specifically, I will examine the personal narrative and subjective cinematic techniques Dong deploys to show how multiple levels of contradiction are sustained throughout the film under its explicitly conformist surface. Some of the film's subthemes—such as domestic imagination and displaced, gendered visions of life—diverge from the official political goals of both the film and the era. Female authorship, as shown in *Small Grass,* is therefore contingent on dynamic negotiations among diverse ideological, institutional, artistic, and personal factors.

SMALL GRASS: FROM SHORT STORY TO FILM

Small Grass is based on Wang Zongyuan's short story "Hui Sao (Hui's Wife)—the Story Within the Story," published in *People's Daily* in 1961; its film adaptation was assigned to Dong by the head of Beijing Film Studio, Wang Yang, in August of the same year. Although Dong had already helped direct several films as assistant director, this was the first film she was asked to direct independently. When it came out in 1962, the film (black and white, 62 minutes) received some critical acclaim and became an instant hit among young audiences. The image and life of the Kunlun grass represented in the film articulated a new, hard-working spirit called for by a period in which China was undergoing huge economic setbacks, international isolation, and natural disasters. The film influenced many young people of the time by encouraging them to confront the difficult situations they faced and to devote their lives to building a strong socialist China.

The story of the film is relatively simple and hardly strays from the plotline of the original story. It tells of Li Wanli, a seventeen-year-old Shanghai woman who, upon graduation from a geological university, enthusiastically volunteers to go to the Qinghai-Tibet Plateau to work, but on the way to her destination, finds herself completely disillusioned by the desolate reality of the mountain areas. As she hesitates about whether she should return to Shanghai, she meets a peasant woman at the Kunlun mountain pass, Hui Sao, a model figure who originally moved there to reunite with her husband and later built a homelike dormitory to house the long-distance drivers who traverse the Plateau by day and night. After listening to Hui Sao's narration of how she overcame her own disillusionment and found meaning in her life by serving those heroic drivers, Li is enlightened and decides to learn from Hui Sao and devote herself to transforming the area.

The film reinscribes dominant tropes developed in socialist literature and film on several levels. First of all, it is a typical education film with an apprenticeship structure, in which an apprentice character learns from a model figure, usually a party member, and grows to become a socialist or revolutionary subject.[2] In the Chinese context, the social roles of apprentice characters vary, and the degree of apprenticeship for various characters also depends on the political and cinematic position of the character in the film. A generally accepted rule, however, is that when intellectuals and women are depicted in literature or film in relation to the working class (workers, peasants, soldiers) or male party members, they are often put in the position of apprentice and witness.[3] The relationships between Li and Hui Sao, and between Hui Sao (who is not a Communist Party member) and her husband, a committed Communist Party member, follow the typical apprenticeship hierarchy.

Second, in addition to the apprenticeship structure of the film, the director deploys a typical flashback device often used in socialist films, in which either heroic or bitter stories of the past are told to educate and enlighten as well as to reveal information to characters in the film and to its audience. According to Chris Berry, "In this trope, memory is not just personal, but part of a collective process of learning from experience."[4] *Small Grass* contains two additional flashback narratives: the second flashback, which is also the major one, is narrated and anchored by Hui Sao and addressed to the targeted listener Li; the third flashback is part of Hui Sao's flashback and narrated by her husband, mostly while speaking, to the targeted listener Hui Sao. Both flashback narratives function to enlighten and change the targeted listeners in the film.

Third, the film ends on a politically satisfactory and personally uplifting note: Li is completely transformed, moving happily forward to her new job.

There is no dispute that Dong's *Small Grass,* like the original short story on which it is based, belongs to mainstream socialist cinema and literature and has a visible pedagogical goal embedded in the narrative. However, while conforming to the overall dominant and collective discourse in socialist film production, the film adaptation of *Small Grass* also enunciates, through its subjective narrative devices and cinematic techniques, some different themes and gendered concerns that, although subdued by the apparent didactic theme toward the film's end, are in fact sustained throughout. These cinematic discourses and subthemes are not necessarily subordinate to the dominant one, as Chris Berry argues,[5] but neither do they form any effective oppositional consciousness. Rather, they reveal, consciously or unconsciously, gaps and contradictions at the heart of the dominant discourse and offer at the same time different subjective perspectives and psychological negotiations. Although the film achieves its pedagogical and collective goal toward the end, it elaborates on particular psychological processes and gendered identification, producing multiple meanings at various points within the diegetic frame.

The following discussion explores some special features and devices of *Small Grass* that not only explain the film's appeal to both past and present audiences, but also reveal a female director's negotiations with the original short story and the dominant mode of film production. Thus I confront questions about the interconnections and interactions among authorship, gender, cinema, and socialist policy.

REVELATION OF IDEOLOGICAL DISCREPANCIES: FEMALE VOICE-OVER AND OFFICIAL REPRESENTATIONS

Jin Fenglan, in her book on Dong Kena's life and films, devotes one chapter to Dong's first film, *Small Grass*.[6] In the section on the cinematic language of the film, Jin points out the devices Dong deploys in *Small Grass*: subjective camera, female voice-over and voice-off, flashbacks, and long takes. The subjective camera, as Jin indicates, was rarely used in socialist films. In fact, not until the early 1980s was it frequently used in personally oriented films, especially those by female directors. Wei Shiyu, in her article on the historical changes in images of Chinese women on the screen and in women's cinema in the twentieth century, declares that it is Dong's *Small Grass*—rather than those films made in the 1980s by female directors such as Zhang Nuanxin, Hu Mei, Huang Shuqin, and Peng Xiaolian—that should be regarded as the first women's film in China.[7] Although she mentions that the elements of female voice-over and voice-off, female perspective, and independent female character establish *Small Grass* as a women's film, she does not elaborate on why these stylistic elements qualify it as such. In fact, these narrative devices have all been employed in other socialist films and have produced quite different meanings and significance.[8] More in-depth studies and analyses are therefore needed to illuminate the significance and effects of Dong's narrative devices and techniques in producing gendered and gender-related meanings in this film.

The film begins with a lone truck bumping along in the great wilderness of China's northwest plateau with literally no road before or after it. As the days and nights pass, the landscape changes to snowy mountains and an endless, snowy mountain path. The camera then cuts to the truck cab to reveal a young male driver and a young woman sitting next to him. Simply by observing their facial expressions and body language, the audience recognizes that the two are not on good terms. When a truck passes by from the opposite direction, the girl turns around, her look following the truck until it disappears. After the girl turns back to her original position, with disappointment legible on her face, the audience is exposed to her inner thoughts through voice-over: "The Plateau, is this the Plateau [I know through other representations]?"

The most salient narrative device in Dong's *Small Grass* is the female voice-over, which is anchored within the diegetic frame, synchronically communicating the inner thoughts and emotions of the character (Li Wanli). The original story by Wang Zongyan has a different narrative device. It begins with a primary first-person narrator (presumably a male writer or reporter) who meets Li at a big celebratory meeting held for young model workers and socialist construction activists in the Qaidam Basin area. He becomes interested in Li, a model young woman with a Shanghai background. When he asks her about her experience of first coming to the Qinghai-Tibet Plateau, she answers him by telling a story of Hui Sao, a peasant woman who helped transform Li's life on the plateau. Although Li narrates the main story from then on, her first-person narration is enveloped by the narrative frame of the male writer.

In their adaptation of the story, Dong and Hua Ming remove both the authorial male narrator and Li's first-person narration and cut instead directly into Li's story as she experiences it. In other words, unlike the story in which Li's experience is mediated by another authorial narrator and told in retrospect, the film begins with her riding in a truck and bumping along the Kunlun mountain road on her way to her working post. This rearrangement of the temporal and spatial frame in the film's opening transforms the entire story from a recounting of a past learning story with a historically vindicated perspective (the character is now herself a model youth)—a narrative device that is often used in revolutionary films—to a direct presentation of what Li experienced in the past. This change in narrative structure fundamentally alters Li's past experience from a provisional and insignificant state moving toward a victorious outcome to a historical reality in which multiple discourses as well as their contradictions are enunciated and sustained.

In addition, the voice-over, which speaks Li's inner thoughts and feelings as she is experiencing a completely new life, emphasizes her particular internal and psychological experience. Indeed, the director prioritizes Li's psychological experience so much that she uses a full reel of her six-reel film to depict Li riding in the truck where she reveals her internal struggles through voice-over. Visually, the story takes much of the pedagogical order of socialist cinema, which is represented literally as the beginning of a (learning) journey in the truck on the mountain road.

Li's voice-over, however, articulates other negotiations, effectively showing her disillusionment, hesitation, and different imagination and emotional longing.

During her two-week voyage on the mountain road, Li suffers severely from altitude sickness symptoms: severe headache, back pain, loss of appetite, and fatigue. She mentions that she is sick and her body is in poor condition (*shenshang nanshou*), possibly implying that she is having her menstrual period. The physical challenges seem to mount beyond what Li can bear, but she is not permitted to complain. The erasure not only of gender difference here but also of human limitations, epitomized in the socialist slogan "Human beings can conquer nature," is implicitly questioned through Li's interior voice-over and the camera's sympathetic gaze. Indeed, her voice-over also indicates the silencing effect produced by her companion, Xiao Liu, a model driver and heroic figure, as the film later reveals, who looks down upon Li when he senses this newcomer may be unable to endure the hardships of working on the plateau.

53

Physical suffering, however, is only a small part of Li's problem. More troubling are her psychological suffering and disillusionment. It turns out, as revealed in her voice-over and flashback, that the major psychological motivation for Li to volunteer to work on the Qinghai-Tibet Plateau came from a magazine cover photo of a young Tibetan woman dressed in colorful ethnic dress and standing happily on the vast green grassland, where the sun above her is bright, the sky behind her is blue, and the sheep surrounding her are white (fig. 1.1). In the first flashback of the film, we see her as a young girl from a well-to-do urban family, gazing at the photo in her cozy bed at home. The desire to meet and become a girl just like the happy and high-spirited one on the magazine cover drives Li to leave home to work in the high mountain area in the far west. Reality, however, completely crushes her dream. Since entering the plateau area two weeks earlier, not only has she seen no one like the girl on the magazine cover but she has seen no women at all. Furthermore, the ruthless natural environment imposes its icy, stormy, and desolate lifelessness. Li is strangled by the environment of the plateau, the same place she once dreamed of beginning a beautiful new life. Psychologically, Li suddenly feels herself completely in the dark: on the one hand, the subject she so desired to identify with and become—the young Tibetan girl on the magazine cover—never appears; on the other hand, the masculine drivers she has met are not appropriate models for self-identification. The vision of oneself and one's future is an important component in self-formation and

FIGURE 1.1 The young Tibetan woman on the cover

transformation; Li's voice-over demonstrates how that vision has been totally shattered by the gap between the official representation of life and gender and their reality on the plateau.

It is important to note that this crucial detail of the Tibetan girl on the magazine cover is not in the original story but was added by Dong and Hua in their adaptation. As a woman and former actress, Dong understood that it is not only simplistic but untruthful to interpret Li's early reaction to the plateau, as the original story did, as motivated by lack of courage or determination. Such a stereotypical and abstract judgment would obscure and dismiss many serious issues. Dong once stressed that her past experience as an actress helped her direct films because it is important for an actress to emotionally identify with her character, not simply to perform her character rationally or externally.[9] Dong found the sudden change that occurs in Li's attitude toward the plateau at the beginning of the original short story to lack convincing internal logic. In an article on the art of film directing, Dong writes, "I make much effort to explore and discover characters' internal worlds in order to move audiences with [appropriate] emotions. . . . My films are full of emotions and artistic appeal because I rely on my own feelings when I direct."[10]

Relying on her own emotions, feelings, and sense of reality, Dong bridged the emotional gaps existing in the original story of *Small Grass* by deploying Li's inner desires and identification models. But when Li's original imagination and desire are revealed, the film inadvertently un-covers enormous ideological gaps: first, between the official public rep-resentation and reality of the plateau, and second, between the public demands on women and women's different psychological and emotional preferences. These ideological contradictions and gaps run deep in social-ist China, and they represent themselves repeatedly in the film narrative.

As the film later reveals, Hui Sao also dwells on the total disillusion-ment caused by her husband's (mis)representation of reality. By employ-ing Hui Sao's first-person voice-off and subjective flashbacks, the film reveals that she had been misled by her husband's letter, in which he described the area in favorable terms and lured her into the dream of building a prosperous new home there. Passionately responding to that representation, Hui Sao traveled all the way from Shanxi to the plateau, bringing with her all the domestic necessities she could possibly carry, including small animals and a variety of vegetable seeds. But the reality appearing before her eyes completely shocked her. The first sentence of Li's voice-over at the beginning of the film rings loud: "The Plateau, is this the Plateau [I know through other representations]?"

Compared with Li, Hui Sao was even more resolute in her decision to return home in Shanxi. Even though her husband had to stay to work in the Kunlun mountain area, she was determined to leave. Hui Sao's sense of home is shown to have nothing to do with her husband. Once again, Hui Sao's determination to leave was not caused by the hardship and difficulty associated with the area. After all, Hui Sao was very differ-ent from Li; she was a strong peasant woman and had endured suffering in the past. When she first arrived in the area, Hui Sao showed no sign of physical fatigue. Instead, she was full of energy and enthusiasm and eager to settle down in her imagined new home. What turned Hui Sao completely around was the huge discrepancy between her husband's rep-resentation of the area and the real situation. Reality bore no trace of her husband's depictions and thus left no space for her imagined sense of self and home. Having no intention to remodel herself after her husband, a Communist Party member, or to embrace the vision he harbored, Hui Sao decided she simply did not belong there.

The official and masculine representation of both present and future life in socialist China, the film implicitly yet critically suggests, was often intended to engage the female imagination, arousing in female audiences and readers a passion for identification and action. After initially embrac-ing the representation, however, most women found that reality was quite

different; it not only ran counter to what they perceived in official representations but also demanded that women repress their own emotions
and required them to cross-identify with masculine models. Xiao Liu,
the model male driver in the film, functions exactly as this silencing and
demanding force. Can women be the same as men? Do (all) women desire to identify with men or with what men represent? Li's and Hui Sao's
voice-overs place such political assumptions under scrutiny and expose
the ideological discrepancies and historical contradictions encountered
in the process of female identification in socialist China.

ARTICULATING GENDERED NEGOTIATIONS
IN SOCIALIST CINEMA

In addition to exposing, intentionally or not, the gaps and contradictions
in the socialist construction of new identities for women, Li's voice-over
in the film, together with the narrative devices of subjective camera and
flashback, articulates a gendered sense of self, identification, and belonging. Following the opening scene in the truck, Dong employs extensive subjective camera shots with voice-over to show what Li sees and
feels when she first meets Hui Sao in the dormitory that is her "Drivers'
Home" at the Kunlun mountain pass. Within the tradition of socialist
cinema, these subjective shots can be conveniently understood as a typical trope in the apprenticeship structure, by which a main character is
introduced from the perspective of a witness, pupil, or both. Obviously
Dong does not discourage such an analysis, but what I hope to illustrate
is that something else is also enunciated through Dong's extensive and
intensive use of subjective camera, shot/reverse shot, and female voice.

The scene of the Drivers' Home contains multilevel significations.
First of all, *siji zhijia* (drivers' home) signifies the socialist concept and
practice of the collective family in which people are related to one another not through blood ties but through class background or working
relationships. Li witnesses the harmonious and happy atmosphere and
relationships in this unique space. At the center of this space is Hui Sao.
Through Li's subjective view and voice-over, the audience also learns that
Hui Sao is a peasant woman who becomes an exemplary socialist figure
by establishing this Drivers' Home and providing a much needed service
to long-distance drivers in the desolate mountain areas. Hui Sao undeni-
ably functions as a model for Li, but from Li's perspective, the significance

of Hui Sao's role lies less in her socialist exemplary status than in being a particular kind of woman. Li acutely senses that although Hui Sao is the very center of this collective family, she is also quite different from its other members. As the only woman, the difference she makes in the area is something only Li can understand and appreciate.

In his study of collective spectacles in socialist revolutionary films, Wang Ban pays particular attention to the aesthetic essence of politics. Rather than endorse the theory that politics represses individual desires, he argues that individual libidinal forces are in fact maintained and reoriented by socialist politics and artistic practice through sublimation and other collective means. Regarding the process of individual identification with the collective or revolutionary subject, Wang Ban quotes Dai Jinhua, arguing that "Giving up oneself to revolution means not only getting a glorious new life and obtaining the meaning of existence, but also taking a final departure from loneliness, weakness, and helplessness, and acquiring a new home, new affection, new concerns, and new power."[11] Wang Ban's characterization of revolutionary films and his argument on the process of individual identification in those films not only capture certain aesthetic effects of revolutionary films but provide insights for our general understanding of socialist films as a whole, made mostly by male directors. Although in a highly centralized society women's artistic practice seldom takes any antagonistic, oppositional stance against the official and dominant practice, it is critically important to examine the specific manner of women's artistic negotiations. Different gendered voices and messages are very often embedded within the overall conforming structure of their works.

On its basic level of signification, Dong's *Small Grass* reflects the major aesthetic and political structure of revolutionary films discussed by Wang Ban, since it fundamentally aims to reorient individual life and imagination toward a socialist collective one; only the latter was endowed with significant social meanings in socialist history. But what distinguishes Dong's *Small Grass* from some other revolutionary films is the way in which individual characters in the film reach the collective goal. Unlike individuals in some other revolutionary films, Hui Sao's and Li's transformations in *Small Grass* are not initiated and facilitated through heterosexual, hierarchical love relationships; empowering scenes of revolutionary movement or socialist construction; male-oriented communal comradeship and pleasure; or help and education from an authoritative party member. In a very significant way, Dong's film refuses to romanticize or dramatize revolutionary or political forces and thus does not contain those empowering processes or scenes of sublimation typical of other revolutionary films.

Sticking to a psychologically and visually realistic style, Dong supplements original stories with more emotionally convincing plots and details, and thus articulates a particular and gendered logic of transformation. In Hui Sao's narration of her own story, which is meant to set an example for Li, Dong uses flashbacks from Hui Sao's perspective to reveal how Hui Sao finally transforms herself and decides to stay in the area. In the original story, Hui Sao's husband, Lao Hui, unsuccessfully tries to persuade her to stay. Finally, he decides to tell Hui Sao a story, despite her refusal to listen, about how, at a most dangerous and desperate moment in his career in the Kunlun mountains, he saw a type of nameless small grass growing vigorously in the adverse climate of the plateau. Inspired by the grass, he thought that as a Communist Party member he should be at least as strong as the small grass. He brought a sample of the grass to his comrades, and then they worked hard together to overcome the difficult situation. Although this story contains some inspiring elements, Dong must have sensed that it would be hard to convince the audience that Hui Sao's strong determination to leave the place could be so suddenly transformed by her husband's story. Furthermore, the crisis Lao Hui and his comrades confronted was related to their careers as party members and their struggle to survive a natural disaster. Even the quotation from Mao Zedong that Lao Hui used to encourage his comrades had been addressed directly to Communist Party members and not to common people. So by turning his story into an educational one intended for everyone, Lao Hui has changed the logic from a political demand for party members and an injunction to survive to a universal masculine model that requires women's sacrifice. Hui Sao has no wish to identify with her husband or his career, nor is she a Communist Party member. Unlike apprentice characters in other revolutionary films, who are often stuck in deadlocked situations and desire to join revolutionary forces in search of new homes and identities, Hui Sao has a home and life of her own in Shanxi, to which she very much desires to return even though her husband must stay in a different place. Though she is in the apprentice position in relation to her husband, in the film Hui Sao is depicted as having her own vision of home, identity, and life.

As a woman herself, Dong understands that Lao Hui's lesson does not address Hui Sao's real problem. So she adds another episode in which a young driver risks his own life to deliver food on a stormy night to a group of workers in another area of the plateau. As soon as this driver, who has not slept or seen real food for days, arrives at the drivers' station where Hui Sao and her husband live, he falls asleep on their bed. At this moment, a silent shot/reverse shot shows Hui Sao looking closely at the driver (fig. 1.2), followed by a shot of the sleeping driver's young, innocent, and exhausted face (fig. 1.3). From this shot/reverse shot, audiences recognize that Hui Sao's maternal instinct is aroused and that some real changes in Hui Sao are beginning to take place. This added scene contributes to smoothing over the original gap in the logic of her transformation. After all, Hui Sao, the peasant woman, does not really buy into the propagated socialist moral obligation or her husband's pressure; she finally stays because she feels emotionally compelled to help those young, brave drivers. This is not to say it is unproblematic to portray maternal love as instinctual and natural; yet in the context of 1960s China, when any kind of intimate intersubjective relationship was strongly discouraged by the Party, and when maternal figures on the big screen became heroes precisely through their sacrifice of relationships with their children, Hui Sao's maternal instinct truly articulates an alternative, gendered approach to the political demands of the era. Furthermore, because Hui Sao follows her own call to stay on the plateau, she also actively brings her own vision of life and home to it. In other words, rather than returning home, Hui Sao transplants her own ideal of home and life to the place of her work, while providing a service to young drivers.

By creating this new episode, which is based on her own understanding of women and their emotions, Dong revises the original story that upholds the masculine ideal of the party and at the same time prevents Hui Sao, her heroine, from being reduced to a symbolic political figure. In a unique and complex way, female individuals in *Small Grass* reach a collective goal not by "giving oneself up" to the cause, as stated by Wang Ban in his discussion of other revolutionary films, nor by totally erasing their gender differences, but by negotiating a way of maintaining and renewing their previous visions of self and life. These gendered visions are more historically constructed than they are essentially determined; that is to say, the meanings they signify are contingent on different historical contexts. As a peasant woman invested with a historically specific vision of life and home, Hui Sao's sense of self offers great insight into the inherently diverse identities of socialist women that are and could be different from the singular model promoted by the state.

FIGURE 1.2 Hui Sao looking at the driver

FIGURE 1.3 The driver's sleeping face

If Hui Sao's transformation hinges implicitly on maternal passion, Li's transformation relies on another gendered psychological and emotional process of identification, which requires maternal/female model figures and a related sense of self. During the journey, prior to arriving at Hui Sao's Drivers' Home, Li's vision and sense of self are completely shattered. Struck with homesickness, she desperately thinks of return-ing home. As a recent university graduate, the seventeen-year-old Li has been looking for a concrete model to whom she can relate. Abstract po-litical reasoning does not help her, and her failure to identify with male drivers in the area close to her age only deepens her sense of loneliness and alienation.

Li's sense of life first comes back when she is greeted by Hui Sao, the first person to directly address her as a beautiful girl and to ask her name. The warm and familial interactions between Hui Sao and all the drivers further help Li to recover from the exhaustion and isolation of the long journey. Later that evening, after most of the drivers have left, Hui Sao takes Li to her bedroom, a scene that begins with a shot of Hui Sao's cat lying on her cozy bed. As discussed earlier, Dong uses subjective camera and voice-over to illustrate Li's gradual revival as she attentively observes Hui Sao and the domestic details of her room. The film further stresses the liveliness of Hui Sao's space by showing a full basket of the little chickens she has raised (fig. 1.4). It is in this alternative space of life and domestic detail that Li begins to feel at home and to feel like herself again. She becomes fascinated with Hui Sao, not necessarily because she is an exemplary socialist figure but because she is a special woman who has, in Li's terms, "magically" transplanted to the area a sense of life and home similar to her own. Li feels relieved that her sense of belonging is restored, and her vision of self and life are confirmed in Hui Sao's space. In this way, Hui Sao functions as a necessary maternal figure for Li's re-birth and transformation. In fact, as the first and only person in the film who asks Li her name, Hui Sao introduces Li to the audience. Later, in Hui Sao's bedroom, it is Li who finds Hui Sao's own name on an award hung on the wall and reads aloud to the audience, "He Lianzhen." This mutual recognition between the two women is especially significant in a context in which nobody pays attention to names or individual identities. Once again, this detail is not in the original story, but was added by Dong in her adaptation.

Although—and probably because—Li is grateful that she finally meets Hui Sao, the model figure for whom she has been consciously or un-consciously looking, she wonders aloud how Hui Sao, the first and only woman in the area, has managed to survive in the environment: "Doesn't she feel lonely?" "What does she think [as a woman]?" Li's questions asked via her voice-over depart significantly from her contemporary pub-lic and political consciousness. In many revolutionary films of the time,

FIGURE 1.4 Basket of little chicks

joining a revolutionary collective force signifies "taking a final departure from loneliness, weakness, and helplessness, and acquiring a new home, new affection, new concerns, and new power."[12] For Li, as well as for Hui Sao, who has her vision of self and life, participating in socialist construction does not require self-repudiation or self-denial. Before they make final commitments based on social demands, they both acquire a context that can validate and value their (gendered) experiences and visions of life and home. Li's questions therefore generate certain effects that reverse the logic of most revolutionary films: for women, loneliness can arise *after* joining a socialist collective force exemplified by a masculine ideal. These questions show how and why Li understands Hui Sao's character and bravery from a woman's perspective; at the same time, these questions implicitly, yet forcefully, problematize socialist public discourse and policy regarding gender, identity, and socialist (re)production.

Hui Sao plays a very significant role in the process of Li's self-identification and transformation. Different from the ideological trope that conflates the image of woman with that of homeland, *mother*land, and socialist new family, and which reduces maternal figures to the embodiment of party and nation in socialist films and Chinese film studies,[13] Hui Sao is represented in Dong's film as a historically specific woman who transforms herself into a socialist subject without completely giving up her previous self. She serves as a model figure for Li in two important ways. First, on the surface or pedagogical level, Hui Sao exemplifies a woman's transformation in socialist China by demonstrating courage, devotion, and a self-sacrificing spirit. On another level, Hui Sao shows Li how women can and probably should maintain and even re-create their own sense of life while contributing to the social and collective goal.

CONCLUSION

In contrast to most revolutionary epic films, *Small Grass*'s narrative process exhibits certain unique features. Instead of being thematically and temporally linear or progressive, it contains many regressions, suspensions, and repetitions. The film has several levels of flashback. Until its very end, the film produces the effect of moving backward, as flashback within flashback continuously defers the force pushing the story forward— the political and symbolic signifier of the small grass. Although the small grass finally comes into view in Hui Sao's husband's flashback—itself framed within Hui Sao's flashback—the small grass has enormous difficulty reversing layers of regressive moves and thus becomes less forceful in its designated political function. At the same time, Hui Sao's flashback, which portrays in detail her own disillusionment after arriving in the area, elaborately and vividly repeats Li's experience in the present. This repetition also significantly impedes the forward, teleological movement and reveals at the same time deeply rooted gender problems. Because Dong insists on an emotionally and psychologically realistic depiction of women, Hui Sao's flashback, which is different from her husband's, also contains significant personal and gendered memories that resist absorption into the teleological structure. The diverse meanings generated through Hui Sao's flashback also render the narrative less linear and unified, which indicates the mechanism of overdetermination in the production of meaning in socialist cinema.

It is therefore understandable that after the film was released in 1962, it received some criticism despite its popular appeal to the public. Some critics pointed out that there was no absolute hero in the film and that Hui Sao was a typical *zhongjian renwu* (middle character); others stated that the way the film depicted heroes was problematic, as it failed to demonstrate the power of the Party's leadership.[14] Indeed, although the film follows the didactic frame of socialist cinema—as discussed at the beginning of this chapter—it also generates and reveals at more local levels

63

many tensions and contradictions. The unfixed relationship between the frame and the dynamic elements within it is thus subject to individual interpretations. In an ironic way, it is through the tensions and contradictions among the dynamic and unstable diegetic elements that *Small Grass* provided its contemporary audience with a more realistic and credible representation of life, which to a large degree accounts for its popularity among young Chinese audiences. For those college graduates who became passionate about socialist construction in remote places, *Small Grass* narrowed the gap between official representation and the reality of those areas, and thus helped young people—especially young women— better prepare themselves to go to those places if they so chose. More importantly, the film also creates an aesthetic and psychological model that differs from the contemporary standard, which instead of suppressing differing visions of life, encourages people to negotiate social demands with their own ideas and to renew their personal visions through their contributions to social and collective work.

Dong's *Small Grass* provides a compelling example for understanding the contingent character of female authorship in socialist cinema and arguably in cinema generally. The film's production process illustrates the necessity of understanding cinematic authorship as fundamentally collective, involving political, institutional, social, and artistic factors. But at the same time, even in socialist cultural production where the social and collective function of authorship is emphatically highlighted, Dong's individual interventions and revisions combined with her gendered experience and imagination play a visible role in making the film a unique and subjectively mediated product. The contingent yet noticeable female cinematic authorship in *Small Grass,* the sustainability of multiple, discrete discourses in the film's diegetic frame, and the overdetermination of the film's production of meaning all effectively indicate the complexity of socialist filmmaking and the role women have played both in promoting mainstream ideologies and in articulating gendered and different voices and visions.

NOTES

1. Among the books that contain significant revisions of previous views on socialist literature, art, and films, see Ban Wang, *The Sublime Figure of History;* Xiaomei Chen, *Acting the Right Part;* and Chris Berry, *Postsocialist Cinema in Post-Mao China.*

2. For a discussion of the apprenticeship structure in Western authoritarian fiction, see Susan Suleiman, *Authoritarian Fictions,* 64–100. For a discussion of the apprenticeship

structure in early Soviet films, see David Bordwell, *Narration in the Fiction Film*, 235–6. For a discussion of Chinese socialist film and the apprenticeship structure, see Chris Berry, "Writing on Blank Paper."

3. During the Cultural Revolution (1966–1976), when Jiang Qing took control over artistic production, women leaders began to appear often in Chinese literature and film.

4. Berry, *Postsocialist Cinema*, 49.

5. Berry, *Postsocialist Cinema*, 22–65.

6. Jin Fenglan, *Yige nüdaoyan de dianying shengya* (The life and career of a female film director), 73–84.

7. Wei Shiyu, "Bainian yinmu nüxing he nüxing dianying chuantong de shanbian" (Transformations of women's screen images and women's cinema in the last one-hundred years), 468.

8. Male directors also occasionally employed these narrative devices and techniques to tell epic and heroic stories of the Chinese Communist revolution. Such examples include *Dang de nüer* (Daughter of the party, 1958), directed by Lin Nong, and *Geming jiating* (A revolutionary family, 1960), directed by Shui Hua.

9. Jin Fenglan, *Yige nüdaoyan de dianying shengya*, 79.

10. Dong Kena, *Wo he dianying yishu* (Film art and me), 14 and 16.

11. Ban Wang, *Sublime Figure of History*, 136.

12. Ban Wang, *Sublime Figure of History*, 136.

13. Ban Wang, in his discussion of imaginary identification and aesthetic ideology, makes a much less convincing argument about maternal figures in revolutionary films. He seems to both question and reproduce the problem of the maternal in socialist cinematic representation. See Ban Wang, *Sublime Figure of History*, 146–54.

14. Jin Fenglan, *Yige nüdaoyan de dianying shengya*, 77.

2

Masochist Men and Normal Women

TANG SHU SHUEN AND *THE ARCH* (1969)[1]

YAU CHING

TANG SHU SHUEN was one of the very few woman directors working in Hong Kong cinema in the 1970s and in Chinese cinemas before the 1980s.[2] In what ways do her films address this special position of hers, explore, and/or challenge the gendered conditions of her times? What are the implications of the strategies found in her films and media representations of her that might further our understanding of feminist politics specific to the cultural-historical context of Hong Kong? This chapter explores these questions, focusing on Tang's debut work *Dong furen* (The Arch, 1969).

SHAME AS FANTASY

Discussion of Tang's work tends to privilege sexual difference by naming her first as a woman. The Hong Kong premiere of *The Arch* in 1969 sparked many writings on the film and Tang Shu Shuen in Hong Kong media. Most notably, *Chinese Students' Weekly,* an influential newspaper that played a key role in introducing international arts and literature to youth from the late 1960s to the 1970s in Hong Kong, responded to the film enthusiastically with a half-page review by film critic Sek Kei on September 26, 1969. The following passage was printed in boldface and concluded the review:

> If only you could just think for a while: it is *she, this woman,* who despite all difficulties, managed to single-handedly create a film truly honest to herself, and further enable the importance of Chinese cinema to be recognized by people around the world; this should suffice to render you *ashamed* of your-self to the utmost [italics mine].[3]

The male discourse propagated by Sek Kei here relates this problem of female authorship to the male psyche (shame) via a national and/or racial discourse ("Chinese cinema"). From a culture in which the construction and propagation of a racial/national discourse (*Chinese* cinema) is a man's job, recognizing the achievement of a woman who makes the first step becomes shameful. Sek Kei chooses a strategic path.

Rey Chow's application of psychoanalysis to Chinese cinema and literature[4] might help us understand Sek Kei's presumptions, positions, and the dilemmas behind his apparently peculiar responses to Tang's work. Examining the cultural premises of "a predominant feeling surrounding the impression of modern Chinese literature: a profound unhappiness, an unabashed sentimentalism, a deep longing for what is impossible,"[5] Rey Chow uses Laplanche and Deleuze to turn Freud's formulation of masochism on its head, by not only prioritizing masochism as the primary position in the structure of sexuality and of subjectivity but also locating its origin in the "preoedipal." The masochist/infant is intricately bound up with the fantasies of submission to the mother figure. To seek pleasure in pain is to know what it is to suffer from pain in the first place, meaning that the subject has to identify with the suffering object. Contrary to Freud's relegation of masochism to a passive role and sadism to an active one, the internalization of a suffering object to produce subjectivity in Laplanche is read as neither active (as in "seeing") nor passive (as in "being seen"), but reflexive (seeing oneself). By identifying with the mother and desiring a fusion with her, the infant sees itself in her idealized image that endures pain. Chow argues that such an emotional excitation and transference of suffering opens up a space where both the mother and the child are activated, and where they achieve their mutually dependent subjectivities through fusion and fantasy, which should be seen as constitutive of culture, rather than preoedipal. Chow suggests, in a later book, that the writing of national culture in modern China typically takes the form of an aesthetic preoccupation with the powerless; the possibility of empowerment amid massive social, political, and cultural destruction might arise from constructing and observing the powerless as a spectacle: "[T]his sympathy becomes a concrete basis of an affirmative national culture precisely because it *secures the distance from the powerless per se.* . . . Such pleasure gives rise, through the illusion of a 'solidarity' with the powerless, to the formation of a 'unified' community."[6]

It is tempting to read these two analyses as continuous rather than distinct. A modern Chinese person, in the process of seeking empowerment and constituting subjectivity for her/himself, exhibits a need to negotiate a position *between* that of (over-)identifying with the powerless, as the masochist, and that of gaining just enough distance to enjoy that suffering self as spectacle, as a narcissist. Both these structures of desire have to be grounded in a fetishizing of one's self-image. By producing an agency based on a certain self-reflexivity via fetishization, narcissism and masochism could then be read as intricately bound up with each other. Sek Kei's words cited previously could be seen as showing masochistic and narcissistic tendencies to (over-)identify with this Hong Kong Chinese woman director, to reclaim her (almost) as the mother, because she has done what he sees as his own responsibilities and desires. On the part of the male critic, his representation of this lone female Chinese artist against the world, who has managed with her integrity to overcome all difficulties and to achieve worldwide recognition for Chinese cinema, betrays an (over-)identification with her via her suffering. This identification with pain is of course facilitated more than anything else by its ability to produce pleasure, through his taking pride in the self-image of his community (Hong Kong) and race (Chinese). Even the self-flagellation, the flaunting of his "shame" at not being able to fully occupy that dominant leadership image of hers, carries an overtone of enjoyment. After all, there wouldn't be any flaunting without pleasure.

The male readiness to submit and condemn himself is here overlaid with an awareness of his distance from the spectacularization of femininity. In this scenario, the more the man whips himself, the safer and the bigger he becomes. He achieves and perpetuates agency as the ultimate inheritor of Chinese culture by assuming a position apparently even lower than that of the female artist. If in Chinese culture, the human subject gains value in the eyes of the beholder through suffering, then by melodramatizing his suffering to a greater extent than the female artist and giving it a higher value, the male critic also gains a voice of greater significance. He reclaims his position of power by locating himself within a however-imagined national and racial conscience via guilt. Sek Kei's critical responses could be seen, therefore, as aiming at a display of his ego more than about Tang's authorship.

Silverman appropriates Lacan's analysis of the "inside-out structure of the gaze" to discuss the ways in which the male psyche is as "fundamentally exhibitionistic" as the female, as dependent upon the gaze of the Other, only that he wants to be seen as (and to see) not just himself but as *the subject looking.*[7] If we use Silverman's argument to read Sek Kei's discussion of Tang's work, the male critic could be seen as precisely exhibiting himself as the subject looking at the woman director whom he sees as similar to him (race), yet different (gender determines entitlement). Contrary to Freud's belief that the male infant progresses from preoedipal to oedipal in linear fashion through a recognition of sexual difference and a separation of identification and desire, the Chinese male subject in question is *simultaneously* obsessed with sameness and difference: the desire to identify and the desire to separate. Because of Tang's perceived/suspected "superiority" within the race, "woman" is used by Chinese male critics repeatedly as a signifier to undermine her entitlement to a cultural authorship; thus she is *always* coined "female/woman director," in order to reduce her threat toward the male entitlement to culture.

69

WOMAN AS ORIGINAL SIN

I have spent time discussing Sek Kei's review not just because he has been widely recognized in Hong Kong as one of the most prominent critics since the 1960s; his writings carry widespread repercussions. He was also one of the few critics who has seriously interpreted Tang's films and has written about all of them. More importantly, Sek Kei's position epitomized many of the problems the authorship of Tang would later encounter. Throughout her career, Tang's work has been consistently ghettoized into the image of the "woman"—into the sexed body—as a means of co-opting her subjectivity into the production of *his* national/racial culture. These interpretations directly contradict Tang's texts, which persistently foreground and challenge the hegemony of the unified race and nation-state.

To name Tang as "woman" is, ironically, a way to exile "woman" from culture, to individualize her and to isolate her to a position that "sounds" historically transcendent. Repeatedly suppressed from the scene of

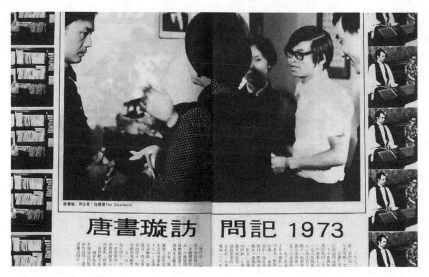

唐書璇訪 問記 1973

FIGURE 2.1 Photo for an interview with Tang Shu Shuen as published in a local magazine (courtesy of Tang Shu Shuen)

history, Tang constructs for herself a subversive location, a place to resist the male spectator's insistence to *look* at her, through her control of her image and her work. From all the photos I have seen of her, Tang is either wearing sunglasses or has her back against the camera (fig. 2.1). Similar to Arzner's underecognized representation of relations between women, as Mayne has observed,[8] Tang is never discussed in the context of the history of other Chinese woman directors, hence systemically depriving her of a cultural tradition and a community of women. Indeed, Tang's singularity is always highlighted: "Lone Rider,"[9] "first and last iconoclast of Hong Kong cinema,"[10] "pioneering."[11] While *The Arch* focuses on relationships among a grandmother, a mother, and her daughter, Tang's later works are increasingly interested in exploring the possibilities and problems of forming communities of women. In her last work, *The Hong Kong Tycoon*, for example, the representations of the talk-show hostess cum porn star Tina Leung and the Miss Hong Kong runner-up Lisa Lui, which exploit their stereotypical personas while at the same time breaking them, calls attention to the collaborative authorship between Tang and her actresses. "Female friendship acquires a resistant function in the way that it exerts a pressure against the supposed 'natural' laws of heterosexual romance."[12] Surprisingly though, none of these female-to-female relationships within the film texts and beyond have ever been discussed.

How is *The Arch* received outside the Chinese context? During the theatrical run of *The Arch* in New York, Vincent Canby critiques the film in a descriptive passage that reads more like a personal attack:

> *The Arch* is a Chinese film conceived, I suspect, after its director, Tang Shu Shuen, a wealthy young Chinese girl who studied at the University of California, saw too many movies that had won film festival prizes in the 1950's and early 1960's. . . . It is a fearfully pretentious little movie that does no real service to Art, whose name it evokes in almost every muted, though anything but subtle, image, any one of which could be hung on a restaurant wall. Blossoms fall, streams burble and valleys are misty in the dawn. Tear off a page, let's see what we have for May. . . . We don't see too many films directed by women, and hardly any directed by Chinese women, which may be why the critics in Paris have been so extravagant in their praise for such a singularly uninteresting talent. . . . They are the pushy devices of an occidental sensibility, of a director without the courage to be modest.[13]

What fascinates me in Vincent Canby's criticism are the grounds he evokes at the expense of discussing the film itself. He starts by critiquing Tang Shu Shuen first for being too young, too wealthy, and most importantly, too Westernized, then somehow his article descends into a series of racist and orientalist images from restaurant wall to misty valleys. The former has little to do with the film except for the stereotype that all Chinese own restaurants. The use of the latter demonstrates, like all other images, that he did not take the film seriously. Why is Tang's employment of cinematic strategies expected to be "modest," except perhaps for the fact that she is "Asian" as well as "woman"? With her biographical data constantly evoked as a source of either speculative idolization or groundless criticism, it seems no surprise that Tang Shu Shuen resists further supply of such information.

CHINESE AS COLONIAL SIN

As a Chinese woman who grew up in Hong Kong and Taiwan, received her college education in the United States, then chose to come back to Hong Kong to work as a filmmaker,[14] Tang Shu Shuen finds herself negotiating, not so much between the so-called East and the so-called West, but rather between several contradictory discourses that expect her, on the one hand, to manifest as much "pure" and "original" Chineseness in her work as possible (the Canby position), and, on the other, to be "Westernized" enough to mark her difference from the "locals" and gain recognition for Chinese cinema abroad (Sek Kei's position). In the latter, however contradictory it might sound, the woman director is still expected to maintain a certain integrity of "being Chinese," because betraying that identity threatens racial unity and pride, to which the male critic has direct access, has rights to protect, and views as part of his property. The paradox of the game is that she is expected to gain recognition for Chinese cinema in the West, but the more recognition she gains from the West, the more suspicious she becomes as a qualified Chinese director. Either way, she is suspicious enough as a woman to start with.

A few days before the theatrical run of *The Arch* in Hong Kong, a review in the *Hong Kong Times* exemplifies this paradox:

72

> *The Arch* has received much praises abroad . . . but all this praise from Europe and America might not be from Orientals. It remains to be seen whether places *that are full of the taste of the Chinese Race,* would accept a film like this. . . . I believe those who like Tang Shu Shuen's work will not miss this opportunity [of watching the film], but it needs to be considered *to what extent Orientals would accept especially stylish films of this kind* [italics mine].[15]

As a translator, I find this last line of quote "but it needs to be considered to what extent Orientals would accept especially stylish films of this kind" extremely difficult to get through. It is one of those language gestures in Chinese posed as modest, reserved, courteous, even objective, but those who read it would sense the deeply harsh and satirical tone underneath. It is intended to work with the entire passage, especially echoing "places that are full of the taste of the Chinese Race." Its criticism targets not only the style of the film as selling out to Westerners, and the Western reception it has enjoyed, but most importantly, all Hong Kong people who might betray their cultural inauthenticity (not Chinese enough) through their enjoyment of a film "like this." All these people, according to the Chinese male critic here, have joined the lot who do not belong to places "full of the taste of Chinese Race." In order to preserve the unity of this "taste," those different are ideologically exiled to where the film and the Westerners are located.

The insistence of the local press on emphasizing (and criticizing) a "Westernized" image of Tang Shu Shuen, in fact in Westernizing Tang Shu Shuen as an image, coincides with the demands of a Hong Kong society caught up in a manufacturing boom tailor-made for Western markets.[16] Hong Kong colonial policies in the late 1960s to 1970s, partly responding to the youth and labor movements of 1966 and 1967, strategically sought to incorporate many emergent youth cultural formations, resulting in institutionalizing a series of trade shows, beauty pageants, concerts, dance balls, the founding of civic centers, and later international film festivals. Many of these programs sought to import Anglo-American culture and fetishize/delegitimize residual Chinese culture. Tang Shu Shuen's work, with its strong assertion of cultural entitlement and hybridity, thus becomes an intensified site for male critics to proclaim their own cultural identity when such identity is constantly under severe pressures of repression and assimilation. The tension produced by the politically constructed binary opposition between the so-called East and the so-called West, to which the whole society is subject, manifests itself in critics' readings of Tang.

Hong Kong was a very unfamiliar place to me. Although I lived in Hong Kong when I was little, my whole family moved to Taiwan during my high school days, then I went to U.S. for college. So, I was a stranger to both the place and the people of Hong Kong. When I shot *The Arch*, I didn't know a single soul in the film scene (Tang as interviewed by Sing Wah).[17]

It is in such a context, in which Tang Shu Shuen's cultural identity has been problematized by her experience of a series of border-crossings to start with (Hong Kong—Taiwan—U. S.—Hong Kong), that she sought to reconstruct and explore an imaginary (Chinese) tradition through representation in her first film. I would argue that this selective tradition was also an interrogation of her own identity, in terms of ethnicity as well as gender. As a stranger returning to a place she knew as a child but had since long lost, Tang chose to map her first feature on a remote and also lost Chinese society, from a piece of legendary history allegedly set in a village of Southwest China in the Ming Dynasty. While Tang deliberately chose to represent female subjectivity within a narrative from a residual culture that was constantly being marginalized and hybridized by dominant narratives of colonialism and Westernization, through *The Arch* she also discovered that the hegemonic processes, the sense of lived dominance and subordination within the ethnocentric Chinese tradition itself, in fact serve to render feminist agency impossible.

The Hong Kong cinema (including Mandarin and Cantonese) of the 1960s and 1970s was dominated by large profit-targeting studios. Not knowing "a single soul in the [local Hong Kong] film scene," Tang finds her own transnational way of producing, writing, shooting, editing, scoring, sound-mixing, and distributing the film in a structure unique at the time, a structure in which the filmmaker has the last word in every step, a way of working similar to what would later be called "independent filmmaking." Law recalls the experience:

> When shooting the film Shu Shuen broke many conventions. Shooting on set at Cathay Studios (now the Golden Harvest Studio), she did not follow normal practice. Subrata Mitra from India, who had worked with Satyajit Ray, imposed his own style of lighting and camerawork on the production. . . . Although local technicians were apparently antagonistic towards Mitra's working methods, he nevertheless succeeded in achieving a visual style appropriate to the film. Shu Shuen also post-dubbed and mixed her film in the United States (practically unique for the time).[18]

Despite the lack of precedence and the antagonism of the Chinese technicians toward Mitra,[19] Tang still insisted on a multiethnic and transnational production structure. This helped contribute to the *difference* of *The Arch* as a hybridized cultural product in the context of 1960s' to 1970s' Hong Kong, which was also struggling to reconcile contradictory forces within its own hybridity.

Tang's body of work demands to be recontextualized in a framework of multiple marginalization. In what ways can *The Arch* be read not as a quintessentially female *or* Chinese text, but rather one that strategically negotiates a woman *and* Chinese, perhaps a Hong Kong authorship, while exposing and challenging the cultural and historical constructions as such? In what ways does *The Arch* mark the beginning of a journey reflecting on sexual and gendered differences caught in the interstices of Chinese and Western imperialisms, and, in the end, become an interrogation of *her* non-identity, her "outsider" status for life?

OF CHASTITY BOUND

The folktale of *The Arch* was first documented in *A History of Humorous Folktales,* later reworked by Lin Yutang and included in his collection of short stories, *Chinese Legends.* In the original story, a widow is seduced by a servant the evening before she is to receive the Tablet of Chastity. She is judged unworthy of the Tablet because of the scandal, and this leads her to commit suicide. Lin reworked the story into a satirical comedy in which a captain seeks shelter in a house with two generations of widows and a teenage daughter, whom he falls in love with and later marries. After their marriage, the widow seduces the servant, knowing that she would have to give up the Tablet. Then her son-in-law suggests arranging a wedding for her and the servant. The story ends on an ironic note with the village peers very disappointed and the village elder saying: The state of a woman's heart is really hard to figure out.

The most radical departure of Tang's film from these texts is the displacement of desire from that of the widow, Madam Tung and servant Chang, onto the mutual attraction between Tung and Captain Yang Kwan. Subsequently, a conflict is established between Tung and her daughter Wei Ling; both are drawn to Yang as their object of desire. This also manifests itself as a conflict between Tung's motherhood and her sexual desire. The film ventures into taboos of intergenerational incest and age (Yang, the man, is younger than Tung, the woman), and also challenges both female and male monogamy legitimized by the institution of marriage and Confucianism to a far greater extent than did the original folktale or Lin's short story. Tang's adaptation has invented strong female characters, revealing the tragedy from the women's points of view, and embodying much greater heterogeneity and contradictions.

After an introduction consisting of credits superimposed on landscape images followed by a series of activities performed by men, from soldiers to farmers, the narrative begins with Wei Ling looking—noting the arrival of the soldiers, and fantasizing—and hoping that they will stay with them. The beginning is framed with this juxtaposition between a male-dominated exterior marked by action, community, violence, and mobility, versus a female-centered interior overlaid with a sense of confinement, stagnancy, and solitude. The rest of the narrative leaves room for a constant challenge to the construction of this dualism.

THE DAUGHTER LOOKS

The classic paradigm of woman as image and man as bearer of the gaze is problematized and subverted at the outset. When this apparently tranquil and secluded world of women is first disturbed by the villager who comes to inquire about providing accommodation for the captain, Tung

FIGURE 2.2 Still from *The Arch*, 1969 (courtesy of Tang Shu Shuen)

is shown in a close-up sizing up the situation before she meets him at the door. Wei Ling rushes to a window, securing a good vantage point to look (fig. 2.2). During their conversation in the courtyard before the captain appears, the camera cuts back three times to a close-up of Wei Ling. In the first close-up, we see her listening intently to the conversation outside while slightly gazing not quite back to camera, pondering her future, which is being decided by this conversation in which she has no voice. In the second close-up, her face and eyes are seen peeping through the door, establishing her as the privileged voyeur of the scene, *before* Yang Kwan comes in (thus he inevitably takes up the position of one to be gazed upon). If the female gaze through the door could still be considered furtive, secret, and therefore quite passive, this change of point of view suggests a shift toward *active*-looking by aligning the camera's gaze (thus the audience's) with Wei Ling's. Yang Kwan's intrusion into this women-only space marks his entry into a site of female desire, offering himself as the object to be framed, surrounded (literally), evaluated, and desired. Tang's mise-en-scène carefully undercuts and challenges the impossibility of female desire under the patriarchal order by aligning our spectatorship with the gaze of women.

The Arch establishes a variety of female gazes, vernacular, desires, and fantasies, so that female subjectivity and agency threaten to penetrate the contrivance of the diegesis at any minute. In this introductory sequence, when Yang Kwan meets Madam Tung and Wei Ling's grand-mother for the first time, Wei Ling is supposed to be hiding. Shielded from Yang's male gaze and carefully using the half-open door to block out most of the camera gaze, Wei Ling is seen, together with the view-ers, as the most active onlooker in the scene, defying the passivity of "hiding." When Yang Kwan is finally accepted into the house, after some negotiation from the villager, Wei Ling is seen, slightly smiling, showing approval and happiness, which also helps the viewers to con-clude the scene with positive expectations from her point of view. After this establishment of the female gaze, Wei Ling is shown in the next scene engaged in a verbal and physical expression of fantasy and desire, slightly rocking her body and gazing at the distance, a posture sugges-tive of longing and imagination. This strategic use of a medium shot of her enables the audience to both observe her body posture, as well as identify with her facial expression.

After this use of mise-en-scène to establish Wei Ling's desire for the only man around, she conversely begins to express something else ver-bally. She asks Grandma if Yang looks like her dad. She then identifies with this male figure: "If I were a man, I would be able to join the army too. Then I could go to many places as well. Only if dad hadn't died." This opening sequence positions our identification with Wei Ling by privileg-ing her physical and emotional experiences, with her vantage point, fan-tasy, and desire even to the point of naming the family taboo of a parent's death. It is noteworthy that her fantasy and desire are expressed via an identification with masculinity. It could well be argued that Wei Ling's de-sire *to have* Yang Kwan is more a symptom of her (repressed) desire *to be like* Yang Kwan herself, a symbol for freedom and power that her mother, as an epitomé of femininity, is deprived of. This sets up a pretext for her further assertion of physical and intellectual independence later on.

Throughout the film Wei Ling's strength is portrayed in her defiance of fixed gender presumptions of femininity ("We don't need the protection of others"); her courage in voicing and pursuing her desire (by initiating all the actions in courting Yang); her intelligence (through her ability to verbalize Tung's anxieties); (her retorts against Grandma and Tung of not wanting to be a woman like Tung or the Confucius *Junzi* ["gentleman"] quoted by Grandma); her beating Yang at chess; the independence of her thinking (an argument with Tung about the meaning of female self-sac-rifice and insisting on continuing her courtship with Yang despite Tung's disapproval); the spontaneity and carefree nature of her actions (playing

77

along the river; exploring the woods without fear); her refusal to bow to social confinement; etc.

As a counterpoint to Tung's concern with normativity and tradition, Wei Ling's ability to externalize her desire through her interaction with the natural environment, including river, horses, trees, and plums, serves as a contrast to Tung's tendency to internalize her feelings and thoughts and renders Tung's silence and aloofness rather denaturalized. The operations of the forces that have brought Tung to where she is become exposed and questionable. This centralization of Wei Ling's subjectivity is particularly radical considering that her character is played by one of the popular teenage idols of the time, Chow Hsuan. The construction of Wei Ling's character in the film significantly departs from the spectacularization of Chow Hsuan's body in the popular press during the production of *The Arch*.[20]

78

THE MOTHER DESIRES

The Chinese title of the film reads *Dong furen,* literally translated as "Madam Tung." In all the newspaper ads for the film during its theatrical release, Tung's head image is used to represent the film. Tung's subjectivity is achieved through variable positions of enunciation, including through silence and repetition. Whereas Yang expresses his desire toward Tung by composing, writing, and reciting poems out loud, Tung's desire is represented through her reading and hearing; both of these activities are marked by an internalization of an external environment while Tung remains silent. Tung's discovery of Yang's love poem amid a classroom full of children's voices and her complicity in keeping that a secret signals to Yang her wavering heart. The more her lips are sealed, the more one sees that internal norm within her (*The Arch*) destabilized. When Wei Ling, the monk, and Yang Kwan are playing the game of drinking wine and composing a poem spontaneously out loud, the camera stays with a close-up of Tung on her bed, keenly listening. Yang's poem about his desire to reach the lonely Princess of the Moon and keep her company becomes the constitutive element in a cinematic centralization of Tung's fantasy and desire, to break away from her own loneliness and be accompanied.

According to Cowie's use of psychoanalysis, "fantasy is not the object of desire, but its setting"; "Fantasy as a mise-en-scène of desire is more a setting out of lack, of what is absent, than a presentation of a having, a being present."[21] The mise-en-scène of Wei Ling and Yang's marriage scene is also the mise-en-scène of Tung's fantasy. The representation of Tung's subjectivity through internalization reaches a climax in this scene, in which the mise-en-scène is done in such a way that the audience is forced to stay with Tung, and does not follow the actions of the newly-weds. Tung's point of view is so privileged that it is almost impossible to witness the marriage from outside her subjectivity. Her desire is most vividly represented in this scene when her object of desire is becoming absent, a lack, right before her eyes (and ours). Not only is she again seen as the one keenly watching (without body movements) and her silence again existing in stark contrast with the hustle and bustle of the rest of the scene, but the marriage is also shown to be internalized and disrupted by her subjectivity through a series of visual and sonoric flashbacks. In (re)experiencing the repetition of Yang's poem in Tung's voice, the audience sees and hears Tung's mind in action and her reconstruction of the entire setting of the marriage for herself. The viewing experience of the audience is forced to be located within her mise-en-scène of desire, fantasy, and loss. "The subject is present and presented through the very form of organization, composition, of the scene."[22] Tung's subject position is clear and invariable as the "I" of the story. In the end, she is the sole subject who "lives out."

79

The repetitiveness and the rapidity in editing highlights the pitch and "speed" of her emotional turmoil, which is in ironic contrast with the apparent immobility of her body. The exaggerated presence of those moments in her psyche foregrounds the stillness of her body. Like the use of freeze-frame in those key moments of her life, the authorial inscriptions are used primarily to disrupt diegetic time in order to highlight a woman's interiority. Tang herself articulates it as such:

> Freeze frame is internal experience; it freezes the important moments and extends them. That's what Proust called "the philosophy of time", and also what we Chinese have as an old saying "Once turning your head you realize a hundred years have passed." You must have this experience too, just a very brief moment, you feel it as very long, very long.[23]

The audience is led to a dialectical experience of time and agency, not one conventionally dominated by words, actions, or a linear progression of events and space, to prioritize a kind of temporality similar to what Modleski adopts from Kristéva's "Women's time" to speak of the "Woman's film," a *different* kind of temporal experience inseparable from space.[24] If we compare *The Arch* with *Charulata* (1964), directed by Satyajit Ray, another film that shares the same cameraman, Subrata Mitra, and which also narrates the repression of a woman's desire and her loneliness pitted against the repressiveness of monogamy and marriage, we find similar strategies used in representing time, such as freeze-frame, flashback, slow zoom, and a minimal use of close-ups. What distinguishes *The Arch,* though, is the representation of the inaccessibility of female bodies, contrasted with an emphasized accessibility of their minds, achieved in part through Tang Shu Shuen's language of repetition: women's bodies turning and their minds returning. When Yang has an extended absence from Tung's house, and both Tung and Wei Ling have been waiting for his return, his appearance at the door is strategically match-cut with both Tung and Wei Ling turning to the camera. The women's slight change of posture produces an emotional significance that registers their desires through space, between a significant absence and presence. After Yang has become Tung's son-in-law, and they meet each other in the courtyard, it is again Tung's extended silence and her body turning around and away that marks her emotional departure. The audience will follow Tung to revisit emotionally and psychologically this site of separation again and again in later parts of the film. The more we see her turning to leave, the more we realize the unlikelihood of her ever leaving.

Repetition and return are perhaps for the women in melodrama "manifestations of *another* relationship to time and space, desire and memory,"[25] and this difference is not sufficiently accounted for in a patriarchal understanding of normativity, subjectivity, or agency. Further, I would contend that it is exactly because a woman like Tung could be moved without moving in a world that prioritizes moving over being moved, that the woman suffers repeatedly. What distinguishes *The Arch* from many conventional melodramas is that it uses the *dominating* forlornness of this particular woman's experience of time and space to critique the dominant society's relationship to time and space. It does not show any attempt to use the male discourse to provide any closure, not even an ironic one. Quite the contrary. During the course of the film, *The Arch* uses various filmic strategies to carve out, to open up, to accelerate an intensity of Tung's interior space, highlighting all the various *open* possibilities of her desire, which is in turn positioned to throw the social, cultural, and political structures that forcibly impose an impossibility onto her into serious question.

PRICE FOR NORMATIVITY

I suggested earlier that the subversiveness of the courtship between Wei Ling and Yang is, in part, based on the possibility of role reversal: of their exchanging positions of active and passive, voice and silence, pursuer and pursued. The scene of "the morning after," however, shows Wei Ling adopting the most stereotypical feminine position, indulging herself in an endless list of caring "do's and don'ts" for her husband about to depart for his routine journey, and ending up in a tiny cuddled position in his embrace. The gender roles once challenged by Wei Ling herself seem to snap back to "normal" once heterosexual desire is consummated. This irony highlights a problem within the strategy of role reversal itself: however attractive to female spectators as a temporary device to equalize power relations, it still relies on and therefore reinforces a dualism that inherently perpetuates the subjugation of women as the Other.

In comparison, role reversal is seen as a possible self-positioning at times in the love affair between Tung and Yang, but it is constantly renegotiated and destabilized. As a woman possessing unusual literary and medical skills, Tung is seen going out to cure the children of neighbors while Yang stays home and reads. Reasserting his masculinity, Yang asks to accompany (and protect) her, but Tung refuses. However, Yang's access to Tung's library also leads to his repossession of a cultural tradition and patriarchal order that "the Word" dominates. Unlike a Eurocentric tradition that might ghettoize the semiotic as the realm of the feminine and the disruptive,[26] a true Chinese *Junzi*, according to Confucianism, is to be capable both as a warrior (*wu*) and as a scholar (*wen*). By accessing Tung's—in fact, her late husband's—literary collection, Yang gains ultimate mobility of *ye wen ye wu:* the privilege to move freely between *wu* and *wen;* the ability to announce his desire to Tung through his use of lyrical words and to Wei Ling through his actions. Tang herself has consciously situated the "origins" of Chinese culture in the formation of its literary tradition. The "Director's Notes" in the publicity pamphlet used for the premiere screening of *The Arch* at Hong Kong City Hall begins like this:

> The Arch departs from the traditional ways of filmmaking in China and attempts to go back to the method by which Chinese characters (word-symbols) were originally constructed.[27]

Tung's struggle in *The Arch* could be read as a constant negotiation *within* a structure that privileges men's access to these word-symbols and men's organization of time and space through the power of signification. When the film begins, the villagers have been waiting for the Word of the Emperor, which will confirm the construction of the Arch. The Emperor's Word and the words on the Arch signify the pride of a community unified only through the members of a group imagining their bonding with one another. While the Chinese Emperor rules by some form of cosmological dispensation and is literally called "Son of Heaven," his possession of the Word is legitimized and demonstrated by his privileged access to ontological truth. Men's privileged access to literacy also legitimizes their dominance and inheritance in the social, political, and cultural order accordingly. The desirability of both men in *Charulata* is marked by their automatic access to words: one using them as a political tool, the other for literary composition and singing songs. Charu's desire toward both of them is negotiated through her seeking access to both privileged realms of literacy. Sexual and gendered difference in *Charulata* manifests itself first and foremost in men's and women's different relations to language, in particular to the written word.

Midway through *The Arch,* just when Tung registers her desire toward Yang by suggesting the planting of some chrysanthemums in their garden, a letter is delivered that announces that a recommendation has been made to the Emperor about the imminent granting of the Arch. The camera pans across the garden, revealing diverse reactions of the characters. Grandma is seen as the most welcoming, Yang the most anguished, and Tung the most ambivalent. The assertion of a political order as signified by the use of an imperial language in the letter, and a specific organization of time through a linear progression of bureaucratic procedures, is seen as an undesirable and irreconcilable disruption to our identification with Tung's experience of her kind of time and desire. The arrival of the Emperor's Word in Tung's life is not unlike the arrival of the television in Cary's life in *All That Heaven Allows* (1956). An omnipresent medium finally formulates a resolution to their lives and presents itself as a material condition, perceived and approved by all. Yet it is also the moment when both women most acutely feel their desires violated and are in a tremendous state of loss about the potential of their lives, which seems to have been brushed aside. In Tung's case, it is compulsory to show gratitude. She has to kneel to receive the Arch.

Public order and its specific organization of time and space is seen in *The Arch* as mediated by an imaginary community spirit and feudal values. When Tung carves out space for expressing her anguish and frustration by killing the chicken and running to the mountains (all done in silence), we witness the villagers carving out their space overarched and protected by the Emperor's privileged words. Like those from male critics who code Tang as the "Woman" (director) because of her demonstrated talent, these words from the Emperor code Tung as the "Woman" through her demonstration of "Chastity." Tung's silence becomes a site of resistance against a system of language that ultimately Otherizes her. In this language, she is positioned to use her dead husband's surname and is, therefore, ultimately nameless. Tung's negotiation could be seen as intrinsically a struggle of a subject seeking the sign of her own existence outside herself, in a discourse at once hegemonic and indifferent. Through maintaining the boundaries of social categories such as "Woman," "demonstrator of Chastity," and "Madam," she subordinates her being for the price of a name, that is, for the possibility of existence. The moment she accepts the Arch is the moment when choice becomes impossible for the subject in order to be.

The film ends with Tang's small, upright, unmoving body pitted against the huge, upright, unmoving Arch. Not unlike the women's catfight on stage in *Dance, Girl, Dance* (1940), which could be read *simultaneously* as a reassertion of patriarchal oppression and a site for theatricalization of female friendship, Tung's minimal body language may be held as both representative of internalized oppression and of resistance to the spectacularization and fetishization of the Chinese female body, especially seen in the context of the actress Lisa Lu Yan's career, who starred in the stage productions of *Flower Drum Song* and *The World of Suzie Wong*, and in films like *The Mountain Road* (1960, opposite James Stewart) and *Tai-Pan* (1986). While the representation of Lisa Lu Yan's body in *The Arch* could be read as a protest to a cross-cultural phallocentric language populated by American cowboys, European sinophiles, Chinese emperors, husbands, scholars, and captains, I would not rule out its potential to be taken as a form of female self-policing and silencing. I read this moment of simultaneous contradiction as a strategy for survival, one that renders various, even oppositional, positions of identification possible, and also makes the authorial inscriptions of the female author to be less explicitly identifiable, thus more difficult to be ghettoized.

PRIVILEGE OF DISTANCE

The mise-en-scène of Tung's fantasies and desires is undercut by the mise-en-scène of the construction of the Arch: the erection of the norm reasserting itself *within* her. Do the men in *The Arch* suffer from the *same* kind of internalization of prohibition that Tung suffers from? Lao Chang says he has been *watching* her in pain. His suffering, the construction of his interiority, stems from the distance imposed by spectatorship; his position and ability to watch the suffering subject and his self-reflexivity produced through his identification with her. It is this privileged distance, of producing power, pleasure, and pain through watching the Other suffer, not the suffering *per se*, I argue, that constitutes a privilege of narcissism and masochism inaccessible to women in Chinese culture.

Without access to a language that registers her name, all the space Tung has is within herself rather than outside. She is deprived of a system that allows her to produce a form of agency through creating a distance from her own suffering. Her killing of the chicken could be seen as a desperate transference of herself onto another being, however temporary. Her running away would then be an attempt to physically take leave of herself. The ultimate mobility of the men is marked by their ability to negotiate their distance with their own emotional identification, which is ideally in direct proportion to the degree of suffering the woman internalizes. When Yang meets Tung in the courtyard as the son-in-law, Tung's emotional signification (her body turning in silence) and Yang's identification with her (his being moved and embarrassed) becomes too much to watch/bear for him and he, therefore, arranges to have Wei Ling leave with him right afterward. Likewise, Chang also chooses to leave the scene, to get farther from the spectacle of the suffering object. The distance between the signification of suffering and the male subject needs to be constantly inspected and reworked in order for the male subject to have any kind of narcissistic and/or masochistic pleasures. The repudiation of an identification without distance constitutes these subject positions of masculinity, at times through physical departure and verbal denunciation, like Yang Kwan and Lao Chang in *The Arch*.

The series of cross-fades of endless misty mountains and valleys that ends and begins the film, which Vincent Canby hates so much, highlights the naturalization of a self-perpetuating order that even Chang the servant can choose to leave and Tung the woman cannot. The ultimate glorification of womanhood is represented as the ultimate condemnation. The moment she enters history is the moment she realizes she will always be left out.

Heaven and earth are not good to the beings that they produce, but treat them like straw dogs.[28]

This well-known Daoist principle acknowledges the constructibility of human society by "Heaven" (the Emperor) and "Earth" (nature), and propagates the inevitable oppressiveness of such constructibility through its absolute (unnegotiated) indifference. Nature is seen as the reason for—and the extension of—the violence of culture.

85

THE FILMMAKER TO BE

In revisiting and analyzing the peculiar position of Tang's as a "woman" filmmaker in the late 1960s, I have attempted to illuminate the psychological and political processes of racialization and feminization, which could very well reinforce similar ideological values comparable to the phallocratic dismissal of female authorship. I argue that the responses of these critics to *The Arch* are directly related to their inability to comprehend the discourses of feminism and anti-nationalism articulated in the film. As a "Chinese film" made by a "woman filmmaker," *The Arch* poses a critique of the values (of "being Chinese" and a "woman") that it ostensibly promotes. In the end, the cinema produced by *The Arch* is a heterogeneous representation that embodies contradictory desires: forces not necessarily reconciled or unified by the cinematic apparatus or the diegesis. Through isolating her into the one-of a-kind "woman director" not directly related to the ethnic context of being Chinese *in Hong Kong* or the cultural, historical context of Hong Kong female authorship *in the 1960s and 1970s,* the local press went through a ritual of partly disowning her. The Hong Kong media culture of the 1960s and 1970s—another budding imagined community not unlike the village in *The Arch*—needed to find a route to simplify the issues of identity that Tang's authorship foregrounds and still be able to claim part of that authorship as its own.

If we regroup Tang's gender and cultural identities, and put her in the context of one of a few Hong Kong Chinese woman film directors, preceded by others like Ren Yizhi and Esther Eng, this signifier will risk an exposure and perhaps even a reexamination of a patriarchal lineage and its inheritance of culture, which is exactly what *The Arch* in part critiques. I argue, in this chapter, that Tang's representation of female subjectivity and its marginalization within a patriarchal *and* nationalistic tradition in *The Arch*, together with the images in which she has been represented, becomes a (self-)representation of marginality produced by a culture of which she is and is not a part of.

NOTES

1. This chapter is rewritten from Chapter 1 of Yau Ching, *Filming Margins*. Most of the arguments have been substantially condensed for this publication.

2. A Chinese woman filmmaker before Tang particularly worth noting is Esther Eng (1915–1970), whose work I have discussed briefly in *Filming Margins* and *Xing/bie guangying* (Sexing shadows). I would like to thank Law Kar for introducing me to Eng's work in the 1990s.

3. Sek Kei, "Dong furen" (The Arch). All translations from Chinese to English in this chapter are mine.

4. Rey Chow, "Loving Women," 121–170.

5. Rey Chow, "Loving Women," 121.

6. Rey Chow, *Primitive Passions,* 135–136.

7. Kaja Silverman, "Fragments of a Fashionable Discourse," 143.

8. Judith Mayne, "Lesbian Looks," 118.

9. Lau Shing-hon, "Tang Shu Shuen," 360.

10. Stephen Teo, "Hong Kong Cinema," 140.

11. Law Kar, "The Significance of *The Arch*," 163.

12. Mayne, "Lesbian Looks," 118.

13. Vincent Canby, "The Arch," 8.

14. All the biographical data was collected through personal interviews with Tang Shu Shuen at her home in Los Angeles in 2002 and 2003.

15. Wai Chi Chuk, "Liangwei guopian qingnian daoyan" (Two young Chinese directors).

16. See, for example, G. B. Endacott, *A History of Hong Kong*, p. 314, and Matthew Turner, "Hong Kong Design and the Roots of the Sino-American Trade Disputes," 51.

17. Sing Wah, "Yu Tang Shuxuan tan dianying" (*Talking about Film with Tung Shu Shuen*), 28.

18. Kar, "The Significance of *The Arch*," 163.

19. Tang recalled in an interview how Subrata Mitra had conflicts with the Hong Kong film crew; one of the examples she cited was that Mitra, in order to achieve a certain kind of cinematic look, rejected the conventional lights available at the Cathay Studios and

chose to build his own lights with paper mounted on wood instead. The Hong Kong film crew members looked down upon these cheaply built lights and threw them down from a slope in the middle of the shoot. The film crew members called Mitra "Ah Cha," the derogatory term for South Asians living in Hong Kong, many of whom were commonly seen at the time as associated with jobs like security guards.

20. See, for example, Lui Yi Tin, "Chow Hsuan Talks about the Love Script," 27.
21. Elizabeth Cowie, "Fantasia," *Representing the Woman: Cinema and Psychoanalysis.* London: Macmillan, 1997, 123–165.
22. Ibid., 134.
23. Lu Li, "Tang Shuxuan fangwen ji" (Interview with Tang Shu Shuen, 1970), 30.
24. Tania Modleski, "Time and Desire in the Woman's Film."
25. Ibid., 336.
26. Julia Kristéva, "Women's Time," 113.
27. Tang Shu Shuen, "Director's Notes," 5.
28. Lao Zi, *Dao De Jing*, 12.

3

Migrating Hearts

THE CULTURAL GEOGRAPHY OF
SYLVIA CHANG'S MELODRAMA

ZHEN ZHANG

CHINESE FILM scholar Chen Feibao's book, *The Art of Taiwan Directors,* has the chapters on Ang Lee and Sylvia Chang back to back.[1] This arrangement occurred simply because the two were born just one year apart. However, the two have more in common beyond this age connection. Both came of age and embraced cinema as their creative medium in the burgeoning Taiwan New Cinema movement in the 1980s and early 1990s, and both have actively pursued a career beyond Taiwan, with Lee shuttling between the island and the United States and Chang operating between Taiwan and Hong Kong (and occasionally Singapore). In subject matter and style, each has demonstrated a shared propensity for family and romantic melodrama and the attendant cultural and ethical concerns with the changing meaning and practice of love and kinship in cross-cultural and transnational contexts. These features set them apart from the rigorous modernist formal experiments and introspective intellectual orientation that underscore the mainstay of the New Taiwan Cinema and post–New Cinema, whose most internationally renowned figureheads are Edward Yang, Hou Hsiao-hsien, and Tsai Ming-liang. In comparison, most of Lee's and Chang's art-pop melodramas seem sentimental fares with their skillful orchestration of broken hearts and torn ties. The audiences they address and the spectatorship their textual and extra-textual systems construct tend to be sinophone and pan-Asian in terms of demographic base, while extending into other intercultural domains. Ang Lee's more recent works have shown a greater variety in genre experimentation, including period pieces, and he is proving himself to be a leading global director who has transcended linguistic and cultural boundaries in terms of artistic identity. Above all, he has, as a naturalized U.S. citizen, entered the pantheon of great American or Hollywood directors.

Where Chang differs from Lee in terms of geocultural affinities and the use of the melodramatic form is where my investigation of the aesthetic and sociocultural significance of her work begins. Chang's work as a whole hardly appeals to conventional masculine auteur criticism and national cinema framework. Straddling independent and commercial modes of production, Chang's films work with the melodramatic tradition, especially the *wenyi pian* strand, in Chinese-language cinema. Yet she refashions and inflects it with accents drawn from various articulations of the genre (or mode) broadly conceived, including the so called "woman's films" (with a pronounced female address) from classical Hollywood that fueled much of the revisionist discourse on melodrama.[2] This chapter will try to contextualize her multifaceted authorship by focusing on three works which she wrote (or co-wrote) and directed, and in which she co-starred, *Zui ai* (Passion, 1986), *Xin dong* (Tempting Heart, 1999), and *20 30 40* (2004), whose onscreen and off-screen settings include Taiwan, Hong Kong, Japan, Canada, and Malaysia, and whose characters are a motley group of evolving subjects with diverse cultural backgrounds, class standings, and sexual orientations. At the emotional center of her films is the perennial struggle over the meaning of home and love. At the same time, Chang's alternately sentimental and reflective treatment of the vulnerability of intergenerational bonds, as well as border-crossing love (and, to an extent, sexuality), is filtered through a restyled maternal melodrama and staged against the backdrop of significant historical and cultural changes in the region and the world at the turn of a new century.

BEYOND THE TREASURE ISLAND

While Chang as a Taiwan-born actress and director is a well-known entity among Chinese-language and pan-Asian audiences and critics, she is conspicuously absent in the growing body of scholarship in English on

89

Taiwan cinema, which has largely followed the often conjoined model of auteur criticism and national cinema. This model highlights a number of male directors—in particular those of the New Cinema movement—and their intellectual and aesthetic meditations on Taiwan's ambivalent colonial legacy and cultural identity in a time of rapid modernization. Chief among these scholarly works is *Taiwan Film Directors: A Treasure Island* by Emilie Yueh-yu Yeh and Darrel Davis, which offers an eloquent yet highly selective presentation of several Taiwan masters of the cinematic art, in particular Edward Yang, Hou Hsiao-hsien, Ang Lee, and Tsai Ming-liang. June Yip's intertextually woven and theoretically driven book, *Envisioning Taiwan: Fiction, Cinema, and the Nation in the Cultural Imaginary,* on the other hand, cuts deeply into the cultural and postcolonial "imaginary" terrain that gave rise to the nativist writer Hwang Chun-ming and Hou Hsiao-hisen, and singles them out as true voices and potent seers for an alternative national consciousness. The list of "national treasures" in Chris Berry and Feii Lu's anthology, *Island on the Edge: Taiwan New Cinema and After,* collects a few more names (or films) such as Wu Nien-jen and Chang Tso-chi, but the large bulk of the volume is again devoted to Yang, Hou, Lee, and Tsai (with four out of twelve essays on Hou alone). Beyond these Taiwan-centered studies, the only woman included in Michael Berry's *Speaking in Images: Interviews with Contemporary Chinese Filmmakers* is the Hong Kong New Wave director Ann Hui, whose film career incidentally was launched with support from Chang.

The almost exclusively male profile of Taiwan New Cinema and overall Taiwan film history,[3] along with the omission of female authorship (in various capacities), in the previously mentioned scholarly works is especially glaring given the relatively more visible presence of female directors in the Hong Kong New Wave and China's Fourth and Fifth Generations, which emerged and flourished in the 1980s and early 1990s.[4] While the fiction writer and scriptwriter Zhu Tianwen has received some attention thanks to her long-lasting collaboration with Hou Hsiao-hsien, Sylvia Chang's prolific and innovative work has not been treated adequately. This is surprising given the fact that she starred in some of the most important New Cinema films (for example, Edward Yang's *Haitan de yitian* [That Day on the Beach, 1983]), and that her career behind the camera started as early as 1980 and seriously took off in the 1990s, punctuated by popularly or critically acclaimed films such as *Shaonü Xiaoyu* (Siao Yu, 1995), *Jintian bu huijia* (Tonight Nobody Goes Home, 1996), and *Xin dong* (Tempting Heart, 1999). Her recent credits include the award-winning *20 30 40,* a refashioned melodrama focusing on the love lives and work lives of three women of different generations in cosmopolitan Taipei today, and *Yige hao baba* (Run Papa Run, 2008). All the while, Sylvia Chang continued to thrive as an actress,[5] performing in both her own and others' films. Her role as a single working mother running a family restaurant in Singapore's Chinatown in *Hainan jifan* (Rice Rhapsody, 2004) won her the coveted Golden Horse Best Actress Award.

Several features of Chang's border-crossing career and films may be clues as to why her name and work have been excluded from the auteurist canons of the New Cinema or post–New Cinema. Like Ang Lee, Chang's home base and work base tend to be more transnational than bound to the "treasure island." She continuously shuffles her life and film locations between Hong Kong and Taiwan, while making occasional forays to New York and Japan. As early as 1972, as a budding teen pop singer and TV music hostess, she moved to Hong Kong for the first time, to play leading roles in Golden Harvest's new kung-fu films. Her craft was garnered, not from attending film schools in the West as many New Wave directors did, but first through her deep immersion in the golden-age commercial cinema of Taiwan and Hong Kong in the 1970s, working as an A-list actress with the preeminent mandarin masters such as Li Han-hsiang (*Hong lou meng*, Dream of the Red Chamber, 1977) and King Hu (*Shanzhong chuanqi*, Legend of the Mountain, 1979). Moving again to Hong Kong in 1979, she inadvertently joined the Hong Kong's first New Wave by producing and starring in Ann Hui's first feature *Feng jie* (The Secret, 1979). Shortly after, she found herself in the midst of the rising Taiwan New Cinema, acting and producing for young directors such as Edward Yang and Yu Kan-ping, causing some critics to call her the "mother of the new directors."[6]

Rather than abandoning acting as she outgrew her teen-idol image and young leading lady roles, Chang's multitasking film career before and behind the camera confounds the conventional wisdom about stardom and authorship, especially with regards to women, as few if any in world film history have been able to do, not to mention succeed in, both aspects of filmmaking over a lifetime. Chinese critics including Chen Feibao thus tend to characterize Sylvia Chang as a one-of-a-kind *cainü* (talented woman), linking her to the genealogy of literary women in premodern Chinese cultural history produced or patronized by the patriarchal order.[7] Since she is also a *jairen* (beauty) by virtue of her profession as a movie star, her talents in areas (in particular directing) usually dominated by men are not taken as seriously as her performance onscreen.

Interestingly, the only existing scholarly article in English that introduces Chang's work as a director connects her with another Taiwan leading actress, Yang Hui-shan.[8] Shiao-ying Shen argues that traces of a feminine writing, or *écriture fèminine* (from the French feminist writer Hélené Cixous), can be located and connected in Yang's performing body and Chang's film *Siao Yu*. A Taiwan-version of Gong Li ahead of the latter's time, Yang's viscerally and emotionally powerful portrait of suffering yet sexually autonomous women in a series of films by Chang Yi in the 1980s (*Yuqing sao,* Jade Love, 1984; *Wo zheyang guole yisheng,* Kuei-mei, A Woman, 1985; *Wo de ai,* This Love of Mine, 1986) generated heated public debates on gender and sexual politics and injected an intense feminine presence in Taiwan's film culture in an era of drastic sociopolitical and economic transformation. If Yang's body-writing remained a circumscribed product of male authorship, the decline of the star system and the rise of the actress-turned-director Sylvia Chang and a new generation of actresses (such as Liu Jo-ying, who stars in *Siao Yu*), observes Shen, allowed the emerging feminine writing initiated by Yang's ambivalent performance to extend and ramify in a new era.

Sylvia Chang's career and work may be better placed in the "sinophone" cultural geography.[9] According to Shu-mei Shih, sinophone applies not only to languages and speeches of sinetic origins that have been historically displaced or relocated to areas away from the Chinese continent, but also to non-sinetic articulations in other forms of hybrid languages and media that permeate the life and expression of overseas Chinese worldwide. Thus Shih sees Ang Lee's films, which are about Chinese past and present, in China, Taiwan, and the United States, who speak "Chinese" with various inflections as well as English, and their transnational reception, both productively and problematically, as "sinophone articulations" par excellence.[10] Chang herself speaks Mandarin, Cantonese, and English fluently; many of her characters do the same or with varying degrees of proficiency or accents. Some even speak Japanese and Malay (as in *Tempting Heart, 20 30 40*), indicating their migrating trajectories. *Siao Yu* is set entirely in New York, focusing on a young Mainland immigrant couple (Siao Yu and her husband) and their emotional and legal entanglements with an aging Italian-American writer through a "green card marriage." Although the film was produced by CMP (Central Motion Picture), a government-sponsored corporation in Taiwan, and the roles played and directed by Taiwanese, the story and sensibility have little to do with or say about Taiwan. The fact that it is based on an original story by Yen Ge-ling, a mainland-born and U.S.-based Chinese woman writer, adds one more layer in Chang's cinematic sinophone writing. Yen's literary imagination, Liu's nuanced performance, and Chang's masterful direction weave a compelling transnational tale of women's capacity for survival and self-transformation.

HOME(LAND) IS NOT WHERE THE HEART IS

Whether melodrama is a genre or a mode has been widely debated in film studies, and critics and scholars of East and West have also contended on the applicability of the term to non-Western forms of melodrama. But one thing has stayed at the focal center of these debates: that the meaning of family and home constitute the central mise-en-scène of the large bulk of film and television melodrama. The groundbreaking volume edited by Christine Gledhill that reshaped the melodrama studies is entitled *Home Is Where the Heart Is*, referring to the centrality of the trope in the melodramatic tradition in the West, particularly in classical Hollywood cinema. *No Place Like Home: Locations of Heimat in German Cinema*,[11] Johannes von Moltke's study on the genealogy of "Heimat film" in modern German cultural history, offers a more recent variation on the enduring trope in the melodramatic imagination in the West.

Chris Berry and Mary Farquhar's engagement with revisionist melodrama studies in the context of Chinese-language cinema also affirms the persistent preoccupation with the home and family, but with an important twist. They stress that Chinese cinema's preoccupation with melodrama and the meaning of home and family is intimately bound to the fate and definition of the nation at different historical moments and places in modern Chinese history. "All in all," they observe, "melodramatic realism is a major strain in the Chinese cinema because its central theme of outraged innocence was often perceived as real in national, and not just personal, terms."[12] As a "mixed mode of the national," melodramatic realism has been continuously utilized and reshaped to account for the "divided families, divided nation" and their restitution in various forms under different sociopolitical arrangements throughout Chinese film history (including Taiwan and Hong Kong). However, these painstaking efforts, often dictated by the hegemonic nation-building interests of the state (be it the People's Republic of China or the Republic of China), began to erode in the late-twentieth century under the parallel and sometimes intersecting forces of postmodern, postcolonial, and postsocialist experimentation. A number of New Wave films in the Chinese-speaking region, notably Allen Fong's *Fuzi qing* (Father and Son, 1981), Chen Kaige's *Huang tudi* (Yellow Earth, 1984), and Tsai Ming-liang's *Aiqing wansui* (Vive L'amour, 1994), visibly articulate the "emptying out" of the family-home in both cinematic registers and cultural imaginary.[13] The term "emptying out" is first coined by the Taiwan feminist scholar Chang Hsiao-hung in her trenchant analysis of *Vive L'amour* in which she argues that the emptied out *jia* (family-home) on screen is indicative of the changing Taiwanese society and culture, beyond that of the traditional family structure.[14] While Fong and Chen's films are deeply steeped in a neo-realist or modernist ethos and aesthetic, Tsai's films, in my view, mark out a new terrain of the melodramatic imagination that goes beyond not just "home" but also homeland, or nation. Tsai Ming-liang's pronounced gay identity and sinophone belonging as a Malay Chinese, along with his Buddhist faith, are important factors to consider in this regard.

Sylvia Chang's take on the family-home trope at the heart of the Chinese film tradition may not appear as philosophically and formally radical as Cai's. Yet her feminist stance and her own less homeland-bound life and career are no less significant clues for understanding her interest in exploring the shifting parameters of the family-home outside the allegorical space of the nation. While the family-home is not exactly emptied out in her films, and sometimes a sense of home may even be restored (several of her films resort to happy endings), Chang's interest in the enduring trope resides in its inherent gender problematic and its everyday expressions below or above the national scale, and beyond the prevalent allegorical deployment centered on "fathers and sons" (which also appears, albeit in a radically transmuted form, in Tsai's films).

An overview of the thematic concerns in Chang's films reveals the recurring motif of the incomplete family and its attendant anxieties and experiments in love relations and family structure. Her films are heavily invested in pairing or clustering of female protagonists, especially mothers, daughters, and sisters or quasi-sisters. *Passion* pivots around the ambivalent friendship of two middle-aged middleclass women, who were close girlfriends until they found themselves in love with the same man—a U.S. trained lawyer. Mingyu marries the lawyer she works for as secretary, fulfilling the typical "marry well" expectation of a socially mobile woman according to the normative gender codes even in a rapidly modernizing Taiwan society. Bai Yun (played by Chang), a designer at an advertising company, has an affair with Mingyu's newlywed husband. This results in a parallel shadow family, as the two friends each gives birth to a daughter. The heteronormative contract in the form of marriage alienates but also strangely binds them together, as Bai Yun seems to knowingly get herself pregnant almost at the same time as Mingyu. (In the middle of the film, the two compare the sizes of their protruding bellies and give birth in the same hospital.) Bai Yun resorts to marrying another man for her daughter's sake; but the lives of the two women and their children are now irrevocably connected through blood ties.

The secret love affair is unraveled—or more precisely, reflected upon—through a series of flashbacks as the two meet for lunch at a country club years later, confessing their mixed feelings about love and marriage. Taiwan film critic Huang Jianye disparages the "hateful" (henyi) theme of two women fighting over one man's love even into his grave as fundamentally conservative, as they seem to linger on painful memories rather than seeking possible liberation. The device of flashback is thereby seen at the service of a regressive "fateful history" (mingding lishi).[15]

The overwhelmingly elaborate sets, deco and color palette of the film, along with the stylized performance of the two women in their maturity (outside of the flashbacks) invite a different perspective on the melodramatic configuration or stylization of gender relations. The film begins with the engagement ceremony at the lawyer's home—(later the couple moves to a brand-new "nuptial" house)—but ends in a relatively open space outside domesticity, in a country club nested in a lushly beautiful setting. This setting seems more theatrical than realistic—a hybrid landscape of an emerging generic global upper-middle-class that cuts across the American suburbs, European country estates, and Hong Kong and Taiwan's nouveau riche playgrounds. (There are frequent references in the film to U.S. or European education of several male characters that are deemed more desirable as husbands at home.) The death of the lawyer, the love of each of their lives, effectively reunites the two lifelong girlfriends, joined by their daughters. As the day cools and the sun sets against an indigo blue sky, the children call the mothers to the dinning table. As if bidding farewell to the guilt-ridden memories associated with the deceased man, Bai Yun suggests to Mingyu that the "past is full of too much fantasy (huanxiang)." She extends her hand to the latter and the two walk with arms intertwined to the patio to join their daughters and a future son-in-law. Two roses stand in the middle of the table, behind them are the two friends smiling at each other intently, with candlelight flickering in their eyes.

The somewhat surprisingly warm glow of the concluding scene fore-grounds the overall artifice of the film's mise-en-scène, especially in scenes set in the houses of the married couple and the country club. Chen Feibao finds, in the lavish deco reeking with "high quality sense of mate-rial life" (*gaozhigan wuzhi shenghuo*), echoes of Qiong Yao film and televi-sion melodramas of the 1970s, and that it serves well for contrasting with Bai Yun's simpler life as a youthful, tender-hearted working woman.[16] I view, however, that the nearly clichéd upper-middle-class paraphernalia (from furniture to dress to tennis-playing), drenched in an overly satu-rated color palette and unnatural lighting, resonates with Douglas Sirk's postwar "Hollywood Baroque." Sirk's "ironic mise-en-scène," observe John Mercer and Martin Schingler, "suggests a critique of bourgeois ideol-ogy that reveals wider conflicts and tensions that manifest themselves through the dominant cinema of the period."[17]

The rejoining of the two girlfriends' hands puts indeed an ironic spin on a key mise-en-scène element in the film—a painting of two inter-twined hands suggesting intense erotic union that Bai Yun brings to her friend at the opening of the film (figs. 3.1, 3.2). It has since been hung in the bedroom of the couple. While it is meant to be a token of Bai Yun's blessing for the newly wed, unwittingly the painting has become the wit-ness to the fractured marriage at its inception. Huang Jianye is right to observe that the plot and the motivations of the characters are utterly "unrealistic," but that critique does not take into account the hyperbolic nature of melodrama, especially the kind poised to expose the often mad-dening strictures of bourgeois sensibilities and values, or illusions of happiness, especially as regards patrilineal family and social structures. In this context, Bai Yun's realization that they as young women had too much "fantasy" about romantic love and marriage makes a more tren-chant sense. They may have been trapped in a historically overdetermined "fate," but the "hatefulness" in their shared act of remembrance is really directed to that past-tense fantasy or illusion that has estranged them.

The redemptive trope of female bonding, reinforced by the friendship and sisterhood between their daughters (who seem oblivious to the family secret), in *Passion* finds continued expression and reconfigurations in her other works to follow. *Shasha Jiajia zhanqilai* (Sisters of the World Unite, 1991) is explicitly structured around a pair of sisters and their divergent fates and choices with regard to love and work. Both struggle with their economic and emotional dependence (as housewife or mistress) on men at home or at the workplace, and also with each other in trying to affirm

FIGURE 3.1 A painting of two intertwined hands suggesting intense erotic union (*Passion*, 1986)

FIGURE 3.2 Two girlfriends rejoin their hands at long last (*Passion*, 1986)

their connection and mutual support. In *Tempting Heart,* two high school best friends, Xiaorou and Chen Li, again find their closeness tested and alienated by their attraction to a young man, a high school senior and an amateur guitarist (played by Kaneshiro Takeshi). However, this tale of female bonding is filtered through a conscious queer lens, through which female affection latent in Chang's earlier films is articulated more saliently (a motif she returns to in *20 30 40*).

FAREWELL TO LOVE

Tempting Heart differs from Chang's earlier efforts in melodrama, while retaining Chang's favored sentimental tonality mixing tears and laughter. Here she shifts her focus to adolescent girls on the brink of social and sexual initiation, and sets a tale of triangular love beyond Hong Kong, in a transurban geography that includes Tokyo (and alludes to other global cities). Here family and home are presented as even more fragmented and unstable ground for individual formation and social and cultural cohesion. More notable is the deliberate framing of a local teen love story and its transnational aftermath within the metanarrative of Cheryl (played by Chang), a middle-aged filmmaker developing the script, as the work-in-progress story based on her own experience unfolds with trials and tribulations.

To begin with, the two female protagonists' bonding may be attributed to their tenuous ties to their own immediate families. Xiaorou lives with her unmarried aunt while her mother has immigrated to Canada (the father is hardly mentioned), where she tries to remarry and settle so that she could bring her daughter over. Xiaorou frequently sleeps over at Chen Li's place, where her parents are barely seen. Several intimate scenes show the two girls sleeping in the same bed, with arms or legs around each other. Chen Li is visibly in love with Xiaorou, whereas the latter perceives their mutual affection as close friendship. Chen has a crash on Haojun when the three meet at a concert. Haojun is the only one among them with a visible but no less troubled nuclear family. His stern father derides his guitar-playing and urges him to study harder for entering college while his soft-hearted mother looks silently on. The budding love between Xiaorou and Haojun is quickly snipped by Lin's father and Xiaorou's mother (who returns for Christmas), after the young lovers have spent a cold night together in a hotel on the Lantau Island. Xiaorou, presumably a virgin, is forced to get a medical check to see whether or not they have had sex. Haojun is ordered to stop seeing her until he has passed the college exam, to fulfill the expectation of Xiaorou's mother that he would be able to provide and care for her daughter. The misunderstanding between the three friends accelerates the premature ending of an innocent romance and a close female friendship.

The plot takes on a surprising turn after Haojun, having failed the exam twice, is sent off to Japan by his father to find a way of life. He becomes a tour guide for Chinese tourists in Tokyo where Chen Li abruptly shows up and intrudes into his lonely life. The two lead a struggling immigrants' life in a cramped apartment in Tokyo and reluctantly pass as a couple as they realize their hearts belong elsewhere, to an aching yet carefree youthful past back in Hong Kong embodied by the memory of Xiaorou. Meanwhile, Xiaorou has grown into a fashion executive cum global jetsetter. She has also taken her mother under her wings in her upscale apartment. On a business trip to Tokyo, she runs into Haojun and the two consummate their love at long last at her hotel room. All the while, Chen Li is in the know and confronts Haojun one day, "Let's get a divorce. . . . The truth is, all this time, we have been in love with the same woman." Sometime later, she literally fades way from the triangulation as she dies of a fatal disease.

A more conventional melodrama aimed for a satisfying resolution might have used Chen Li's convenient disappearance to propel the reunion of the heterosexual couple, now that obstacles including parents' objection and socially unsanctioned same-sex love are out of the way. Instead, the pathos induced by the "too-lateness" of a finally consummated love is not recuperated by the "just in time" effort to create a happy ending. Haojun flies to Hong Kong to propose to Xiaorou, beseeching her to move to Japan. Xiaorou hesitates, but no clear indication is given as to exactly why. In discussing this scene with her co-writer—a young man on the brink of marriage, Cheryl interprets it in terms of Xiaorou's (her younger self) pragmatism or lack of courage for a risk-taking move to a foreign country. Yet other elements in the film suggest that Xiaorou's feelings and situations are constantly in flux. She has a coworker boyfriend who shares her everyday reality in Hong Kong; and she is practically her aging mother's sole caretaker. Her ambition as a professional woman and her responsibility as a filial daughter (despite their earlier unhappy frictions) intertwine in a paradoxical present tense, compounding modern aspirations and traditional moral obligations, whereas her love for both

FIGURE 3.3 "These are the days when I missed you . . . Now I return them to you." (*Tempting Heart*, 1999)

Lin and Chen Li have remained in the past. Encountering her youthful flame in Tokyo, while solving the mystery of Haojun's sudden disappearance, only helps to affirm her distance from her past self—a teen girl at the mercy of others' emotional and economical provisions. Now in full possession of herself and her future, she chooses not to marry Haojun even though she could and with her mother's endorsement this time.

But this choice comes at a cost—a profound sense of loss pervades the film's epilogue, now overlapped onto Cheryl's present life. Haojun moves on to marry a young Japanese woman, drifting further away from the orbit of his paternal homeland. After attending Chen Li's funeral, Haojun (now in the gestalt of an older man played by a different Japanese actor) bids Cheryl (the middle-aged Xiaorou) farewell at the airport and gives her a box. She opens it on the plane—it's filled with the snapshots of clouds that he took during his first wandering days after leaving Hong Kong, on top of them is her high school portrait (fig. 3.3). Every picture is dated clearly— "these are the days when I missed you . . . Now I return them to you." Cheryl looks tearfully out of the cabin window and her mind is swept away by the floating clouds and an unmitigated sense of loss. The box has in essence delivered to her a broken heart and a time bomb that blasts open a deep-seated crate in her seemingly well-balanced life as a successful professional woman as well as a mother and wife (yes, in that order).

The image of Xiaorou/Cheryl the jetsetter holding the box that contains a photographically condensed passion not fully lived is underscored by a chanting female voice overlaying the cosmic force of the vanishing clouds, inducing an overwhelming pathos. This scene resonates with what Rey Chow has identified as a modern tradition of Chinese feminine expression of a deeply ambivalent "psychic interiority."[18] From Bing Xin's fiction in the 1930s to Ann Hui's film *Ketu qiuhen* (Song of the Exile, 1990), Chow traces the recurrence of the motif of an educated woman's struggle for self-identity vis-à-vis an enduring patriarchal kinship system that marginalizes deviant conducts and affect. Qiuxin (or "Autumn Heart") in Bing Xin's short story experiences a moment of regret or "belated illumination" for giving up love (and marriage) for individual growth and social worth after encountering her youthful lover (now a mature career/family man). Hueyin, the more world-weary female protagonist in Ann Hui's autobiographical film is less trapped in a heteronormative fantasy than a more entrenched Chinese patriarchal politico-ethical fortress that first excluded and then assimilated her Japanese mother. Their sense of melancholy and homelessness are "semiotically reexternalized or metaphorized as nature in the form of elements of seasons, west wind, late autumn, and so forth."[19] Even Hui's ingenious use of the layered flashback and voiceover that unveil the impossibility of "psychic interiority" as a solution to modern female subjectivity cannot seem to counter the excess of the "ethnosocial stronghold" or "'natural' environment" of the Chinese family tradition.[20]

Despite the many affinities between *Tempting Heart* and *Song of the Exile*—in the uses of flashbacks, voiceover, images of nature, not to mention the two filmmakers' early collaboration—the sentimentalism culminating in Chang's film has a skewed relation to patriarchal tradition. In fact, fathers are seen largely missing or inept in directing the young generation into a normative ethnocentric kinship system. The mothers are themselves adrift between conflicting values and sentiments, and, in the case of Xiaorou's, between Hong Kong and Canada. As Hong Kong itself is faced with the historical rupture of the handover of 1997 (the film was made in its immediate aftermath), its equivocal and even painful relationships to its two competing sovereign "homelands" (Britain and China) are often reflected in the multifarious explorations of gender and sexual identities, as well as cultural belonging on the Hong Kong screen in that period. If many pre-1997 Hong Kong films articulate a nostalgic longing for China as sources of cultural roots (as embodied by the benign yet authoritative grandfather in *Song of the Exile*), the Taiwan-born Chang seems less lured by the "Mainland complex."[21] The sense of loss as evoked by the "natural image" of the floating clouds at the film's end flows not out of a regret for a failed personal life (unmarried or childless) for an educated and socially ambitious woman (as in Bing Xin's text), or for the passing of a paternal figure associated with an authentic cultural home (as in Hui's film). Xiaorou/Cheryl in fact seems to have it all—career, family (child, husband, mother), and romance, except for a father. What she mourns on the plane is really her severed bonds with two sweethearts of her formative period—a culturally doubly marginalized young man and a queer girl.[22] She herself may have realized that she is the survivor of a tumultuous recent past with confusing passions and identities, and is now paradoxically the arbiter of a heteronormative "ethnosocial stronghold." In the end, her heart-wrenching tears call for a renewed probing of the all-powerful affective machinery of the Chinese kinship system, which has shown its insidious capacity to recruit women for lubricating its operation and rejuvenation. Even though Cheryl is en route home to Hong Kong, a piece of her heart has been stolen and left among the vanished clouds the young Haojun meditated upon, and with Chen Li in her burial ground in Japan.

SEISMIC SHIFTS IN A GENERATIONAL SAGA

Sylvia Chang's fascination with generational bonds and rifts, especially those between mothers and daughters, is articulated with different emphasis in *Passion* and *Tempting Heart,* and with varying scales and styles of the transnational imaginary. In *20 30 40,* this thematic concern receives a more playful treatment. What connects these three films—and, to an extent, *Xin tongju shidai* (Conjugal Affairs, 1994), which Chang co-produced, co-starred, and co-directed—is Chang's multifarious authorial signature as writer, director, and actress. More interestingly, she consistently casts herself in the role of a middle-aged woman, and a mother at that, who juggles her multiple responsibilities, as well as her own desires. If Bai Yun in *Passion* remains mired in the sacrificial mold of the maternal melodrama and its stylized mise-en-scène, Cheryl's role as a para-diegetic mother figure in relation to her off-screen daughter and to the evolving project as her brain-child shows a more experimental impulse in redefining the borders of love, home, and melodrama in a volatile time for Hong

Kong society. *20 30 40* showcases, however, the polyrhythmic everyday life of a post-Y2K Taiwan through three parallel women's tales wrought locally, regionally, and globally.

Chang, Liu Ro-ying, and Lee Sin-je play three women in convergent and divergent transitions. Their first simultaneous (unbeknownst to each other) appearance is at the airport. Lily (Chang), a forty-year-old florist, is busy video-filming her daughter and husband, both distracted by their cellphone calls. (They have just returned from a family vacation abroad.) Early in the film, she divorces her husband after she discovers that he has kept another family in the same city—an unimaginable act for Mingyu in *Passion*. Xiang (Liu) is a thirty-year-old flight attendant who has several boyfriends but is eager to find the right one to settle down with. She blames her itinerant profession as a hindrance to finding true love. Jie (Lee) is the wide-eyed twenty-year-old arriving from Malaysia, excited about her prospect of becoming a singer, only to be stranded in a foreign city where she experiences a first love of sorts—with a girl named Tong from Hong Kong. The latter, as it turns out, is in turn on a private mission to figure out her mother's secret love object, a recording artist and agent whose career goes nowhere (recalling the character Haojun in *Tempting Heart*).

In the DVD bonus feature for *20 30 40*, Sylvia Chang and her co-stars relate the creative process behind the film. The title and the film initially came from a song album idea—a collaborative project between the three screen-pop music idols of different generations.[23] After realizing the broad significance behind the emblematic title connoting the best years of a woman's life, Chang and her co-stars started a collective brainstorming, with each contributing autobiographical or semiautobiographical writings to an eventual script. This method invokes the metanarrative frame of the collaborative "script-developing" in *Tempting Heart*. While *20 30 40* does not explicitly include a similar metanarrative gesture, it redistributes it in other manners, such as Lily's home-video filming (which Cheryl does in *Tempting Heart* as well, especially in the opening and ending scenes at the airport), and Jie and Tong's shared audio dairy. As a result, the film, with its multidirectional narrative lines crisscrossing Taipei's urban geography, is by far the most polyphonic in articulating a sinophone feminine world among Chang's works. Here Chang probes the ambivalent generational relations beyond that of family confines by extending them to both the actors' personal experiences and the larger world of women's lives. Chang confesses that she initially found it hard to communicate with Lee (perhaps in part because of her far younger age and a different national

103

background), but the making of the film allowed her to "grasp" (*buzhuo*) Lee. Likewise, Lee is grateful for the opportunity to reflect on her experience as a newcomer to Taiwan from the Chinese diaspora in Malaysia years ago; writing about it enabled her to connect with the subtle feelings her character has toward another girl.

The making of the film in fact created an ad hoc family, enabling the three actresses to solidify their feminine and professional "kinship." Through a skillful orchestration of the mise-en-scène and deliberately loose-fitting narrative weaving, the film literally draws the three women—who remain strangers throughout the film—into the same neighborhood toward the end of the film. Resolute about changing her life's direction, Xiang moves to an apartment near Lily's flower shop. While hailing a taxi in front of the shop one morning, she meets the widower who had knocked on her door before, wanting to buy her old piano—a memento from her dead mother (a single mom and piano teacher)—for his young daughter. It turns out that the inn where Jie has been staying is also nearby. Homesick and broke, she wanders by the shop and peeks inside—perhaps the image of Lily surrounded by tropical flowers has reminded her of her mother back in Malaysia? Sensing her gaze, Lily turns around and is also reminded of her own daughter in Canada, who has decided not to come home for Christmas holidays. Lily has been struggling with loneliness and the daunting task of finding a new mate at the "too late" age of forty.[24] The melodramatic coincidence at one urban intersection—here refigured as haphazard proximity—shows how the metropolis at once generates painful alienation for striving women, young or older, and connects them in "fateful" ways.

The motif of earthquake provides a crucial linchpin of the three parallel tales of displacement and attachment. After Xiang gets home from the airport and barely utters the words "home, sweet home," an earthquake strikes and she ducks under for protection. A little while later, she turns on the TV for updates. On screen, Jie and her new friend are giggling, relating their earthquake experience to the reporter on the street outside of their inn. What actually transpired between them in their room during the brief period of shock is revealed in the next sequence (the film as a whole is structured around synchrony and contiguity rather than linearity). The two girls, strangers a minute ago, are brought into a tight embrace by forces of nature when the heart of the earth experiences a sudden seizure. Lily's life also takes a dramatic turn after the quake. Her shop is a mess but it's only when she has to deliver flowers, unwittingly, to her husband's mistress's home, that she is really hit by the "aftershock." A "family" portrait on the wall shows her husband smiling gleefully; and his young son emerges from the hallway. She immediately obtains a divorce and plunges herself headlong into the date scene—"why not? I'll go for it if there is a good catch out there," she says emphatically to herself in front of her bathroom mirror. She also takes up another project—caring for and talking to an older woman in a permanent coma at a hospital.[25] The film ends with an echo to the earlier quake, after Lily experiences another shock of betrayal (her love interest decides to follow his fiancée and her career to Beijing). Once again we find her shaving her armpits in front of the mirror, sobbing and repeating "I'm an abandoned woman." Just then, another earthquake hits the city. She shakes in fear but resolves to withstand the shocks by standing tall and holding up the shaving blade in the air. Her final utterance of "I'm an abandoned woman" is energized by the shockwaves and now carries the tone of defiance, implying "so what!"

Earthquake as a metaphor for fateful change—shifts and new forma- 105 tions—is poignantly encapsulated in Jie's and Tong's relationship. When Jie finally decides to go back to Malaysia, Tong bids her farewell at the airport. She gives Jie a parting gift—a cassette tape with sounds of their shared moments in Taipei—the earthquake and many ordinary days and nights, including their breathing during sleep. "There are you and me inside it," says Tong tenderly (fig. 3.4). The cassette tape, like the box containing pictures of floating clouds in *Tempting Heart*, becomes a miniature time machine that rekindles murmurs of the heart and tremors of passion. The two may have failed in becoming "Twins"—a pop brand embodying a "hybrid and borderless world" concocted by their ineffective agent—but they have formed a deep bond and come to embrace their affection for each other. (Jie kisses Tong on her lips before proceeding toward the security check and passport control.) The earthquake has precipitated their rites of passage from home and homeland, as well as their discoveries of both the pain and richness of becoming women and citizens of the world.

The lighthearted feminist sentimentalism—no major accident, no death, no outrageous rebelliousness—of 20 30 40 departs from the more somber tone of the two earlier films in its investment in action over meditation, in future rather than in past (hence the absence of the flashback structure and voiceover). Here Chang's storytelling is not just from the regretful or circumspect perspective of a middle-aged professional woman, which more or less harks back to the tradition of feminine melancholy

Of course! I'm on there too!

FIGURE 3.4 Tearful parting at the airport (*20 30 40*, 2004)

106

in modern Chinese culture that Rey Chow incisively dissects. In refiguring the popular Chinese narrative formula "three women stage a drama" (*sange nüren yitaixi*) into a transregional cross-generational saga, *20 30 40* offers a new romantic melodrama without centering the affective energy on a single male protagonist. The stage the three women share is the city of Taipei and the multiple worlds with which it is connected. By virtue of their symbolic ages, they also perform the varying stages of womanhood—a lifelong process of becoming rather than attaining prescribed identities or roles. The objects of affection in turn become plural and more diffusive, heterosexual, or queer.

Suspending momentarily national and sociocultural references, the earthquake binds these women and people around them affected by it, and reminds us that each human being exists, moves, and changes *with* fellow beings. The earthquake motif accentuates what the contemporary French philosopher Jean-Luc Nancy calls the "turning" of the everyday. They are both extraordinary (in terms of frequency) and ordinary earthly events —intensely localized yet regionally and globally resonant. The scattered narrative lines of *20 30 40* that loosely connect the particular phases each of the three (or four) women undergoes illustrate the "*inter*lacing" (l'entre*croisement*) of strands whose extremities remain separate even at the very center of the "knot."[26] The "knot," or the earthquake, may have pulled these lines together for a contingent period of time but does not subsume all the extensions that may lead to other points of interlacing and knot-tying. In its reiteration of the constant "local turning" or "circulation" of the everyday and the crisscrossing of individual existence in contiguous temporal and spatial relations, we begin to appreciate in a serious way the seeming "middlebrow" sentimentalism of Chang's films and its implications for an everyday feminist agenda. Such an agenda acknowledges the persistent social fantasy about a "normal" family structure as embodied by Xiang's longing. She is the only one among the three who receives a happy ending in the form of (an implied) heterosexual union, albeit to a widower single-father, and thus takes on the role of the mother herself. At the same time, this hardly militant agenda pushes the envelop of the "ethnosocial stronghold" of Chinese patrilineal kinship by allowing a range of other female characters in Chang's work as a whole to seek alternative forms of attachment and intimacy without necessarily resorting to normative expectations or closures.

CONCLUSION

This chapter is a tentative attempt to situate the unique work of Sylvia Chang within the contexts of the sinophone film culture and transcultural melodrama studies. My interest in the versatile authorship of this "renaissance woman"[27] has led me to focus on her triple screen signatures as actress, writer, and director, as most visibly inscribed in *Passion, Tempting Heart,* and *20 30 40.* Her comprehensive skill sets in filmmaking make her nearly a one-of-a-kind phenomenon in the Chinese-language film world. The conspicuous lack of scholarly interest in her work may, in part, be attributed to the tenacious traditions of auteur criticism and art cinema canon-making underlying the foundation of film studies as an academic discipline, which became more entrenched when a whole generation of scholars and critics was preoccupied with a narrowly interpreted model of national cinema (and "national style"). The preference for an austere and largely masculine modernist and intellectual style of (non-Western) filmmaking has created a certain critical myopia and even discrimination against middlebrow melodrama, especially those addressed to women or by women, regarding it aesthetically conventional and socially conformist. This kind of blanket perception risks relinquishing opportunities for understanding the richness and complexity of melodrama as the thermometer of a society's fluctuating body temperature, especially when a woman filmmaker creatively rewrites this globally favored mode of storytelling in Chinese-language cinema. Moreover, the transnational horizon of Chang's themes and characters and her worldly feminism place her films in a broader cultural geography of gender and sexual politics,[28] in relation to reconsiderations of the meanings of the individual, the family and kinship, and community. The deep bonds between women—sisters, daughters, mothers, girlfriends, and coworkers—in Chang's films manifest a sustained effort to construct a feminine world empowered by memory, affect, and solidarity. In consistently playing the role of the mother herself, varying from the sacrificial mistress to the confident provider with her own desires, Chang has also refashioned the maternal melodrama in this set of films with an embodied authorial signature. Whereas Ang Lee famously made his contribution to the post–New Cinema and Chinese-language melodrama film through his "Father Knows Best" trilogy (*Tuishou*, Pushing Hands, 1991; *Xiyan*, Wedding Banquet, 1993; and *Yinshi nannü*, Eat, Drink, Man and Woman, 1994), the three films by Sylvia Chang discussed in this chapter demonstrate that mothers know no less. Not merely a "mother of the new directors" in her capacity as producer and leading actress, Chang is also the proud mother of her own films.

ACKNOWLEDGMENT

Thanks to Shi-yan Chao and Dan Gao for their research assistance. I am grateful to Professor Yang Junlei for inviting me to present an earlier version of this essay at Fu Dan University in Shanghai in the summer of 2009.

NOTES

1. Chen Feibao, *Taiwan dianying daoyan yishu* (The Art of Taiwan Directors).
2. On *wenyi pian*, see Stephen Teo's succinct article, "Chinese Melodrama." For seminal studies on film melodrama and "woman's film," see Christine Gledhill, ed., *Home Is Where the Heart Is*, especially her own comprehensively and astutely argued essay, "The Melodramatic Field." See also Mary Ann Doane, *The Desire to Desire*.
3. Recently, the highly popular and influential woman writer and producer Qiong Yao has received some scholarly attention, but hardly any substantial work in English on her has been produced so far. Yingjin Zhang's chapter on Taiwan cinema in his *Chinese National*

108

Cinema has but one page on her as fiction writer (p. 140). For an excellent study in Chinese on Yao's work and its cultural significance, see Lin Fangmei, *Jiedu Qiong Yao aiqing wangguo* (Interpreting Qiong Yao's Kingdom of Love).

4. For an early study on and interviews with Fourth and Fifth Generations women directors, see Chris Berry, "China's New 'Women's Cinema.'" Hong Kong female filmmakers, in particular Ann Hui and Clara Law, have been studied extensively, though still limited in comparison to their male counterparts. For an important study on a forerunner of the New Wave filmmakers, see Yau Ching, *Filming Margins*.

5. To date, Sylvia Chang has starred or appeared in more than ninety Chinese or non-Chinese language films.

6. Chen, *Taiwan dianying daoyan yishu*, 232.

7. On the tradition of "talented beauty" in late imperial China, see, among other things, Dorothy Ko, *Teachers of the Inner Chamber;* and Ellen Widmer and Kang-i Sun eds., *Writing Women in Late Imperial China.*

8. Shiao-ying Shen, "Locating Feminine Writing in Taiwan Cinema."

9. Shu-mei Shih, *Visuality and Identity.*

10. Ibid., chapters 1–2.

11. Johannes von Moltke, *No Place Like Home.* As the author indicates in his preface, the book title and his main approach are inspired by Dorothy's famous line at the end of *Wizard of Oz.*

12. Chris Berry and Mary Farquhar, *China on Screen*, 82.

13. Ibid., 98–107.

14. Ibid., 98–99.

15. Huang Jinaye, *Renwen dianyingde zhuixun* (In Search of a Humanist Cinema), p. 202.

16. Chen, *Taiwan dianying daoyan yishu*, p. 234. Incidentally, Sylvia Chang's first award-winning role is a poor school girl struggling with economic survival and moral obligations in *Biyun tian* (Posterity and Perplexity, 1976), adapted from Qiong Yao's novel of the same title.

17. John Mercer and Martin Schingler, *Melodrama, Genre, Style, Sensibility*, 39–40.

18. Rey Chow, "Autumn Hearts," 85–104.

19. Ibid., 88–89.

20. Ibid., 102.

21. On the "Mainland Complex" or the "China Syndrome" in Hong Kong cinema of the 1980s and 1990s, see, Li Cheuk-to, "The Return of the Father"; and Esther Yau, "Border Crossing: Mainland China's Presence in Hong Kong Cinema"; and Stephen Teo, chapter 13, "Reverence and Fear."

22. The male musician—often "emotionally or psychologically disturbed"—is a significant companion figuration of the "feminine" emotions in classical women's film. See Heather Laing, *The Gendered Score*, especially chapter 5. The casting of Kaneshiro as the young Haojun is not without significance here. Born in Taiwan, to a Japanese father and a Taiwanese mother, Kaneshiro's biethnic identity and multilingual gift has made him a darling of contemporary East Asian cinema with a trans-Asian appeal. For an incisive analysis of his stardom, see Eva Tsai, "Kaneshiro Takeshi."

23. *20 30 40* DVD (Columbia Pictures Film Production Asia Limited, 2004).

109

24. Ibid. Liu says, "Thirty is a paradoxical age in search of a sense of security. . . . But it'd be just too late at forty . . . [to settle]."

25. This is an interesting variation of a similar motif in Edward Yang's *Yiyi* (Yi Yi: A One and a Two, 2000), in which an extended Taipei family is thrown into a crisis after the matriarch falls into a coma. Members of the family reconfront the family's history and their own place in it by taking turns talking or confessing to the comatose old woman.

26. Jean-luc Nancy, *Being Singular Plural*, 5; 9–10.

27. The remark is made by an online fan, see *http://www.brns.com/pages3/sylvia1.html* (accessed May 15, 2009).

28. The queer subtexts in Chang's films partake in a broad cultural discourse and social formation. For some recent scholarly work on queer cultural practices in Hong Kong and Taiwan, see Helen Hok-sze Leung, "Queerscapes in Contemporary Hong Kong Cinema"; Fran Martin, *Situating Sexualities;* Song Hwee Lim, *Celluloid Comrades.*

Part II

GENDERED VOICES: IMAGES AND AFFECT

4

The Voice of History and the Voice of Women

A STUDY OF HUANG SHUQIN'S WOMEN'S FILMS

XINGYANG LI

TRANSLATED BY THOMAS MORAN

MANY CONSIDER Huang Shuqin to be one of the first female directors in China to be a self-aware possessor of women's consciousness (*nüxing yishi*), and one critic has praised Huang's *Ren, gui, qing* (Woman, Demon, Human, 1987) as contemporary China's "sole film that can unequivocally be called a 'women's film.'"[1] Among some dozen films directed by Huang, six are about women: the feature films *Qingchun wansui* (Forever Young, 1983); *Woman, Demon, Human; Hua hun* (The Soul of the Painter, 1994), and *Hei, Fulanke* (Hey, Frank, 2001), and the made-for-television movies *Hongfen* (Rouge, 1994) and *Cun ji* (The Village Whore, 2000), which is also known as *Zhangfu* (Husband). Closest to Huang Shuqin's own experience as a woman are *Forever Young*, which is about the lives of female middle-school students, and *Woman, Demon, Human* and *The Soul of the Painter*, both of which are about the lives of female artists.[2] Huang Shuqin has said, "[T]o give a film personality a director must put her self into the film, and the most important factor in the makeup of the self is gender. First there is gender, then there is the person. If gender gets lost, how can you have an authentic individuality? In the work of a female director, including in my own previous work, the narrative mode is not, however, entirely the product of women's consciousness. Without one really being aware of it, the specific features of women's narrative are assimilated and diluted by mainstream ideology; they get trapped inside a centuries old, superstable narrative schema and can't get out."[3] Indeed, in *Forever Young, Woman, Demon, Human,* and *The Soul of the Painter* we find both "the loud, recognized, reigning voices of the epoch, that is, the reigning dominant ideas (official and unofficial)"[4] and "the voices of women," which carry women's consciousness and are among the "voices still weak, ideas not yet fully emerged."[5] In Huang Shuqin's women's films there is a complicated dialogic relationship between these two different sorts of voices. In this chapter, I intend to listen closely to and decode the voices of the epoch, the voices of women and the dialogic relationship between these types of voices as expressed in each of Huang Shuqin's three women's films.

FOREVER YOUNG: THE EXPRESSION OF WOMEN'S CONSCIOUSNESS WITHIN THE PARAMETERS SET BY POLITICAL DISCOURSE

Huang Shuqin said she directed *Forever Young* because it was both a task assigned to her by the government and her own choice.[6] Zhang Xian's screenplay *Chu chun* (Early Spring, 1981), an adaptation of Wang Meng's novel *Qingchun wansui* (Forever Young, 1979), was published in 1981 but was met with criticism from readers and was ignored by other directors, and Huang Shuqin's decision to direct the film was met with perplexity: "Why make a film about the lives of 1950s' middle school students? Why in this day and age make a movie about characters with empty heads and why celebrate the 'left'?" Huang Shuqin was not dissuaded; she has said, "Regardless of what anybody else thought, when the Shanghai Film Studio gave the green light to the screenplay of *Forever Young* and named me director, I was excited."[7] In short, *Forever Young* was caught in contested ground between the discourse of official political ideology and the discourse of intellectual liberation and historical reflection that was sweeping through Chinese society in the late 1970s and early 1980s, which undoubtedly influenced the film's content and form.

Huang Shuqin began by changing the artistic orientation of *Forever Young.* Wang Meng's *Forever Young* is an ode to youth—and in particular an ode to the youth of one particular era. Zhang Xian's screenplay is about "the springtime of the People's Republic, that ever so wonderful time" (this is Yang Qiangyun's line at the end of the screenplay). Huang Shuqin turned homage in the direction of investigation and changed the implicit subjectivity behind the text from a champion of the revolution to a bearer of nostalgia or a historian bent on discovering historical truth. As Huang Shuqin has said, "It was very clear to me that my duty was to be as authentic as possible in recreating the period and capturing the way in which the people of those times lived and thought. If the film was authentic, I was sure people could learn something from it and benefit from seeing it. As far as any conclusion about what was right or wrong about those times goes, that is not something the film has to provide. That should be something for audiences to think about and debate after they leave the theater."[8] The film has three narrative threads: the conflict between progressive students and one typical arrogant student; the assistance given to the unfortunate Su Ning by the warm-hearted Yang Qiangyun; and the rescuing of the Catholic believer Hu Mali by members of the Communist Party. Through the detailed depiction of the lives of a group of students in a girls' middle school, the film captures a broad array of social experience at a time when the Communist Party was first establishing its power in China and when the official, mainstream political ideology was promoting socialism, collectivism, and patriotism while disparaging individualism (i.e., individuality) and religious belief. The film shows the omnipresence of the new political authority and the youthful vigor of the epoch. This comprises the film's "authentic history" of Chinese society in the 1950s, but the theme of the film is maturation—"the beauty and charm of youth"[9] as people come of age—and the keynote to this theme is the joy and passion of youth.

As a witness to history, Huang Shuqin took a "simple, candid look back" at "the vitality, intimacy and youthful spirit of life at a girls' middle school."[10] In interpretations and readings of the film, however, commentators have overlooked *Forever Young*'s second subject, which is the women's consciousness particular to any given epoch. The film's women's consciousness is evident in two ways. First, the historical, epochal, and political discourses just mentioned are subsumed by the quotidian and private experiences of women, and second, youth in the film is specifically the youthful vitality, character, and beauty of women growing up at that time.

Huang Shuqin has said that at a girls' middle school boys are absent, there is no voyeuristic gaze of the Other, and the sense of gender inferiority and constraint felt by female students weakens or disappears.

In consequence, all the details of daily life, such as "going to class, taking tests, eating, sleeping, going to town, watching movies, and laughing, crying, fighting and making up,"[11] are infused with the specific qualities of female identity. Most of these details in the film are taken from Wang Meng's novel, but some are the creation of Huang Shuqin and her colleagues. The film focuses on and foregrounds the details of women's lives and in so doing not only re-creates the special atmosphere of a girls' middle school but also shows us what women students are like when they can mature in relative freedom. Particularly deserving of analysis here are the stories of several of the characters. These stories speak not only to political discourse but also to the private life experiences of women. First, we can consider the story of Catholic believer Hu Mali. Hu Mali is a victim of history who is rescued. Her pale, haggard face, her worn-out, patched clothing, which tears at a touch, her fear of her foreign nanny, and her devout praying are symbolic of imperialist oppression and the

poison of religion. Hu Mali gradually opens her eyes; she joins the group, takes part in a running race, falls down, gets up, dentifies with Zheng Bo, who represents the Communist Party, takes part in Youth League Day activities, and rebuilds her belief system. This is all an allegory for the healing of the wounds of history and the emergence of a new socialist subject. The real impetus for Hu Mali's awakening and conversion is not political propaganda but friendship among women. Both Zheng Bo and Yang Qiangyun attempt to use political discourse to help Hu Mali see the true nature of her foreign nanny, who is a symbol of imperialism and religious ideology, but what truly influences Hu Mali is that as social subjects and as gendered subjects, Zheng Bo, Yang Qiangyun, and Yuan Xinzhi represent a community of women (to be distinguished from a community of students) and are the bearers of the consciousness of the modern notion of the equality of the sexes. Hu Mali's plight is not her material poverty but is rather her loneliness and fear, which is the result of her life as a helpless orphan, uncared for and living under subjugation. Hu Mali aspires to join the women's community not because of increasing political awareness and a transformation of faith but because she discovers a feeling of belonging that allows her to overcome her loneliness and fear. Hu Mali's sense of inferiority becomes confidence; her melancholy becomes optimism; and she undergoes a transformation of faith. Her maturation is not so much the result of an education gained from political propaganda as it is the result of her acceptance into a community of women and the power of friendship among women. Of course, the women's community that allows Hu Mali to gradually find a sense of belonging is the product of its particular historical era. In their "tears, laughter, and philosophizing" (from the prologue) and in their ideals, beliefs, and aspirations, the women in the film clearly display the imprint of the times. To some degree what they think and feel is determined as much by their historical context as by their individual agency.

Su Ning is a character much like Hu Mali in that she is a victim of history who is saved. The source of the hurt deep in Su Ning's soul is the decline of her family's fortunes and her anxiety over her class standing, and more importantly the sexual assault she has endured. But what causes Su Ning the greatest suffering is not that she has suffered sexual assault—despite the fact that this has left her with psychic wounds that are slow to heal—but the consequences of this assault, namely her rejection by men. This, of course, is a sign of Su Ning's identification with and fear of patriarchal society. When Yang Qiangyun comes to understand Su Ning's true worry, she consoles Su Ning by saying, "Why should we worry about whether some man likes us or not? What a nuisance that is! You and I will be friends and that's that, okay? . . . Forever!" The two young women then hook their little fingers together in promise. This is close to being a homosexual scene, and it is the scene in the film that is most imbued with modern women's consciousness. Yang Qiangyun's words of consolation carry at least three layers of meaning, the first being a declaration of female independence that is a rejection of the female psychology of dependence on men, a "nuisance" according to Yang Qiangyun, and a denunciation of the social oppression of women. The second layer of meaning is the assertion of gender equality, including equality in sexual morality. The third layer of meaning is the implicit claim that friendship among women can replace male-female love or compensate for its lack. To make Su Ning feel better and ease her depression over her loss of chastity, Yang Qiangyun does not invoke the exemplars of the female heroes Zhuo Ya and Liu Hulan, instead she suggests that the cure for Su Ning's anxiety is to stand up against the ideology and social formations of male-dominated society. In this scene, the narrative's engagement with political discourse slips toward the expression of women's consciousness. The oath of alliance between Yang and Su can therefore be understood to express a women's consciousness that goes beyond 1950s' political, economic, and social women's liberation and gestures toward a more profound female consciousness of gender and self. The Chinese women's liberation movement of the 1950s, which was promoted as one aspect

117

of a political revolution, had great influence but was flawed. First, it was something granted to women; a certain amount of political and economic power was granted to women, and in truth only a very limited number of representative women got to enjoy a bit of power. Second, it was a defeminization of women under the slogan "men and women are the same," which in fact meant that women are to be the same as men. This was gender equality achieved by the eradication of gender differences, which not only caused women to lose what they were in and of themselves but also put increased social pressure on them to behave like men. Third, the movement was external; it advocated gender equality but paid little attention to the awakening of an internal and self-aware women's consciousness, which is where its difference from the West's feminist movement lies. The modern women's consciousness expressed in the scene of the oath of alliance between Yang and Su is an internal coming to consciousness—Yang and Su become conscious of their identity as women—and in this scene, therefore, the film transcends the time in which it is set.

The characters in Wang Meng's novel and in Zhang Xian's screenplay were created with similar intent; Hu Mali stands for opposition to imperialism, and Su Ning stands for the repudiation of the Nationalist Party's political authority and bureaucrat-capitalism. The two young women bear symbolic responsibility for overturning the "three big mountains."[12] When women are defined solely as the victims of the disasters and humiliations of history, feminists recognize a trope of the discourse of the patriarchy. In Huang Shuqin's women's narrative, in contrast, while Hu Mali and Su Ning do not entirely escape entrapment within political discourse, they begin to express women's consciousness, and this is Huang Shuqin's realignment of the point of view in the novel and the screenplay.

While *Forever Young* is not a women's film by a strict definition, its initial experiment with the expression of women's consciousness prepared the way for the women's films *Woman, Demon, Human* and also *The Soul of the Painter*, which is suffused with a self-aware women's consciousness.

WOMAN, DEMON, HUMAN: CULTURAL CRITICISM AND THE LIMITED EXPRESSION OF WOMEN'S CONSCIOUSNESS

Woman, Demon, Human, the film that made Huang Shuqin's name, is considered by some critics to be what Dai Jinhua has argued it is: contemporary China's "sole film that can unequivocally be called a 'women's film.'"[13] Qian Guomin was one of the first to point out that *Woman, Demon, Human* has women's consciousness,[14] Shao Mujun was one of the first to undertake a detailed analysis of the film's women's consciousness using Freudian psychoanalytic theory,[15] and after the publication of Dai Jinhua's influential article,[16] most commentators understood and read the film from the perspective of women's consciousness/women's film, obscuring the complicity of this layered artistic work. Huang Shuqin was moved to make the film because she was inspired by the career of Pei Yanling, a female performer of male heroes in Hebei opera. Huang Shuqin has said, "What astonished me about Pei Yanling was that such a pretty and charming actress was playing the rugged, ugly ghost catcher Zhong Kui. It struck me that in this was an extraordinary spiritual journey that was worth delving into."[17] The film delves into the personal/spiritual/artistic maturation of the female protagonist Qiu Yun, who is modeled on Pei Yanling, by considering the complicated relations between Qiu Yun and the Other and between Qiu Yun and her self. This lends the film a multiplicity of different voices, including the voice of women's consciousness.

In the film, Qiu Yun's interactions with the Other are, in the main, the occasion for cultural critique. This critique is directed at cultural failings, including male chauvinism, that are ingrained in the national collective unconscious. In the course of her complicated interactions with the Other, Qiu Yun is simultaneously unsuccessful in her personal life and successful in her professional artistic life. Qiu Yun's day-to-day experiences, from childhood through her time as a wife and mother, are difficult and wounding. Throughout her acting career, Qiu Yun endures hardship and repeated misfortune and wins her successes only with difficulty. There are three events that cause Qiu Yun pain: first, she sees her mother in an act of adultery; second, her childhood friends, in particular the boy Erwa, bully and humiliate her; and third, her colleagues plot to harm her by placing a nail on a prop table so that it will stab her hand. The scene in which she sees her mother having sex with her lover in a haystack is for Qiu Yun what Freud called a primal scene, and it launches a tragedy for women of two different generations. Wang Lingzhen argues that:

> When the young Qiu Yun at last discovers her mother lying in the haystack under an unknown man (who is in fact Qiu Yun's biological father), Qiu Yun not only subconsciously sees what she has been unconsciously seeking—her mother—but she also sees her own future, a future that declares that she

will not be a bride (she will not be a traditional woman): this future is in the dark surroundings, which lie distant from all others (from society) and which are suffused with taboo, solitude and hopelessness. Although the young Qiu Yun does not fully comprehend what her mother is doing, she quite clearly understands that this is taboo ground; she quite clearly sees the hopelessness and flight in her mother's eyes. Can this really be the price one must pay for choosing to be something other than a traditional woman? When the high haystacks suddenly collapse and bury Qiu Yun's mother and that "back of a head" (the unknown man) together, Qiu Yun is alarmed and suddenly comes to the realization that her mother's choice—which is also her own subconscious choice—must proceed in darkness and, moreover, will result in the severe punishment of banishment to the margins of life.[18]

Indeed, after Qiu Yun's chance stolen look at this scene of adultery, the object of her identification shifts from her mother to traditional morality; her identification with her mother is "sublimated, becoming a latent desire."[19] In the discourse of modern Chinese enlightenment, Qiu Yun's mother's adulterous love and her elopement constitute rebellion against traditional moral ethics, but to upholders of the old feudal moral code, her behavior constitutes moral degeneracy and is disgraceful. Qiu Yun's mother's actions are also the cause of the gossip that the anonymous crowd uses to insult and hurt Qiu Yun unceasingly. Although Qiu Yun is a victim of traditional ideas, in her ignorance she also at the same time identifies with these ideas, and this is why she clashes with her childhood friends, is unlucky in love, has an unhappy marriage, is distant from her mother, and why she and her biological father meet but do not acknowledge each other. Qiu Yun's conflict with her childhood friends, particularly with Erwa, wounds her in several ways. First, the conflict strengthens Qiu Yun's identification with traditional notions of morality, because the boys who bully and humiliate her do so because her mother has a lover. The boys, too, are mindless supporters and defenders of tradition. Second, it blocks Qiu Yun's gender identification, in that from this moment Qiu Yun rejects her identity as (biologically/socially) female. Three, it impresses upon Qiu Yun in intense, painful fashion how weak, alone, and helpless she is and how cold and heartless the Other can be. This impression is reinforced when Qiu Yun falls victim to the conspiracy that plants a nail on the prop table to stab her hand. The cultural significance and implicit meaning of this incident are multifaceted: it exposes the deviousness of those who are jealous of talent; it satirizes the hypocrisy of those who make a display of virtue; and it laments the way in which the vulgar masses take pleasure in the pain of others. Almost all the others who surround Qiu Yun hurt her, but none is truly evil. The evil lies in the traditional cultural ideology that inhabits their bodies like a virus. Qiu Yun's father calls these Others devils who are "cannibals, misers, gamblers, lechers, liars, degenerates, flatterers, and perverts," but Qiu Yun's understanding is more profound: "The real devils are those things we cannot see and cannot touch." The "real devils," in other words, are the cultural ills in the hearts of the Others and the wickedness in human nature; these are the "devils—or ghosts—that Zhong Kui cannot catch."

The voice of cultural critique in the film is Huang Shuqin's voice and the voice of the history at the same time. In the late 1980s, the Chinese mainland was experiencing a second tide of cultural critique much like that of the May Fourth period. The main current of the roots-seeking movement in literature popular at the time was the reconsideration and criticism of traditional Chinese culture. This is seen not only in roots-seeking literature but also in films of the fourth- and fifth-generation directors that are oriented toward cultural reflection. *Woman, Demon, Human* was conceived and produced in this particular cultural context and so it is natural that it speaks with the voice of cultural criticism. The film, like roots-seeking literature, employs symbolism to convey its cultural critique. For example, *Woman, Demon, Human* uses the language of film (the close-up, for example) to portray besiegement (by boys who have been steeped in the "soy sauce vat" of Chinese culture), the encircling gaze of the crowd (the faces of the audience), and gossip and slander (the hissing and chatting of the clamoring public) and other instances in which the crowd obliterates the individual. The frequent use of the close-up not only foregrounds and emphasizes the cultural deviousness and wickedness of the crowd but also makes it plain that the storyteller herself has perhaps experienced similar emotions of fear and detestation of these national failings. For a second example, the simpleton who appears several times in the film is another symbol of reflection and critique of traditional culture that is often seen in literary works of the time (the metaphorical meaning of the simpleton is ambiguous and complicated). Among the terrible "devils" or "ghosts" of traditional culture that are criticized in the film, the refusal of traditional culture to allow women, in particular remarkable women, full standing as people is the object of Huang Shuqin's most pointed criticism. As a critic has said, "*Woman, Demon, Human* is a film about women made by a woman, and so the

121

film's women's consciousness and women's psychology (including that which is latent in the film) is particularly deserving of our attention."[20]

Qiu Yun interacts with several Others, and it may seem at first glance that the disappointments in her personal life and her professional successes alike are the result of her interactions with those Others, but in truth her disappointments and her successes always result from her either yielding to the demands of patriarchal culture or rebelling against those demands. The predicament faced by women is the product of patriarchal culture, and Qiu Yun is caught short by the question "What can a woman do?" and is even more bewildered by the question "What is a woman?" Here begins Qiu Yun's interaction with her self. Here begins the process of Qiu Yun's self-inquiry, her self-searching, and her journey to the awakening of her women's consciousness.

During the course of Qiu Yun's interaction with her self, she first encounters obstacles to her gender identification as (biologically/socially) female. "What is a woman?" is a difficult question of gender identity to which she is never able to find a final answer. Qiu Yun's gender identification evolves through several stages, which in the discourse of traditional culture would be called the stages of normality, abnormality, return/regression, and confusion/loss. At the beginning, Qiu Yun's gender identification is "normal"; in the bride-gets-married game that she plays with the little boys, she plays the bride. Qiu Yun's change to an "abnormal" gender identification begins when she is besieged by the boys and Erwa beats her up, leaving her wounded in spirit. From this point, Qiu Yun changes her gender identity; if she cannot change her biological gender identity, she can change her socially determined gender identity; she can dress herself as male and act in a seemingly masculine fashion, becoming the fake boy that others see her as and playing male roles on stage. Qiu Yun's choice to be a woman playing a male stems from her deep fear of men and also is an answer to her father's challenge: "No actress comes to a good end; either some bad guy takes advantage of her or, day by day, she turns bad herself, just like your mom." But after playing Zhong Kui for an extended period, Qiu Yun internalizes the character of the ghost catcher; he becomes her alternate self. When Qiu Yun makes a categorical declaration to her colleagues in the provincial opera troupe that she is "a real girl," it marks her "return/regression" to identification with her (biological/social) female gender identity. This declaration is prompted by her secret love for Maestro Zhang. As a critic has argued, "When she experiences her first thoughts of love and feels longing for a man, she cannot but be frightened by the thought of the repression of her feminine qualities. Her feelings of love for Maestro Zhang are best understood as the first awakening of her women's consciousness. Her strong attraction to the man in front of her drives away the ideas about men she was left with after seeing that 'back of a head.'"[21] Qiu Yun's enters married life, and although her husband is not a good man she becomes a so-called "good wife and mother," what patriarchal society defines as a good woman. While yielding to patriarchal society, Qiu Yun makes another effort to recover her self. Ignoring her husband's objections ("If I play male roles, he thinks I'm ugly; if I play female roles, it worries him"), she resumes playing Zhong Kui, a role she could not play during the Cultural Revolution, and is successful. But this success comes only when Qiu Yun obscures her female gender identity and female beauty and appears on stage as a man, and as an ugly man at that. Her success is accompanied by a "confusion/loss" of identity. The answer to "What can a woman do?" is "What women do," but this cannot answer the existential question, "What is a woman?" When Qiu Yun says, "I have married myself to the stage," it is not so much a declaration of her commitment to her art as a bleak soliloquy on her loss of identity. There are several objective reasons for the various changes that Qiu Yun's gender identification undergoes, but the fundamental cause of these changes is Qiu Yun's intense personal experience of the predicament of women in patriarchal society and her attempt to break out from the trap in which she finds herself. Regardless of how we might judge each change she undergoes, each change can be seen as contributing to Qiu Yun's awakening to women's consciousness.

123

To be direct, the women's consciousness to which Qiu Yun gradually awakens is not entirely modern. The salvation that Qiu Yun finds in life is different from the salvation she longs for in her heart, and there is no necessary connection between the two. In life, Qiu Yun is a woman who saves herself at each difficult turn by relying on her artistic talent and by resisting the gender hierarchy of patriarchal society. In her heart, however, Qiu Yun entrusts the salvation of women to men; Zhong Kui is her ideal male savior: "Don't be fooled by Zhong Kui's demonic visage. The most important thing to him is a woman's fate. . . . He is always trying to help women find good men." This explains why whenever Qiu Yun is frightened by men and whenever she is troubled by the thought that she does not enjoy the happiness a woman should enjoy, the vision of Zhong Kui catching ghosts and marrying off his sister appears in her grieving and angry imagination.[22] In real life, Qiu Yun does everything she can to save herself, but in her imagination she becomes her own male savior; this split between her outer and inner worlds perhaps can be understood as a reflection of the fact that in contemporary China, liberation and equality were granted to women from the outside and were not the product of an internal awakening of modern women's consciousness. The incomplete modernity of Qiu Yun's women's consciousness is also seen in her beliefs about what good women and good men are. It is not entirely clear what "good" means in Qiu Yun's ideal, but it certainly has more to do with the ideas of traditional morality than it does with the rationality of modern enlightenment. The mingling of tradition and modernity in Qiu Yun's women's consciousness ensures that she will be unable to complete her journey to find herself as a woman in the modern meaning. In an era where men are still in charge, the times will never allow a woman to make her own way alone.

Qiu Yun, who is not permitted by history to make her own way, follows the opera troupe along country roads and through urban spaces in foreign countries. Her face is covered in greasepaint and marked by the dust and dirt of the everyday world, but the film shows us almost no sign of the clamor of the times in which she lives. In a flash forward, the film even skips the Cultural Revolution without mention. Instead, through the use of close-ups, the film brings us into women's psychological space, with its desires, passions, anxieties, fears, loneliness, and confusion. The de-emphasizing of historical background and the resulting de-emphasis on mimetic meaning somewhat surprisingly lends the film symbolic unity. Huang Shuqin has said, "The traveling opera troupe isn't a symbol of the times, and it isn't a symbol of sacrifice; it is an allegory of life."[23] Huang Shuqin was initially inspired by Pei Yanling's extraordinary artistic career; she "delved into" Pei's life and career; and she has argued that the film is "an allegory of life." Huang Shuqin has, in other words, not only put her own experiences as a woman into the creation of Qiu Yun and the world she inhabits, but she has contributed an interpretation of the film, enriching our understanding of the implicit meanings of the film. According to Huang, "a good film shouldn't be about only one thing; it should be worth going into from a number of different angles; it should welcome inquiry from many perspectives, rather than offering up a single meaning."[24] *Woman, Demon, Human* is indeed a film that may be viewed from a variety of perspectives. The film was produced in the context of contemporary China's ongoing cultural critique, and though it has been called by critics a women's film, its most prominent discourse is that of cultural criticism; its expression of a women's consciousness that mingles tradition with modernity comes second. We may even say that the latter is derived from the former. If we cannot say that the film is an allegorical text about human/woman, we can say that the polyphonic voices the film contains ensure that it may be regarded in a variety of ways.

THE SOUL OF THE PAINTER: MASS CULTURE AND THE PHYSICAL EXPRESSION OF WOMEN'S CONSCIOUSNESS

Huang Shuqin's *The Soul of the Painter* is also about a woman artist, and while its critical reception was not as positive as that of *Woman, Demon, Human,* it was quite successful as what the director herself proudly calls a commercial film. The film's release was stalled for a time by the government because of a problem with a nude scene, but after this ban was lifted *The Soul of the Painter* became a contemporary box office champion and the subject of widespread public discussion. Huang Shuqin has said, "I've never rejected commercialism. The more people see my films the better. That's what I hope for." She also has said, "When I was making *The Soul of the Painter* I was going after box office success and I did my best to make it commercial."[25] Huang Shuqin's life has always been her art, but because of a transformation in the nature of Chinese society, she had no choice but to try her hand at a commercial film. In the 1990s, China moved from a planned economy to a market economy, and the profit motive became the driving force behind everything happening in society. The ensuing emergence of a mass culture that was driven by economic considerations encroached upon the discursive hegemony once enjoyed by elite culture, driving out the spirit of rationality and cultural criticism that had been reestablished in the wake of the Cultural Revolution and substituting instead the pleasure of entertainment and the joy of profit. *The Soul of the Painter* was made in the early 1990s and was influenced by the cultural atmosphere of the time, and therefore it buzzes with a rather disharmonious noise in which are mixed a variety of cultural signifiers.

The Soul of the Painter employs several of the features of a commercial film with seasoned skill and packages itself in appropriate fashion. The first of these features is the employment of source material that reads like a romantic myth: Zhang Yuliang, the real person upon whom the character Pan Yuliang is based, started in a brothel and became the concubine of a member of the Revolutionary Party; she metamorphosed from a prostitute with a talent for embroidery into a professor at a famous Chinese institute of higher learning and a world-famous artist. Second, the film uses the trope of the hero rescuing the beauty and a story of a talented woman and a beautiful man (a transfiguration of the conventional romance about the talented man and the beautiful woman). Zhang Yuliang, the prototype, was a talented woman, but she was not a beautiful woman; judging from extant photographs she might even be termed an ugly woman. In the film, Pan Yuliang becomes a beautiful woman as played by Gong Li. The third commercial feature of the film is its nude scene, which despite being motivated by Pan Yuliang's actual artistic practice still has an extremely obvious commercial purpose. As one would expect, the nude scene was a reason for the government's banning of the film and a focus of public debate. These commercial elements of the film were added to it with men in mind and are a submission to patriarchal society, but at the same time they expose the patriarchal nature of society. Huang Shuqin has said with resignation, "When politics was everything, equality between the sexes was accomplished by eliminating any difference between the sexes. The type of woman demanded by society was a masculinized woman, a Hua Mulan who hides all of her feminine characteristics, a female hero who gives of herself and has no needs. Today China is on the path to a commodity economy, and all cultural production, especially film because it is expensive, of course takes market value as its most important value. Consumer society has resurrected the idea of woman as accessory and decoration in male-dominated society."[26] *The Soul of the Painter* is not, however, a purely commercial film. All the elements that seem to make the film commercial are superficial, merely packaging for a film that, both in the story it tells and in the way in which it tells it, still is art. Pan Yuliang suffers the misfortune of becoming a marketable visual object, but she also has a chance to tell the story of how she went from being "'a woman who is less than human,' to being a 'woman who is fully human,' to being 'a woman in full possession of her dignity,'. . . . who establishes a 'self' once and for all."[27] This constitutes female self-narration. Huang Shuqin's concern for women and her interest in women's self-directed growth and liberation are as evident in *The Soul of the Painter* as in any of her films.

The Soul of the Painter does not set out to represent the entirety of the historical fate of the modern Chinese woman but instead pursues its fascination with the romantic life and emotional journey of one female artist. Nevertheless, in Pan Yuliang's indefatigable efforts to save herself and fight for liberation despite difficulty, we can find an allegory of the fate of the modern Chinese woman. Pan Yuliang moves through three cultural contexts: premodern Chinese culture, modern Chinese culture, and modern Western culture. The first half of her life is lived during China's historical transformation from premodern culture to modern culture. She spends the last half of her life in France in a modern Western cultural context where she observes both the humanism and the inhumanity of Western capitalist culture and is cut off from modernizing China. There are also three aspects to Pan's salvation or liberation. First, there is the physical liberation of the female body. Pan Zanhua rescues Pan Yuliang from the brothel, taking her body, which had been used for the pleasure of many, as his own possession. From this point on, Pan Yuliang has a least some measure of liberty and dignity. Second, there is change in her social identity and status. She begins as a prostitute, becomes a concubine, then an art major and a student who goes abroad, and finally a college professor and a famous artist. The third and last aspect to Pan Yuliang's liberation is the liberation of her individuality and the establishment of her modern women's consciousness. In France, Pan Yuliang is directly influenced and educated by modern Western culture. In China, she is saved and awakened to the ideas of modernity by Pan Zanhua, an early member of the Revolutionary Party, Chen Duxiu, one of giants of the Chinese enlightenment, and Liu Haisu, one of the pioneers of modern Chinese art. Pan Yuliang is helped by Chinese progressives who see the liberation of women as their duty, but when women are saved by men, it is a sign we are within the discourse of male-dominated society.

127

CONCLUSION

The Soul of the Painter continues the strain of cultural critique found in *Woman, Demon, Human* and identifies the hypocrisy, ignorance, and inhumanity of traditional Chinese culture as the cause of Pan Yuliang's misfortune and the obstacle to her salvation. As Huang Shuqin has said, "Just as my earlier films do, *The Soul of the Painter* offers a frank examination of the despicable national mindset that refuses to recognize the full personhood of women." In the film, the camera several times brings to us in immediate fashion the sights and sounds of crowd scenes, including the scene of the furor at the college over nude models, the scene in which Pan Yuliang draws from life in a bath house, the scenes in which

Pan's classmates gossip about Pan and plot against her, and the scene of the chaos that breaks out at Pan's exhibition. In these scenes, the film provides a concentrated laying bare of the hypocrisy, ignorance, and inhumanity of traditional Chinese ethical codes. The film pays particular attention to the psychological split and moral quandary that Pan Yuliang experiences as an enlightened new woman living in a time of social transformation. In her ideas about education, love, and marriage and family, Pan Yuliang is half old and half new. Pan Yuliang's clash with Pan Zanhua's first wife is not the clichéd jealous fight between wife and concubine for a man's attention or a struggle between positive and negative characters; it is a clash between two types of women's consciousness, traditional and modern. In her belief in the crucial importance of having a son, Pan Yuliang is very traditional. Her experience in the brothel, namely the harm done to her reproductive capacity there, leaves her unable to provide an heir for the Pan family. To show her gratitude to Pan Zanhua, she does everything she can to get him back together with his wife, who becomes pregnant with a son. In her ideas about love, Pan Yuliang is likewise both modern and traditional. She is faithful to Pan Zanhua but maintains her friendship with Wang Shouxin. At every turn, Pan Yuliang remains half new and half old and so cannot escape moral quandary and the pain of a psychological split, which we may see as the representation of the inner landscape of a Chinese society that was in transition.

For Brecht, "the dismantling of our given identities through art is inseparable from the practice of producing a new kind of human subject altogether."[28] Indeed, the steady changes in Pan Yuliang's social identity, the steady advancement of her standing in the social hierarchy, and the steady coming into being of her new subjectivity are tied to her art. Pan Yuliang says, "I am my own model. I create art, and art creates me." Pan Yuliang's actions violate the conventions of Chinese patriarchal society; they violate sexual taboo. She becomes her own model; she gazes at herself in the mirror and with her pencil re-creates herself; she puts her own naked body and all the passion and pain her body carries into the figure she draws. At the same time that Pan creates a work of art, she creates a new female self. Huang Shuqin makes a break with the hypocritical sexual taboos of the period by turning her camera on the female body; through the use of a mirror image, Huang reveals the way in which the female body has been obscured by male discourse, offers symbolic comfort for the wounds the female body bears, and celebrates the beauty of the female body. In so doing, Huang dismantles the given identities of women in patriarchal culture and allows woman to become visible as a new kind of human subject.

According to a critic, "It is quite clear that in both its general conception and in its telling of the story of its protagonist, *The Soul of the Painter* is more infused [than *Woman, Demon, Human*] with the ideas of feminism. As a work of art, however, *The Soul of the Painter* is obviously inferior to *Woman, Demon, Human*. This leaves us with a lot to think about."[29] Huang Shuqin has said she wanted to make a commercial film and say something new about women's consciousness and the state of Chinese society and culture, but it was difficult to bring these things together, leaving her feeling it was all a little "forced."[30]

Huang Shuqin's "women's films" *Forever Young, Woman, Demon, Human*, and *The Soul of the Painter* were made in the early 1980s, the mid- to late 1980s, and the early 1990s, respectively, and during these three historical periods Chinese society was dominated by the discourses of politics, cultural criticism, and mass culture, respectively. These dominant discourses not only formed the underlying structures[31] upon which these films were built as women's films but also provided the discursive bridges over which women's stories had to pass to enter into public discussion. Huang Shuqin's identity as a women, her acute sensitivity as an artist, her natural interest in women's issues, and her at first spontaneous and later conscious decision to take the woman's perspective have ensured that both wittingly and unwittingly she has brought her own experience as a woman into the public discourses that she joins; by giving expression to her experience within these discourses, she changes them. This makes Huang Shuqin's films polyphonic. Even if the voice of women is not the dominant voice in this polyphony, it nevertheless is the most moving voice. The women's consciousness found in Huang's films is not a pure women's consciousness that pushes aside the discourses of history and the patriarchy but is rather connected to the social, political, and cultural context of its time. The question "What is a woman?" may transcend history, but it is exceedingly difficult for the women's consciousness of any particular woman or of the women of any particular generation to transcend history. Huang Shuqin remains optimistic: "The establishment of women's consciousness of self is a matter of the establishment and awakening of the other half of humanity. For film, this can open up new vistas and lead to the exploration of new worlds. I am confident that as human civilization progresses, society will increasingly respect and recognize the culture that women create."[32]

NOTES

1. See Dai Jinhua, "Bu ke jian de nüxing" (Invisible Women), p. 277. In recent scholarship on women directors and women's films, in step with increased understanding of the work of women directors such as Wang Ping and Dong Kenan, Dai's claim has been subjected to challenges of varying intensity.

2. Huang Shuqin says that like the characters in *Forever Young*, she went to a girls' middle school, and like the main characters in *Woman, Demon, Human* and *The Soul of the Painter*, she is a female artist. On several occasions, Huang has argued that society does not give women, especially extraordinary women, full standing as people and therefore successful women artists cannot escape loneliness, bewilderment, and pain. This, Huang says, is why she decided to make movies about female artists. See her essay about *Forever Young* titled "Zhenzhi de shenghuo/zhencheng de fanying" (Honest Lives/Faithful Record); as well as "Zhuiwen ziwo" (Questioning the Self) by Huang, et al., which is an interview with Huang that touches upon *Woman, Demon, Human* and *The Soul of the Painter* among other films; "Xie zai *Hua hun* gongying zhi ji" (On the Occasion of the Premiere of *The Soul of the Painter*); and "Nüxing dianying" (Women's Film). In "Nüxing, zai dianyingye de nanren shijieli" (Women, in the Male World of Cinema), Huang Shuqin has said, "The image of the Chinese woman that I want to present is that of a woman who has through difficult experiences gradually come to the realization of her own worth." Qiu Yun and Pan Yuliang fit this description, as does Huang Shuqin herself.

3. Huang Shuqin, "Nüxing, zai dianyingye de nanren shijieli" (Women, in the Male World of Cinema).

4. Mikhail Bakhtin, *Tuosituoyefusiji shixue wenti* (Problems of Dostoevsky's Poetics), p. 117 in the original and p. 90 in the translation.

5. "Voice" is an important term in Bakhtin's *Tuosituoyefusiji shixue wenti* (Problems of Dostoevsky's Poetics) and refers to the expression in language of thoughts, world views, and attitudes. For the quoted passage see the citation in the previous endnote. In feminist theory, "voice" has been an important term: "Despite compelling interrogations of 'voice' as a humanist fiction, for the collectively and personally silenced the term has become a trope of identity and power: as Luce Irigaray suggests, to find a voice (*voix*) is to find a way (*voie*)." Susan Sniader Lanser, *Fictions of Authority*, 3.

6. Huang Shuqin and Xu Feng, "Liushi yu chenji" (Time Passes, Much Remains).

7. Huang Shuqin, "Zhenzhi de shenghuo" (Honest Lives).

8. Ibid.

9. "When we were discussing the script, Huang Shuqin told me that in the film she wanted to do everything she could to represent the beauty and charm of youth, which was very sound judgment on her part. Foreigners have their youth films, and we should have ours; we should have socialist youth films that can move and inspire the young, the middle aged and the old with the beauty, emotions, vigor and strength of youth." See Zhang Xian, "Guanyu *Qingchun wansui* gaibian de yi feng xin" (A Letter about the Screen Adaptation of *Forever Young*).

10. Huang Shuqin, "Zhenzhi de shenghuo" (Honest Lives).

11. When talking about her film's reliance on the description of the details of the girls' lives as found in the original novel, Huang Shuqin praises Wang Meng for his sensitive observations but also repeatedly mentions her memories of her own life in a girls' middle school, saying for example, "I remember that once two friends and I kept diaries. Mine was all about the trivia of school life, who was sad, who was happy, what homework we did, how we tried to make up for our shortcomings, but I really cherished it and I've gone back from time to time to read my little diary. It's ridiculous, notes on stuff that doesn't amount to anything, but it is so sincere and such a treasure." Huang, "Zhenzhi de shenghuo" (Honest Lives).

12. Translator's note: the "three mountains" are imperialism, feudalism, and bureaucrat-capitalism.

13. Dai Jinhua, "Bu ke jian de nüxing" (Invisible Women), 277.

14. See "Zhizhe de yishu zhuiqiu" (A Steadfast Artistic Ambition).

15. Shao Mujun, "Yayi nüxing benwo de tongku" (The Suffering of the Oppressed Female Self).

16. See Dai Jinhua, "Ren, gui, qing" (Woman, Demon, Human).

17. Huang Shuqin and Gu Zhengnan, "Fang Huang Shuqin tan Ren, gui, qing (An Interview with Huang Shuqin about Woman, Demon, Human).

18. Wang Lingzhen, "Hua Mulan xushi de beihou" (The Other Side of the Hua Mulan Story), 662.

19. Ibid., 663.

20. Shao Mujun, "Yayi nüxing benwo de tongku" (The Suffering of the Oppressed Female Self).

21. Ibid.

22. Ibid.

23. Huang Shuqin, "Nüxing, zai dianyingye de nanren shijieli" (Women, in the Male World of Cinema).

24. Huang Shuqin, "Zhongguo ru jin yi meiyou nüxing dianying" (To this Day China Still Has No Women's Film).

25. Huang Shuqin, et al., "Zhuiwen ziwo" (Questioning the Self), 113.

26. Huang Shuqin, "Nüxing, zai dianyingye de nanren shijieli" (Women, in the Male World of Cinema).

27. Huang Shuqin, "Xie zai Hua hun gongying zhi ji" (On the Occasion of the Premiere of The Soul of the Painter), 149.

28. Terry Eagleton, Literary Theory, p. 191, trans. Wu Xiaoming as Ershi shiji Xifang wenxue lilun, 239.

29. Ni Zhen, "Yige wanmei de ren shi gudu de" (A Person Complete in Herself is Lonely), 44.

30. Huang Shuqin, et al., "Zhuiwen ziwo" (Questioning the Self), 113.

31. For an explanation of the notion of xianxing jiegou, here rendered as "underlying structures," see Niu Hongbao, Xifang xiandai meixue (Modern Western Aesthetics), 550–551.

32. Huang Shuqin, "Nüxing, zai dianyingye de nanren shijieli" (Women, in the Male World of Cinema).

5

Post–Taiwan New Cinema Women Directors and Their Films

AUTEURS, IMAGES, LANGUAGE

YU-SHAN HUANG AND CHUN-CHI WANG

TRANSLATED BY ROBIN VISSER AND THOMAS MORAN

PIONEERING TAIWANESE WOMEN DIRECTORS

Participation by women directors in Taiwanese cinema began during the era of Taiwanese (Hokkienese)-language cinema, which was launched by (male) director Ho Chi-ming's *Xue Pinggui yu Wang Baochuan* (Xue Pinggui and Wang Baochuan, 1956), a thirty-five millimeter film adaptation of the Taiwanese opera (*koa-a-hi*, in Mandarin *gezaixi*). During the post-War period, many mainland filmmakers followed the Nationalist Party (Kuomintang, KMT) to Taiwan; Mandarin-language films could not initially be produced, while Taiwanese directors who had worked under Japanese occupation and studied in Japan had relatively more creative freedom. The popularity of Taiwanese-language film helped woman filmmaker Ch'en Wen-min gain prominence by directing *Mangmang niao* (The Dazzling Bird, 1957), *Ku lian* (Bitter Love, 1957), and other films. In the 1960s, Taiwanese-language cinema flourished, yet most artistically talented women took up acting because opportunities for female directors were rare.

More women directors emerged in the late 1970s, making Mandarin-language films,[1] including Wang Ying, who had studied in the United

States, Li Mei-mi, Yang Chia-yün, and Liu Li-li, all of whom paved the way for New Cinema women directors. The incorporation of feminist ideology into world women's cinema in the 1970s became a media tool for the women's movement in Europe and North American, while in Taiwan Lü Hsiu-lien (Annette Lu) launched a women's rights movement by promoting feminism after her return from the United States.[2] After the 1979 Formosa Incident (Kao-hsiung Incident), Taiwan's women's movement was thwarted, yet research on feminist theory and feminism by women scholars such as Li Yüan-chen, founder and editor of the magazine *Funü xin zhi* (Women Awakening), replaced social movement protests with information dissemination.

THE BIRTH OF WOMEN'S CINEMA DURING THE NEW CINEMA ERA

The 1980s were a turbulent era for Taiwan and Taiwanese New Cinema. In the 1970s, Taiwan's withdrawal from the United Nations had provoked a sense of escapism in society, and film production became increasingly removed from civil society. Military education films and romances denied the angst and anomie caused by international crises such as the Diaoyu Islands Movement and the oil crisis. Scholars agree that the emergence of Taiwan New Cinema was partially a reaction against the escapism of the 1970s. During the New Cinema Era in the 1980s, many works of literature by Nativist writers (*xiangtu wenxue zuojia*) and women writers were adapted to film, putting women on screen in determined, resolute roles, often in coming-of-age stories and often offering a perspective on Taiwan's history. Examples of nativist fiction from which film adaptations were made include Hwang Chun-ming's "Kan hai de rizi" (A Flower in the Rainy Night), Wang Chen-ho's *Jiazhuang yi niuche* (An Oxcart for a Dowry), and Wang T'o's *Jinshui shen* (Auntie Jinshui). Film adaptations of works by women writers or films with screenplays by women writers delved into human nature while representing women's sexual and emotional worlds. Films made from Liao Hui-ying's story "Youma caizi" (Ah Fei), Chu T'ien-wen's screenplay for *Fenggui lai de ren* (The Boys from Fengkuei), and Li Ang's novella *Sha fu* (The Woman of Wrath) portray the inner life of women from different social classes who take charge of their marriages, acknowledge their sexual desires, and resist male authoritarian control.

THE GROWTH OF WOMEN'S CINEMA IN THE MID-1980s

The international acclaim of Taiwanese New Cinema did not provide much space for women to create independently.[3] Sylvia Chang and Wang Hsiao-ti began directing and producing films in the early 1980s, but opportunities for other women did not come until the latter stage of New Cinema's development. Sylvia Chang worked as an actress and did screenwriting and production work for the Taiwan Television (TTV) series *Eleven Women* before finally attracting the attention of the film world by directing *Zui ai* (Passion, 1986). Wang Hsiao-ti wrote *Huangse gushi* (The Game They Call Sex, 1987) for Tomson Company and invited Sylvia Chang and Chin Kuo-chao to co-direct this film, which traces a woman's emotional journey as she reflects on marriage and sexual awakening. From the late 1980s through the 1990s, the Central Motion Pictures Corporation (CMPC) nurtured a second wave of directors, including the men Ang Lee, Tsai Ming-liang, and Ho P'ing, and woman director Huang Yu-shan.

134

Images of women in the films of this era primarily focused on female desire and the changing social roles of women. More women were participating in politics at that time, and the emergence of women's voices in cinema signified the entry of women into the public sphere and the possibility for changing the conditions of women in a patriarchal society. In the 1980s, efforts by democratic movements to topple the Kuomintang (KMT) dictatorship addressed issues of social disenfranchisement, and stories about women in the films of this era often highlighted the exploitative restrictions placed upon them by a patriarchal system.

THE RAPID DEVELOPMENT OF WOMEN'S CINEMA IN THE 1990s

During the development of Taiwan New Cinema in the 1980s, women directors were provided only limited opportunities in the film industry. In response to societal pressures that discouraged women from pursuing directorial work,[4] Li Yüan-chen and Wang P'ing of the magazine *Women Awakening* collaborated with the Black and White Film Studio, managed by Huang Yu-shan, feminist scholars Chang Hsiao-Hung and Fifi Naifei Ding (Ting Nai-fei), and women artists Shu Lea Cheang (Cheng Shu-li), Yen Ming-Hui, and Hou I-Jen to hold Taiwan's first women's film festival, Women's Visual Arts Festival, at the Huo K'o Gallery in early 1993. The screened films explored issues including women's activism, women and work, women and immigration, the media's representation of women, and women's desire. A women's film festival, later named Women Make Waves Film Festival, has been held annually in Taiwan ever since. The film festival is sponsored by the Taipei Women's Film Association (precursor to the Taiwan Women's Film Association), which was established in 1998 with financial support from the state and civic arts foundations to promote films by women filmmakers in Taiwan and worldwide that express female sensibilities and viewpoints. The festival showcases the potential and diversity of women filmmakers by screening feature films, animated films, experimental films, and documentaries.

The emerging field of documentary filmmaking has provided essential resources for women directors.[5] Documentary filmmaking in Taiwan was encouraged by the establishment in 1995 of the Graduate Institute of Sound & Image Studies in Documentary at Tainan National College of the Arts (now Tainan National University of the Arts) and by the Taiwan Documentary Film Festival and documentary channels, such as Viewpoint on Taiwan Public Television. Documentaries such as Yang Chia-yün's *A Ma de mimi: Taiji "weianfu" de gushi* (A Secret Buried for Fifty Years: A Story of Taiwanese "Comfort Women," 1995), Chien Wei-ssu's *Hui shou lai shi lu* (Echoing with Women's Voices, 1997), and Hu T'ai-li's *Chuanguo pojiacun* (Passing through My Mother-in-Law's Village, 1998), reveal women filmmakers' concern with women's collective memory and women's historical narrative. These films enrich the historical material on women's lives from various eras and provide an alternative version of so-called historical knowledge. As feminist historian Joan Wallach Scott points out, the "appearance" of women in history is not merely a question of excavating and compiling new historical materials, but provides a new methodology for reading politics, nation, and gender.[6]

Starting in 1995, the number of feature films directed by women gradually trended upward, but their distribution and run time in theatres was under attack. Nevertheless, the younger generation of women filmmakers has taken advantage of state subsidies and advances in technology. Digital technology and broadband Internet have reduced production costs and diversified distribution platforms, enabling women filmmakers to establish themselves in traditionally male-centered film circles.[7]

Younger women have joined forces with experienced women filmmakers, and the numbers of films by women has increased in recent years, in diverse genres extending to art films, commercial films, and documentaries. Commercially successful feature films directed by women include Chen Ying-jung (DJ Chen)'s *Shiqi sui de tiankong* (Formula 17, 2004), Tseng Wen-chen's *Dengdai feiyu* (Fishing Luck, 2005), and Zero Chou's *Ciqing* (Spider Lilies, 2007). Films by women directors Alice Wang, Chiang Hsiu-ch'iung, and Li Yün-ch'an, among others, have also succeeded at the box office and have attracted increasing critical attention. In addition to their rich stories and forms, these films established a marketing model independent of government support. New-generation films have returned to the market not to replicate Hollywood but to engage the public in dialogue in order to find a market for domestic films. These films are commercially oriented but retain uniquely Taiwanese social, cultural, and historical characteristics, including cultural and aesthetic hybridity.[8]

Given the number of women filmmakers in Taiwan, choosing any as representative is risky, but the differences in creative direction, style, and market appeal among Sylvia Chang, Huang Yu-shang, and Zero Chou will be taken to represent the diversity of women's films within Taiwan cinema.

THE FILMS OF SYLVIA CHANG

Taiwan-born Sylvia Chang began her career as an actor and producer in the mid-1970s. Since 1992, Chang has done half her work in Hong Kong and half in Taiwan, and her peripatetic life is the reason her films evince little in the way of concern with a specific regional identity. Instead, Chang's films are set against a background of a "cultural China" (*Hua wenhua*) and use the love story, Chang's strong suit, as a vehicle for investigating the subjectivity and experiences of women of different generations, backgrounds, careers, and sexual orientation. Chang's favored narrative motif is the intermingling of fantasies and disappointments in women's lives, and her films convey the sense that passionate aspirations are always accompanied by alienation in the face of reality.

Chang's *Shaonü Xiao Yu* (Siao Yu, 1995), based on a short story of the same name by Yan Geling, is about a young woman, Siao Yu (played by René Liu), who comes to New York from mainland China illegally to work and reunite with her boyfriend, Chiang Wei. In order to make ends meet and secure a green card, she enters into a sham marriage with an older white man named Mario. While living together (in different rooms), the two find warmth and comfort in looking after each other. This makes

Siao Yu's boyfriend jealous and changes their relationship. The story is told from Siao Yu's point of view, and this narrative choice adds gender and racial elements to a story of immigration. Siao Yu comes to New York because Chiang Wei's mother is concerned that Chiang Wei may take a foreign woman as his wife; this and the fact that Siao Yu's access to permanent residency is through marriage to a citizen manifest the idea that nations, which depend on heterosexual reproduction, are of course always already gendered.[9] Siao Yu's heterosexual body represents both the dream of the protection of the purity of the native race and the prospect of the assimilation of the foreigner. The plot in part hinges on the meek, obedient character of the traditional Chinese woman, which is the source of Siao Yu's predicament and its solution. She obeys Chiang Wei's mother and ends up as an illegal immigrant in New York; she follows Chiang Wei's instructions and moves in with a man who is a stranger to her. On the other hand, the reason Mario gradually begins to treat Siao Yu with kindness and Mario's estranged wife Rita has to give in to Siao Yu is because Siao Yu is meek and obedient. Older Americans take a paternalistic attitude toward Siao Yu. With Siao Yu, Mario plays the role of teacher and philosophical guide. Mario is even the one who leads Siao Yu to the realization that she does not, in fact, "belong to Chiang Wei." When the white, male Mario lectures to Siao Yu, an Asian and a citizen of China, we seem to see an image from the history of American colonialism. At the end of the film, Chiang Wei has left and Mario is dead. This highlights Siao Yu's independence, but Siao Yu's awakening to her identity as a woman has been dependent from first to last on the lessons taught to her by Mario, who is a symbolic colonial father.

137

The depiction of the negotiation between Chinese women and the patriarchy—Siao Yu submits to Mario as a father and authority figure—leaves room for a more radical statement.

The subject of the plight and flight in the life of a woman are once again the concern in Chang's 2002 film *Xiang fei* (Princess D, 2002). The game designer Joker (played by Daniel Wu) encounters the middle-class barmaid Ah-ling (played by Lee Sin-jie) and decides she possesses exactly the romantic charm he is looking for as the prototype for the adventurous princess of the video game he is designing. Joker asks for Ah-ling's help in producing the video game of his dreams, and their lives become entwined. In this film, Sylvia Chang uses special effects to create a sense of magical realism to accentuate the way in which we now move back and forth unsteadily between the virtual world and the real world.

The story of Princess D was Sylvia Chang's experiment in engaging the world of computer games from a woman's perspective. She ensured that the female character in the computer game at the center of her story does not exist solely to fulfill the fantasies of male game designers and male players, whether as a virginal damsel in distress or a sexy female warrior, as is the case with the character of Zumi created by a competitor of Joker's. Virtual reality for Joker should be an *extension* of the real world, and that is why his princess is not perfect, even though it is true that the imperfect can be improved by manipulation in the world of video games. Joker's computer-generated princess is called Princess D (Digital), and she is the avatar of the Princess D of reality—Princess Diana, who made a meteoric rise from her status as a kindergarten teacher to the heights of society. By becoming Princess D, Ah-ling can temporarily escape the circumstances at home: her father is in jail, her mother is suffering from a mental breakdown, her brother is involved with gangsters, and she bears the responsibility of finding a way to pay the family debts.

138

While Sylvia Chang believes that, in a world driven by the new media and Internet culture, the line between the virtual world and the real world has become blurred, she also seems to believe that while phenomena now appear to us in new and different forms, the intrinsic nature of the phenomena themselves will never change. In the real world, Joker cannot help Ah-ling pay her family's debts or escape from the pressures at home, but in the virtual world he can give Princess D wings, weapons, and the power to defeat monsters. The irony is that as the design of the Princess D video game is improved, the burden Ah-ling carries in life worsens. Sylvia Chang does not, however, deny that the events in the virtual world have an influence on human mental perception. When Ah-ling is about to take the risk of crossing the border into China with drugs so that she can make the money she needs to pay her debts, she slips into Joker's workspace and places her hands on the computer screen so that they meet the hands of Princess D, her digital self. When Princess D's hands move slightly, it seems that Princess D has responded and wishes to encourage Ah-ling, giving her strength as she goes forward. At the end of the film, when Ah-ling and her family leave Hong Kong, it is as if Princess D will finally be able to put on her wings and fly away.

20, 30, 40 (2004), one of Sylvia Chang's more recent directorial efforts, involved René Liu and Lee Sin-jie, both of whom Chang mentored. Chang, Liu, and Lee all act in the film and the three wrote it together. The film was a collaborative effort but is very much in the style of Sylvia

Chang's romantic comedies, and the characters are portrayed in a manner that is reminiscent of Chang's earlier films. Chang, Liu, and Lee play
the roles of the middle-aged Lily, thirty-something Hsiang-hsiang, and
the young girl Hsiao-chieh, and each wrote the story of her character. The
forty-year-old Lily discovers her husband is having an affair and divorces,
exactly what happens to Chia-chia in *Shasha Jiajia zhanqilai* (Sisters of
the World Unite, 1991). Lily's decision to pursue sexual fulfillment recalls
the story of not only Chia-chia but also Mrs. Ch'en in *Jintian bu huijia*
(Tonight Nobody Goes Home, 1996).[10] The stories of Hsiang-hsiang and
Hsiao-chieh were written by René Liu and Lee Sin-jie, but Hsiang-hsiang
moves from man to man and shares a man with another woman, which
combines the story of Sha-sha with that of Coco in "Weihun Mama" (The
Unwed Mother), the third story in *Xin tongju shidai* (In Between, 1994).[11]
Hsiao-chieh is admired by her singing partner T'ung (who is female),
making her resemble the character of Hsiao-jou in *Xin dong* (Tempting
Heart, 1999),[12] and their developing romantic friendship is subsequently
undermined by the younger man Jay, an echo of the love triangle in
Tempting Heart involving Hsiao-jou, Ch'en Li, and Hao-chün. At the end
of *20, 30, 40*, Hsiao-chieh stands outside Lily's flower shop and the two exchange a gaze, creating a strong metafictional and extratextual mirroring
effect (in the story, Lily and Hsiao-chieh do not know each other). Hsiao-
chieh is desired by the woman T'ung, making her like *Tempting Heart*'s
Hsiao-jou, who is loved by the woman Ch'en Li. In *Tempting Heart*, Sylvia
Chang plays a director, Cheryl, who is making a movie about love, and
the character of Hsiao-jou is Cheryl's (and therefore Chang's) alter ego.
Therefore, when at the end of *20, 30, 40* Hsiao-chieh (an echo of Hsiao-
jou) and Lily (played by Sylvia Chang) exchange a look, an intertexual link
is established between the two films.

Even though the film's female protagonists subvert the image of the
traditional woman—they are not faithful to their husbands until death,
they do not deny their own sexual desires, and they pursue sexual fulfillment actively—their experiences as women adhere to heterosexual
ideology. Hsiang-hsiang disbelieves in marriage until she finds her Mr.
Right. The divorced, middle-aged Lily decides she will live the rest of
her life for herself, but the film introduces a man who shows an interest
in her, endorsing the same ideology affirmed by Hsiang-hsiang's story.
Hsiao-chieh and T'ung are drawn to each other but do not transgress or
challenge the ideology of heteronormativity. The feelings between Hsiao-
chieh and T'ung grow out of horseplay and curiosity and conform to the

heteronormative disavowal of same-sex desire among young women, which holds that before women enter into mature heterosexual relationships they go through a transitional period of homosexual affection.[13]

Chang tells stories from a woman's perspective that are finely wrought, moving, and accompanied by striking cinematography, but they rarely address questions of history and non-heteronormative gender identification, which are the preoccupations of the films of Huang Yu-shan and Zero Chou.

THE FILMS OF HUANG YU-SHAN

Huang Yu-shan's films take the narrative point of view of women, but unlike Sylvia Chang, whose orientation is as a female director from broader cultural China, Huang Yu-shan makes films that strongly identify with Taiwan as place. Her films straddle the boundary between documentary film and feature film and attempt to tell the story of Taiwan's history and society in images. Huang was born in P'eng-hu, Taiwan, and grew up in Kao-hsiung. After graduating from college, Huang met director Li Hsing and went to work at his studio. From 1977 to 1979, she worked for Li Hsing as he made *Wangyang zhong de yi tiao chuan* (He Never Gives Up, 1978), *Xiao cheng gushi* (Story of a Small Town, 1979), and *Zao'an Taibei* (Good Morning, Taipei, 1979). She next went to the United States to study film and began to make documentaries. Huang went on to make documentaries about a number of personages important in the history of women in Taiwan, including Hsü Shih-hsien, who was born during the period of the Japanese occupation and studied medicine in Japan before becoming Taiwan's first elected woman town mayor; dancer and choreographer Ts'ai Jui-yüeh, who was also born under the Japanese occupation and later brought modern dance to Taiwan; Chiang Fang-liang, wife of Chiang Ching-kuo; and the female architect Hsiu Tse-lan.

Huang Yu-shan's first feature film *Luoshan feng* (Autumn Tempest, 1988) became the topic of much conversation during its production because it deals with women's sexual desire. Subsequently Huang was invited to go to Hong Kong to make a film for Cosmopolitan Film Productions (a company founded by Shaw Brothers {HK} Ltd.), which sent her to Hui'an in Fujian to shoot *Shuang zhuo* (Twin Bracelets, 1990). The next year she returned to Taiwan and made *Mudan niao* (Peony Birds, 1991). These films are collectively known as Huang's "women's trilogy"

FIGURE 5.1 *Twin Bracelets*, 1990

and share common themes: All explore the discovery of self-awareness by young women as they come of age, and all lay bare how traditional social morality and conventional marriage fetter the individual woman. As Azed Yu has written, "In Huang Yu-shan's films resistance to the power of the patriarchy and denunciation of the unequal treatment of woman comprise a powerful defense of women's rights."[14] The story of *Autumn Tempest* revolves around protagonist Su-pi's sexual awakening. The scene in which Su-pi strokes her body in the bath and gazes at herself in the mirror signifies her physical craving inspired by her closeness to male protagonist Wen-hsiang. These images, which caused an uproar in the 1980s, show women's sexual desire and advocate for women taking possession of their bodies.

The subject matter of the 1990 *Twin Bracelets* is taken from the tradition of the *"Zishu nü"* (the "women who comb their own hair," a term for women who are self-sufficient) in Hui'an, Fujian, and its environs and tells the story of a homosexual bond between women that can defer or even defy heterosexual marriage (fig. 5.1). As Yu points out, the suicide of protagonist Hui-hua is "the film's strong protest at the way in which patriarchal ideology oppresses women."[15] The film was not understood as a "lesbian film" when it was shown in Taiwan, but in the West because of the way in which the film treats same-sex romantic love and friendship among women, it was taken as a lesbian story. Vivian Price explains this is as happening because "The film's representation of women rejecting oppression resembles the lesbian utopia envisioned in the West."[16] *Peony Birds* explores female sexual desire and looks at career women, using the lives of Ch'an-chüan and her family to show the changes in Taiwan society. *Peony Birds* has a touch of the surreal in its use of color, lighting, and music, and in its plot, which includes melodramatic conflict and an emphasis on the clash between an individual inner life and the outside world. The attempt to depict a woman's pursuit of love and sexual fulfillment in the context of Taiwan society is continued in Huang's 1998 *Zhen qing kuang ai* (Spring Cactus, 1998), but the narrative focus shifts to the working class and touches upon the issues of family and education. Both *Spring Cactus* and *Peony Birds* include moments of dream or fantasy imagery but in the main combine elements of the theatrical film and the documentary film.

Nanfang jishi zhi fushi guangying (The Strait Story, 2006) is a docudrama that continues Huang's concern with the cultural history of Taiwan. It uses montage, collage, and juxtaposition to convey the individual human memories, dreams, and fantasies that exist in interdependence with the grand sweep of history. As Lai Hsien-tsung has written, "The film, on the one hand, reflects on Taiwan's cultural history realistically, and on the other hand, it represents Taiwan's bitter history poetically. Its employment of a poetic visual language does not aim to convey a sense of self-pity but to transcend the historical traumas that this island has experienced."[17]

The Strait Story employs a parallel narrative structure that depicts the life stories of artist Huang Ch'ing-ch'eng, who was born in P'eng-hu during the time of the Japanese occupation, and contemporary art restorer Hsiu-hsiu, who grows interested in Huang Ch'ing-ch'eng's work and is drawn to uncover the details of his life (fig. 5.2). By making brilliant use of a search for Huang's muse, the film writes the women in Huang's life into the history of art. For a male artist, the muse is the woman who stands behind him as his foil, inspiration, and advocate. The film, however, tells its story from Hsiu-hsiu's point of view (which is also the point of view of the filmmaker) and so changes the power relation between the genders. Hsiu-hsiu takes the authority to uncover and write history as a woman. Huang Ch'ing-ch'eng is Hsiu-hsiu's muse, and like him, Hsiu-hsiu pursues her ambition with a daring disregard of all else. Her boyfriend Kuo-chün stands behind her as her foil and advocate.

While the women who fit Huang Ch'ing-ch'eng's ideal remain in his shadow, each is nevertheless portrayed vividly and powerfully.[18] Huang's

FIGURE 5.2 *The Strait Story,* 2006

childhood sweetheart Yü-lan may be uneducated, but she defies the puritanical mores of the traditional countryside and boldly agrees to be Huang's nude model. Huang finds his second muse in the person of Li Kuei-hsiang, who is studying music in Japan and represents the self-aware modern woman. Li Kuei-hsiang repeatedly questions or challenges Huang's male-centered world view. By sticking to her own beliefs and values throughout her involvement with Huang, she shakes up his male egocentrism. Huang Ch'ing-ch'eng's sister-in-law Ah-ho represents a dispirited woman who lives in the home of the patriarch as nothing but a wife to her husband and a mother to her children. Each time Kuei-hsiang and Ch'ing-ch'eng return to P'eng-hu to visit relatives, the frame is taken up by the figures of Ch'ing-ch'eng, his elder brother Ch'ing-shun, and Kuei-hsiang as they eat and chat, while Ah-ho is relegated to the frame's lower left-hand corner, her back to the others as she eats and feeds her children. The lives of Ch'ing-shun, Ch'ing-ch'eng, and Kuei-hsiang change—sometimes in response to social changes and sometimes following personal choices—but Ah-ho's life doesn't change at all, she just has more mouths to feed. Her entrapment by the patriarchy renders her life meaningless, and Hsiu-hsiu, having learned a lesson from Ah-ho's life, rejects Kuo-chün's marriage proposal.

The Strait Story is much more than a biography of a male artist told with realist devices; Huang places documentary within a fictional plot and

uses flashbacks, dream sequences, shots of newspaper clippings, mono-
logues, and collage to free her narrative from chronology and liberate the
film's re-representation of history. *The Strait Story* also becomes Huang's
personal story: in telling the story of Hsiu-hsiu, Huang Yu-shan looks
back at the lives of her parents during the war in the Pacific and their
memories of that time.

In *Chatianshan zhi ge* (The Song of Chatien Mountain, 2007), which is
based on a novel of the same name by Hakka author Chung Chao-cheng,
Huang Yu-shan continues to explore the way in which the war inflicted
trauma and ruthlessly changed the course of lives. The sinking of the
Takachiho Maru in 1934 by a torpedo from an American submarine as
the Japanese ship steamed from Kobe, Japan, to Keelung, Taiwan, establishes the complex emotional tone of both *The Strait Story* and *The Song of
Chatien Mountain*. These films are Huang Yu-shan's experiment in telling
the story of the young love, passion, and dreams of the generation that
was coming of age during the war.

THE FILMS OF ZERO CHOU

Before becoming a director of feature films, Zero Chou worked as a political reporter for a television news channel opposed to the KMT. This
impressed upon her the power and influence of the filmed image. Zero
Chou came to the public's attention as a producer and one of twelve directors who did work for a 2000 film project called "Liu li dao ying" (Floating
Islands).[19] The directors involved in the project used their subjective ideas
and emotions in filming each of Taiwan's twelve outlying islands and
took the "rejection of objectivity" as their guiding principle, shunning the
pretense of objective realism that dominates mainstream documentary
filmmaking.[20] Chou next turned her attention to her own creative ideas,
focusing on the topic of Taiwan's *tongzhi*[21] community in several documentaries and feature films. *Si jiaoluo* (Corner's, 2001), Chou's first documentary about *tongzhi* culture, concerns a *tongzhi* bar in Taipei called *The
Corner's* during the two months before it will go out of business. Poetic
imagery and first-person monologue in French carry the film's visual and
verbal alternative to the language of the dominant culture. After *Si jiaoluo*,
Chou began to make her "*tongzhi* trilogy." The second film of the trilogy,
Spider Lilies, won the Berlin Film Festival Teddy Award, known as the Gay
Oscar, in 2007. This was when Chou talked candidly about her sexual

orientation with the media, becoming Taiwan's first out-of-the-closet lesbian director.

The first film of the trilogy was the sixteen millimeter feature film *Yanguang sishe gewutuan* (Splendid Float, 2004), which tells the story of a group of cross-dressing *tongzhi* performers and looks at the impossibility of gay men finding themselves within the confines of heteronormative society. At the start of the film we see a drag cabaret troupe called Splendid Float in the midst of a dazzling nighttime performance. The stage is surrounded by inky darkness that contrasts with the lights of a city glowing behind the far bank of a river, the image collapsing a world into a small space. After a few medium shots of the performers and the audience, Zero Chou uses an extreme long shot to place the utopian visage of the troupe in the lower right-hand corner of the frame, with the rest of the shot taken up by the surroundings, symbolizing the way in which the social environment overwhelms the world of the cabaret and showing us that the troupe is marginalized but still vibrant. The main character is a drag queen, and the film is concerned with drag and with gender performance. Zero Chou has said, "In fact, every one of us is in drag, both in order to gain socially recognized identity and to self-identify." Indeed, the idea that life is theater (*rensheng ru xi*) is important to the affective structures of the *tongzhi* sensibility (*tongzhi ganxing*); the queer person, disparaged by society for violating the norm, imitates heterosexual romantic conventions or adopts passing as a strategy—dressing so as to appear to fit social gender conventions—to get by in the world.[22] Revolving as it does around the onstage and offstage life of a drag queen, *Splendid Float* gives expression to Judith Butler's argument in *Gender Trouble*: "In imitating gender, drag implicitly reveals the imitative structure of gender itself—as well as its contingency."[23] The heterosexual law that asserts that the three dimensions of anatomical sex, gender, and gender performance are consistent is a fiction. The performance onstage by the anatomically male performers may seem to be an imitation, but taking into account their gender self-identification as female, we understand that it is when they are offstage dressed as men that they are involved in the imitation of gender (fig. 5.3).

Zero Chou also uses the subject of gender performance to challenge the customs and ideology of the patriarchy. Rose is the star drag performer of the cabaret troupe during the evening, but during the day he is Ah-wei, a Taoist priest who conducts funeral rites to guide the dead to the next world. When practicing the ritual of summoning the soul of his departed

145

FIGURE 5.3 *Splendid Float,* 2004

lover Sunny,[24] Ah-wei is confronted with the fact that he has no right to Sunny's spirit tablet, meaning he will be unable to live out his years with Sunny's soul as company. Ah-Wei therefore decides that he will use his authority as a Taoist priest to conduct a ceremony to "divide the spirit tablet" (*fen ling*),[25] and through divination he secures Sunny's approval to do so. Ah-wei's wish to keep Sunny's soul with him critiques the compulsory heterosexuality imposed not only on the living but also on the souls of the departed. At the end of the film, the cabaret troupe organizes a performance for the enjoyment of Sunny's spirit and as a memorial to him, and this is a second appropriation by the queer community of the rites of the entrenched patriarchal authority. The cabaret troupe's stage is built onto a truck, making the troupe mobile, which is a reference to the custom of using trucks decorated with electric lights (*dianzi huache*) in funeral ceremonies. The performances on the backs of these trucks feature scantily dressed pretty young girls who sing and dance to please the gods and the departed; the nature and the popularity of these performances conforms to a culture in which the female body is displayed for the pleasure of a male audience. Zero Chou uses the drag culture of the *tongzhi* community to appropriate the *dianzi huache* for use in a *tongzhi* funeral ceremony.

The Taiwan *tongzhi* culture represented in *Splendid Float* is that of the working class and, therefore, different from the *tongzhi* culture of the urban middle classes. Zero Chou's focus on grassroots *tongzhi* culture stems from her realization that the aesthetic of Taiwan's urban *tongzhi* culture is overly imitative of European and North American queer culture. In interviews, Chou has repeatedly said that she hopes to ground *tongzhi* culture in the discursive context of Taiwan's indigenous culture so that it will no longer be rootless and homeless. In her *tongzhi* trilogy, Chou not only tells the story of Taiwan's *tongzhi* in images but also pursues the Taiwan *tongzhi* aesthetic of her ideal, which is vulgar and exaggerated but vibrant and suffused with the poetics of desolation.

Spider Lilies tells a story of lesbian love and deals with the tattoo parlors and webcam girls of Taiwan's mass culture, and also makes the earthquake of September 21, 1999, which was a major event in the history of Taiwan, pivotal in the lives of the characters. The film depicts the lives of female tattoo artist Takeko and her traumatized brother and their memories of the earthquake, but gives equal emphasis to the story of Jade, who is from the same hometown as Takeko and now makes her living as a webcam girl. The film uses Internet culture to drive the plot—misunderstanding is created by the disconnect between the virtual world and the real world—and to overturn and reverse the gender power relations that exist in the world of online images. Jade is not a passive subject put on display but rather an agent who manipulates the viewer's desire by what she says and how she moves. Indeed, Jade can go offline whenever she likes: she can sever the viewer's connection to the object of his desire at her whim. The film uses self-reflexivity to direct its critique at the film's audience: the audience is made aware that as it watches *Spider Lilies* it also watches Jade's webcam girl broadcasts. The camera takes the point of view of Jade's customers, putting Jade in front of Zero Chou's camera, facing it, looking straight at the film's audience. The film's ability to get the audience to reflect critically on the activity of looking is especially apparent in the subplot involving a policeman who goes by the name Silence in an undercover investigation of Internet pornography and who urges Jade to quit working as a webcam girl. When Jade scolds the policeman (who represents society and the media), she is directing criticism at society for rarely making the consumers of webcam girl images the objects of its moral criticism. A second reversal of the dominant culture of the Internet occurs through the involvement of Takeko. Jade's online performances are not directed only at the heterosexual world; her erotic performances are intended to arouse Takeko, who is a woman (Jade thinks that Takeko, to whom Jade is attracted, is online watching her, but the person she thinks is Takeko is actually Silence), which upsets the uniformity of gender identification and sexual desire among customers for Internet pornography. This self-reflexive device disrupts the structures of Taiwan's male-centered Internet visual culture.

Spider Lilies also challenges the stereotypical images of gender and tongzhi common in mass culture. When Takeko's Japanese tattoo instructor tells her that he does not accept female students, she offers the fact that she cut the tattoo of a Manjusaka flower from the arm of her dead father as proof that while she is a woman, she is not afraid of blood or of putting her knife to skin. Both Jade and another customer named Ah-Tung call Takeko a nan ren po (butch) and a tie T (iron T, roughly equivalent to "stone butch"), but in fact Takeko, played by Isabella Leong Lok-Sze (Luisa Isabella Nolasco da Silva), is fair-complexioned and refined and does not match in either facial appearance, figure, or temperament the conventional image of the tie T as understood in Taiwan tongzhi culture. Through the character of Takeko, Zero Chou seems out to upset the conventional idea of the tie T. Similarly, Takeko's customer Ah-tung is an idle high school tough guy, but to the audience's surprise he turns out to be gay, even though he could not be more unlike the image of the male tongzhi common in Taiwan's middle-class gay culture. In Spider Lilies, Zero Chou not only deconstructs the relationship of the watcher and the watched as it exists under the hegemony of heteronormative authority but also enriches and complicates the representation of Taiwan's tongzhi identity.[26]

Conversations about issues in the lives of lesbians in Taiwan that are begun but not concluded in Spider Lilies are dealt with more thoroughly in Piaolang qingchun (Drifting Flowers, 2008), the last film in Chou's "tongzhi trilogy"; these issues include the awakening to Po (femme) identity, the life experiences of the tie T, and the experiences of tongzhi as they grow old in a heterosexual society. In Spider Lilies, the good feelings that overcome Jade when she is with Takeko at the age of nine are not fleeting; they are the sign of a girl beginning to self-identify as a Po lesbian. In like manner, the eight-year-old May in the first story of Drifting Flowers, "May," falls in love at first sight with the tie T woman Diego, the girlfriend of her older sister Ch'ing-ch'ing. May's self-identification as Po thus commences. The film depicts the lesbian relationship between the blind singer Ch'ing-ch'ing and Diego from May's perspective, and May's mixed emotions of jealously and longing for the T (butch) object of her desire ensure that the movie is about how Po identity is constructed. May's innate sexual orientation is reaffirmed when she declares her adoration

FIGURE 5.4 *Drifting Flowers*, 2008

for another girl in front of their entire class and when she is indifferent to the boys who pursue her (fig. 5.4).

In the second story, "Lily," Chou addresses the collective historical memory of the Taiwan *tongzhi* community, which includes strategic marriages between lesbians and gay men, the inability to appease families,[27] and social discrimination against gays and lesbians. Lily (the very first out lesbian person whom Diego meets in her life) is a lesbian, and Ah-yen (Diego's high school friend) is gay. They wed in a marriage of convenience that allows them to escape pressure from their families while each continues to live with his or her homosexual partner. The next time Lily and Ah-yen encounter each another they are elderly; Ah-yen has AIDS, and Lily has Alzheimer's disease. Because of her disease, Lily mistakes Ah-yen for her long-dead female companion Ah-hai. Ah-yen has come to see Lily to say goodbye, but with nowhere else to go, he allows Lily's mistake to stand and takes the part of Ah-hai. Lily is stuck in her memories of the past and frets that Ah-yen, whom she believes to be Ah-hai, is too masculine and so she is careful to keep their relationship within bounds. At the end of the film, Ah-yen agrees to get treatment for AIDS so that he will be around to care for Lily, and we see the formation of a queer family, a rewriting of the notion of "family," which has always adhered to heterosexual norms.

The third story, "Diego," is about how the *tie* T Diego comes to realize who she is. In comparison with Takeko in *Spider Lilies,* Diego better fits the image of the T in the minds of members of Taiwan's lesbian subculture who are of Zero Chou's generation.[28] Diego's experiences as she comes of age can be taken to represent the collective memories of the generation of butch lesbians who grew up in Taiwan in the 1960s. The film calls attention to the way in which the binary discourse of sexuality caused awkwardness and pain for the T. Because society divides gender into the binary opposition of male and female, someone like Diego, who has a female body but a male appearance, finds herself with no way out of a predicament. To help provide for her daughter, Diego's mother and her brother-in-law (Diego's uncle) decide to allow Diego to have part of the family business. Diego's older brother, however, is firmly opposed to this idea because while Diego may look like a man, she is still a woman, and women have no right to inherit family property because they are to be married off into someone else's family. At the end of "Diego," Diego is on a train, leaving home to make a life for herself by herself, and because the film does not follow a chronological sequence, we already know that Diego will find Ch'ing-ch'ing, and the two will spend their lives together, which indicates that in a heterosexual society there is a place for lifetime lesbian companionship.

150

Derek Elley wrote in *Variety* that *Drifting Flowers* is "content to speak largely in lesbian clichés" and is about "a group of femmes struggling with that old gay chestnut, 'identity.'" Elley has applied the concepts of Anglo-American gay culture to *Drifting Flowers,* and that leads to misreadings and the sort of mistake Elley makes when he takes the characterization of Diego to be the film's comment on *femme* gender identity politics.[29] In the context of Taiwan's *tongzhi* culture, Diego is not *femme;* she is an American-style *butch.* In creating characters, crafting the plot, arranging the mise-en-scène, and designing the soundtrack, Chou has connected the specific lesbian culture of Taiwan to Taiwan's specific history and society. For Taiwan's lesbian community, *Drifting Flowers* is anything but "cliché" in that it is the very first film that tells their story.

FILMS BY OTHER WOMEN DIRECTORS

While not many women have been able to make films in Taiwan since the appearance of New Cinema, the women's films that have been made leave behind the stereotypical images of women offered in films from the period of Healthy Realism (*jiankang xieshi zhuyi*) and in the romance films and film noirs of the 1970s. They have given us a variety of perspectives on women's lives and have told stories about the cultural and social realities of women's pursuit of desire and self-identity. In the 1990s, contemporary Taiwan women film directors began to emphasize the individual character of their work, over which they exerted increasing control, and more and more of them began to include in their feature films a documentary-tinged look at social issues. For example, Singing Chen's first sixteen millimeter long feature, *Wo jiao A Ming la* (Bundled, 2000), mixes drama and documentary and weaves together several different plotlines to represent the world of vagabonds.[30] Through the stories of marginalized city dwellers who live outside the orthodox social order, the film deals with the subject of collective social amnesia and the search for a sense of spiritual companionship. Chen Ying-jung (DJ Chen) made her name with her film *Formula 17*, which earned a strong response from audiences because Chen applies a lighthearted style to the usually serious subject of the lives of gay men. The success of *Formula 17* indicates that audiences have grown more accepting of films about gay characters; it also tells us first, that thirty years of work by feminists has ensured that the need for gender equality and the acceptance of different sexual orientations have become part of the mainstream discourse about gender in Taiwan, and second, that since the late 1990s, discussion about gender in Taiwan has no longer been limited to talk of "two sexes" but has broadened to include the subjects of gay, lesbian, transsexual, and transgender identity.

The foundation for women's filmmaking in Taiwan was put in place during the postwar period and the 1970s and 1980s, and beginning in the 1990s the passion, tenacity, and stamina of women filmmakers finally began to bear fruit. For decades, women filmmakers have been addressing personal subjects and also subjects to do with questions of gender, sexuality, history, and society, and gradually their films have broken free of the stylistic and thematic conventions of domestic dramas and film diaries, infusing personal filmmaking with an epic spirit and vision. As we undertake the work of writing the history of women's film and analyzing examples of women's film, the presence of these women directors reminds us that the world of Taiwan film is populated not only by men but by women as well.

ACKNOWLEDGMENTS

The authors wish to thank Lingzhen Wang for her response to earlier drafts of this essay. Please contact Chunchi Wang at chunchiwang@mail.ndhu.edu.tw with any comments or questions.

151

NOTES

1. Taiwan-language films disappeared in the late 1970s, whereas the production of Mandarin-language cinema grew stably since the mid-60s and has since become dominant.

2. Annette Lu's *Xin nüxing zhuyi* (New Feminism) introduced feminist thought into 1970s' Taiwan society. Her agitation for equality of the sexes is acknowledged by Taiwan feminists as the origin of the women's movement in Taiwan.

3. In the documentary *Bai ge jihua* (Our Time Our Story: 20 Years' New Taiwan Cinema, 2002), directed by Hsiao Chü-chen, Sylvia Chang discusses how she was invited to act in, but not direct, the first New Cinema Era film, *Guangyin de gushi* (In Our Time, 1982), produced by the Central Motion Picture Corporation.

4. Vita H.S. Lin, "Jiaohan 'Kaimaila' de nüxing" (Women Who Shout "Action"), 32.

5. Ibid.

6. Joan Wallach Scott, introduction to *Feminism and History*, 3.

7. The primary funding for women feature film directors came from the Government Information Office feature film grants, whereas the Public Television Service *Life Story* series (*Rensheng juzhan*) and Da Ai Television provided training grounds for women filmmakers; civic funding sources for women directors later emerged gradually.

8. *Formula 17*, for example, incorporates elements borrowed from Japanese animation, and the lead roles are played by Taiwanese and Hong Kong actors.

9. Geraldine Heng and Janadas Devan, "State Fatherhood," 344.

10. In this film, Lang Hsiung and Kua Ah-leh (Kuei Ya-lei) play an older married couple, and each has an affair when each sets out to find adventure. First Lang Hsiung's character gets involved with a young married woman played by Yang Kuei-mei, and then Kua Ah-leh's character, Mrs. Ch'en, unwilling to be alone and after revenge, goes to a bar looking for fun, meets the handsome, understanding gigolo, Ah-tu (played by Alex To), and allows herself to relax and enjoy a night of happy conversation.

11. This film combines three stories directed by Yonfan, Samson Chiu (Chiu Leung-chun), and Sylvia Chang, respectively. Chang directed "The Unwed Mother"; the story directed by Yonfon is called "The Wronged Wives Club," and the story directed by Samson Chiu is titled "Catching Stars."

12. Ch'en Li (played by Karen Mok) has a crush on her classmate and good friend Hsiao-jou (played by Gigi Leung) who is drawn to the man Hao-chün (played by Takeshi Kaneshiro). Hao-chün's entry into their lives upsets their friendship, and they grow distant. Years later, Ch'en Li and Hao-chün are married, and this keeps Hsiao-jou and Hao-chün apart. Similarly, in *20, 30, 40*, T'ung first shows her affection toward Hsiao-chieh but later is with Jay, who was at first attracted to Hsiao-chieh.

13. In her *The Emerging Lesbian*, Tze-lan D. Sang offers a detailed discussion of the connections between Chinese lesbian identity and the discourses of romantic love in China and the West.

14. Azed Yu, "Wenxue bichu xia de nüxing shenying" (Literary Images of Women). *Taiwan dianying biji* 台湾电影笔记 (Taiwan Film Notes), May 8, 2004. http://movie.cca.gov.tw/files/15-1000-753,c138-1.php. Accessed Nov 15, 2009.

15. Ibid.

16. Vivian Price, "Nütongzhi zhuti zai Zhongwen dianying zhong de jueqi" (Emerging Lesbian Subjectivities in Chinese Films), 15.

17. Lai Hsien-tsung, "Chaoyue fushi de yishu guanghua" (The Glory of Transcendent Art). (The Liberty Times), November 3, 2005. http://www.libertytimes.com.tw/2005/new/nov/3/life/article-1.htm. And this quote is from paragraph 3. Accessed Nov 27, 2009.

18. Ibid.

19. "Dianying dangan" (About *Floating Islands* by Zero Chou).

20. "Dianying gongzuozhe" (About Zero Chou).

21. The discourses about homosexual identity are different in East and West, and neither concepts nor terms match exactly. The use of "*tongzhi*," which means "comrade/s," is equivalent to the use of "LGBT" or "gay" in the United States, but for the rest of this chapter *tongzhi* will be used instead of a translation.

22. Jack Babuscio, "Camp and Gay Sensibility," 44–46.

23. Judith Butler, *Gender Trouble*, 175.

24. "Summoning the soul" (*qian wanghun*) is a Taoist folk custom found in Taiwan. When a family member dies suddenly or dies without having made a last behest, surviving family members can enlist the help of a Taoist priest or a spirit medium to put them in touch with the departed.

25. Taiwan folk belief endows the soul with the ability to divide like a cell and, therefore, with the permission of the soul of the deceased, a second spirit tablet can be created, allowing the soul of the deceased to reside in more than one place at a time.

26. There are several different identities in Taiwan's lesbian subculture, including those of the obviously masculine T (tomboy), and in contrast to the T, the obviously feminine *Po* (the *po* or wife of a T), and an identity that is neither T nor *Po*. The distinction between T and *Po* is much like the distinction in American lesbian culture between butch and femme.

27. Many scholars of Asian *tongzhi* identity have pointed out that the LGBT identity created by "coming out" and breaking with one's family is a Western individualistic identity. See Chris Berry, "Asian Values, Family Values"; Gayatri Gopinath, *Impossible Desire;* Martin F. Manalansan IV, *Global Divas*.

28. In an interview with the *Zhongguo shibao* (China Times), Zero Chou said that she put the detail about breast binding into *Drifting Flowers* because many lesbians said that Chou had yet to give expression to the true voice of the *tie* T. See Chang Shih-ta, "Zhou Meiling haodu, wei tongzhi zuqun zuozhuan" (Zero Chou Bets Big in Telling the Life Story of the *Tongzhi* community). http://news.chinatimes.com/Chinatimes/Philology/Philology-artnews/0,3409,112008081600028+110513+20080816+news,00.html. Accessed Dec 21, 2009.

29. Derek Elley, "Berlin Film Festival Review."

30. Li Chih-Ch'iang, 李志薔. "Yi ze chuzou de yuyan—*Wo jiao A Ming la*" 則出走的寓言—《叫我阿銘啦》 (A Parable about Flight: *Bundled*). *Ziyou shibao* 自由時報 *Liberty Times*) August 7, 2001. http://www.libertytimes.com.tw/2001/new/aug/7/life/article-1.htm (paragraph 3). Accessed Jan 5, 2010.

153

6

Affect, Memory, and Trauma Past Tense

HU MEI'S *ARMY NURSE* (1985) AND XU JINGLEI'S *LETTER FROM AN UNKNOWN WOMAN* (2004)

E. ANN KAPLAN

IN RECENT years, interest in affect has increased in humanities research and has found its way into cinema studies. Walter Benjamin, sensitive to the modernist shocks of new cinema technology, implicitly recognized issues of affect as linked to time and technological medium that are a main focus of this chapter.[1] His insights, however, were for a long time marginalized by cinema studies' methods, which focused on somewhat limited psychoanalytic and ideological readings of film, and on interest in how viewers negotiated meanings. In the period since Benjamin wrote, the role of affect in the public sphere has expanded. As Brian Massumi notes, "Affect holds a key to rethinking postmodern power after ideology."[2] Ideology is still with us, but, Massumi argues, "it no longer defines the global mode of functioning of power."

In this situation, we need as never before information about how emotions are communicated through the media, more knowledge of which emotions are provoked with what related meanings, and more information about the different kinds of emotions that constitute spectator affects/meanings, as well as those that (relatedly) drive the characters. For in both Eurocentric nations and Mainland China (my focus here), public emotional sets partly *structure* filmic emotions and are partly *structured by* cinema in circular fashion. While I see humans as vulnerable to having their emotions "managed" by pervasive media intent on creating specific subjective (spectator) feelings for political or commercial ends, I also see a place for media imaging subjectivities that contest social pressures for conformity, as in the films studied here.[3]

In related research, I have distinguished three distinct temporalities for dealing with trauma, namely trauma-time present tense, trauma past tense, and trauma future tense.[4] I argue that publics exist in lived experience simultaneously within these linked trauma temporalities. But, given my focus on media, it is important that each temporality is associated with specific media technology or site of performance—film, TV, internet, memorial sites. Each technology arouses a different set of traumatic emotions in spectators. Trauma past tense, relevant to the films analyzed here, relates to a culture traumatized by memory of past national horrors—a culture thus of traumatic memory.

Cinema's affect (including traumatic affects) depends on the kind of cinema involved, whether commercial, state supervised, independent, or avant-garde. Commercial or state-controlled dominant cinema tends either to utilize affects already present in a culture, and produce more of such affects, or to use cinema to instill new feelings and related subjectivities in audiences. In many nations, independent or underground cinema challenges authorized public feelings, offering alternative affective sets to the normative ones in play. Or filmmakers find ways to offer images that resist norms through comedy, allegory, or both. Such films may draw these alternative sets from personal experience, which does not mean that the perspective is limited. Rather, films like these become case studies for *understanding* differently.[5]

Ann Cvetkovich has argued that films carry an archive of feelings, especially public feelings; they embody historical constructions that may continue as legacies over time and are important as opening up repressed memories.[6] Both of the Chinese films to be studied here (although to different degrees) offer a window through the heroines' flashbacks onto repressed traumatic historical memories in Mainland China—those of the 1930s Japanese invasion and of the 1970s Cultural Revolution—and produce new meanings of these events.

The framework of affect, memory, and trauma developed here avoids some of the old critical pitfalls in two ways. First, prior focus solely on nation and ideology is no longer sufficient. In the new globalized economy, old concepts of "nation" have to be reworked. The collapse of European empires resulted in increasing flows of peoples and goods across ever more porous borders, while a global Internet now enables instantaneous transmission of ideas, images, and cross-cultural communication—a transfer of affects and memories amongst other things. Surveillance of literal or Internet borders fails to completely prevent such interchanges because people always find underground networks.[7] If, paradoxically, globalization reinvents the category of "nation," it is no longer in the sense of a closed unit consisting of homogenous ethnic group, but now in the sense of a multidirectional largely geographical designation—the space from which, and to which, goods, peoples, and ideas flow, with accompanying affects.[8] This conception allows me to show the change in the case of China from a nation in the 1980s more or less keeping its borders intact, its population relatively stable, and its public affects tightly monitored, to a "nation" in the new sense just noted.

Second, in selecting the framework of affect and trauma past tense for looking at films by Hu Mei and Xu Jinglei, I hope to move beyond the monolithic "East/West" binary critics often use. It is a binary I believe Xu is deliberately seeking to dispel (while also benefiting from) in choosing to base her 2004 film on Stefan Zweig's *Brief Einer Unbekannten* (Letter from an Unknown Woman, 1938), and in addition remaking Ophüls's 1948 Hollywood film with the same title; Hu is arguably also reworking this binary in drawing on European New Wave cinematic strategies in her 1985 film, *Nüer lou* (Army Nurse, 1985). I will focus on changes in how affect, politics, and memory are mobilized by Hu Mei and Xu Jinglei in regard to female subjectivity by comparing their films about sacrificial love. In both periods, China was undergoing political and social transformation, and it is in such times that a gap opens for new (in this case female) subjects.

A useful way of elaborating the different conceptions of female subjectivity and related feelings as they pertain to differing politicocultural conditions between 1980 and 2004 is through looking at the varied filmic techniques each director uses to represent feelings on screen. Brian Massumi's distinction between affect and emotion helps foreground in what ways Hu's technical use of the traumatic memory flashback enables a less normative female subject, yet paradoxically a subject who also has less agency than does Xu's heroine. In his "The Autonomy of Affect," Massumi (influenced somewhat by Deleuze) distinguishes two parallel systems of feeling in images—a level of what he calls emotional "intensity" and one of "quality." Via psychological case studies, Massumi argues that the signifying order is disconnected from "intensity." For Massumi, "intensity" is a kind of feeling that he distinguishes from "quality" which is linked to cognition: Intensity is "disconnected from meaningful sequencing, from narration." He notes that "Language, though head-strong, is not simply in opposition to intensity. It would seem to function differentially in relation to it."[9] And he concludes the discussion by saying, "Approaches to the image in its relation to language are incomplete if they operate only on the semantic or semiotic level . . . what they lose precisely is the expression *event*—in favor of structure."[10] The expression event is what the spectator feels, then, but which does not get interpreted, put into language; this kind of expression is not often paid attention in film analyses. While both affect and emotion require language (neither Deleuze nor Massumi pretend otherwise), "affect" connotes feeling as trace, resonance, uncertainty, whereas "emotion" indicates fixing of a specific feeling. Focus on the different effects of each technique will reveal different (somewhat contradictory) implications for female subjectivity and agency in the two films.[11]

Army Nurse needs to be situated in the context of China's 1980s' revocation of the Cultural Revolution lasting from 1966 to 1976, with 1979 normally seen as the year of "opening up." This was when Deng Xiaoping's government initiated reforms that sanctioned greater initiative taking and instituted an "era of recovery from the traumas of the last decade," as Chris Berry demonstrates in *Postsocialist Cinema in Post-Mao China*.[12] Prior to Deng Xiaoping's rise to power, as Berry also notes, "all action, including academic research and publication, waited on orders from above."[13] Part of Deng's reform was to encourage greater autonomy in the arts, the media, and academia, but this was sometimes mistakenly confused with allowing open dissent or questioning of authority or politics.[14] Such direct openness turned out to be dangerous, so within the new, more generous limits, filmmakers did their best to communicate new kinds of affects and to include indirect commentary on China's recent past and new present.

It was with this context in mind that Jameson wrote his hotly debated theory of third-world texts as national allegories. As I argued in 1997 (and as Imre Szeman has more recently argued),[15] Jameson's position has been misread. As Szeman puts it, "If in the third world, private stories are *always* allegories of public situations, this does not thereby imply that of necessity third world writing is narratively simplistic or overtly moralistic."[16] And Szeman continues to note that "The claim is rather that the text speaks

157

to its context in a way that is more than simply an example of Western texts' familiar 'auto-referentiality': It necessarily and directly speaks to and of the overdetermined situation of the struggles for national independence and cultural autonomy in the context of imperialism and its aftermath."[17] What we are seeing in the 1980s, then, and arguably in Hu's film, is a change in the relationship between the libidinal and the political that Deng's reformist Party made possible and that tempered the necessity for "allegory" while leaving open the possibility that some films could still be read allegorically. Chris Berry considers the change just before and in the 1980s to be qualitative enough to require the term "postsocialist" that he coins for his purposes. In addition, Berry's analogy for what is going on in 1980s' (and earlier) cinema perhaps offers a more successful model than Jameson's: "The feints, ambiguities, and doubly coded signals in Chinese public discourse that can be seen as signs of difference and dissent by some, and transparent and devoid of meaning for others, are structurally similar to the language and practices of pre-Stonewall gay subcultures."[18]

As Xiaoning Lu argues persuasively in her dissertation,[19] the start of the Cultural Revolution in 1966 initiated a "process of dis-embedding and re-embedding social subjects."[20] Above all, Lu argues, "socialist modernization entailed and facilitated the formation of socialist subjects."[21] These "new persons" were "productive socialist builders who were healthy in body and sound in mind," and Lu proceeds to examine how individuals "became recipients of and actors within the multiple powers that transformed them into the desired 'new socialist persons.'" As Lu notes, Mao was in fact implementing a "remoulding" that exemplifies, in Michel Foucault's terminology, a kind of biopower, bringing "life and its mechanisms into the realm of political economy." Mao's proposals were in effect to "discipline the body and regulate the population" in the manner Foucault details for earlier European cultures.[22]

In the 1980s, women filmmakers like Hu Mei found ways to develop female subjectivity through flashback narration remembering intimate emotions, and thus to open up new ways of being unable to be represented during the Cultural Revolution. Hu's film was made as Fifth-Generation directors were building out from the traditions of Fourth-Generation filmmakers, who (Berry argues) had already begun to challenge the status quo: The Chinese Film System was opening up to new themes and subjectivities generated by young directors often sent to work on films in remote regions. Hu sets her film back in the 1970s so as to remember how controlled that generation was, and to image new Chinese subjects.

One of the main aims, then, of Hu's *Army Nurse,* as a reflection of trauma past tense, is precisely to invite contemporary audiences in 1985 to remember the traumas of the Cultural Revolution and of Mao's bio-power as well. The importance of affect, in this story of sacrificial love set in the 1970s, is partly shown through the flashback narration that invites spectators to contemplate the disastrous attempts to discipline the body, especially in regard to sexuality, and to register the psychic pain that such disciplining produced. Rather than arguing that the film also offers an "al-legory" for China qua nation, I see the film as perhaps displacing (to use a psychoanalytic concept) disenchantment with China's still restrictive poli-cies in the 1980s onto the sacrificial love that is a main theme in the film. Hu had to bear in mind what the Chinese Film Bureau of her era would permit in regard to theme and style—something Hu mentioned specifi-cally in my 1987 talk with her, as I later note. While Deng's reforms had indeed liberalized film production to some extent, enabling some reflec-tion on party policy not allowable before, directors still had to be mindful of how far they could go. On the other hand, as Chris Berry points out, it did seem newly possible "for cinema to be treated as an autonomous dis-course without appearing to threaten the Party or the State."[23] This new cinema discourse, in turn, influenced Chinese culture through spectators recognizing repression of feeling—something the party most likely did not anticipate.

Hu Mei's film is difficult to categorize as a genre within Western frames; it straddles a realism quite close to Italian Neo-Realism with a few surprising avant-garde effects similar to the New Wave Cinema (European films were newly available to Chinese directors at the time). Xu's film, by contrast, as will be clear in the text that follows, fits the psy-chological melodrama genre of Ophüls's original, with the difference of being less sentimental and melancholy.

Army Nurse opens with an enigmatic slow panning shot of key char-acters in the film, accompanied by a voice-over reading a poem signifi-cantly about a bird flying away, being looked for again, and not returning. Hu here sets up the theme of presence/absence and loss. One assumes the last shot in the panning sequence—that of a woman—is the heroine, Xiaoyu, who picks up the voice-over narration in the abrupt cut to the Cultural Revolution and young people destroying bourgeois households. Xiaoyu is caught up in these historical events without understanding what is going on. "Everything suddenly changed," she says in the flashback voice-over. History seizes hold of the heroine: History violently uproots

FIGURE 6.1 *Army Nurse,* 1985

her, confusing her; history is turmoil, violence, noise. Xiaoyu seems not to understand or be able to insert herself into what's happening.

But the film carries an apparent personal archive of intimate feelings, as Hu constructs her heroine's subjectivity newly for the time through Xiaoyu's strong but frustrated desire for the wounded soldier, Ding Zhu. This desire is first expressed through Xiaoyu's desiring gaze; later it emerges in a mutual desiring gaze and silent intimacy as Xiaoyu bandages Zhu's wound.

Because of the biopolitics that characterized the 1970s, Hu's characters can't act on their desire (it is forbidden, and they are under constant surveillance about bodily actions). Hu has to use other techniques to convey sexual arousal, such as close-ups of eyes looking into eyes, of Xiaoyu's fast breathing, of the way her head rests on Zhu's shoulder (fig. 6.1). As a result, the entire film might be said to function in the modality of Massumi's "expression event," of intensity rather than "quality" (emotion linked to language and cognition). Fragmentation of the discourse was Hu's deliberate aim. In my 1987 interview with Hu, she noted that women were characterized by a fragmentation and disorientation—a shorter attention span than men—all of which she attributed to conflicting demands.[24] Women, Hu said, had a less linear way of thinking than men; women are split, disoriented by the many demands on them. She had wanted to convey this sense of her heroine's fragmented, dispersed thinking in a voice-over that would have included unfinished sentences, meaningless phrases, and disjointed series of sentences (perhaps such as could be found in European New Wave films in the 1970s). But the studio leadership refused to allow a soundtrack that did not accord with realist conventions. Elements of this aim remain, however, and result in a striking contrast between the official male discourse in Chinese culture of the time, and that of Xiaoyu in the film.

Sessions with the party officer overseeing the nurses and the hospital make this difference clear. We see how the female subjects are constantly under surveillance, subject to the patriarchal and official party biopower, to the paternal gaze, and rendered abject; yet Hu also allows us to see the constraints under which they labor. In a talk between Xiaoyu and the official, it is clear that wind of Xiaoyu's interest in Ding Zhu has reached him. He warns Xiaoyu to put her work and study first: "Devote yourself to your duty," he says, reminding one of the Red Guards' Cultural Revolution directives.[25] If she can't get her personal life in order, the official says, she must write more thought pieces and join the party.

Yet despite this, Xiaoyu finds ways to assert her subjectivity as her love for the soldier deepens and intensifies. It becomes her reason for being, and yet, once he leaves, she has no recourse for finding him. The Party finds an appropriate husband for Xiaoyu after she moves to a city and the Cultural Revolution is over, but she is unable to carry the marriage through because of her unfulfilled love. She returns to work in the mountain hospital where she met Ding Zhu.

Despite this melancholy ending, perhaps signaling Hu's hopelessness about real change in Chinese culture at the time, some of Hu's original aim to show a different feminine discourse remains in *Army Nurse*. Though the Film Bureau forbade Hu from carrying the disjuncture she wanted further, something remains of an attempt to reveal a feminine difference, and a feminine resistance via use of the flashback. After all, Xiaoyu stays attached to her love object and defies convention in not following through on the arranged marriage. This very fact suggests a change in female subjectivity. And in a sense, even the portrayal of melancholy defies the prior robust but "false selves" Mao commandeered during the Cultural Revolution. Melancholy seems to have been an appropriate emotion for women in 1980s' China, and its direct expression in film advances resisting the prior sanctioned types of subjectivity.

Xu Jinglei's millennial China is a far cry from that of Hu's 1980s. Known foremost as a brilliant actress, Xu belongs to a young group of new

Chinese filmmakers who have been dubbed "The Urban Generation." In her edited book with that title, Zhang Zhen notes that while 1980s' reforms did have an impact, "all the while, the concrete mantle of the socialist economy and social order stayed mostly intact."[26] In the new millennium, however, socialism, while still upheld, now functions "as a window-dressing ideology affirming its legitimacy in the name of continuity and stability, while the tides of commercialization and globalization which it helped to bring in . . . have resulted in widespread privatization and a blatant form of capitalism," which mixes the rawness of industrial capitalism and its slickness with the residues of socialism.[27] It is in the spaces made available by this mixture of economic modes and the somewhat contradictory stance on the part of the ruling Communist regime that these new young filmmakers and actors find a space to offer a very different image of contemporary China.[28]

If these new filmmakers have benefited in recent years from the relaxation of state censorship of film scripts, enabling them, as Zhang shows, to bring onto the screen new kinds of characters including the marginalized and people from varied ethnic groups, the simultaneous reduction of government funding for films has had contradictory results. On the one hand, directors are now freer to make a diversity of films, and independent filmmaking has developed enormously; but on the other, these same filmmakers are now prey to market forces as they seek funding for their projects. In addition, not all films made with independent funding can be shown in Mainland China (as in the case of Lous Ye's Yihe yuan, Summer Palace, 2006), and the government still sets severe limits on which foreign films can be shown and for how long.[29] The ironies of this situation are complex and interesting, but the upshot is that new films, often centered on the cities where the young filmmakers live, sometimes mixing documentary footage with fiction, are now being produced.

Xu's film is, then, made in the contemporary situation of a dramatically changed China, inevitably opened up to global trends in media, Internet, and popular culture.[30] The subjectivities Xu is interested in, in Yige mosheng nüren de laixin (Letter from an Unknown Woman, 2004; hereafter Letter) are inspired by Western literature and film, but I will argue for an important difference related to the specific Mainland interest in foregrounding a female desire hitherto blocked as we saw in Hu's film. Relatedly, Xu's film offers a dramatic contrast to Hu's film in production values, relationship to genre cinema, and national/international distribution and exhibition. But once again, Xu surely intends (on one level) to say something about female subjectivity in the "new" China—its advances, its remaining limits—and at the same time (on a second level) to comment on the new face that China now offers the world.

What interested me about *Letter* was the ways in which a fiction of sacrificial love, not that dissimilar from Hu's, also using a flashback structure complete with affect and memory of past trauma, took on a different dimension because of the vastly differing national and political contexts of the "China" in which the directors lived. In what follows, I consider what Xu might want to say about female subjectivity by remaking the Ophüls film, and think about what she intends to communicate via the obvious contrast between the two films—Ophüls's and hers. I will suggest that in many ways, Xu continues to build on perspectives about female subjectivity begun by Hu under a far more restrictive China than the one Xu enjoys.

Letter is Xu's second film, but she has acted before in some of the new urban films now possible for young directors to make. According to Zhang, Xu's character in Zhang Yuan's *Wo ai ni* (I Love You, 2003) allowed her to play a semiautobiographical role relating to her troubled marital relationship.[31] The personal experience of troubled love might explain Xu's interest in Stefan Zweig's novel and Ophüls's film, which also dwell on a complex, passionate, if one-sided, relationship. But I'll show how her setting the film in the China of the 1920s to 1930s may make possible indirect commentary about contemporary China perhaps still less easy to undertake directly in a film aimed at a wide audience. In this way, her strategy echoes that of Hu previously.

Army Nurse and *Letter* share a structure of looking back to a past of frustrated female desire within a specific historical moment, but the degree of female autonomy each heroine is able to sustain differs markedly. If the gesture of history marking female subjectivity in each film figures loss or constraint, in Xu's film the heroine's, Miss Jiang's, control of the discourse and her life suggests a degree of hope that we might expect of the new millennial China despite the paradoxical heroine's death that the narrative requires. Her letter, having arrived at its destination, is at the center of the film's action; it drives the narrative through the flashback to Jiang's experiences as a child, and then as an adult. What Maureen Turim says of the Ophüls's version of *Letter*, "Death is the price that ironically allows the secret of a female's desire to be told,"[32] applies in a slightly different way to Xu's remake. For death as such is less emphasized in Xu's version than in Ophüls's, and while Miss Jiang does not speak directly to

163

FIGURE 6.2 Jiang gazes at the writer from window

her lover, the writer Mr. Xu Aiyou, until she has died, she explains in her letter to him that this refusal is her deliberate choice. She ultimately finds a way to express her desire to her lover, to make a connection after death, to reach into him by means of the letter—something that Xiaoyu fails to do since *her* letter to Ding Zhu never reaches him. Miss Jiang's letter, an extended remembering of her one-sided relationship to the writer whom she has loved since a child, does reach its destination and provides the structure for the entire film. Importantly, Miss Jiang situates herself as a subject in history in ways Hu's heroine could not do.[33]

Xu's film by contrast to Hu's, then, offers a coherent story of a life-long obsession on the part of a woman who, despite her fixation on the writer, is able to retain control of her life. She knows what she wants despite its pain. She chooses. She is seen owning the gaze, staring out windows and through doors to catch a glimpse of her lover (figs. 6.2, 6.3). It is she who sets up the meetings with the writer by being where he is (the one exception is when the writer pulls her out of the march protesting Japan's invasion). Far more than Lisa in Ophüls's version, or Xiaoyu in Hu's film, Miss Jiang offers an example of a female subjectivity that controls the discourse. Just because of this, Xu's film evidences for the most part emotion (quality, cognition) rather than affect or intensity. The visual track is "fixed" by the language that states her feelings and her conscious decisions. For example, in the middle sequence of the film after Miss

FIGURE 6.3 Writer caught by Jiang's gaze

Jiang knows she's pregnant, her voice-over accompanies images of her journey away from Shandong. In this voice-over, Jiang states clearly why she chose not to tell the reporter about the child: "You would never have believed me. You would have been suspicious of me. There would have been a shadow of mistrust between us." Jiang says she had her pride, and, perhaps most forcefully that she "wanted to be the unique one amongst all your women." She had the power to keep her lover, she says, because of the child growing inside her, but this is not how she wanted to be loved. Jiang is also the one to actually initiate the first sexual contact once in the writer's home. Contrast this with Xiaoyu's hesitancy, her inability to speak or to make decisions, her inability to challenge the authorities who control her.

Miss Jiang situates herself as a subject in history: History does not confuse her even as it deprives her of loved ones. She moves with history rather than, as in Xiaoyu's case, being moved by it. And perhaps because of this, or because her emotional life (her love for the reporter) is so consuming, she does not dwell on the trauma of the Japanese invasion, although she mentions it in a moving sequence. The trauma is conveyed through her voice-over stating her loss of friends and family and her urgent need to move away from danger for the sake of the child, while the darkness of the screen as she talks and shots of the boat taking her away in the blue night express her grief. Her life's goal, however, is focused

FIGURE 6.4 Jiang in modern city

on her beloved son and the sacrificial love for the male hero. While she is still in a sense subject to patriarchal law, nevertheless, she has choices and some leeway to determine her fate—something that was completely unavailable to Xiaoyu in Hu's film.

In contrast to the dark, dreary, and ascetic environment of the world in Hu's film, Xu's heroine lives in an exciting China newly modernizing in the 1930s. Miss Jiang is seen moving around in the city, with crowds around her, and one scene shows a cinema advertising 1930s' American female melodramas, like *Woman of the Year* (fig. 6.4). It's possible that it is this experience of relative freedom for women in the 1930s that attracted Xu to Zweig's novel and Ophüls's film as suggesting changes going on in Xu's contemporary China. That is, if in setting his 1948 film at the turn of the century in Germany, Ophüls saw that earlier period "as the foremost generator of our current sensibility,"[34] perhaps Xu was doing something similar. In her case, she perhaps saw 1930s' China as the "generator" of China in 2004 in two ways. First, the 1930s' class discrepancies exacerbated by a modernizing China (and a Western-focused elite class) may be seen as generating Mao's revolution. Second, the 1930s was a period when women had more choices, even within a still patriarchal and male-dominated culture. While in the 1930s women still had fewer choices than men (Miss Jiang ends up a high-class prostitute), Xu possibly sees

Jiang's cultural freedom as a model for women in the China of 2004 who sought more artistic, sexual, and aesthetic possibilities.

CONCLUSION

Hu's and Xu's films, then, offer a glimpse into a process of increasing female subjectivity in China through the cinematic technique of the flashback spoken by each heroine—a discourse that illustrates affective memory. We identify with both heroines, but there is a difference: Identification with Miss Jiang is easy because of the way Xu deploys the flashback narration. Her heroine is in charge of the film's discourse throughout; it is less easy to identify with Hu's heroine because she does not control her discourse throughout the film. While *Army Nurse* is also constructed as a flashback narration, Xiaoyu's voice-over moves in and out, and is not consistent.

So we have a paradox: Hu's comments, as we saw, suggest that Xiaoyu's fragmented discourse was deliberate, and the effect of this is, instead of identification, an experience for spectators of what Massumi called an "expressive event." We experience loss, absence, melancholy as a feeling that moves beyond Xiaoyu as an individual subject. It is possible that Hu used the "expressive event" technique to also communicate a view of female subjectivity close to that of French feminist and postmodern concepts in which female subjectivity is not tied to a teleological order in the manner of male discourse.

There are two arguments to make, then, in regard to contrasting Hu's and Xu's films: One could see Xu's film as making a stronger case for women in having her heroine's voice-over dominate throughout, and in presenting a woman who, while fixed on an impossible love for a man outside her reach, at least owns this love, is connected to her lover through the child, and is the subject of the gaze (she all but stalks the writer). Miss Jiang regrets nothing, and even offers an implicit critique of the male hero as unable to feel deeply.[35] She also situates herself in history through joining protests and being aware of political dangers the reporter ignores.

On the other hand, one could argue that Hu's idea of subjectivity is closer to recent theories to do with splitting, fragmentation, and dispersal across a range of identities as how subjectivity, in fact, functions. In this sense, Hu's film would reflect aspects similar to those found in European

New Wave Cinema, whereas Xu's film corresponds rather to commercial Hollywood-style melodrama.

But if we consider the issue of agency, we see that Xu's film allows her heroine far more agency than Hu's protagonist. Xu perhaps situated her film back in the 1930s precisely to permit her to show such agency, whereas Hu's film, set in 1980s' China, had to image the controlling power of the state. Xiaoyu's place in history is as subjected, while Miss Jiang clearly has much more freedom and possibility to act, to be a subject in history. Xu may be seen as continuing a movement toward imaging inner-female psychic and sexual lives initiated by directors of Hu's generation. Xu's film suggests that young Chinese women today are interested in exploring such themes.

The comparison of Hu's and Xu's films has, then, revealed interesting paradoxes: Massumi's distinction between affect and emotion has allowed me to illustrate some important differences in how female subjectivity is expressed in the two films—a difference partly produced via the different cinematic genres and styles. Hu's neo-New Wave technique of "affect" (expressive events rather than "fixing" emotions) at once suggests less agency to her heroine and paradoxically allows her to be less "normative." Using affect as expressive event also extends critique of patriarchal oppression beyond one individual's life to a more generalized resistance to dominant values. Xu's melodrama genre, on the other hand, with production values closer to Hollywood, entails fixing her heroine's emotions through language. This conveys a sense of agency and purpose, a control of her fate, but also produces a more individualist and normative heroine. In addition, traumatic memory in a psychoanalytic sense pervades Hu's film, whereas Xu's offers some vibrancy and hope. Hu's heroine does not know or cannot represent her loss, and yet this pervades the film. Miss Jiang's life includes trauma (the Japanese invasion), but she lives for love. She is resigned to keeping her love secret, and in this way also keeps it idealized and safe. She lives in its (largely imaginary) emotional energy, and in the pleasures of the rare unrecognized sexual encounters the lover's "forgetfulness" makes possible. She chooses to write the letter to be sent after her death, and this letter finally brings the reporter to knowledge of what he has missed through his carelessness about love. In this sense, Jiang has agency enough to bring about change, embodying, perhaps, desires of Xu's new Chinese generation. With the efforts of Hu's 1980s' generation behind her, Xu is able to build on the advances in regard to female subjectivity that generation made while, through her

168

glance back to 1920s' and 1930s' China before the revolution Mao led, suggesting what may still be lacking in regard to artistic culture, sexuality, and aesthetic freedoms.

NOTES

1. See Walter Benjamin, "The Work of Art in the Age of Mechanical Reproduction."
2. Brian Massumi, "The Autonomy of Affect," 235.
3. Before we can engage productively in projects dealing with emotions in culture, we need to know more about how emotions circulate; how emotions function within the individual; about differences among the various kinds of emotions; the relationships among cognition, emotion, and the body; and about cultural differences vis-à-vis emotions. This project offers merely an initial contribution from the specific perspective of film studies.
4. E. Ann Kaplan, "Trauma Future Tense."
5. E. Ann Kaplan, "European Art Cinema, Affect and Postcolonialism."
6. Ann Cvetkovich, An Archive of Feeling.
7. The example of Google in China is a case in point: Google had been cooperating with the Chinese government in recent years, but with its sites attacked in 2010, it was threatening to withdraw its services from China, putting the Chinese government in a tricky position. Some accommodation was reached in 2011. The Chinese government, like everyone, wants access to the flows of new knowledge Google offers but is afraid of the impact of some of this knowledge on its power.
8. See research by Arjun Appadurai, especially his Fear of Small Numbers.
9. Massumi, "The Autonomy of Affect," 219.
10. Ibid., 220.
11. Massumi's use of Deleuze does not invalidate psychoanalytic understandings of the unconscious and of traumatic memory. His formulations offer a useful way of distinguishing how feelings are represented in film and how affects are communicated to spectators. Classical psychoanalysis focused on the drives and their vicissitudes rather than on affective relations between subjects, and so is less useful for discussing such relations. It retains its use in regard to traumatic memory and issues of displacement of cultural malaise into filmic narratives. See his "The Autonomy of Affect."
12. Chris Berry, Postsocialist Cinema in Post-Mao China, 5–14.
13. Ibid., 9.
14. Ibid., 10.
15. Imre Szeman, "Who's Afraid of National Allegory?"
16. Ibid., 806.
17. Ibid.
18. Berry, Postsocialist, 10.
19. Xiaoning Lu, "Performing, Embodying and Constructing Socialist Subjectivity."
20. Ibid., introduction, 4.
21. Ibid., 4.

22. Ibid., 6. For more details about Mao's statements and policies, see Scott Watson and Shengtian Zhung, *Art of the Great Proletarian Cultural Revolution.*

23. Berry, *Postsocialist*, 11.

24. E. Ann Kaplan, "Problematizing Cross-Cultural Analysis," 151.

25. Some of these directives are quoted in the exhibition catalogue by Watson and Zhung, 28–34. For example, "Ladies and young masters (nurses and doctors), you-all wear large white gowns and work in hospitals. . . . The world is now dominated by the proletariat. You must overturn the traditional institution. You should work with the proletariat and devote all your efforts to serve the workers, farmers and soldiers." Or "If you are a revolutionary, you will welcome the revolutionary rebellion with joy. You will give enthusiastic support and impetus to the revolution. You will also take part in it. You will carry the revolutionary rebellion to the end!"

26. Zhang Zhen, ed., *The Urban Generation*, 5.

27. Ibid.

28. For more on Xu's complex and changing star image, as well as on the frustrations facing young directors like Xu in contemporary China, see Shaohua Guo, "Modern Woman in Conflict."

29. In 2010, there were reports of James Cameron's new film *Avatar* (shown on 2,600 or so screens in China) being abruptly withdrawn because of its overwhelming popularity at the expense of Chinese films locally made. It is not clear if there were objections to the film's Utopian themes about race, class, and war.

30. For details regarding changes in film production and themes in the new millennium, see Yingjin Zhang, *Screening China;* Paul Pickowicz and Yingjin Zhang, *From Underground to Independent;* Gary Xu, *Sinascape.* There is no room here to show the dramatic changes in how films may now be produced in China as against the 1980s or to detail the complexities of exhibition.

31. Shuo's films, according to Zhang, offered "an alternative, oppositional vision of China, taking into account the collapse of the socialist master narrative, the blasé, amoral, and self-destructive behavior of many urban youths and the disintegration of the traditional texture of society." See Zhang, *The Urban Generation*, 286.

32. Maureen Turim, *Flashbacks in Film*, 156.

33. For more on history in *Letter,* and issues relating to gender and the phallic order, see E. K. Tan, "Transcultural Adaptation of the Unknown Woman: Chronotope and Transtextuality in the Repositioning of the Female Subject in Xu Jinglei's *A Letter From an Unknown Woman.*"

34. Virginia Wright Wexman, ed. *Letter from an Unknown Woman,* 4.

35. In Zweig's novel, which Xu's film follows more closely than does Ophüls's film, the novelist is described as being moved to recognize his loss more than it is possible for Xu to show within the constraints of cinema. That is, the first page of the novel describes the novelist's reception of the letter, and the feelings it evokes. Xu attempts something similar in the opening sequence of her film, but the close-in camera and darkness of the sequence make the figure shadowy.

Part III

THE VISUAL SUBJECT AND FEMINIST CINEMA

7

The Encoding of Female Subjectivity

FOUR FILMS BY CHINA'S FIFTH-GENERATION
WOMEN DIRECTORS

S. LOUISA WEI

I REMEMBER the experience of watching Hu Mei's *Nüer lou* (Army Nurse, 1985) as a teenager; I felt very touched and immediately identified with the protagonist, who was my age at the beginning of the movie. I did not know how to express my feelings then, but I knew the film was very "different." In my early twenties, I was exposed to feminist theories in Canada, first as a masters student in comparative literature and then as a PhD student in film studies. Excited and inspired by feminist film theorists' dynamic readings of Hollywood's "women's films" and experimental films that emerged during and after the feminist movement, I have been consciously looking for works by Chinese women directors that may also answer to Claire Johnston's call for a "counter-cinema" within the mainstream of feature filmmaking and Teresa de Lauretis's incitement to a women's cinema that not only points to a "feminist *deaesthetic*" but also redefines "both private and public space" in "a new language of desire."[1] Meanwhile, as a former science student from China, I was hoping to "prove" to what extent Western feminist film theories are valid and useful in the context of Chinese women's cinema. From 2002 to 2008, I extensively researched the development of women's cinema in China and interviewed fourteen important female directors from four generations.

I find that China's socialist system did allow a large number of female directors to work in the state-owned studios from the mid-1950s to the early 1990s, and as a result, there exists a remarkable though not large repertoire that can be considered women's cinema.[2]

From this repertoire, I chose four films to discuss here: Hu Mei's *Army Nurse,* Liu Miaomiao's *Mati sheng sui* (Women on the Long March, 1987), Li Shaohong's *Hongfen* (Blush, 1994), and Peng Xiaolian's *Jiazhuang mei ganjue* (Shanghai Women, 2002). These four women directors belong to China's "Fifth Generation" and are among a small number of women directors who succeeded in their transition from the socialist system to the market-oriented mode of film production.[3] As members of the Fifth Generation, these women participated in a movement that renewed both film form and film content in the 1980s, and, like their male peers, revealed a strong concern for the individual's fate set against the backdrop of social transformations. In their works focusing on female characters, they often construct a distinctive female subjectivity that is absent in works by their male counterparts. Unlike many women directors from older generations, who prioritize "humanity" as a larger and more significant theme than "womanhood," Fifth-Generation women embrace the significance of feminine consciousness and perspectives. They may not make films for women all the time, but all of them have contributed works to the corpus of women's cinema. My choice of films here is determined by their strength in encoding female subjectivity into film narratives, which (re)write women's histories/stories, (re)construct women's speeches/voices, and/or (re)map women's spaces/places. My discussions will help to, in the words of Mary Ann Doane, "specify female subjectivity via narrative mechanisms" and to "trace the contours of female subjectivity."[4]

China did not have a feminist movement like that which took place in Western countries from the 1960s to the 1970s, but this does not necessarily mean that China lacks the preconditions of cinefeminism. When women filmmakers in the West liberated their works from "illusionist representations" of Hollywood films and turned to experimental cinema "in search for an outlet for their inner experiences, sensations, feelings, [and] thoughts,"[5] Chinese women directors had their battles mainly within their own sociocultural context and the mode of feature melodrama. Most films by these women directors are not as visually shocking as such early Fifth-Generation classics like *Yige he bage* (One and Eight, 1983) and *Huang tudi* (Yellow Earth, 1984) and thus are not recognized as avant-garde works of their times. What I hope to prove is that these films are avant-garde in their own sense, as a kind of double-layered countercinema. They are countering traditional Chinese cinema as Fifth-Generation films and, simultaneously, countering the mainstream of Fifth-Generation films as women's cinema. To me, such an extension may well be the practice of cinefeminism.

(RE)WRITING WOMEN'S HISTORIES/STORIES

In one way or another, all four films selected here may serve as historical recounting of Chinese women's state of living in different eras. Liu Miaomiao's *Women on the Long March*—the first Chinese film to fill in a blank in China's revolutionary history, is extremely compelling. Liu Miaomiao told me in a 2006 interview that she read the original novella by Jiang Qitao—a male military writer who specializes in wartime stories— during a seminar commemorating the Long March.[6] Liu Miaomiao was attracted to the story because it was the only one about female soldiers. She began her preproduction process by traveling along the route of the Long March and interviewing some veteran soldiers of the Red Army, who told her stories about the female soldiers—mostly aged from 10 to 20 years old—and taught her some songs sung by them, which she later used in her film. This research process is not only important in searching for historical locations for the filming purpose but also for learning about the realities that female soldiers faced. Without knowing their day-to-day struggle on the Long March, it is impossible for Liu Miaomiao to assert the female subjectivity in her presentation of these women. Even though the writing credit is given to Jiang Qitao only, Liu Miaomiao's female authorship is most distinct in many discrepancies between her film and Jiang's novella.

The film narrative is arranged in chronological order and eliminates all but one flashback from the original story. The plot is quite simple: A Red Army commander sends a troop of eight women away to deliver telephone cables to a military post on the Tibetan plateau. The women soon find out that the main troop has continued on without them, most possibly with the consideration that it would be difficult for the women to survive the Long March. Having chosen the path of revolution, however, the women see no option but to catch up with the main troop. As Helen Praeger Young writes in her oral history, *Choosing Revolution: Chinese*

Women Soldiers on the Long March, women's stories can "reconfigure the body of knowledge that has been considered history"; rather than relating "Mao's progression to power," their stories are about "how they adapted to the political, military, physical, and social demands of being soldiers" and how they "integrate and absorb unusual occurrences into their daily lives."[7]

In Liu Miaomiao's film, there is no mention of Mao Zedong or other Chinese Communist Party (CCP) leaders, who are often the main characters of stories about the Long March. The film is made to remember the women soldiers—psychically and historically. Near the beginning of the film, the women gather together when the troop leader, Guizhen, warns them to watch out when they answer the call of nature in the wilderness and to bury their menstruation cloths "as far away as possible." In the middle of the film, Liu Miaomiao adds several scenes that are not in the original novella. One scene reveals the women gathering around a campfire. First they sing a folksong about a girl's ill fate and worries, after which they talk about their past and their expectations for the future. From the women's own recounting, we learned that they chose revolution to escape the possibility of dying in poverty, being sold as a child bride, or being married off to a much younger boy whose family would, in fact, keep her as a servant: Revolution gives them hope. In a later scene, after two women die, Guizhen gathers her soldiers and takes out a piece of cloth with the names of all eight women written on it. Each woman presses her fingerprint under her name and under the name of a dead comrade. Liu Miaomiao creates this ritual to remember every woman's existence and to resist the easy oblivion of the official history. The presence of the group is significant here as it reinforces the vulnerable memories of individuals (fig. 7.1).

Although Mao pointed out various significances of the Long March in the course of the Communist Revolution, for these women, it is nothing more than a day-to-day struggle to survive when traveling through the vast barren land and endless swamps. In the film, a series of actions are loosely organized around three major "events." First, a "Colonel Chen" falls for one of the women soldiers—Shaozhi—and has a rendezvous with her at night near the military camp. The colonel later loses his legs in battle, and Shaozhi is assigned to look after him. He commits suicide before she finds him, and she returns to her troop. Second, the troop leader, Guizhen, and a slightly older soldier, Sister Deaf, together witness women soldiers from another detachment being captured by Tibetan

FIGURE 7.1 Abandoned female soldiers sent away on a false mission (*Women on the Long March*, 1987)

bandits. Considering her troop is seriously outnumbered and has only two guns, Guizhen decides not to take any action. Members of the troop are angry and elect another soldier, Big Feet, to be the leader. Third, Junfen—a former singer in the performance troop—and Xiaohuazi see a dead horse on the other side of the river. They decide to cross the river to procure the horse for food but are swept away in the current. This loss greatly saddens the other women.

In the film's road movie plotline, Liu Miaomiao encodes a feminine narrative by a very special plot arrangement: each of the eight women cries at a different point in the story. Although the logical connection between actions and events is rather loose, the constant shift of emotional intensity from one woman to another maintains a good rhythm and tempo in the narrative. First, the youngest girl, Yaomei, cries over a nightmare she had about war. Then the pretty Junfen cries out of jealousy when she sees the handsome colonel holding Shaozhi in his arms. She cries again when learning that they have been left behind by the main troop. When Xiaohuazi and Junfen die in the river, Jinqiu cries first and then Shaozhi also bursts into tears—she was just reconciled with Junfen by confessing that her "love affair" with the colonel was only brief and platonic.[8] When learning that Guizhen decides not to save the women soldiers captured by the Tibetan bandits, Big Feet cries, thinking of what will become of those women. Sister Deaf cries at the sight of dead soldiers near the swamp. Guizhen is the last one to cry when she confesses that she hid the truth about the main troop's leaving them behind on purpose. She makes it clear that there is no turning back for her after she left her loving father to join the army. These points of emotional intensity not only help to configure eight different women characters, but also avoid turning the entire film into a "weepie" and reducing its historical significance.

Many women directors I interviewed emphasize the use of *emotion* or *mood* as the narrative drive to push the story forward, which is not exclusively a feminine trait but is often skillfully employed by women. In Liu Miaomiao's film, the narrative tension and rhythm correspond to the emotional ups and downs of female characters: the repressed romance, the dispute and reconciliation between girls, the moments of desperation and hope, the hallucination from starvation, and so forth. In the soundtrack are cues of rather dismantled music without a distinct melody, setting a sharp contrast to the heroic tunes often heard in other revolutionary films. This simple music that is strange to the ear of a Chinese audience creates an audio space corresponding to the barren lands and empty battlefields where the women soldiers are placed most of the time, forming the audiovisual impression of a historical vacuum. Liu Miaomiao makes no attempt at all to construct a grand narrative of a typical Chinese revolutionary film.[9] These women's history of the Long March is a survival story without a real contribution to the advancement of the CCP; but who can say that their history—"their gradual losing of womanhood" in the war—is less important?[10] With no movie stars in the film, *Women on the Long March* was not commercially successful when it was theatrically released, but people who have watched it cannot forget it.

The CCP has repressed many histories of women in its official history. Li Shaohong's *Blush* relates the stories of some former prostitutes who went through the labor reform around 1951, two years after the CCP set up the new regime. The two female protagonists of *Blush*, Qiuyi and Xiao Eh, are former prostitutes—"everyone's lady" in a sense—played by two of China's most talented star-actresses—Wang Ji and He Saifei, who helped to make the film a huge commercial success in 1994.[11] Doane observes that films "organized around a woman's act of remembering" often repress "her own history," the "cinematic abstraction of the woman is represented as *in tension* with the complex articulation of memory, history and narrative."[12] This is quite true in *Blush*'s original novella, which is authored by a male writer, Su Tong (fig. 7.2).

FIGURE 7.2 A poster acknowledging the original novel writer (*Blush*, 1994)

The greatest dramatic tension in the plot of *Blush* is also historical. In the actual process of reform, the conflict lies between the officials' assumption that "labor" can "cleanse" the corrupt minds of prostitutes (who are classified as lumpenproletariats in Communist China, after Karl Marx) and these women's difficulty in coping with hard labor. At the narrative level, such tension is presented by the resistance of both female protagonists. Qiuyi runs away from the labor camp and becomes a nun after a failed attempt to stay longer with her lover, Lao Pu; Xiao Eh tries to hang herself when she cannot finish her assigned work during the day. Both of them were once "stars" in the Happy Red Inn brothel and did quite well financially in the "Old Society," but they have to relinquish both money and freedom to be with men in the "New Society."[13] The film *Blush,* however, remembers these historical women differently from the original novella, which presents them as women who victimized the male protagonist, Lao Pu, and who have no control at all over their destinies. The film's emphasis is placed on how they adapt to the social transformation much better than Lao Pu, and how they make the best out of their situation after the central man of their lives dies.

(RE)CONSTRUCTING WOMEN'S SPEECHES/VOICES

The most "unfaithful" part in Li Shaohong's adaptation of *Blush* is her (re)construction of women's speech and voices. First, in the film, the army officers all speak in standard Mandarin—representing the government in the North, while all other characters speak the Shanghai dialect with different accents. Both Xiao Eh and Lao Pu are quite articulate when speaking in their local language and not eloquent at all when speaking Mandarin in public places. Second, indirect speeches given by the omniscient narrator in the novella are often distributed among women characters in the film, establishing the female subjectivity in a Bakhtinian *polyphony*—a carnival of voices with a heteroglossia. A good example is the meeting scene after Xiao Eh's failed suicide attempt. In the novella, the dialogue between Xiao Eh and the Chief Army Officer is very brief and private, in the presence of only a couple of other female officers who want to find out what happened to Xiao Eh and who see her as a potential key speaker in the upcoming denouncement meeting against the brothel-keeper.[14] In the film, the dialogue is elaborated to a lengthy meeting, where Xiao Eh sits with around forty former prostitutes in a classroom, while the Chief Army Officer in charge of the reform camp stands in front of a blackboard with two of her colleagues sitting on the side.

> CHIEF ARMY OFFICER: (*Speaking to all women*) We, women of the new society, must learn self-respect and independence. The old society treated women as chattel; we're our own masters now. (*Turning to Xiao Eh*) Wang Xiao Eh, would you tell us frankly why you attempted suicide.
>
> XIAO EH: (*Speaking honestly*) My hands are bleeding. There is no end to the work; I couldn't take it any more.
>
> CHIEF ARMY OFFICER: This is not the real reason. You were oppressed and exploited by the brothel keeper for many years. Your suffering is bitter and hatred deep. You're afraid you'll end up in such position again, isn't that it?
>
> XIAO EH: (*Speaking in hesitation*) I don't know. I am so scared.
>
> CHIEF ARMY OFFICER: Don't be afraid. We've abolished prostitution. No one will harm you again. You are not criminals. The brothel-keepers are the criminals. They should be denounced.
>
> XIAO EH: I'd be too ashamed to talk about those matters.
>
> FEMALE OFFICER B: (*Speaking out loud, impatiently*) We're not asking for those dirty details. Do you know what it means to denounce? Tell us how you were tricked into the brothel, how they beat you up when you tried to escape. . . . The point is to call in the blood debt with your enemy.

Women begin to whisper to each other and not all their speeches can be heard clearly.

WOMAN A: You know, they made us take a dozen johns a day!

WOMAN B: Xiao Eh, you could tell about how the madam swore at you.

WOMAN C: She forced us to swallow tadpoles so we'd miscarry.

WOMAN D: And we never had enough to eat.

XIAO EH: (*Speaking truthfully and bashfully*) Maybe you don't know this, but I was born at the Red Happiness Inn. No one's ever taken care of me. I've always had to look after myself. You all come from normal families, but I was born to be a whore.

CHIEF ARMY OFFICER: (*Looking at Xiao Eh with sympathy*) Sit down, Xiao Eh. Let me tell you a true story. There was a girl whose father died when she was two. She lived with her mother. Her mother struggled to put her through university. One day, someone told her that her mother was a prostitute. She'd never dreamed such a thing. Many years passed before she appreciated her mother's suffering.

181

The Chief Army Officer's voice is choked and the room is silent. Women's heads are lowered. Xiao Eh remains silent but she does not seem to be touched at all. The meeting scene is 3 minutes 40 seconds and one of the longest scenes in the film.

The female subjectivity is established here within Mao's predominant ideology of class struggle. The Chief Army Officer always addresses the former prostitutes as "sisters" and makes every effort to win them over. When she asks Xiao Eh to speak "frankly," Xiao Eh speaks of her own "truth." The Chief denies her "truth" as not "the main reason" and offers her own thoughts, but Xiao Eh refuses to confirm or accept them. When the Chief then asks Xiao Eh to denounce the brothel-keeper, she again fails to understand. Another army officer is impatient and gives examples of the kind of things they want to hear. Other women in the classroom immediately pick up the signal and start to give a list of the brothel-keeper's crimes. Xiao Eh, however, interrupts them and confronts them all by stating that her case is different. Asking her to sit down, the Chief Army Officer ends up giving secondhand testimony by telling the story of a prostitute's daughter, which is most likely her own story. Both the officer's verbal repression and Xiao Eh's resistance can be clearly felt. The women in the classroom form a spectatorship that is absent in the novel. The diegetic spectatorship here is set in tension with that of the film audience, whose identification with Xiao Eh's perspective and position is established earlier in the film.

In addition to the diegetic voices of characters used in the film *Blush*, there is an interesting female voice-over at the extra-diegetic level, which speaks both in the women's language and about their desire. This voice-over opens the film even before the first frame appears from the dark screen: "So many things changed after liberation. One morning, all the girls in the Green Cloud Lane were taken away. What a scene it was!" Then we see the red-light district guarded by lines of soldiers, and prostitutes in their cheongsam are being taken on a boat to a temporary clinic for check-ups. Although this voice-over, acting like the omniscient narrator in a fiction, naturally claims a higher level of reliability and authority from the audience, Li Shaohong does not construct it to dominate the overall narrative. First, this voice speaks in a soft-toned Shanghai dialect and in a chatty manner, as opposed to the male, Mandarin-speaking voice of authority—the voice Chinese people often hear on radios and in films, especially news or historical documentaries. Second, the role of the voice-over is not fixed. Every time it appears, it has a different narrative function: bridging the informational gaps in the story, explaining a character's state of mind, predicting the fate of women, or, analyzing two characters' relationship. Third, the narrative suggests different possibilities regarding the source of this disembodied voice. We see the town's storytellers—a man and a woman—singing in a tea house when Qiuyi leaves Lao Pu's home. We see women exchanging gossip at Xiao Eh's wedding about her pre-marriage pregnancy. We see Qiuyi hearing stories about Xiao Eh and Lao Pu in a food stall run by Ruifeng, another former prostitute. Following Ruifeng's words, the voice-over says: "And so Ruifeng told Qiuyi about Xiao Eh's baby. No big deal really. But what moved her to tell Mrs. Zhang about Qiuyi having lost Lao Pu's baby? Mrs. Zhang told Lao Pu. He was shocked. His old feelings for Qiuyi came back in a rush. He felt terrible. He wondered how he could ever make it up to her." The voice-over here tells how a secret is being passed around. At this moment, the voice-over could be linked to one of the women in the film who knows all the main characters, or to Mrs. Zhang who is a storyteller herself, or to a collective voice combining different versions from different people.

Like the female voice used in Helke Sander's *The All-Round Reduced Personality—Redupers* (1977), this voice-over "exists as an ungrounded presence, emanating from a number of sources, none of them privileged as the center of the film."[15] Compassionate but detached, the voice-over interacts with other voices as well as the visuals in storytelling. In Bakhtin's words, this voice is to "express authorial intentions but in a refracted way" or to form a dialogue "between two intentions."[16] The film is a dialogic text that is "open to dispute" and is "charged with value," especially in the context of feminist filmmaking.[17] The voice-over in *Blush* "emphasizes the plurality of truths, the proliferation of perspectives that are possible"[18] and contributes to an excellent dialogic narrative with a distinct female subjectivity. Through such a voice with a concern to relate, Li Shaohong fulfils her passion in "writing women's own history."[19]

Ten years before *Blush*, Hu Mei also experimented with the heroine's voice-over in her directorial debut, *Army Nurse*. She tells Chris Berry in an interview that her original voice-over of Xiaoyu—the central character—was less "precise. It was scattered and fragmentary. She might be doing one thing, but she is talking about something else." When Xiaoyu separates from her first love, she watches him leaving with the voice-over saying: "What is a shadow? I really don't understand. . . . When I want to grab hold of it, it goes far away, and when I want to get rid of it, it insists on following me." The leaders of the August First Film Studio that produced the film did not understand it.[20] Hu Mei had to delete a lot of narration in this voice-over, which lends the film an extended space of psychological exploration. E. Ann Kaplan observes that "the heroine's voice-over narration increases the spectator's close identification with her. In this way, the film arguably offers more resistance to dominant Chinese sexual and political codes" by "asserting the heroine's subjectivity, and in making us identify with her sexual desire and its impossibility."[21] *Army Nurse*'s female subjectivity, however, is encoded not only by this voice-over. Xiaoyu is not an articulate person and is often caught between other more outspoken nurses with different opinions. Her voice-over is thus necessary to reveal her internal thoughts and her habits of "turning things over in her mind." This voice-over only works through its mismatching with the vision of "the world from what is completely a woman's angle."[22] The construction of her "vision" depends on how the space surrounding her is presented and how she maps out this space in her daily life.

(RE)MAPPING WOMEN'S SPACES/PLACE

The film *Army Nurse*, like Xiaoyu's life, is set mostly in a hospital. Che walks through the corridors to bring medication to the wards and collects used sheets from the wards; in the X-ray room, she listens to Lingling's secret when the latter is examining a half-naked soldier; she plays volley-ball with other nurses and soldiers in the playground; she hangs washed sheets in the courtyard with the other girls while listening to the gossip about a handsome patient, Ding Zhu, on whom she has a crush. She does not have a room of her own. Her dormitory is shared with other nurses. (The title of the original story of *Army Nurse* is *Maiden House,* referring to the dormitory building for the nurses.) Xiaoyu's first intimate moment with Ding Zhu is in his ward. When she tests his blood pressure and announces the result as "70/110," he challenges her and says it should be higher, asking her to test again. The soldier in the next bed cannot bear this and coughs loudly when Xiaoyu leaves the room. Even the most erotic scene of the film, when Xiaoyu changes the bandages on Ding's wound and cannot help pressing her face on his bare shoulder, takes place in the treatment room. Hearing footsteps in the corridor, Ding has to interrupt her moment of indulgence by calling her name softly and asking her "to hurry" (fig. 7.3).

184

The army hospital in the mountains is like a big home for nurses and sojourning soldiers, as well as for Xiaoyu and Ding Zhu. After the blood pressure scene, Xiaoyu constantly gazes at him through a doorway (when he plays his harmonica to a dying man) and through a window (when he wanders in the moonlit courtyard). This "domestic voyeurism"[23]

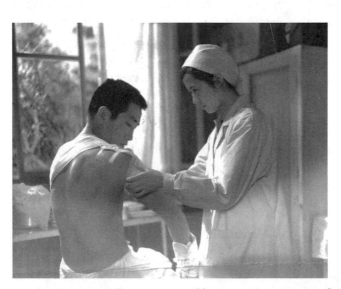

FIGURE 7.3 A private moment in a public space (*Army Nurse,* 1985)

soothes her, even though her gaze is not always returned. Her desire for him reaches another climax when she learns that he has left the hospital early. She chases him over a hill to say goodbye to him. At the road under the hill, the two are alone, but they have to part. When Xiaoyu finds the first letter from him in the mailroom, a fellow nurse, Yamei, is reporting to their commissar about another girl Xiuxiu, accusing her of keeping a love letter. Xiaoyu is eager to read the letter and so she goes into the lady's room. She barely finishes reading the love letter when someone knocks on the door. In panic, she throws the letter into the toilet, and as it is being flushed away, Xiaoyu immediately regrets it. Her only private space is in her diary, in which she pastes his address from the envelope.

Beatriz Colomina suggests that the "politics of space are always sexual, even if space is central to the mechanisms of the erasure of sexuality."[24] In *Army Nurse,* such politics are presented as the constant erasure of sexuality. Following the lady's room scene, Xiaoyu's "absentmindedness" is reported to the army's commissar, who speaks to her in the meeting room about her future. An inscription of Mao's writing occupies the entire wall in the background, while the commissar and Xiaoyu sit at one end of the table in the middle ground. The foreground is composed of a long table and empty chairs turned on their sides. Such framing is meaningful: the most "public" space in the hospital is now turned into the place for discussion about a girl's private matters. The result of this talk is Xiaoyu's repression of her personal desire and her devotion to work for the next ten years. When Xiaoyu is nearly thirty, the commissar talks to her again while walking up the hill, asking her forgiveness for having checked the background of Tu Jianli, a potential future husband introduced to her by a friend. Xiaoyu's courtship with Tu is brief and unromantic in a city setting. Being a "model of late marriage," Tu is awarded an apartment by the army, which he prepares as a home for him and Xiaoyu, but Xiaoyu refuses to rest in the bed as he suggests. Tu shows Xiaoyu the hospital that he will get Xiaoyu transferred to, but the sight of medical equipment only reminds Xiaoyu of her mountain hospital. Xiaoyu spends part of the evening with Tu in a hotel room, where she knits a sweater and he reads a newspaper. She feels that she is suffocating and pushes open the window. The next day, she returns to the army hospital where she sacrificed her youth, when her voice-over asserts that only there can she find a meaningful place for herself.

The sexual politics of space plays more bluntly in Peng Xiaolian's *Shanghai Women.*[25] The film begins with the daughter, Ah Xia, leaving

185

for school on her father's motorcycle. A call to her father's cell-phone, forgotten at home and picked up by her mother, brings the first moment of narrative tension. By the eleventh shot, the daughter's cheerful conversation with her father is interrupted by the sound of a crashing dish in the kitchen. The girl rushes in there to find her mother in tears. The horizontal frame is constantly divided by the vertical lines of the door and window frames separating the domestic space. The daughter is asked to go back to her room when her parents need a private conversation. The camera is in the daughter's room, showing the girl standing by the partly open door and peeping at the mother sitting in the living room. The father attempts to close the door once in the middle of the long talk, but the door is ajar again. The focus is on the mother first, and then switched to the girl's face in the end after the father yells out: "It is you who wants a divorce! You can take anything. You can take our girl too. But this apartment was given to me by my work unit!" The claim of the space's ownership here will soon be a curse on the mother and daughter.

"A cultivated man does not look out of the window,"[26] but an unhappy girl stares from her window all the time. When the camera pulls out from a close-up of her gaze while her mother asks her to hurry, we see a divided space again: the father is typing on a computer in the room on the left, while the girl is sitting on a chair in her room on the right. Her mother moves in the foreground, packing up things. The girl tries to say goodbye to her father, but he goes into the washroom. She leaves while he is flushing the toilet.

With many things hanging from their bicycles, the mother and daughter arrive at the grandmother's place on a sunny morning, but are not welcomed. The grandmother smokes in the background when the mother unpacks in the foreground. We learn that this is the third time the mother has returned to the grandmother's home, in a rage, after learning that her husband's affair with another woman has continued for two years. The grandmother blames her daughter for being too easy to agree to a divorce, and asks her to start looking for another place as her brother will soon be married: "Even if my place is a hotel, you cannot live here forever." The mother's salary is not enough to rent a place of their own and the director wastes no time placing her in an arranged marriage with a widower who has a teenage boy. Problems in their new life still revolve around space issues. The boy is annoyed that he has to give up half of his room to the girl. A sliding door is installed, and closing the door becomes an act of war between the boy and the girl. When the couple makes love, the kids do their homework on the other side of the thin wall, of which the boy's soccer star posters are shaken off. Although the mother tries her best to keep her new family together by willingly doing all the housework and buying a pair of new shoes for the boy, when the water bill comes with a doubled amount, the stepfather accuses her and her daughter of showering every day. The mother finally snaps when her husband says that he worked hard to pay for the apartment and that she is using "him as a meal ticket" (fig. 7.4).

Going back to the grandmother's is not easy this time, as the girl's uncle is already married and cannot spare a room for the mother and daughter. When the uncle's wife reveals her discontent, the grandmother defends her daughter and granddaughter and shuts the wife out of her room. The scene where the three generations of women lie in three parallel beds is very touching; they are united in one space, but under such sad circumstances. The grandmother's room is like a box in the middle of a house, where another family lives downstairs. The original living room is now used as a shared kitchen. Such a setting is normal in Shanghai's old houses, where privacy is about never speaking loudly and leaking out family secrets. In such a place, the girl does not even have her own chest. When she catches her mother reading her diary, she is very mad.

187

FIGURE 7.4 The bathroom is the only space where the mother and her daughter can have a private conversation in her second husband's home. (*Shanghai Women*, 2002)

The grandmother stops her from throwing things at her mother: "She is your mother. Can she harm you even if she reads your diary?"

By this time, the girl's father has finished his affair with the other woman, who went abroad, and he proposes to her mother again for their daughter's sake. The grandmother asks the mother to accept the proposal, but the daughter stops her mother on her way to her ex-husband's: "He is not a man that you can trust. Don't ever marry him again for my sake!" The reconciliation between the mother and the daughter is compensated by her father's agreement to split his property with her mother, with which she purchases a small flat for herself and her daughter. The message seems to be that a woman needs her own room more than she needs a man; but the "happy ending" (which was also required by the studio leaders) does not completely reduce the harsh reality of Chinese women's search for living and spiritual spaces. *Shanghai Women* won several awards from international film festivals and was released in Japanese theatres for thirteen weeks in 2003, after it was "discovered" by a *Yoriumi Shimbun* reporter in Shanghai.

188

LOOKING INTO THE FUTURE

While studying the history of Chinese women's cinema and approaches taken by female directors, I find that the theoretical frameworks of psychoanalysis, Marxist, and other feminist film theories are not readily applicable to the Chinese context and cases, but many concepts are quite useful in textual analyses. (They did help me, for instance, to explain why I was moved by a film like *Army Nurse* in a much more crystallized way.)

As Chinese cinema has become increasingly commercialized over the past decade, fewer films present the realities of China, let alone films concerning ordinary Chinese women. The full recognition and dynamic reading of existing works by Chinese female directors are very important as they are still trying their best to work within the mainstream production system. As long as a group of women directors can stay in the business, there are chances for female subjectivity to be reaffirmed and for them to produce their own counter-cinema, even a cinefeminism, if "feminism" is defined as "personal growth (gaining independence, sexual and intellectual self-fulfillment)," as "political activism (changing laws and policies affecting women with a view to changing the world)," and as "scholarship (developing new interdisciplinary insights through taking up female perspectives and topics)."[27] Or, as Teresa de Laurctis states in her speech at The 10th International Women's Film Festival in Seoul in 2008, for a "cinema by and for women," she might be "willing to give up the word *feminist*."[28]

NOTES

1. Claire Johnston, "Women's Cinema as Counter-Cinema," 29; Teresa de Lauretis, "Rethinking Women's Cinema," 145–146.

2. A survey shows that 59 female directors directed 180 films from 1979 to 1989, see Huang Shuqin, "Nüxing–zai dianyingye de nanxing shijie li" (Women in the Male World of Film Industry), 59. For historical reasons, a majority of these women directors belong to China's Fourth Generation. A more detailed introduction to the four generations of women directors in China can be found in S. Louisa Wei, "Women's Trajectories in Chinese and Japanese Cinemas."

3. Most women directors in the Third and Fourth Generations did not succeed in such a transition.

4. Mary Ann Doane, *The Desire to Desire*, 35 36.

5. E. Ann Kaplan, *Women and Film*, 88–89.

6. The Long March was a massive military retreat undertaken by the Red Army of the Chinese Communist Party (CCP), to evade the pursuit of the Nationalist Party army. There were several Long Marches, but the most well known is the march from Jiangxi province, which began in October 1934 and reportedly traversed some 12,500 kilometers (or 8000 miles) over 370 days. As the Long March began the ascent to power of Mao Zedong, it is represented in films and musicals as a monument of the CCP history. Only one-tenth of the force that left Jiangxi completed the march; most died of starvation along the way. Over 2000 women took part in the Long March, though this number may not be accurate. For my interviews with Liu Miaomiao, see S. Louisa Wei and Yang Yuanying, *Nüxing de dianying* (Women's Films), 189–193.

7. Helen Praeger Young, *Choosing Revolution*, 8.

8. All erotic scenes that involved sexuality and nudity in the original story are not shown in the film. The colonel's desire for Shaozhi is indicated by a long gaze and his throwing a pair of straw shoes to her feet. This is partially per the request of director Liu Miaomiao's studio leaders, who also revised the beginning of the film where women soldiers are sitting on the bridge so it cannot be bombed as there are other soldiers coming. In the released film, it seems that the women soldiers are sitting because they are tired.

9. Ironically, the belated release of the film's DVD by Xiaoxiang Film Studio's Home Video Division has printed on its cover the caption "prelude to Feng Xiaogang's Assembly," falsely promoting it as a "grand war piece."

10. Wei and Yang, *Nüxing de dianying*, 192.

11. *Blush* is one of the earliest cooperated films that adopted the production and distribution mode of Hong Kong. With an investment of 2 million yuan (roughly $230,000 U.S.

in 1994), it grossed 38 million yuan. This is also the biggest commercial success ever enjoyed by a Chinese woman director to date.

12. Mary Ann Doane, *Femmes Fatales*, 76.

13. See more discussion on this matter in Xu Jian, "Blush from Novella to Film."

14. Su Tong, "Hongfen" (Blush), 204–205.

15. Judith Mayne, "Female Narration, Women's Cinema," 389.

16. M. M. Bakhtin, *The Dialogic Imagination*, 325.

17. Ibid., 276; Lucy Fischer, *Shot/Countershot*, 301.

18. Mayne, "Female Narration, Women's Cinema," 389.

19. Li Shaohong, "Wo de nüxing juewu" (My Feminine Consciousness), 155.

20. Chris Berry, "Interview with Hu Mei," 34.

21. E. Ann Kaplan, "Melodrama/Subjectivity/Ideology," 22.

22. Berry, "Interview with Hu Mei," 34.

23. Beatriz Colomina, "The Split Wall," in *Sexuality and Space*, 73.

24. Beatriz Colomina, introduction to her ed., *Sexuality and Space*, iii.

25. This film is inspired by a composition written by Xu Minxia titled "At the End of My Teenage Years," which describes how she and her mother have to move to her uncle's flat after her parents' divorce, and move again to her aunt's flat when her uncle's son needs to get married. In my interview with Peng Xiaolian, she said that she had been feeling constantly unsettled, though she's been living in Shanghai most of her life. The action of "moving" here provides her with an action necessary to a film story. Keeping the teenaged Ah Xia's feelings about her mother and two boys in her school and neighborhood, Xiaolian adds a very strong grandmother figure and constructs the plot around the relationship between grandmother, mother, and daughter.

26. Beatriz Colomina, *Privacy and Publicity*, 74.

27. E. Ann Kaplan, "Feminism, Aging and Changing Paradigms," 21.

28. Teresa de Lauretis, "Cine-feminism and the Creation of Vision," 10.

8

From Mao's "Continuous Revolution" to Ning Ying's *Perpetual Motion* (2005)

SEXUAL POLITICS, NEOLIBERALISM, AND POSTMODERN CHINA[1]

GINA MARCHETTI

SIXTY YEARS after the founding of the People's Republic of China in 1949, a generation of women, who grew up with Mao Zedong and revolutionary "new" China, reached middle age. Coming of age during the Cultural Revolution (1966 to 1976) and crafting their adult identities in a dramatically different post-Mao cultural landscape, these women "of a certain age" find themselves positioned between old notions of the Chinese "new" woman and new conceptions of "success" for women within an increasingly cosmopolitan, globalized, neoliberal Chinese present. In *Desiring China: Experiments in Neoliberalism, Sexuality, and Public Culture*, Lisa Rofel describes this ideological shift as follows:

A sea-change has swept through China in the last fifteen years: to replace socialist experimentation with the "universal human nature" imagined as the essential ingredient of cosmopolitan worldliness. This model of human nature has the desiring subject at its core: the individual who operates through sexual, material, and affective self-interest . . . "Desire" is a key cultural practice in which both the government and its citizens reconfigure their relationship to the postsocialist world. In official, intellectual, and popular discourses, this desiring subject is portrayed as a new human being who will help to usher in a new era in China.[2]

Ning Ying's film *Wu qiong dong* (Perpetual Motion, 2005) captures middle-aged women from a particular class (educated, urban, professional, and apparently "liberated") in "perpetual motion" in Beijing as they confront these enormous social, political, economic, and ideological changes. As artists, intellectuals, and entrepreneurs, these women, who can claim a burgeoning public sphere in the arts and commerce, remain sequestered behind the walls of a domestic compound in one of Beijing's *hutong* alleyways. Obsessed with questions of possession and loss (ranging from romantic love to real estate), these women belie the promises of both Mao and Deng that they can "hold up half the sky" while glorifying the nation through the accumulation of capital.

In *Perpetual Motion,* Ning Ying works candidly with performers who, in many respects, "play themselves." Magazine publisher Hung Huang portrays Niu Niu; musician and author Liu Suola plays La La; business consultant Ping Yanni needs to do very little acting in the role of Ms. Ye; and professional actress Li Qinqin takes up the role of the "actress" Qin Qin. All come together ostensibly to celebrate the Lunar New Year, but the hostess has a bit of detective work in mind as she attempts to determine which of her "girlfriends" may be sleeping with her husband. Within this very closed world of Beijing's female cultural and commercial elite, Ning Ying opens up the contemporary Chinese public sphere to the complexity of self-criticism. However, in post-Mao China, the self-criticism sessions of the Cultural Revolution and the consciousness-raising groups of Second Wave feminism have given way to chick lit/chick flicks of Third Wave and postfeminist postmodern culture. *Perpetual Motion* stays on the verbal and visual move, within the very private world peopled by some of China's most public women, in order to explore the malaise at the heart of this merger of Mao's "iron girls"/*tie guniang* and neoliberalism's iron ladies of China's current spectacle of consumerism.

Perpetual Motion traces China's turn to neoliberalism, which accelerated after its inclusion in the World Trade Organization (WTO) in 2001, as the basis for its exploration of women's lives. As Lisa Rofel points out, the relationship between the WTO and the creation of a particular type of "desire" in China cannot be underestimated:

> The goal of the negotiations over China's entry into the WTO was to craft a "desiring China" that would not only cultivate an internal desiring machine yielding endlessly proliferating desires for foreign goods and services but also turn China into an object which others could desire freely, without obstruction.[3]

192

Clearly, the "iron girls" of the Mao era needed to be transformed into global models of erotic femininity, female consumers, light assembly workers, domestic laborers, and managerial and design professionals to fit into a new economy in which the "workers, peasants, and soldiers" of the past no longer played a defining role. As trendsetters and members of the cultural elite, the women featured in *Perpetual Motion* work in industries that transform women's lives—physically, socially, emotionally, and ideologically— as writers, entertainers, artists, and entrepreneurs. However, for them, feminism has been an "incomplete project."[4] Western liberal feminism and socialist feminism fail to give them personal satisfaction, emotional security, sexual fulfillment, or social relevance. Focusing on the cultural elite, *Perpetual Motion* indicts Chinese society at large. As the economy expands, even the most educated and affluent women fail to navigate smoothly the rough waters of global consumer capitalism.

SITUATING *PERPETUAL MOTION:* HOLLYWOOD, MAO, AND POSTMODERN CHINA

Self-consciously engaged with the "spectacle" of contemporary China, *Perpetual Motion* pastiches past and present cultural forms from the People's Republic and elsewhere. This juxtaposition moves from satire on the vacuity of global popular culture to an acknowledgement of the way in which postmodernity shapes women's sexuality, consciousness, and presence in society. Revolving around the personal lives of women, the film fits most clearly within the genre Molly Haskell has defined as the "woman's film."[5] Haskell characterizes this much-maligned genre as follows:

> Held at arm's length, it is, indeed, the untouchable of film genres. The concept of a "woman's film" and "women's fiction" as a separate category of art (and/or kitsch), impl[ies] a generically shared world of misery and masochism the individual work is designed to indulge . . .[6]

Given that postmodern culture questions the divisions between "high" art and "low"/popular/commercial culture, *Perpetual Motion* navigates the line between the Chinese "art" film, which has won critical accolades in festivals around the world for the weighty treatment of political issues and aesthetic daring, and the Hollywood "woman's film," a commercial genre dealing with the quotidian lives of women in the domestic sphere.

In line with the Hollywood "woman's film," *Perpetual Motion* fits within the thematic category of "competition," which Haskell characterizes as:

> . . . the heroine meets and does battle with the woman whose husband (fiancé, lover) she loves . . . While deciding the man's fate, the women will discover, without explicitly acknowledging it, that they prefer each other's company to his.[7]

This describes *Perpetual Motion*'s plot in a nutshell, and the film bears a very strong resemblance to George Cukor's *The Women* (1939), one of the better-known iterations of this type of film. Based on a play by Clare Booth Luce (screenplay by Anita Loos and Jane Murfin), *The Women* features an all-female cast in which the women battle over the right to the affections of the men absent from the screen. Similarly, the four women featured in *Perpetual Motion* define themselves in relation to Niu Niu's husband, George, who appears only in a framed photograph, but who puts the plot into action by leaving evidence of his affair with another woman behind. No men take part in the drama that unfolds, and even the supporting players are all female.

Ironically, from Depression-era America to China at the millennium, these absent men continue to define and circumscribe women's lives, and both films revolve around women eager to compete for the love of a "good" man of "quality." However, as the stories unfold, this initial competition gives way to a potentially subversive narrative undercurrent that brings the women together as comrades rather than competitors. The tension between the very conservative narrative trajectory that keeps the women apart and attached to the male figure and the potentially feminist countercurrent that brings the women together as allies provides a generic dynamic that keeps the plotline germane to a postfeminist cultural context. Director Diane English remade *The Women* in 2008, and, clearly, a similar narrative resonates with Ning Ying's concerns in China in 2005. Competition among women over men, the centrality of the male figure within the family as well as the wider society, the importance patriarchy puts on the youth and physical attractiveness of women, and the pressure the society of the spectacle places on women to conform to specific notions of "beauty" defined by consumer capitalism, continue to play a role in these films. The women operate in a world in which they are scrutinized by each other within the context of a male-defined society.

As global popular culture operates within more diffuse and increasingly specialized niche markets, "chick flicks" and "chick lit" emerge in the wake of the Hollywood woman's film, the romance novel, and other popular culture products associated with the female consumer. After the sexual revolution and women's liberation, these stories become free to discuss female sexuality more explicitly and directly. In this way, *Perpetual Motion* also seems to be in conversation with popular American television shows, such as *Sex and the City* and *Desperate Housewives,* which deal with female sexual desire and taboo subjects such as female orgasm, lesbianism, and masturbation, among other topics.

Perpetual Motion recognizes and parodies this trend within Chinese popular fiction by poking fun at the crass and explicit email that Niu Niu's anonymous rival sends to George in order to express her passion. However, the language found in this email, which refers to women's sexuality as coming into flower during menopause, is echoed by more than one of the women invited to Niu Niu's New Year party. The soft-porn language of romance fiction has seeped into the consciousness of even this very privileged, sophisticated group of women who talk about phallic "shafts" penetrating expectant vaginal "flowers." Consumer fiction speaks through them and masquerades as "authentic" female desire. Ironically, these middle-aged women find themselves created through the clichés of popular culture. However, the film does not let these clichés stand unchallenged. When La La describes sex during menopause as "a fresh flower opened to the stem, very slow and sexy . . . bursting with sensuality, so damp and hot," Ye chimes in that she is likely more like "wilted cauliflower" or "old tofu."[8]

While referencing the popularity of explicit "tell-all" books by Chinese women such as Wei Hui's *Shanghai Baby,*[9] *Perpetual Motion* can also be situated within the context of other postfeminist works that take the group confessional mode as a starting point. As a popular outgrowth of the "consciousness raising" groups of Second Wave feminism, films such as the Madonna-vehicle *Truth or Dare* (1991) or Hong Kong filmmaker Barbara Wong Chun-Chun's *Liulou houzuo* (Truth or Dare: 6th Floor Rear Flat, 2003) feature mixed-male/female, gay/straight groups taking up where an earlier wave of feminists left off by confessing their deepest fears and feelings about their sexuality and identity. *Perpetual Motion* revolves around a series of confessions made by the women in the film, and, at one point, features its own version of the "truth or dare" game in which the loser in a round of mahjong must reveal a sexual secret. Qin Qin, as the loser, talks about her two marriages—one to a Japanese, and the other to an American. Although the confession starts

195

off on a light note, it soon turns dark when Qin Qin begins to reveal her feelings of guilt surrounding the death of her first husband, whom she had divorced to marry the second. Single again after a second divorce, she still dreams of her departed first husband and continues to feel guilty about giving in to her second husband's demand not to attend the funeral.

When the darker side of Qin Qin's inner life emerges, *Perpetual Motion* as a film also edges closer to another cinematic tradition featuring women's subjectivity and sexuality. As an international art film, *Perpetual Motion* lays claim to the screen territory associated with Ingmar Bergman, Michelangelo Antonioni, and other European *auteurs* who have dealt with the inner lives and sexual traumas of middle-class women in their fiction. However, the film also takes up the Chinese literary and screen tradition of focusing on the status of women as emblems of the society at large. Going back at least to the late-Qing dynasty, the treatment of women has been used as an indictment of China's relative "backwardness" in relation to other nations or to a more abstract notion of "modernity." Writers associated with the May Fourth Movement, filmmakers coming out of the leftist studios in Shanghai before the Japanese Occupation, and revolutionary artists associated with Mao Zedong and the Chinese Communist Party all lay claim to this tradition.

From this perspective, *Perpetual Motion* comments allegorically on contemporary China through the lives of its female protagonists. Films of this sort figure prominently in post-1949 Chinese cinema. Many revolutionary dramas deal with groups of women fighting collectively (e.g., Xie Jin's *Hongse niangzijun,* The Red Detachment of Women, 1961), and melodramas such as Wang Qiming and Sun Yu's *Ren dao zhongnian* (At Middle Age, 1982) portray women in the same age category as *Perpetual Motion* as representative of a specific period in Chinese history. Ning Ying is, in fact, in good company with other Chinese women filmmakers who have focused on women's lives collectively and individually. Designated as "women's cinema,"[10] some of these films made by women associated with the so-called Fourth, Fifth, and Sixth Generations of Chinese filmmakers deal with the power of women's relationships (e.g., Peng Xiaolian's *Nüren de gushi,* Women's Story, 1989; Li Shaohong's *Hongfen,* Blush, 1994; Zhang Nuanxin's *Sha'ou,* The Drive to Win, 1981), while others focus on individual women at odds with a lingering Chinese patriarchy (e.g., films by Hu Mei and Huang Shuqing, among others). Films by younger women, including Li Yu's *Jinnian xiatian* (Fish and Elephant, 2001) and

196

Liu Jiayin's *Niupi* (Oxhide, 2005), also take up issues of women's desires, sexuality, and the new economy in China today.

In fact, what many of these films by Chinese women filmmakers have in common consists of a cinematic portrait of the changing lives of women in post-Mao China. These films chronicle the ambivalence experienced by women who may have suffered enormously during the Cultural Revolution and/or had opportunities open up for them because of Mao's insistence that "women hold up half the sky" and the power exerted by women near the seat of power, most notably Mao's wife, Jiang Qing, putative leader of the Gang of Four. With the trial of the Gang of Four, the repudiation of the policies associated with the Cultural Revolution, and a backlash against the "iron girls" associated with Maoism, Deng Xiaoping took Chinese women into a new era of momentous economic shifts— including the globalization of commerce, neoliberal economic restructuring, class stratification, and the growth of consumerism. From this perspective, the "truth or dare" game the women in *Perpetual Motion* play comes to resemble the line separating the Mao and Deng years, moving from political self-criticisms associated with the confessions of the Cultural Revolution to the confessional tell-alls of women's post-Mao consumer culture.

However, few of these films deal with middle-aged or older women. Hong Kong director Ann Hui's *Yima de houxiandai shenghuo* (The Postmodern Life of My Aunt, 2006) is a notable exception.[11] Although *The Postmodern Life of My Aunt* does not deal with the art and media elite of Beijing, but the marginalized women of Shanghai, it does deal with many of the same issues found in *Perpetual Motion*, specifically, the question of the survival of aging women in China's rapidly changing global economy.

While *The Postmodern Life of My Aunt* focuses on the decline of its central character during the course of the film as an indictment of the society that created her predicament, *Perpetual Motion* turns a critical eye on the ostensible female winners in the new neoliberal economy and shows that their public success belies personal torment. Not new, this tension appears to be an outgrowth of China's entry into the global marketplace and adoption of neoliberal policies. Although written in 1993, this statement by Dai Jinhua still holds true and resonates with Ning Ying's film:

> It is evident that today's China is experiencing an unprecedented and dramatic historical transformation, and is currently negotiating an especially difficult historical passage. In this process of rapid modernization and

commercialization, the social and cultural status of women is undergoing a tragic decline. It seems China's historical progress will be completed at the expense of, and through the retrogression of, women's social position. It may be that such an overt suppression of women and their very visible status decline will usher in a more self-conscious and more fundamental women's resistance. In this process, will women really become a visible portion of humankind? Will women's film and television, as a sort of marginal culture, perhaps become a force in the newly established "public space" *(gonggong kongjian)*? Perhaps, but this writer does not dare to be optimistic or certain.[12]

Perpetual Motion explores the contradictions between the public and the private in the lives of Chinese women. It deals with very public women, who have considerable control over issues of style, consumption, and media, but who lead private lives troubled by the givens of male dominance, female subservience, and domestic inequality. Rather than drawing a line between the public and private spheres, however, *Perpetual Motion* shows how the two are inexorably linked. Visions of Western consumer goods, images of impossible cosmetic beauty, and the ventriloquism of popular romance literature create a public sphere for women, which defines their private lives.

Off-screen, director/co-screenwriter Ning Ying has much in common with the fictional characters in *Perpetual Motion* and the performers who portray them in the film. She operates on the borders of consumer culture, working transnationally between China and Europe. She has had a hand in international co-productions, such as Bernardo Bertolucci's *The Last Emperor* (1987), as well as in small-scale, small-format digital video (DV) films such as *Perpetual Motion*. Although part of the Beijing Film Academy's graduating class that defined the Fifth Generation, Ning Ying has charted her own course by making urban films (e.g., *Zhao le*, For Run, 1993; *Minjing gushi,* On the Beat, 1995; *Xiari nuanyangyang,* I Love Beijing, 2000) when her classmates Chen Kaige and Zhang Yimou went to the countryside for their first features. Also, unlike Chen and Zhang, she has moved in the direction of low-budget DV rather than going in the other digital direction of big-budget, CGI-enhanced epics. Since *Perpetual Motion* deals with artists and works within an experimental narrative tradition, it seems to have more in common with urban films about artists and intellectuals made by Sixth Generation filmmakers (e.g., Wang Xiaoshuai's *Dongtian de rizi,* The Days, 1993, and *Jidu hanleng,* Frozen, 1996). More generally, *Perpetual Motion* appears to be in conversation with other films set in Beijing that take up critical commentary on the capital as the seat of political power in the People's Republic of China, including Jiang Wen's *Yangguang canlan de rizi* (In the Heat of the Sun, 1994), Chen Kaige's *Bawang bieji* (Farewell My Concubine, 1993), and Tian Zhuangzhuang's *Lan fengzheng* (Blue Kite, 1993), among others.

However, *Perpetual Motion* is a collaborative project and not just the vision of its director. Hung Huang, Liu Suola, and Ning Ying co-wrote the script, and Liu Suola composed the score. As such, its aesthetic is more in keeping with a postmodernist distrust of singular authorship, consistency, and coherence. Rather, the film operates as a pastiche of performance styles, personal anecdotes, and visual perspectives. Li Qinqin/Qin Qin is the film's only professional actress; however, all the women in the film perform in public professionally; i.e., Liu Suola/La La as a musician and avant-garde performance artist, Hung Huang/Niu Niu as a radio personality, and Ping Yanni/Mrs. Ye as a prominent businesswoman. Even Zhang Hanzhi, who plays the maid Zhang Mama (and is, in fact, Hung Huang's mother who passed away in 2008), has a very public, international presence as Mao Zedong's English tutor and interpreter, who translated for Henry Kissinger and Richard Nixon during their visits to China in 1971 and 1972. (In fact, Ye comments Zhang Mama still has the "look of class struggle" about her and fears she may want to eat her pampered pet dog.) Off-screen, these women collectively provide a very public face inside and outside of China, and they represent two distinct generations of women with very different relationships to the Mao and post-Mao eras. *Perpetual Motion* plays with these tensions and contradictions between the public and the private, the domestic and the international, the past and the present in both the casting and creation of the characters within the narrative.

Ironically, although very vulnerable in their private lives, these women are trendsetters who exercise considerable professional power in defining women's lives in contemporary China. As a real estate broker, Ye defines their physical habitat. Qin Qin provides a visual model for their dress and deportment as a desirable film and television star. La La represents the artistic "cutting edge" as a musician and "art" celebrity. As a writer, Niu Niu narrates women's lives, telling their stories as they should be told. In her control of the depiction of space, time, visual design, and narrative in the film, Ning Ying critically redefines women's roles in her capacity as a critical commentator on the media that depict them. All negotiate ideology as cultural brokers and critics.

Because of the play between the public personae of the performers and the fictional characters on screen, the women enact a number of "versions" of who they are or could possibly be. In Brechtian fashion, they stand at a distance from themselves and the characters they play, interpreting their roles as they perform, alienating themselves from the off-screen public images, as well as from their on-screen constructions of the very visible public roles they inhabit. Each character satirizes a certain type of fashionable Beijing woman with outrageous flaws and affectations, including colored cigarettes with gold tips, a pampered pet dog, a kiss on each cheek in the French fashion, and a cell phone glued to the head like a third ear, as well as spouting dialogue straight out of erotic chick lit. Done up for the holidays, the women overdo it with fashion accessories; e.g., oversized jewelry, silk scarves, high heels, trendy glasses, elaborate coiffures, and sequined clothing.

As Mary Ann Doane, drawing on the work of Joan Riviere, has pointed out, femininity involves a masquerade that disguises women's non-identity as human beings. In this case, the "hyperbolization of the accoutrements of femininity"[13] allows the women in *Perpetual Motion* to hide behind the masks of cosmopolitanism and urbanity. However, in each case, the mask camouflages an ulterior motive. Niu Niu, of course, schemes to smoke out her rival. Qin Qin wants to get closer to her lover and seems surprised he is not at the party. La La plans to seduce Niu Niu. Ye tries to convince Niu Niu to sell her house, so she can profit from the commission on the sale. All the women hide behind the feminine mask of conviviality, passivity, and guilelessness in order to achieve their aims.

This inauthentic femininity, which characterizes the postmodern fragmentation of subjectivity, has its own ambiguities. As Stephanie Hemelryk Donald points out in her study of Chinese film, *Public Secrets, Public Spaces: Cinema and Civility in China*:

> Inauthenticity is a sign that the subject is flexible and comfortable in the contemporary mode. The inauthentic subject must engage in dialogue within herself to achieve fleeting reconciliation between the material and the symbolic elements of her experience. Artists and critics function as mediators, prizing their way into the social imaginary with aesthetic tricks and barbed wit. Therefore, they must be silenced in a different nexus of exclusion, which is the discourse of the authentic. As inauthentic they have neither the confidence of the narcissistic Self, nor the doubtful honor of necessary Otherness. They hover between one subjectivity and another, seeing both and inhabiting neither.[14]

The characters in *Perpetual Motion,* as cultural mediators, prove to be inconsistent and move in and out of type, poignantly revealing multiple aspects of their psyches constructed between Maoism and global capitalism, traditional patriarchy and consumerism, Chinese culture and Western style.

For example, in addition to her failed marriages, Qin Qin reveals a problematic relationship to her father, who does not approve of the Western blue jeans that take her away from the Chinese Communist definition of style. Niu Niu struggles with her husband's infidelity and her growing suspicion that George may simply not be worth all the emotional effort she has put into the marriage. Ye fluctuates between being a crass businesswoman and Niu Niu's loyal confidante. Perhaps the most complex character, the bisexual La La has the particular privilege of being the only character granted voice-over narration to reveal her inner thoughts. She gradually distances herself from the group through her queer desires, odd behavior, and eventual nervous breakdown. Still suffering from the consequences of her father's imprisonment and humiliation during the Cultural Revolution, La La cannot get beyond the impact this period had on her mother and her own future. Even after eight years in prison, her father clung to Mao, and La La cannot fathom that he could cry copious tears for Mao's death but none on being reunited with his daughter. When she decided to go abroad, her father maintained she was betraying the nation.

This presentation of what feels like a collective, fictionalized autobiography can be shocking. Not only do these women talk about taboo subjects, such as sex during menopause and the continuing impact of the Cultural Revolution, they also speak frankly about other topics central to women's lives but usually excluded by the commercial media, including the impact of adultery on married women, divorce, bisexuality and lesbian desire, childlessness, and mental illness. Glimpses of life close to the inner circles of the Chinese Communist Party are even more infrequent, and the fact that these characters share a privileged past places them outside the experience of most Chinese women. These characters bounced back from the Cultural Revolution to study and work abroad, marry foreign husbands, and return to lucrative jobs within the burgeoning cultural and commercial marketplace in China. Apparently abroad during the upheavals leading to the June 4, 1989, crackdown, they now live in a world that revolves around real estate, interior design, fashion, media, consumption, and sexual expression.

THE NEW YEAR AND THE NEW WOMAN

At one point in *Perpetual Motion*, a bird gets trapped in the attic of Niu Niu's house during the New Year party. Niu Niu and her friends go up to deal with the feathered intruder and come across a collection of old manuscripts, Mao buttons, and recordings (fig. 8.1). Qin Qin discovers some old feudal manuscripts she cannot read, but she manages to make out the characters for "female, woman, concubine, and wife." Ye uncovers a box of Mao buttons and enthuses over records from her youth such as "Song of the Little Red Guards," "I Love Beijing Tian'anmen," and "When I Grow Up, I'll Carry a Rifle." Between the concubine of the late-Qing and the Cultural Revolution's "iron girls," *Perpetual Motion* situates the postmodern women of the new economy living under the roof of feudalism and socialist modernity. The past continues to define their present through the neglected residue of history.

202   The attic, in fact, gestures toward a history of modern Chinese women. As women took center stage after the fall of the Qing Dynasty in 1911 and during the May 4 Movement of 1919, the "New Woman" became an emblem of "modernity" by throwing off old traditions like arranged marriages and foot-binding, agitating for political reforms and influenced by the rise of women internationally (e.g., popularity of translations of

FIGURE 8.1 Mao button collection

Henrik Ibsen's *A Doll's House*, 1879). Mao took up the cause of women as part of the Revolution, and the "iron girls" associated with Mao's policies became an emblem of national as well as female strength. They were key players in his vision of "continuous revolution" in which social hierarchies (including divisions within the Communist Party) would be subject to constant scrutiny through a process of class struggle. For some, Mao's state-sponsored gender equity opened doors; while, for others, the Cultural Revolution interrupted educations, ruined families, created unlikely marital alliances, and uprooted many young women who were "sent down" to be reeducated in the countryside.

Although Ye maintains that "revolutionaries stay young forever," the women in *Perpetual Motion* must negotiate a postfeminist world often closer to the feudal patriarchal past than to Mao's unisex revolutionary vision. The events of May to June 1989, as the public expression of these ideological vicissitudes, are conspicuous by their absence. Skipping over the June 4 crackdown, *Perpetual Motion* places its cosmopolitan women abroad during the late-1980s, cultivating transnational contacts and absorbing Western expertise. The implied return to Beijing after 1989 finds expression through their ambivalence about China as a nation, as well as an "ideal" allegorized by their romances with George. After sampling men outside of China, both Niu Niu and Qin Qin end up with George as a way to reconnect with China sensually. Niu Niu, for example, narrates George's seduction as culminating with a trip on a crowded public bus to a public park. At that point, after rubbing shoulders with the masses, she knew that marrying George would somehow reestablish her connection to China. George, like many in Tian'anmen Square in 1989, represents a progressive vision for China and an idealism stemming from a desire for equality. However, George's rise from avant-garde obscurity to popular celebrity parallels the rise of consumerism after Deng's drive toward privatization in his famous trip to China's south in 1992. As Deng's reforms opened markets for pulp fiction for George, this success also paved the path for his infidelity. As Rofel points out, the post-1989 economic reforms and an ideology of individual desire are inextricably linked:

> After the June 4th crisis of legitimacy, the constitution of a postsocialist humanity in China entailed not merely the demolition of those politics portrayed as hindering human nature but a positive encouragement and elaboration of people's sexual, material, and affective self-interest in order to become cosmopolitan citizens of a post-Cold War world.[15]

The idealized China of Niu Niu's imagination had little to do with George and the commercial literary marketplace. Niu Niu may have wanted to return to her roots, but China (and George) had already gone global, picking up Qin Qin, a glamorous television star, as a trophy along the way.

The New Year season provides an ironic backdrop to the investigation of George's adultery. The Lunar New Year is traditionally a time for family reunions. However, instead of spending time with her family, Niu Niu is holed up with women whom she suspects of betraying her. George is conspicuous by his absence, and each of Niu Niu's guests asks about his whereabouts. With firecrackers and festive foods, the Spring Festival celebrates the joys of childhood. However, in *Perpetual Motion,* the New Year decorations with cheerful children in traditional costumes only underscore the fact she has no children. In fact, all the women appear to be childless. The New Year couplets that decorate the home provide an ironic reminder that the doorways do not lead to any marital bliss or familial unity. The festive gambling that should provide the winner with good fortune, instead gives the loser a platform to share very depressing personal stories.

Removed from the festivities, Niu Niu listens to the firecrackers in the distance as she stands in her empty courtyard, and the women celebrate the New Year by watching it on television rather than participating in any direct way. The jingoistic display of People's Liberation Army performers and women in garish costumes singing "I am Chinese," enervate Niu Niu and her guests. As they doze off, New Year becomes an empty event drained of any significance other than national chauvinism and commercial display.

Ye has her own version of a New Year greeting for the new neoliberal economy:

> . . . money follows you, the mafia aids you, the police protect you, your career will reward you, the stock market will grow with you, real estate will find you, and your lover loves you.

Although facetious, this sentiment does not vary greatly from the more traditional, pre-Revolutionary wishes for material prosperity and family harmony. Niu Niu also has her own ironic, post-1949 New Year chronology:

- 1950—"first" spring festival of the PRC
- 1969—Chinese youth spend spring festival in the countryside
- 1972—sale of fluorescent watches

- 1979—new hair salons open so there are no lines for New Year haircuts
- 1981—polyester men's jackets sell out—some arrested for buying more than their quota
- 1985—hot gift—quota certificates for imported cameras
- 1992—first messaging center
- 2001—email greetings used
- 2005—Niu Niu invites three friends for mahjong

Marking key dates with political events and commercial commodities, note how time accelerates on this list after Mao's death in 1976. The New Year and China's "New Woman" become a part of this redefinition of identity through global consumerism and new technologies. Returning to the traditional pastime of mahjong, Niu Niu takes her friends back to pre-1949 China and the concerns of women cloistered in the patriarchal home.

This finds concrete expression in the film's choice of the *siheyuan* as its principal location. Although they occupy a very public place professionally and remain "modern" in their Maoist upbringing, the women are visually imprisoned behind the thick walls and closed doors of the *siheyuan*, the traditional Chinese courtyard home found along Beijing's *hutong* alleyways.

205

WOMEN AND SPACE IN *PERPETUAL MOTION*

Even though time accelerates in post-Mao China, the space associated with the *siheyuan* appears stubbornly to remain static over the decades. The *siheyuan* in *Perpetual Motion* is, in many ways, reminiscent of the stifling home Nora closes the door on at the end of Ibsen's *A Doll's House*. It consists of four buildings designed to form a courtyard surrounded by a wall with an entrance gate opening onto the *hutong*. Lin Haiyin's novel *My Memories of Old Peking* (1960) famously captures the fading of traditional life in the *siheyuan*. PRC filmmaker Wu Yigong took the Taiwan-based writer's classic up in 1983 as one of the first films made after the Cultural Revolution to deal with the pre-Revolutionary past from a distinctly nonrevolutionary point of view.

Although the book deals with the southern rather than the elite northern part of the city, Ning Ying's use of the *siheyuan* continues the saga of the closed world of women within the confines of the domestic sphere, and *Perpetual Motion* uses the location to full advantage in its examination of this prison house of privileged Beijing women. The opening shots of the film emphasize the boxlike enclosure of the courtyard through window frames, and the female form is dwarfed by a high-angle shot that emphasizes the empty center enclosed by the walls of the compound.

The tension between the sequestered world of the *siheyuan* and the very public fact of the presence of the camera becomes an important theme throughout *Perpetual Motion*. Close-ups of fish in a tank visually resonate with shots of Niu Niu behind the windows of her home, the courtyard reflected on her face, behind glass like the fish (fig. 8.2). She is part of the domestic space—a detail of the environment like the pet fish—as well as available for public scrutiny by her female guests as well as the camera. Other reminders of public scrutiny pepper the mise-en-scène. For example, when Niu Niu gets up in the morning, a low-level *tatami* shot shows a photomontage of women's eyes on the floor of her bedroom watching her as she leaves the room (fig. 8.3). Not only does the camera intrude into the closed world of the *siheyuan*, but popular culture, fragmented parts of the female form likely taken from advertising, has already been there to judge Niu Niu and implicitly "see" her middle-aged form as lacking. Niu Niu's quick check of her sagging belly in the mirror confirms that she has internalized this commercial gaze. As night falls during the course of the party and the interior lights come up, exterior

FIGURE 8.2 Life behind glass

FIGURE 8.3 Women in fragments

shots of the home exacerbate this visual point. Niu Niu appears to be both trapped and on display in the composition of the frame.

After 1949, a hierarchy emerged in the Communist Party. Most *siheyuan* were divided up for multifamily use (mentioned by Qin Qin in the film). However, as Ye says, other compounds remained single-family residences used by high-ranking cadres. After Deng's reforms, these homes reverted to the families, and Niu Niu's grandfather's books in the attic seem to point to her family's continuous habitation of the *siheyuan*. In fact, each part of the *siheyuan* tells a different aspect of the story of women in China from the Mao buttons and sex manuals in the attic to the color television in the parlor. Each character in the film has memories associated with living in a *siheyuan,* and Niu Niu's New Year invitation allows them to travel back in time and explore their own understanding of claims the past has on their current lives. In many ways, as the women play at being girls and skip rope in the courtyard, the *siheyuan* becomes a concrete emblem of this interior journey into their private lives as women, as well as the impact the vicissitudes of modern Chinese history has had on their sense of self.

In contrast to the traditional courtyard, Niu Niu's study, with its oversize Western desk, speaks to her adult, professional life and her reliance on new technologies to communicate and, ironically, to uncover her husband's affair. The global dimension of this room allows the outside to intrude, and publishers, students, as well as the unintended voice of her husband's mistress bombard her on answering machines and through email messages. George's[16] framed portrait on the desk emphasizes that he belongs to this room, part of Niu Niu's public life, but remains removed from her inner world. Apparently a social climber, outside the closed world of Niu Niu and her privileged friends, his joining her household reverses the tradition of patrilocality associated with feudal China.

Since food is at the heart of any home and any celebration, the contrast between the kitchen and the dining room in the *siheyuan* proves telling. Spotless and modern, the kitchen, for example, also has its share of blood and guts. As the realm of the maid Zhang Mama, the kitchen, like the Mao buttons in the attic, still elicits thoughts of "class struggle" and the unfinished project of class leveling. Zhang Hanzhi, of course, as Mao's translator, both represents and stands outside those policies. She functions as a reminder, too, that women have been literally and figuratively "sent back to the kitchen" in the new society. As public services erode, women fill the gaps, increasing their paid and unpaid domestic burden as cooks, housecleaners, childcare providers, caregivers for the elderly and disabled, and household servants.

Playing her daughter's maid, she remains silent throughout most of the film, a mute witness to history and a domestic fixture in the household. However, close-ups of her slaughter of the white chickens and the bowl she uses to collect the blood point to the blood on the hands of even the most menial members of the household or the society at large. The women may suffer from the remnants of feudalism and failed Maoism, but they also are complicit in jockeying for advantage. In this case, the mistress and the maid plot to smoke out George's mistress, and butchering the chicken graphically attests to their ruthlessness. They must kill to eat and survive.

Zhang Mama may be good enough for the kitchen; however, she cannot serve in the dining room, the place where Niu Niu displays her wealth and status as mistress of the *siheyuan*. Rather than offering the chicken Zhang Mama has prepared to her guests, Niu Niu caters the New Year luncheon with chicken feet served by young women in elegant attire. A blend of China and the West, the interior design of the room also conveys a sense of luxury, which could be found in wealthy domiciles in New York, Paris, Tokyo, or London. The chicken feet may be a distinctly local Chinese delicacy, but the setting for the gathering speaks volumes about these women's access to global style as well as capital. Known euphemistically as "phoenix claws" in Chinese, the chicken feet, like the phoenix, have a feminine connotation. They supposedly enhance a woman's complexion, and their consumption can connote female vanity. In voice-over, La La notes that the claws remind her of female relentlessness as she envisions the claws selfishly scratching out the best crumbs for consumption by bullying any competing hens.

The montage of the women's mouths lustily eating the chicken feet points to the erotic ways in which the claws can be devoured as well as the potential viciousness of the women (fig. 8.4). Niu Niu's sharp eye on this display of her competitors' sensuality and lustiness, however, does not bring any specific suspect to the surface. Under the façade of elegance and worldliness, all the women seem base when free to fulfill their carnal desires. Like the hens they consume, they remain trapped in a pecking order they have little power to control.

Even though Niu Niu defines the rules of her gathering and determines the menu, she has little power over the system of scarcity, value, and romantic competitiveness that forces them to treat each other with suspicion. Later, Niu Niu must soak her own sore feet in the bathroom because the fashionable heels she wore as part of her New Year finery hurt her. With this image within the even more private space of the bathroom, the visual motif of the feet comes full circle as standards of beauty within

209

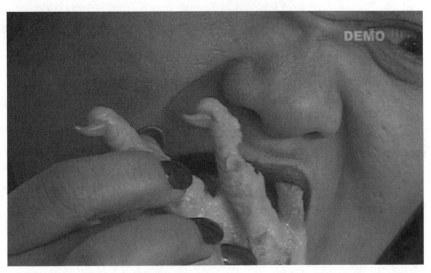

FIGURE 8.4 Chomping on chicken feet

a society of consumption give Niu Niu aching feet while she digests the expensive chicken feet she enjoyed for lunch.

Only La La seems able to opt out of this situation. When she insinuates interest in pursuing a lesbian affair with Niu Niu in the pantry, La La steps out of the "closet" by acknowledging her bisexuality. La La also takes the film away from the "woman's film" genre associated with Hollywood conventions of romance. Her sexual identity has little, if any, bearing on her mental collapse. As the performer Liu Suola uses gestures reminiscent of avant-garde dance and mime to indicate La La's self-absorption and interior turmoil, the film moves away from what has become a somewhat petty concern over George's infidelity into the realm of state history and personal trauma. In voice-over, La La repeats her mother's question of why things never seem to change. Within the postmodern condition, Chinese women always seem to be in "perpetual motion" at the same time that they are trapped in a perpetual present that promises little change from the male-defined limitations of the traditional patriarchy or global capitalism.

Ultimately, the *siheyuan,* as Ye points out, remains a piece of real estate, to be bought and sold like any other building in Beijing or in any other global metropolis. With the elimination or gentrification of the *hutong* districts of Beijing, the commercial value of the *siheyuan* becomes paramount in importance. As historical buildings with cultural significance, these decaying, but grand, courtyard homes attract artists, intellectuals, writers, design professionals, gallery owners, and other cultural entrepreneurs before gentrification puts them financially out of the reach of these individuals. With a change in the neighborhood, Ye sees the prospect of a commission, and she advises Niu Niu to sell her *siheyuan* and buy a modern condominium or a villa in the suburbs with the proceeds.

THE NEXT MOVE OR BACK TO THE FUTURE

Even though the *siheyuan* exudes a feeling of continuity and cultural stability, it is, as a piece of real estate, also in perpetual motion as a circulating commodity. With the domestic space of the *siheyuan* symbolizing their private lives and subjective thoughts, the women, although they appear to be pillars of the new society, remain mercurial. They move between China and the rest of the world, change careers, change husbands and lovers, move between sexual orientations, and change moods and topics of conversation. Mao advocated "continuous revolution," but he likely did not have in mind the vicissitudes of these women's lives. At the very heart of China, in the middle of its capital city of Beijing, in its most traditional domestic architectural feature, these women represent a storm churning in the teapot—marriages unhinged, lives defined by commercial aims, traumatized by the past, as uncertain of their present identities as they are of their future direction.

At the end of *Perpetual Motion*, after La La has been sent to the hospital, Niu Niu, Qin Qin, and Ye leave the *siheyuan* and the *hutong* behind as they march toward the camera. On the road in Beijing, they walk past construction workers engaging in the urban development gradually encroaching on the *hutong*. Niu Niu has a spring in her step, and the women seem to be walking away from the one hundred years of stagnation La La's mother had decried. Although women's "perpetual motion" may be a perpetual repetition of a sexist past in the new trappings of global consumer capitalism, this motion may gesture toward change. Niu Niu manages to take a breath of fresh air away from George and the *siheyuan*, which may signal hope. The fact that *Perpetual Motion*, a film made by a woman about the lives of Chinese women, has found a place within the transnational circulation of Chinese-language cinema may also point toward the possibility that women's creativity will not be marginalized or undervalued within global film culture.

211

NOTES

1. A version of this paper was presented as "'New Women,' Postmodern China, and the Legacy of the Cultural Revolution," *Between Public and Private: A Space for Independent Chinese Cinema*, 33rd Hong Kong International Film Festival, April 12, 2009. I am grateful to Sebastian Veg for inviting me to participate and to Louisa Wei for chairing the panel. I also want to thank Ning Ying for her kind encouragement of this project.
2. Lisa Rofel, *Desiring China*, 3.
3. Ibid., 159.
4. See Jurgen Habermas, "Modernity—an Incomplete Project," 3–15.
5. Molly Haskell, *From Reverence to Rape.*
6. Ibid., 153.
7. Ibid., 163–164.
8. The reference to "tofu" involves the Chinese euphemism for the woman's body; e.g., "to eat tofu" means "to flirt," etc.
9. Wei Hui, *Shanghai Baby.*

10. The term came into use in the 1980s. See Chris Berry, "China's New 'Women's Cinema.'"

11. See my essay for more on this film, Gina Marchetti, "Gender Politics and Neoliberalism in China."

12. Dai Jinhua, "Invisible Women," 279.

13. Mary Ann Doane, "Film and the Masquerade," 49.

14. Stephanie Hemelryk Donald, *Public Secrets, Public Spaces*, 100.

15. Rofel, *Desiring China*, 13.

16. George's distance from this world is accentuated by the fact that he is "played" in the still image by Hong Kong cultural studies scholar, Ackbar Abbas, who is Liu Suola's husband.

9

Searching for Female Sexuality and Negotiating with Feminism

LI YU'S FILM TRILOGY

SHUQIN CUI

THE HISTORY of filmmaking in China does not lack women's films or female directors. But woman's cinema—marked by female subjectivity, perspective, and aesthetics—remains ambivalent, a result of the paradox that woman as gendered subject and discursive mode remains subordinated to mainstream rhetoric. In the domain of socialist politics, individual interests yield to national ideologies and class categories overpower gender difference, so the female body recedes behind a collective identity as her screen image becomes a social-political signifier. Works such as *Hongse nianzijun* (The Red Detachment of Women, 1961) and *Baimao nü* (The White Haired Girl, 1950) exemplify how class oppression can enslave women but how political ideology can enlighten them and make them vanguards of the proletariat.[1] Moreover, the cinematic image is articulated to ensure that woman's release from subjugation to emancipation occurs only when gender difference is erased.

In post-socialist China, where a market economy drives cultural production and the mainstream mass media encourage consumption, the female body image is valued for its power of sexual and visual attraction. Under these conditions, women may not need to disguise their gender identity to make films, but in a male-dominated and commercially measured cultural production industry, women filmmakers face multiple challenges. In addition to ideological censorship, commercial expectations and distribution restraints have forced women directors to either shun the film industry or seek alternative ways to enter the mainstream. For instance, a group of filmmakers who began to make women's films in the 1980s have shifted their interests dramatically. We rarely hear much from Huang Shuqin since her highly regarded feminist film, *Ren, gui, qing* (Woman, Demon, Human, 1987). Hu Mei, after *Nüer lou* (Army Nurse, 1985), which explores the female-self split between submission to sociopolitical ideology and allegiance to personal desires, switched to historical soap operas made for television. Peng Xiaolian, who made *Nüren de gushi* (Women's Story, 1989) about three peasant women leaving the countryside for the city, now creates urban narratives. Li Shaohong, director of *Hongfen* (Blush, 1994), a film about female sexuality and prostitution, currently makes thrillers. A subjective women's cinema, let alone a feminist one, finds scant possibilities in a limited market in China.[2]

Nevertheless, recent film releases by new female directors have brought renewed interest in the making of women's cinema. Ning Ying's *Wu qiong dong* (Perpetual Motion, 2005) subverts existing conventions of female images and the image-making system. Xu Jinglei's *Wo he baba* (My Father and I, 2003) interweaves a father-daughter plot that transgresses constantly against the Oedipus complex. Xiao Jiang's *Tongnian wangshi* (Electric Shadows, 2005) returns to a social-familial past when a young girl's coming-of-age narrative was integral to film history. The return to women's cinema calls attention to the question of how women directors—a minority on the margins of the film industry—make works that run counter to the mainstream while also yielding to it. Among the young or new female directors bringing the subject of women's cinema to the forefront is Li Yu, whose film trilogy—*Jinnian xiatian* (Fish and Elephant, 2001), *Hongyan* (Dam Street, 2005), and *Pingguo* (Lost in Beijing, 2007)—emphasizes female sexuality.[3] *Fish and Elephant*, the first Chinese feature on a lesbian relationship, presents homosexuality against a heterosexual social-cultural environment. Although this cinematic representation of a homosexual identity marks the possibility of asserting sexual diversity against "regimes of the normal," the confinement of homosexual experience within heterosexual discourse inhibits a potentially queer discourse and cinema that might go beyond homo/hetero binary conventions. In *Dam Street*, Li Yu continues the search for female sexuality with a focus on the female body as a site of sociocultural punishment and sexual spectacle. Considering the body in terms of spectacle and politics, I argue that sociocultural norms punish the female body for sexual abnormality even as the film offers resistance in a female protagonist who defies subordination. In addition, a voyeuristic spectatorship, first surveillant, then adolescent, complicates the female body as unwanted on the one hand, while desired on the other.

Finally, this chapter analyzes how Li Yu's new release, *Lost in Beijing,* locates female sexuality against a commercial society in which the female body is commodified for its exchange value. The displacement of a female migrant, especially her pregnant body, between two men—her boss and her husband—constitutes a transaction made through the female body/sexuality. Analysis of Li's three works, taken together, demonstrates why women's filmmaking in China persists on the social-cultural margins while remaining ambivalent about feminist representation. As feminist theories and film practices cross the lines between local and global, national and transnational, what they say to and about one another requires a rethinking and rereading of feminism(s) from transnational and translocal perspectives.

NEGOTIATING HOMOSEXUAL RELATIONS WITHIN HETEROSEXUAL DISCOURSE

Female sexuality, especially homosexuality, is a subject that film directors in China hesitate to address. Li Yu's *Fish and Elephant,* the director's debut, is the first feature from mainland China to portray a lesbian identity and relationship, a sexuality normally invisible and unspeakable in social-cultural discourse and cinematic representation.[4] Unlike new queer cinema in the independent circuit that deals openly with queer culture and identity politics,[5] *Fish and Elephant* shows how lesbians negotiate their identities and relationships *within* the heterosexual system. The film is neither a popular lesbian romance nor a coming-out film, but rather, in the director's words, an "exploration of how a lesbian relationship deals with family and society."[6] Or, in the view of Carol Guess, the representation attempts "to incorporate lesbian existence into a world view that excludes it, and to expose the mechanisms of compulsory heterosexuality."[7]

Familial pressures and social denial act to negate lesbian identity and silence lesbian voices. Heterosexual conventions of marriage and sexuality permit little room for alternatives. The film interweaves narrative sequences of Xiaoqun, the lesbian protagonist, dating an assortment of males. The mother has arranged these meetings for Xiaoqun, ignorant of her daughter's sexual identity, and Xiaoqun participates out of filial piety, thus dislocating the lesbian narrative within heterosexual conventions. To reinforce the dislocated homo-and-hetero encounter, the film director sent out actual date-seeking advertisements, and a number of men responded to the ads without knowing that the offer was a ruse for filmmaking. The dating scenes become real-life engagements. Each of the potential dates says that his girlfriend should be virtuous, beautiful, and feminine. By having the lesbian protagonist confront compulsory heterosexuality, the film allows her to affirm her lesbian identity and voice: "I'm interested not in man but in woman." "Embracing the word 'lesbian,'" as Carol Guess cites Adrienne Rich, "is a political imperative, a brave and necessary gesture which serves as a speech act, challenging the hegemonic forces opposing the identity the speaker claims with the very act of speaking."[8] But no male partner finds the lesbian voice comprehensible. The denial of lesbian identity in the face of its declaration reflects how social-cultural perception remains willfully blind to lesbianism in contemporary China.

The dual identity and lifestyle that the lesbian embodies becomes apparent in cinematic juxtapositions between homosexual and heterosexual engagements. The spatial mise-en-scène of public places and underground space divides and defines the shifting identities. The dating scenes occur in public settings—tea houses, restaurants, and parks—and the dates are often accompanied by family members. The public setting suggests that finding a date and getting married are not simply personal choices but also familial and social obligations. The film crosscuts frequently from public to private spaces, however, such as basement apartments and the elephant house, as the lesbian relationship unfolds. The divided spaces indicate an identity split: a legitimate heterosexual in public but an unacceptable homosexual in private. The lesbian figure oscillates between spatial and gendered boundaries.

In addition to spatial divisions, the hetero/homosexual contrast is also marked by a mother-daughter relationship, with the daughter subordinate to the maternal figure's heterosexual regulation. As Xiaoqun narrates her mother's story, she explains why her mother cannot acknowledge a homosexual identity. Xiaoqun reveals that her mother divorced because of her husband's affair with another woman. As a single mother, she raised two children: Xiaoqun and a son who dies in a car accident. The film shows the mother, victim of marital conventions, expecting her daughter to marry and settle down. The heterosexual maternal discourse is demanding and places the lesbian daughter in a difficult situation: maintaining her lesbian identity while fulfilling a daughter's piety. Xiaoqun's former lover, Junjun, reveals how *her* mother pretended until the last moment of her life not to acknowledge that her husband was sexually violating their daughter. The mother's silence about the incest further victimizes Junjun and pushes her to retaliate against the heterosexual hegemony. The film's mother-daughter narratives suggest that while the mothers rely on the heterosexual discourse of marriage and family to regulate the daughters' sexuality, the daughters' homosexual behavior subverts such norms within the limits of heterosexuality.

Compounding the maternal restrictions over the lesbian daughter's sexual choices is the authority imposed by father figures, individual or collective. Junjun is a criminal suspected of murdering her father. The film inserts Junjun's voice to explain how her father sexually violated her body since childhood. Memories of the rape scenes drive Junjun to seek justice through violence and to turn to lesbian relations for support. She relies on Xiaoqun and uses the elephant house for shelter. Junjun fails to realize that using violence against violence makes her the target of another fatherly authority, the police. In a confrontational mise-en-scène, the single lesbian figure is trapped inside the elephant house, facing the armed police outside. Junjun owns a handgun, symbol of social and phallic power, and fires at one policeman. The critical moment comes, in a close-up, when Junjun confronts the police officer, both with guns drawn, and she runs out of bullets. The officer persuades her that it's unwise for a woman to challenge armed force. The suppression of female criminality in the name of security implies similar consequences for displays of lesbianism: any overt challenge to heterosexual orthodoxy will be punished. Thus the possible utterance of a woman and her control over her body is blocked by sexual abuse by the father and silenced by the state. Junjun's intention to rebel and fight the forces of heterosexuality ends in tragedy.

In contrast to the violent heterosexual world, we see a peaceful homosexual space shown in cross-cutting from gunfight sequences to scenes of lesbian lovemaking. Sexual gestures, a fish tank, sounds of rain, and the color red all forge a moment of intimacy (fig. 9.1). The accelerated sequences reinforce the contrast between love and death, violence and peace. Nonetheless, homosexual interaction in a private, hidden place presents only a fleeting pleasure and moment of escape from the

FIGURE 9.1 Homosexual intimacy (*Fish and Elephant,* 2001)

dominant heterosexuality. The constant cross-cutting emphasizes how the world of the homosexual is surrounded by heterosexual regulations. Like Junjun confronting the police, anyone who crosses the line faces punishment. Thus the film implies that in China lesbian identity and practice remain pushed underground.

Fish and Elephant also raises the issue of spectatorship: what happens when the spectator identifies with the lesbian-as-spectacle? With two lesbians playing themselves, and as the first Chinese feature on the subject of lesbianism, the film allows the spectator to project empathy outside heterosexual conventions. Placement of the lesbian relation within a heterosexual framework, however, inhibits this identification, and spectatorship as well as the lesbian relationship shifts between the two realms of sexual identity. A succession of scenes dramatically juxtaposes hetero- and homosexual spaces. Xiaoqun, for example, regularly goes on blind dates in public at her mother's request, but in private she falls in love with a young woman. Her lover, Xiaolin, oscillates between their relationship and one with her boyfriend. Similarly, spectatorship also alternates, identifying with the "homoerotic" at one moment and heterosexual norms at another.

The accentuated juxtapositions destabilize spectatorship, especially female spectatorship, as the lesbian image/identity shifts across boundaries. As Rosemary Hennessy describes lesbian identity, it can be considered "as an ensemble of unstable and multiple positions, [which] contests traditional formulations of identity politics by challenging the array of assumptions on which empiricist notions of the person depend."[9] In *Fish and Elephant*, the director uses an observing, nonintrusive camera lens to locate the audience's position, although shifting and uncertain, at a distance in respect to the lesbian images. "It's a perfectly poised distance," as Shelly Kraicer points out, "one that ironizes without alienating, observes without fetishizing."[10] The film ends happily for the mother when she marries one of her daughter's older dates, thus returning to the tradition of heterosexual mating after years of divorce. Meanwhile, the lesbian daughter(s) remain hidden from the public eye.

From this analysis, one can conclude that the content of the film stresses homosexual negotiation *within* heterosexual norms. While the lesbian protagonists search for recognition of their homosexual identity, the women's film tries to assert a homosexual discourse. Both, however, situate the representation of homosexuality within rather than against heterosexual normality. In a culture and society where familial order regulates sociocultural positions and heterosexual marriage defines gender roles, issues that concern homosexuality are less a question of sexual orientation than of a lifestyle that seeks recognition or acceptance by adherents to conventional norms. Cinematic explorations of homosexuality, including Li Yu's *Fish and Elephant,* thus seek screen space where social outsiders perform their sexual identities while the audience comprehends the mechanism of sociocultural regulation.[11] With origins in neither a political movement nor a theoretical position, the subject of homosexuality and its representation in China continue to negotiate with rather than directly challenge heterosexual conventions. Homosexual identity and sexuality thus appear shifting and multifaceted in the context of changing social-cultural conditions.

BODY POLITICS AND SEXUAL SPECTACLE

In *Dam Street,* Li Yu continues her search for female sexuality but with a focus on punishment of the female body and the body as spectacle. From its opening, *Dam Street* situates the deviant body against the social-political era of 1980s' China, when teenage pregnancy was seen as "moral decadence." Various parties with different concerns punish the female body for its sexuality; together they compose a network of force, institutional or familial. The question of how a social network exercises power over the female body, specifically the teenage pregnant body, is answered in visual tropes. Xiaoyun, the teenage protagonist, is hidden in a public toilet, with contrast lighting and a confined mise-en-scène. A tracking shot, through the teacher's point of view, leads our gaze to the frightened young girl, wrapping her belly with belts of fabric. The revealed pregnant body receives official condemnation as the diegetic sound of a loudspeaker denounces the pregnant student for her deviant sexual activity. The film then situates the disgraceful figure under the watchful eye of the local townspeople in a domestic setting, where the enraged maternal figure expresses her anger by lashing the pregnant girl.

The film foregrounds the body as a site where institutional disciplinary and sociocultural norms are inscribed and reinforced. The punishment meted out in school and at home recalls Michel Foucault's "culture of spectacle," which equates public punishment and torture with the exercise of power.[12] When the punished body is not a prisoner but a pregnant girl, the culture of spectacle foregrounds female sexuality or the sexed body against a network of disciplinary practices. The film demonstrates how the female body, especially the pregnant one, becomes the site of cultural inscription and social regulation. In gendering the Foucauldian notions of the body and power, this Chinese woman's film displays teen pregnancy and its consequent social punishment to bring sex and gender into the discourse of power, adding a feminist perspective.[13] Although the film director invites us to rethink issues of body and power, she does not re-vision women themselves as subversive and empowered bodies. The film forecloses the unspeakable teen pregnancy with a rupture. The mother figure arranges an adoption but tells her daughter that the baby has died.

Dam Street uses an inter-title explanation to move ahead ten years in the female protagonist's life and further explore the question of the female body and sexuality in the China of the 1990s. We learn that in a commercially driven society a woman with a "history of inappropriate sexual conduct" faces fierce hostility when she tries to regain good standing in terms of heterosexual norms. Now a Chuan Opera singer in her local town, Xiaoyun embodies a theatrical image as she performs and sings on stage. Despite her transformation from pregnant teenager to opera singer, her status as a sexual spectacle for viewers on and off screen has not changed, however. The on-screen audience refuses her theatrical persona and requests that she sing popular songs. Performing pop songs but in a traditional mask, the female body has to enact her gender identity for the collective and commercial spectatorship.

One may read the sequence in light of Judith Butler's statement that "Gender reality is performative . . . it is real only to the extent that it is performed."[14] The performance of gender, sex, and sexuality derives from "regulative discourse," whereby the body is expected to repetitively act according to social-cultural norms. While locating its female protagonist within the regulative discourse and depicting gender performativity, the film seeks an alternative. Xiaoyun ignores the compulsory heterosexuality of getting married and has sexual relations with a married man, despite the social gossip. By refusing to act according to social and sexual norms, the female body rejects phallocentric readings and problematizes the viewing of women's bodies. The subversion is temporary, however, as the heterosexual hierarchy does not permit alternatives. The film presents a striking mise-en-scène; performing on stage, Xiaoyun is humiliated by a family. The film positions Xiaoyun on an open stage performing pop songs for the street audience. Three members of a family force their way through the crowd and attack Xiaoyun with verbal and physical violence. They bite her arms, strangle her throat, tear off her clothes and call her a hooker who has seduced the man in their family. In a bird's-eye shot, the bruised Xiaoyun is nakedly displayed in public under bright daylight (fig. 9.2). Once again the female body becomes a public spectacle, punished and humiliated for its deviant sexuality.

The world framed in *Dam Street* is a female one, with women left behind or divorced, striving to survive on their own. By contrast, the male figures are either absent or ambiguous. The mother-daughter dyad thus becomes a central subject. *Dam Street* may be called a daughterly film, as the relationship unfolds from the daughter's point of view. She tries to recover what has been oppressed as she struggles to find a voice of resistance through the visual reconstruction of mother-daughter conflicts. Nonetheless, in the representation of the conflict the mother and the daughter are subject positions characterized not by clarity and stability but rather by confusion and contradiction.

The film's authoritative maternal figure participates in the network that disciplines through punishment. As the mother lashes her daughter's pregnant body with a feather duster, the maternal voice speaks in the law of heterosexual discourse. In the violent mise-en-scène, for instance, the film cuts to a photographic image of the father on the wall. The mother challenges the daughter to explain her "immoral" deeds to

221

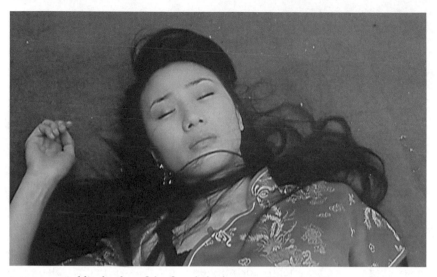

FIGURE 9.2 Public display of the female body (*Dam Street*, 2005)

her father and accuses her of ruining the family reputation. In this sequence, the film situates the maternal figure as the voice of heterosexual
mores; she exercises power over her daughter's body at the end of a lash.
The single mother is a lonely figure, consigned to the social-sexual periphery of her world. As the unhappy and mad mother figure imposes the
culturally dominant notion of gender discipline on her daughter's sexed
body, she doubly reinforces female victimization: first her own, then her
daughter's. The conflict thus indicates the link between a mother and
daughter hemmed in by the harsh limits of their social world.

Conflict or alienation is not the only problem vexing the mother-daughter relationship. The paradox of psychological distance and filial commitment complicates the dyad. Xiaoyun brings money home regularly but
chooses not to live a life like her mother's. With a past that includes a
teenage pregnancy and an affair with a married man, the daughter refuses to settle into heterosexual marriage and normality. By rejecting her
mother's expectations and social regulations, Xiaoyun raises the possibility of a daughterly autonomy. Such defiance, however, brings the daughter figure to the social-sexual periphery, where men take her for sexual
pleasure and audiences see her as a stage commodity. Her confrontation
with and denial of the maternal figure fails to foster a daughterly subjectivity, as woman's body remains in a patriarchal and commercial economy

that denies the possibility of achieving a subject position. Xiaoyun leaves her mother behind to go to Shenzhen. The departure from the maternal house does not imply entrance into the law of the father, however; the film has already hinted that local women who go to Shenzhen end up as prostitutes.

The film critiques a society dominated by sex and commerce, where women find neither space to settle down nor men to trust. In parallel to the mother-daughter narrative, however, the film introduces a young boy who takes Xiaoyun as the desiring subject and acts as her protector. In so doing, the film establishes an adolescent gaze through which Xiaoyun's personal life unfolds. As the relationship between Xiaoyun and the boy grows, each finds in the other the love and care missing from their lives. The choice of an adolescent for the roles of voyeuristic spectator and Xiaoyun's young lover frames a scopophilic gaze through which adolescent curiosity and erotic desire find a site of projection. Through the adolescent point of view, the camera reveals intimate moments of the female protagonist: nude in the shower, a sexual affair with a married man, and lonely moments backstage. The voyeuristic acts of the young boy in his observation of the female body challenge the "male gaze" as an exclusive and monolithic concept. The adolescent gaze leads to different possible viewing positions: curiosity of the young innocent, voyeurism of the adult pervert, and recognition of female spectatorship. Different positions in looking, in Kaja Silverman's argument, engender "differentiation between the look as a carrier of desire and lack and the gaze as a carrier of symbolic patriarchal dominance."[15]

The innocent loving relationship or friendship is destroyed when the film reveals—except to the boy—that he is Xiaoyun's son, the child said to have died shortly after birth. Thus *Dam Street* complicates the film narrative and the character relationship with the Oedipus complex: a loving bond between friends becomes a mother-son relationship. The transgression jeopardizes the established adolescent perspective and the unconventional friendship. Nonetheless, the film rejects a potential construction of Freudian mother-son narcissism and forecloses the narrative with Xiaoyun leaving the boy/son behind for another city. Her exit eliminates the possibility of identification with the mother as lover. The separation ends not only the boy's desire for his loving subject but also the audience's desire for the scopophilic gaze. The questions of what a woman can do after she chooses to leave her problems behind and how much further a woman's film can explore remain ambiguous.

223

From *Fish and Elephant* to *Dam Street,* Li Yu's films clearly take women and sexuality as central concerns. *Dam Street* positions the female body against restrictive social-economic conditions when sexual alternatives to the heterosexual hierarchy meet with punishment. The film also locates the female protagonist in a psychological confusion that problematizes female self-identity. Feminist Foucauldian interpretations help us to understand how social-cultural disciplinary practices exercise power over the sexed body. But feminist assumptions do not bring empowerment to this Chinese women's film, as the director expresses her concern for women's issues but rejects a feminist position. This reluctance is difficult to explain, and the film and its protagonist are left disillusioned with reality.

LOST IN BEIJING AND LOST IN REPRESENTATION

Li Yu's recent release, *Lost in Beijing,* considers how rural migrants, especially females, feel lost in the metropolis as they struggle to survive. The spatial mapping of the rural onto the urban raises the question of how a woman's film negotiates the relationship between gender identity and urban space. In assuming that urban space is gendered, one realizes that gender relations and spatial divisions manifest each other.[16] The credit sequence in *Lost in Beijing,* for instance, uses rapid handheld camerawork and accelerated montage to connect the audience immediately to radically changing Beijing, where proliferating high-rises and highways make one's head swim. Against the setting of an urban center, the camera lens focuses on a migrant couple on the social and spatial margins. The husband is framed as a high-rise window cleaner and the wife Pingguo (Apple) as a massage girl, whose responsibility is to wash and massage customers' feet. Both occupy positions on Beijing's urban periphery; the husband sells his labor in public places while the wife offers a bodily service in a confined private space.

Foot massage centers have recently emerged in China as commercial places where customers often seek sexual pleasure as well as physical relaxation. The young and unmarried girls employed there are expected not only to massage feet but also to provide sexual services. A massage girl embraces a customer's feet with her bare hands, soaks the feet in an herbal medicine bath, and massages them along acupuncture points. As the business bespeaks a new luxury in Chinese lifestyle, it poses issues of sexual exploitation and gender politics. The bodily engagement between hands and feet or legs allows customers, especially males, not only to engage their sexual imagination but also to make sexual requests. The paying customer gains temporary ownership of the massage girl, who often becomes a sex worker, a thinly disguised prostitute in this urban space.

The film director understands and visualizes how "the social construction of gender difference establishes some spaces as women's and others as men's; those meanings then serve to reconstitute the power relations of gendered identity."[17] But the film does not see "the space or spatial politics of difference as central both to masculinist power and to potential feminist resistance."[18] The film narrative thus neglects a potential feminist construction. The gendering of space and the woman's position in it make the rural female migrant doubly displaced: onto the social-economic margins on the one hand and into the sexual domain on the other. Although a site of opportunity for migrants, the city can also become a place of imprisonment and exploitation. The film's protagonist feels trapped; the imperative of social-economic survival comes at the cost of sexual exploitation. The film director seems uncertain about how to portray this dilemma, in effect how to negotiate her woman's film within or against the mainstream discourse. In other words, the film feels lost about whether to foreground the female character as a socially and sexually exploited victim or as a woman with her own voice and perspective. The directorial ambiguity renders the protagonist as a passive character: one who appeals to her boss not to fire her after he rapes her, who advises her co-worker to let a customer touch her hands if he wants her breast. A moment of resistance does occur when the film introduces a foot-massage girl who takes off a customer's toenails after he sexually harasses her. But the director presents this behavior as inappropriate; the rebellious girl becomes a prostitute, selling her body as a profession.

As a woman's film with a marginalized female migrant at the center of the narrative, *Lost in Beijing* has possibilities for alternative representation. "To be in the margin," bell hooks writes, "is to be part of the whole but outside the main body . . . a central location for the production of a counter-hegemonic discourse," and here one has "the possibility of a radical perspective from which to see and create, to imagine alternatives, new worlds."[19] *Lost in Beijing,* however, seems disinterested in the "production of a counter-hegemonic discourse," and rather than "a radical perspective" the representation of female body signifies a desiring or sacrificing object. Because the woman is trapped in the gendered spatial confinement of her workplace and in the transactions of sexual commodity exchange, the central narrative and cinematic configuration fail to provide a fresh perspective. Exploitation of the female body as a commodity in the sex/money nexus leaves the film fatally flawed.

The entanglement of Apple, the female migrant, between two men, her window-washer husband and the owner of the foot-massage parlor, illustrates the crude enactment of sexual exchange. Apple gets drunk and passes out in one of the massage rooms. The film uses a telephoto lens to foreground a scene in which the boss rapes the unconscious Apple. As the boss forces himself into the female body, Apple's husband happens to witness the rape through a window. Male force claims the female body as sexual property, one man physically, the other with his gaze. The following montage sequence through a handheld camera concerns not the victim so much as the collision between the two men. The husband yells: "How can another man rape my wife!" The boss declares that the act is accidental, not intentional. The film casts Apple as property of common ownership: wife in a heterosexual marriage and victim of sexual violence. Framing the female protagonist so she is silent and off screen, the film misses an opportunity to insert a woman's voice, let alone a feminist perspective.

In addition to presenting woman as a sexual commodity, *Lost in Beijing* further reinforces her use and exchange values. Apple becomes pregnant, but who is the father? A two-shot of the husband and the boss on a rooftop shows them agreeing that the one whose blood type matches the baby's will be the father. The marginal figure of the migrant and the successful entrepreneur share possession of the female body, but for different desires. The boss of the foot-massage parlor wants to claim fatherhood to fulfill his desperate desire to have a child, so he offers to buy the pregnant body to possess woman and child. In the transaction sequence, the film cross-cuts between the two men signing a contract guaranteeing that the parlor boss will pay the husband 22,000 yuan after the birth. For the husband, the exchange of 22,000 yuan for his wife's body and the baby is the easy road to wealth. Money is power. The social conditions in the film certainly illustrate Luce Irigaray's claim that "woman is traditionally a use-value for man, an exchange value among men . . . a commodity" and, as such, she is "a dualistic entity," possessing her own "natural body" as well as a "social and cultural body . . . imbued with a symbolic

FIGURE 9.3 Two men signing a contract to exchange the pregnant female body (*Lost in Beijing*, 2007)

227

value because of its exchangeability."[20] The female protagonist, present but silent, watches her pregnant body and unborn baby turned into a transaction between men (fig. 9.3).

The film presents explicitly how the female body is exploited to satisfy male sexual desires and exchanged for its reproductive capacity. But the question of how the woman responds to the sexual-political economy needs explanation. The film allows the female protagonist a temporary possession of her own body. After discovering that she's pregnant, Apple pursues an abortion. She announces to her husband, "This belly is not yours!" but her declaration of self-possession indicates an intention, not a fact. Unable to afford medical expenses, Apple tries to obtain an illegal abortion. At an unauthorized clinic, the off-screen sound of a teenage girl screaming makes Apple realize that a botched abortion puts her life at risk. Thus she acquiesces to the deal between husband and boss, a film narrative governed by male desire. Her submission reflects, on the one hand, the social-commercial reality in China, and, on the other, the visual construction of the film. In a market-driven society that treats the female body as a sexual commodity, *Lost in Beijing* feels lost, with Li unsure how to configure her female protagonist. The question of how the image of female migrant might appear when prevailing social-economic conditions offer her hardly any choice or autonomy remains open. A further challenge is how a woman's film can negotiate with mainstream film production without invoking either censorship or subordination.[21] The possibilities for a feminist cinema or practice in China remain uncertain, no matter how woman-centered the film might be.

While *Lost in Beijing* draws our attention to the issue of woman reduced to her exchange value, the film further configures the female image as a signifier of lack. What power has the migrant woman apart from her working, reproductive body? And the rich man's wife, consigned to idleness, unable to get pregnant, what value has she? Thus, the former's lack of social-economic status and the latter's lack of children pose the question of how a woman's film deals with the notion of lack and its symbolic meanings. A psychoanalytical perspective considers lack "one of the primary concepts that has structured female identification and desire"; moreover, lack has "haunted women's attempts to enter a representational economy in which our only mandated positions are either invisibility, or object rather than subject of the gaze."[22]

Indeed, *Lost in Beijing* represents woman as defined by lack, with the female body as a split signifier: the lack of social-economic status, on the one hand, and reproductive capacity, on the other. Thus the film captures a reality in contemporary China where women are subordinated to class-specific gender norms. The woman who does not bear children or the woman without material means are both marked as failed, devalued, disempowered. In the sequence in which the two men sign their contract, for instance, the pregnant woman up for sale and the manager's wife are present but silent. Significantly, however, the woman's film rejects gender conventions to include a scene of potential resistance. The boss's wife initiates sexual intercourse with the migrant woman's husband. In the mise-en-scène of the woman on top, the man on bottom with eyes covered by sunglasses, the wife figure revenges her husband by "fucking" another man. She may be childless, but she retains the sexual power to challenge male privilege. Exchanging sexual partners as a means of revenge and punishment subverts conventional gender norms and replaces the woman's lack with a phallic power.

In another scene of resistance, the film ends with Apple leaving the two men behind as she walks away from the boss's house with her newborn baby. The final sequence suggests that Apple's refusal to go back to her husband or her boss signifies her ownership of her body and legitimizes her motherhood over her baby. At that moment, the film presents the migrant woman in a position of agency and offers a feminist gesture in representation. Nonetheless, the closing scene calls to mind Lu Xun's classic inquiry, what else can a woman be after she leaves her husband's house?[23] The question remains as the female image fades off and the final credits fade in.

The representation of female experience reflects problems in gender politics and the conditions for woman's filmmaking in contemporary China. As the market economy turns migrant bodies, male and female, into commodities in the accelerating urbanization of China, the female body carries a double value, labor and sex. While the female migrant struggles to survive economically as well as sexually in the urban milieu, women directors face the challenge of how to make a woman's film when mainstream production is so male-dominated. Whereas making a woman's film may compromise commercial success, achieving commercial success may require rendering the female body as a commodity. In addition, woman directors must deal with administrative censorship and the absence of an art-house network. The dilemma has trapped directors within survival strategies rather than the subjective pursuit of feminist filmmaking. As Li Yu oscillates between her concern for women's issues and for audience/market reception, female sexuality serves both ends. Women's films thus find it difficult to claim a subjective position or an independent sexual identity within the Chinese filmmaking industry.

229

CONCLUSION

Li Yu's film trilogy is an example of how female moviemakers are working persistently, albeit on the margins, to negotiate their presence in the male-dominated, commercial film industry. By foregrounding issues of female sexuality and homosexuality, directors have been able to create female images and voices counter to the mainstream. In spite of its significance, however, women's filmmaking in contemporary China presents paradoxical problems. Li's *Fish and Elephant* has to frame the lesbian relationship within the discourse of heterosexuality. *Dam Street* attempts to insert daughterly insubordination against heterosexual regulation and maternal discipline but ends in frustration; circumstances change only by fleeing them. In *Lost in Beijing*, while the migrant becomes lost in the social-economic upheaval of China's urbanization, the director is drawn toward the conflicting imperatives of commercial or feminist representation. The concern for female sexuality combined with uncertainty about feminist rhetoric leaves Li Yu's films with the contradiction of woman-centered narratives in the context of social-economic regulation. In addition, women's filmmaking faces pressure from censorship and market expectations. *Lost in Beijing* had to submit to more than fifty cuts before it could be sent to the Berlin Film Festival.[24]

The dilemma that female directors encounter is how to deconstruct the conventional representation of woman while also defining "what it means to be a woman" and thus expressing female subjectivity. With woman as the speaking subject and central image, women's filmmaking has challenged mainstream discourse but without yet defining "all points of identification (with character, image, camera) as female, feminine, or feminist."[25] When one reads Chinese women's films in terms of a conversation with feminist assumptions, one realizes the paradoxical contradictions. Also pertinent is the question of the comprehensibility of feminist readings of Chinese films. Why are Li Yu's films unable to turn marginality into counter-hegemonic discourse? Why is homosexuality located within rather than against heterosexual normality? To make matters even more confusing is the fact that Li Yu rejects feminism as a position or a discourse, as she states in an interview: "I am neither a feminist nor do I pursue gender equality in my films. Sexual difference is essentially contradictive and I have no intention of seeking resistance or changes in my works. Concern for women's issues or a female perspective is naturally embedded in myself, which doesn't require special gender consciousness."[26]

The director's stance and practice pose the question of whether in an ideological and commercially driven film industry it is possible to have a woman's cinema defined by feminism with "all identifications." We are challenged to rethink feminism under local/global conditions. "Feminism," as Dorothy Ko and Wang Zheng explain, "is always already a global discourse, and the history of its local reception is a history of the politics of translation."[27] As theories in translation or translingual practices in the era of globalization, feminist theories and practices require that we consider global feminisms in light of local social-cultural conditions. In the process of negotiation and translation, women's filmmaking, hence female discourse and enunciation, will become increasingly interwoven with multiple canons: official, mainstream, masculine, commercial, and local/global.

NOTES

1. On the concept of socialist cinema, see my chapter, "Constructing and Consuming the Revolutionary Narratives."

2. On women's cinema in the 1980s and 1990s, see my chapter, "Feminism with Chinese Characteristics?"

3. Before becoming a film director, Li Yu worked as a television anchorwoman for a local station and as a documentary film director for CCTV. *Fish and Elephant, Dam Street*, and *Lost in Beijing* are her three feature films to date. Young and talented, Li and her works have drawn notice from film festivals and film critics. *Lost in Beijing* incited controversy before it was sent to the Berlin Film Festival, and it was openly attacked by the Film Bureau after the festival.

4. *Fish and Elephant* is Li's first feature. In the film, two lesbians play themselves. In order to make this film, the first-time amateur director borrowed money, emptied her savings, and sold her house. The film did not reach a mass audience, but it received an award from the Venice Film Festival.

5. See Ruby Rich, "New Queer Cinema," 30.

6. Director's comments from Q&A session after the screening of her film, *Fish and Elephant*. See Su Qiqi, "The True Story of Two Lesbians," http://www.hsw.cn/fun/2003-08/29/content_719924.htm.

7. Carol Guess, "Que(e)rying Lesbian Identity," 19.

8. Ibid., 19.

9. Rosemary Hennessy, "Queer Theory," 964.

10. Shelly Kraicer, "Film Review," 3.

11. Queer cinema in China remains on the social-cultural margins. But film works on male gay identity and issues, both features and independent documentaries, are increasing. Zhang Yuan and Cui Zi'en are two representative figures. In comparison, films on the subject of lesbianism still have an open field.

12. On the notion of punishment as spectacle, see Michel Foucault, "The Spectacle of the Scaffold."

13. On feminism, Foucault, and the body, see Margaret A. McLaren, *Feminism, Foucault, and Embodied Subjectivity*, 81–116.

14. Judith Butler, "Performative Acts and Gender Constitution," 278.

15. Kaja Silverman, *Threshold of the Visible World*, 168.

16. On urban space as gendered space, see Alison Blunt and Gillian Rose, "Introduction."

17. Ibid., 3.

18. Ibid., 1.

19. bell hooks, *Yearning*, 206–207.

20. Luce Irigaray, *This Sex Which is Not One*, 31.

21. The lack of a counter-discourse or radical perspective despite the centrality of women's issues and female figures challenges us to rethink feminism(s) under different social-cultural conditions. In China, scholars, especially women, promote "softer" or "smiling" feminism(s) in confrontation with the "malestream" and mainstream.

22. On the notion of "female lack," see Rosalind Minsky, "Commentary on 'The Significa-
    tion of the Phallus'"; and B. J. Wray, "Performing Clits and Other Lesbian Tricks," 188.
23. In his speech to the Beijing Women's Normal College in 1923, Lu Xun challenged the au-
    dience with the question, "what else could Nora be after she left her husband's house?"
24. The SARFT (State Administration of Radio, Film and Television) required more than
    fifty cuts in the film and banned the film from screening for five months because of
    sexual scenes. There are two versions of the film, the original and the cut version fifteen
    minutes shorter.
25. Teresa De Lauretis, *Technologies of Gender*, 133.
26. See Li Yu, interview by Professor Cui Weiping, http://www.xschina.org/, April 18, 2007.
27. Dorothy Ko and Wang Zheng, "Introduction," 463.

Part IV

FEMALE WRITING, PERFORMANCE, AND
ISSUES OF CINEMATIC AGENCY

10

To Write or to Act, That Is the Question

1920S TO 1930S SHANGHAI ACTRESS-WRITERS AND THE DEATH OF THE "NEW WOMAN"

YIMAN WANG

WOMEN SCRIPTWRITERS in early cinema are conventionally seen as pioneering figures who ventured beyond acting, exercising their authorship, thereby potentially more effectively shaping the early Chinese film industry. This perception, self-evident as it may seem, categorically privileges writing over acting and fails to examine the specific circumstances and ramifications of women writing versus acting at the embryonic stage of filmmaking. In this essay, I focus on two Chinese female actresses from 1920s' and 1930s' Shanghai, Yang Naimei (1904 to 1960) and Ai Xia (1912 to 1934), each of whom wrote a script and played the female lead. Whereas the films they "authored" no longer exist, the remaining film stills, print materials, public discourses, and the actress-writers' nonfictional writings invite us to examine the promise *and* risks inherent in the role of actress-writer as played out in early twentieth-century China. Studying these print and visual "traces," I explore the ways in which the "modern working girl" image became visible, desirable, problematized, contained, and disavowed. My argument is divided into four parts that deal with three interconnected issues: (1) the history of female writing versus female acting; (2) the actress-writers' embodied enactment of the "modern working girl" image on and off the screen; and (3) the multifarious political discourses on what I call the mise-en-abyme "dead new woman" phenomenon.

THE STORIES ABOUT THE ACTRESS-WRITERS AND THE ACTRESS-WRITERS' STORIES

Strictly speaking, the two actress-writers I study, Yang Naimei and Ai Xia, were not professional scriptwriters since their scripts were a one-shot project that contributed to self-aggrandizement to a degree. However, their rendition of the "woman question" participated in the larger discursive debate on the new woman/modern girl phenomenon. Furthermore, the media coverage of their acting and writing indicated the public desire to negotiate a new mode of female visibility in tandem with new sensorial experiences born out of the emerging commercial, urban culture—a process described by Miriam Hansen in terms of "vernacular modernism."[1]

Coming from very different family backgrounds, both Yang Naimei and Ai Xia started acting in the silent era, and both were, for a period of time, affiliated with a major Shanghai film company, Star Motion Pictures Company. Contradicting her entrepreneur father's wish for her to obtain a Western education overseas, Yang Naimei joined Star Motion Pictures Company in the mid-1920s, and became a member of what Michael Chang calls the first generation of Chinese actresses.[2] This first generation was not professionally trained. Their unprecedented public visibility rendered them eccentric in the early 1920s, simultaneously alluring and scandalous. Riding on the waves of the time, Yang soon made a reputation by flaunting a fashionable lifestyle and provoking media publicity.[3] The promotion of her film, *Liangxin de fuhuo* (Confession, 1926 [adapted from Tolstoy's novel, *Resurrection*]), both cashed upon and augmented her sensational appeal by placing her on the stage, dressed like her character, performing live her character's lullaby featured in the film.

At the height of her "modern girl" fame in 1928, she left Star Motion Pictures and established her own film company, Naimei Film Studio, reputedly financed by a Shandong Province warlord with whom Yang presumably had an affair. This company produced a film, *Qi nüzi* (A Wondrous Woman, 1928), which Yang wrote as her own star vehicle. Inspired by a contemporary news story, "Miss Yu Meiyan's suicide," which concerned a woman killing herself to escape from an arranged marriage, Yang wrote *A Wondrous Woman*. Interestingly, Yang's version retained the element of the woman's death, yet changed everything else. Different from the Miss Yu Meiyan incident, that was mobilized to express the awakening female subjectivity as part of the collective quest for societal renewal, Yang Naimei's *A Wondrous Woman* portrayed a female protagonist who is both extravagant and conservative.

According to the synopsis, the female protagonist, Yu Meiying (played by Yang Naimei), is a socialite who ignores her hard-working husband and young daughter while indulging in extravagant social occasions. Suspecting that she is involved in an extramarital affair, her husband turns her away from home. She decides to "sacrifice" and obtains a divorce, then soon gets remarried to a dandy boy. Meanwhile, she gives a sum of money to a woman friend and asks the latter to help take care of her daughter. Twelve years later, Yu and her second husband return from another city and are warmly welcomed by their old friends. At the welcome party, Yu's dandy boy husband meets and tries to seduce a girl student, who turns out to be Yu's daughter. Rushing to her rescue, Yu kills her second husband and is shot by the latter's bodyguard. Yu's first husband finally understands the situation, but he only gets to see Yu right before she breathes her last.

The real-life Yu Meiyan and the fictional "wondrous woman" begin from two opposite ends, one being single and commonplace, the other being married and unruly. However, they meet the same end—death—for different reasons. The previously commonplace woman dies rebellious and single. Indeed, her suicide reinforced her insistence on singlehood and integrity. By contrast, the previously "wondrous woman" dies reincorporated—as a self-sacrificial mother. Her initial unruliness, which marks her as a decadent "modern girl," is revealed to be an extravagant surface hiding the underlying traditional feminine virtue.

The female protagonist's shedding of the wondrous extravaganza parallels Yang Naimei's life trajectory to an extent. Yang's company folded shortly after producing this film. Before long, the inception of the sound era led the Nationalist government to enforce Mandarin Chinese as the only sanctioned language for talkies. Yang Naimei, a Cantonese native raised in Shanghai who did not speak Mandarin, faded out of the industry. By 1935, Yang, the erstwhile screen idol and "modern girl" model, was listed as one of the "forgotten stars."[4] Married and relocated to Hong Kong during the war, Yang lived a declining life. During her last years, she was spotted begging on Kowloon streets. In 1960, she died penniless.

Yang's excessive allure as a first-generation actress and a modern girl/
new woman in the early twentieth-century was manifested in three commentaries written in the 1920s, 1930s, and 1940s, respectively. In *Naimei
nüshi xiaoshi* (A Sketch of Miss Naimei), written by a director, Cheng
Bugao, in 1925, shortly after Yang joined Star Motion Pictures, Yang was
described as a versatile actress, smart, lively, and trendy, who could very
effectively play a wide range of roles.[5] Ten years later, Zhang Shichuan,
the boss of Star Motion Pictures who initially recruited Yang, commented
that Yang led a loose life, and was therefore best-suited for romantic,
seductive female roles.[6] By 1942, when Yang had pretty much dwindled
into oblivion, an article announced, "Yang Naimei Made Her Comeback,"
in which the author described her as a "courageous new woman" (*xin
nüxing*) who scorned the traditional notion of feminine fidelity and did
not think much of marriage or divorce.[7]

Summarizing the discursive emphasis on her new-fangled lifestyle and
her pathetic ending, one may label her as a woman made and *un*made by
"newness." That is, she seemed to have lived out a cautionary tale prog-
nosticated in her script, *A Wondrous Woman*. If Yang's writing, acting, and
life implied the inevitability of failure regarding the new woman/modern
girl figure, what kind of new woman sensibility can we find in the case
of Ai Xia?

Ai Xia began as a stage actress affiliated with South China Theater
Society (*Nanguo jushe*), founded by Tian Han. She then joined the Leftist
Dramatists League (*Zuoyi juzuojia lianmeng*), founded in 1930, and was
then introduced to Star Motion Pictures Company in 1932. Compared
with Yang Naimei's single-shot scriptwriting, Ai was a more committed
writer of commentaries as well as scripts, and was therefore dubbed the
"writer star" (*Zuojia mingxing*). Furthermore, Ai Xia's importance as an
actress-writer needs to be considered in relation to her historical time.
Following Japan's occupation of northeast China in 1931 and the bomb-
ing of Shanghai in 1932, the leftists restrategized their position by shifting the focus from class struggle to nationalism, thereby obtaining popular support. As a result, China's sociopolitics and cultural production
were reshaped profoundly. Leftist writers and critics were solicited first
by Star Motion Pictures; other Shanghai-based film companies soon followed suit. This led to a rich turnout of left-leaning films in 1933, which
came to be known as the "Year of Leftist Cinema." Given this historical
transition and Ai Xia's affiliation with the Leftist Dramatist League, it is
not surprising that many of her writings indicated distinct sociopolitical

consciousness, which offered a new angle for studying the writer-actress phenomenon.

Let us first take a look at Ai Xia's script, *Xiandai yi nüxing* (A Woman of Today, 1933). The script portrays the fall and rise of a "modern girl," Putao (Grape), an employee of a real estate company. It begins with the setting: "the night of Shanghai, a dream of debauchery," which is followed by a generous "offer": "'Get drunk tonight when there is wine.' The world is yours." Grape is then introduced as "a little pigeon, clever, pretty, sassy . . . yet suffering from an epidemic of the time; she desires excitements, and uses excitements to fill her empty heart." A chance encounter with Yu Leng, a journalist and a married man, precipitates complications. "Boating, strolling in the park . . . nothing is missing in their homework of love." In due time, trouble erupts. Grape is fired for rejecting her boss's sexual advance; Yu Leng's wife comes to the city with their sick child. Grape eventually resorts to sleeping with her former boss in exchange for money that satisfies her desires and Yu Leng's needs—until one day, she steals a large sum of money from her boss. "Men may voluntarily give money to women. But women cannot voluntarily take money from men. Grape has committed—yes, she's committed a crime. The law allows the rich to grab money by civilized means, but prohibits the poor from *illegally* taking money from the rich." In prison, Grape meets a woman friend, An Lin, "a woman with radical thoughts and a revolutionary mind," thus also a criminal. Educated by An Lin to look beyond love and romance, Grape is finally released, spiritually as well as physically. "The prison of love can no longer constrain her. A bright road lies ahead. Keep going, the ocean is wide and the sky is open. Today's Grape is no longer yesterday's Grape."[8]

Released in 1933, the year of leftist cinema, and produced by Star Motion Pictures, the first film company that actively recruited leftist writers, Ai Xia's script, *A Woman of Today*, was unsurprisingly imbued with progressive rhetoric, as indicated in Grape's transformation from a "modern girl" with an empty heart to liberated girl with a bright future, from "yesterday's Grape" to "today's Grape." Contrary to Yang Naimei's "wondrous woman" who walks from one husband to another while remaining a self-sacrificial mother, Ai Xia's Grape walks out the prison of love—the modern "epidemic" of individualism and narcissism—presumably toward the collective bright future as envisioned by An Lin, the revolutionary girl who devotes herself to teaching workers' children.

In her afterthoughts on the script, Ai Xia explained that the leading characters' "epidemic"—the empty heart that desires excitements—stemmed

239

from the "problem of the entire society." "If they are given the right things to do, if they invest their strength and life in a proper career, they'll be too tired to need excitements, or suffering or comfort."[9] The proposal of society as the proper site for individual psychic as well as physical investment recurred in Ai Xia's instructions on how to become a good actress. In her essay, "*Gei youzhi dianying de jiemei men*" (To My Sisters Interested in Film Acting), Ai argues that film develops along with societal shifts. Thus, "an actress of her time should not only produce expressions of happiness, anger, sadness and joy; but more importantly, she should try to *recognize the various aspects of society through praxis.*" She concludes by requesting that actresses "shoulder social responsibility, and obtain clear-minded recognition of society and participate in social practice."[10]

Interestingly, in the same essay, Ai admits her own lack of social praxis, which led to her improper depiction of Yu Leng, the male protagonist in *A Woman of Today.* To redeem the weakness, she resorted to *fiction* that portrays rural bankruptcy in order to better prepare for her next film, *Feng nian* (Bumper Harvest, 1933), which narrates peasants' redoubled suffering in the year of bumper harvest because of imperialist economic incursion. Ai Xia's reliance on fiction (presumably the social exposé type), instead of physical experience of the countryside life, suggests not so much a naïve categorical confusion (i.e., mistaking fictional representation for reality) as her self-identification as a writer-reader as well as actress. Ideological transformation for her took place more through education (in the form of reading and writing) than through firsthand social praxis. As a commentator pointed out, Ai Xia demonstrated her "modern girl" quality (original English) not through materialist indulgence, but rather through her writings that "are not only beautiful, fluent and feminine, but also terse and scintillating."[11]

Positioned as an educator (vis-à-vis her "sisters" who aspired for an acting career) and an educatee (vis-à-vis advanced exposé writers), Ai Xia emphasized suturing the new female subjectivity (through writing and acting) into the broad social history. To accomplish this, she bypassed the domain of the family, which conventionally sat between the female individual and the society as a blockage as much as a linkage. This was clearly demonstrated in Ai Xia's playful beginning of "To My Sisters Interested in Film Acting." Referring to her nickname "yemao" (wild cat), Ai Xia quipped, "Too bad! How could they [the magazine editors] ask a 'Wild Cat' to talk about 'Women and Family' [the assigned title]? She is not a human being, nor has a family. Maybe she has a cat home, maybe not even that."

Having joked her way out of a woman's default task of talking about her family, Ai Xia leapt straight from an individual actress to society, thus leaving out the intermediary or barrier of the family.

Ai Xia's desire to transform female consciousness in her script and other writings corresponded with her enthusiastic expectations for the unfolding historical shifts. In "*1933 nian, wo de xiwang*" (1933—My Hope), she exclaimed, "The giant wheel of history relentlessly rolls forward; all is swept along. The films made in 1932 and 1933 are epoch-making. No one can deny that they are no longer luxury goods for the leisurely class."[12]

If Yang Naimei's "wondrous woman" in the late 1920s had to die, that is, to exchange her life for a respectable reputation as a good wife and mother, Ai Xia's early 1930s' "modern girl" was encouraged to live a radically different life, a life ready to be dedicated to (if not necessarily sacrificed for) a new social cause. If both scripts begin with an abject "modern girl" (i.e., excessive material indulgence being gendered as feminine), then this abject figure is eventually disavowed and sublimated in different manners. In "A Wondrous Woman," the disavowal and sublimation are achieved through domestication that presumes the stable authority of the nuclear, monogamous family structure. In "Modernity," they take the form of conscientization and radicalization that prioritize society and the collective good that supposedly liberate the female individual from the family.

THE RUNAWAY "NEW WOMAN/MODERN GIRL"

Both Yang's "wondrous woman" and Ai's "modern girl" clearly resulted from interlocution with contemporaneous debates on the role of women in relation to China's modernization. This role was generally defined vis-à-vis three terms: the individual subjectivity of the woman, the family of the woman, and the society made up of women as well as men. Given the Confucian doctrine that one should "*xiushen qijia zhiguo ping tianxia*" ("refine the self, stabilize the family, flourish the country and finally harmonize the world"), the three domains seem to constitute a harmonious and concatenated relationship. However, the introduction of the modern notion of individual subjectivity, combined with the emerging commercial culture that encouraged individual *jouissant* (or *jouissant* in the individual), made the harmonious relationship problematic, if not completely obsolete. An important event that fueled the early twentieth-century

Chinese debate on individual subjectivity, especially female consciousness, was the translation, adaptation, and staging of Henrik Ibsen's *A
Doll's House,* often simply known as "Nora" in China.

The introduction of Ibsen as an iconoclastic playwright began with
two essays written in 1907 by Lu Xun, the commonly recognized pioneer
of modern Chinese literature. Shortly after, Hu Shi, a would-be founding figure of the early twentieth-century New Literary Movement, was
exposed to Ibsen while studying in United States. His translation of *A
Doll's House* and theorization of Ibsenism appeared in the 1918 Ibsen special issue of *Xin qingnian* (New Youth), the flagship journal of the New
Literary Movement.[13] In March 1919, right on the eve of the students' protest against the Paris peace conference that settled World War I, yet further compromising China's sovereignty, Hu published his short comedy,
Zhongsheng dashi (The Greatest Event of My Life, 1919), which relates a
young woman's resistance of an arranged marriage and elopement with
her boyfriend.[14] Announcing that "This is the greatest event of my life;
and I should make my own decision," the female protagonist came to be
crowned "the first Nora of China." Regarding the play's debunking of the
traditional marriage system, Lu Xun observed, "the marriage that is so
crucial to 'mandarin duke and butterfly fiction' [a low-brow genre featuring dramatic and sentimental excess] now runs away like Nora."[15]

Such iconoclasm was soon distilled into a very specific image—the
runaway woman. In her examination of the shifting Nora image in early
twentieth-century Chinese literature and sociocultural discourses, Hsu
Hui-chi, a contemporary Taiwan scholar, argues that the broad parameters that Ibsen opened up for women's liberation was shrunken and
reified into a singular model of "running away" (*chuzou*) as a result of
the China-specific antifeudal compulsion.[16] The metaphor of "running
away" signaled not only the emergence of female subjectivity, but the new
consciousness of individualism on the part of the entire generation of
Chinese youth. A contemporary Chinese writer, Lin Xianzhi, aptly describes the 1919 May 4th Movement, triggered by the Paris peace conference, as a significant event of "collective running away" (*jiti chuzou*);
and "Nora thus transcended the ethical confines to become a symbol of
modern China."[17]

The optimism of individualist running-away in the 1910s soon gave
way to three forms of skepticism and critique. The first stemmed from the
increasing realization that women who ran away from home tended to fall
victim to social evils (especially prostitution). The second was concerned

with subsuming women's emerging individual subjectivity into communal and nationalist interests that acquired increasing urgency because of Japan's invasion. The third had to do with the conservative backlash engineered by the Nationalist Party's New Life Movement launched in the early 1930s, which sought to contain women by molding them into new good wives/wise mothers. By aligning the running-away woman with conservative social, political, and gender concerns, such critique continued to explore the promise of the Nora image while disavowing its subversive power.

It was in the context of the ebbing and flowing discourses on the Nora image that Yang Naimei's "wondrous woman" and Ai Xia's "Modernity" acquired symbolic significance. To the extent that they both foregrounded the damage of female self-indulgence, they invited women to reorient themselves toward the family and the society. Ai Xia, in particular, voiced her enthusiasm for the epochal shift, as figured in the sublimation of "yesterday's Grape" into "today's Grape." The desire for renewal and sublimation continued and reinforced the turn-of-the-century discursive privileging of the "new" (as opposed to the old, traditional China), as reflected in the proliferating terms such as "new woman," "new youth," "new literature," and "new citizen."

A significant difference, however, is that, unlike male authors and critics who theorized Ibsenism and only *wrote* about the Nora-like "new woman," the writer-actresses not only wrote about, but also enacted and embodied, the figure on and off the screen. It is by embodying and enacting the "new" that the writer-actresses not only fantasized but also *tested* and *challenged* the boundaries of the new woman/modern girl figure in actual social context. To borrow Kelly Oliver's terminology, they enacted the new female "subjectivity" (or agency) as a way of testing and reshaping the female "subject position" (i.e., the positioning in the power structure).[18] As a result, their biographical experiences functioned as a barometer of what was allowed, what was prohibited, thereby illustrating the tension between the production and containment of the "new."

Such embodiment was precarious in the early twentieth-century, given the fact that acting in general and female acting in particular had traditionally been viewed as conducive to promiscuity and moral debauchery. Meanwhile, the inherent female labor that resulted from the emerging urban, commercial economy was rarely recognized, let alone acknowledged. The myopic understanding of acting as degrading reinforced the ambivalence of the "new," associated both with the character and with the writer-actresses. In Ai Xia's case, the coexisting promise and risks of the "new" reached the climax with her suicide in 1934 and its chain effects (to be elaborated below). The frenzied public interpretation of the writer-actresses' experiences (especially suicide) constituted a mechanism of rationalizing, instrumentalizing, and interpellating the "new." This larger interpretive frame raised questions regarding the subjectivity or agency of the writer-actresses. If they were allowed to write, were they allowed to act; furthermore, were they allowed to interpret? How did the public conceptualize the relationship between writing and acting? What do we miss if we unquestioningly follow the conventional argument that female authorship entails more agency than mere acting? With these questions, I segue to the next part.

TO WRITE OR TO ACT—CONUNDRUM OF THE "NEW"

The question of how to *embody* the "new," making it visible and tangible, perplexed the "new woman" discourse from the very beginning. The first Chinese "new woman" literature, Hu Shi's 1919 one-act comedy, "The Greatest Event of My Life," for instance, had trouble finding a woman willing to play the running-away woman, even though the figure was optimistically welcomed by iconoclastic intellectuals (mostly male). Commenting upon the ironic gap between the intellectual vision and reality, Hu wrote self-mockingly, "since nobody dares to play this role, the role must be unrealistic."[19] This gap that stemmed from the taboo against women acting with men on the same stage made the figure of film actress an unrepresentable yet exciting scandal from the very beginning. Metaphorically speaking, a woman deigned to acting (as in Yang Naimei's case) or forced into acting for financial reasons (as was the case with a large number of early actresses) was already placing herself in the abject "new woman" position, a position signifying the loss of her proper social niche, hence stigmatization of her body. As a result, how to discipline and refine the film actress became a staple concern throughout the early twentieth-century discourses on film industry.[20] The disciplining of the unruly body involved the spectrum from the body's embellishment (including makeup, dressing, and physique), to *suzhi* (quality), *xiuyang* (cultivation), and utility (the last being manifested in discussions on the actresses' right to moonlight as dance hall hostesses, salon owners, etc.).

The compulsion to discipline the female body both on and off the screen/stage bespoke the assumption that the female body was an ineluctable material presence that determined a woman's writing and acting. That is, the materiality of the body (especially when staged in public, on and off the screen) was so overwhelming that a woman's acting would inevitably elicit some public somatic correspondences. As a result, the acting woman with a hypervisibilised body became a trope that galvanized and confronted variegated anxieties, concerns, and interests surrounding the interconnected issues of gender, nation, and class.

Under such circumstances, female writing and female acting were consistently coded *differentially* in the multilayered processes of monitoring, resignification, and interpellation.[21] Whereas acting was viewed as morally compromising and potentially degenerate, writing (along with reading) was viewed as elevating and salutary. Actresses were constantly encouraged to read good books in order to improve their quality and cultivation. Thus, Ai Xia was deemed different from the superficial, materialist Shanghai "modern girls," since her "favorite hobby [was] to sit at home and write with her vigorous pen." Moreover, her elegant writings were published widely in various art and cinema columns of major Shanghai newspapers.[22] As a new, positive model of the "modern girl," she was crowned the *"zuojia mingxing"* (writer star), an appellation that implicitly realigned her star status with writing (instead of acting).

The consistent discursive privileging of writing (and reading) over acting manifested what we may call a somatophobia, which escalated with the increasing public visibility of the female body in early twentieth-century urban China. As a result of somatophobia, writing (along with reading) was used to curtail women acting in the public sphere, and instead to place them back in the domestic private sphere. The association between female writing and domesticity was already an important phenomenon during the late Ming (mid sixteenth-century) to the high Qing era (the eighteenth to early nineteenth-century). Known as *cainü* (or talented women), female writers from elite family backgrounds formed poetry societies, published anthologies, and played an important role in constructing women's social position.[23] As Hu Ying argues in her study of the emergent new woman at the turn of the twentieth century, the talented writing women and their active role demand that we take a more nuanced look at the women's agency in Chinese history. Contrary to the conventional belief that women in feudal China constituted a monolithic figure of victim, they actually produced a stage of self-expression and community formation, which, in turn, made them an important socio-cultural presence.

Whereas I agree that the *cainü* phenomenon does indeed foreground women's heterogeneous modes of existence and production, I argue that this does not contradict the fact that women's writing came to be coded as domesticating and containing, and was thus encouraged as a means of self-cultivation and providing *service* to the family and society. A brief outlining of the discourse on self-cultivation and self-discipline can help clarify this point. As mentioned previously, a cardinal Confucian principal is precisely to start with *xiushen* (self-refining), which eventually leads to *ping tianxia* (harmonizing the world). It is important to note, however, that the concentric expansion from the self all the way to the world applied only to men; whereas the domain of women was more or less confined to the two inner circles of the self and the family. A woman invested in writing perhaps diverged from the more familiar image of a woman busy with housework. However, to the extent that an important part of homemaking was to properly educate the next generation—a task that the early twentieth-century male reformists redefined as cultivating "new citizens"—then it becomes clear that women's writing could easily become complicit with the Confucian familial ethic and gender hierarchy, even as it might also allow women the freedom of self-expression and building a quasi-sorority relationship.

Thus, both the late feudal "talented women" phenomenon and the early twentieth-century discursive emphasis on film actresses' reading and writing as a means of self-cultivation shared the agenda of containing women's excessive bodily presence in public. A 1925 magazine article rationalized this by alluding to a German experiment that proved girls were born scriptwriters since they were better at writing fiction filled with details and excitements, with little regard for logic or reasoning. The work of directorship, however, was more suitable for men, since it combined the roles of executor, diplomat, artist, dramatist, sportsman, and businessman. Thus, "even educated women are not strong enough for the job."[24] Under the pretext that women lacked the physical strength to direct, one may detect the real concern that directorship would require too much publicity that women (especially "educated women") should not be subjected to. The same could be said for women's acting, which was symptomatically missing in the article.

Thus, we should not conflate female writing with female agency. On the contrary, the actresses' writing was often highlighted and encouraged because it could serve as a disciplining mechanism. Acting, on the other hand, potentially challenged the attempt of sublimation by displaying intractable somatic materiality on and off the screen. The public's wrestling with the somatic materiality of the writer-actress resulted in the latter's literal and symbolic death.

TO LIVE, THEN TO DIE—DETRITUS OF THE BODY

Death of a star is a public event, perhaps even more so in early twentieth-century China, since the dead star was also a prototypical new woman/modern girl whose death immediately acquired social and political ramifications.

As mentioned in the first section, Yang Naimei, the 1920s modern girl/new woman, died penniless in 1960 in Hong Kong. Her era of raging glory was as brief as her one-shot script, "A Wondrous Woman." And her death analogized with the death of the "wondrous woman," with the important difference that the latter dies with a good reputation (recognized by her repentant first husband as a good wife and mother), whereas Yang's death signaled the meaninglessness and perhaps failure of the modern girl/new woman vision. The female body that ran away from her high-pressure home and flaunted high fashion was ultimately consigned to a living spectacle of shame and oblivion and then, a death devoid of any spectacle.

Contrary to Yang Naimei's eclipse, Ai Xia's suicide in 1934 at the prime of her reputation catapulted her from lifetime glory to postmortem spectacle. One year after writing and starring in her progressive film, *A Woman of Today*, Ai Xia was found dead—from an overdose of opium. As the first high-profile Chinese film actress who committed suicide, Ai instantly became a topic for fans and critics of all persuasions. One reason given for her suicide was betrayal by her lover (*shilian*), which echoed what happens to her *A Woman of Today* with a twist. Contrary to Grape, her female protagonist (or her alter ego), who sees through the illusion of love and decisively walks out of self-indulgence toward the bright future, Ai failed precisely at the last minute. This failure became the very focus of the avalanche of memorial and critical writings triggered by her death.[25]

In the effort to treat Ai's suicide as a symptomatic social event, various commentaries strived to decode Ai Xia's last words, "To live is to suffer. I now feel satisfied." "Again, I learned a lesson today/The world is full of lies/

Now I give up everything/to stay true to my conscience."²⁶ Interestingly, the diagnoses mostly followed the scenario laid out in Ai's script, namely, bifurcating the modern girl/new woman (Ai Xia herself) into the old "yesterday" and the new "today," then using the disjuncture between the two to explain Ai's failure to enact her own writing. The consensual conclusions of these commentaries were that the failure stemmed from Ai Xia's "*xiao shimin*" (petty urbanite) or "*xiao youchanzhe*" (petty bourgeois) mentality.

In the memorial issue of *The Screen Pictorial*, Li Sha described Ai Xia's eventful life as a puzzle that galvanized so many speculations that it resembled a set of funhouse mirror refractions. Upon her death, "lo and behold, the concaves and convexes all of a sudden become clear flat mirrors, showing to the world the real Ai Xia. And people all start to feel sorrow and regret."²⁷ The real Ai Xia, the author tells us, wished to jump out of what Wang Ying, who was Ai Xia's good friend, also a writer-actress, called the "*heian de dianying quan*" (dark film circle). Yet, she failed, according to the author, by being caught in a "perpetual dilemma between proactive or progressive hopes ("today" and "tomorrow") and retroactive habits ("yesterday"): "Every possibility she thought of could have delivered her from her physical and psychic suffering. Yet she didn't have the courage to pursue any of the possibilities."²⁸

Tang Na, a well-known 1930s' film critic, similarly attributed Ai Xia's failure and suicide to her "*xiao shiming genxing*" (petty urbanite mentality). Again, Ai Xia was said to have died of the "internal contradiction between the 'yesterday's I' and 'today's I,'" and the overpowering of the new Ai Xia by the old Ai Xia.²⁹ Likewise, Yin Di described the internal contradiction as between "living" versus "thinking."³⁰ Xia Yan, a major leftist cultural critic and writer involved in the Shanghai film industry in the 1930s, aligned Ai Xia's dilemma between living and thinking with the contradiction between flesh and spirit:

> "The wound of love, the contradictions between living and thinking, passion for progress and the un-remedied body, the dark, cold environment and impenetrable personality, . . . the murderous system, murderous prejudice, murderous *scandal* [original English]—a weak person exhausted by life's torment, how was it possible for her to live on?"³¹

All these commentaries unanimously lamented Ai Xia's death, while affirming its inevitability. It was inevitable because of her internal contradiction that was seen as endemic to the "new woman." Furthermore, the contradiction was attributed to the "dark society" and the microcosmic "dark film circle" that "swallowed" Ai Xia. Failing to enact the "newness" that she scripted for her character, Ai Xia had to escape via suicide.

An alternative and oppositional argument, advanced by Katherine Hui-ling Chou, a Taiwanese scholar, is that, instead of accusing Ai Xia of sticking to the retroactive "petty urbanite" and "petty bourgeois" mentality, one must consider her sexy "modern girl" persona that contradicted the leftist ideology. By leaving out Ai's urbane decadence, Chou argues, the leftist straightjacket erases the heterogeneity of the 1930s film culture, which led to "schizophrenia."[32] Chou's critique of the dogmatic leftist discourse is valid. Yet, it also risks reifying leftism into a single argument, and lumping all social conscious discourses together as leftism. Thus, the effort to rescue Ai Xia from the leftist straitjacket may end up denying her difficult (and perhaps schizophrenic) negotiation with (rather than simple opposition to) the social conscious imperative, a negotiation that was amply demonstrated in her writings (if not acting). It is her constantly negotiating stance that made Ai Xia a contended site, dead as well as alive.

Thus, instead of subsuming social conscious discourses to leftism, and holding the latter responsible for repressing heterogeneous desires and positions, I understand the rhetoric of binary (old versus new, living versus thinking, retroactive versus progressive) that governed the social diagnosis as a logical mechanism for grappling with Ai Xia's conundrum as a self-contradictory actress-writer. The logic goes: if Ai Xia wrote in one way but acted in another, that must reflect her internal contradictions between two compartments—living and thinking, body and mind, the negative and the positive. By severing one thing from another so as to disavow the negative side, this logic denied the dialectic and co-implicating relationship between the two. The side that was disavowed in the actress-writer case was her material body, which was deemed retrogressive, corrupted and corrupting, incapable of sublimation.

The exorcism of the female body was literalized in Ai Xia's suicide (i.e., self-initiated physical disappearance). The materiality of the body was further erased when it was transfixed as the perpetual *image* of death subjected to the microscopic scrutiny of social critique.[33] To recall Li Sha's vivid description of the living Ai Xia as a baffling conundrum as if refracted from a set of funhouse mirrors, contrary to her death, which made all the mirrors flat and clear, one may surmise that the mirrors became reflective (instead of refractive) because the dead Ai Xia was now finally rendered fixable (perceived as still life or rather, nonlife). In other words,

249

by making Ai Xia's death an inevitable result of the binary contradiction, the socially conscious critics (leftist or not) could finally make her body disappear as the symptom of failure.

The gender-specific death drive and imaging of death did not stop with Ai Xia. One year later in 1935, the scenario repeated itself with uncanny poignancy with the suicide of a more famous actress, Ruan Lingyu (1910 to 1935). Ruan's suicide was uncanny because of its misc-en-abyme quality. After Ai Xia's death, Cai Chusheng, a sympathetic director of the United Photoplay Service (UPS [one of the three major film companies in 1930s' Shanghai]), decided to make a film to expose how the dark society destroyed such a talented writer-actress with its slanderous and profit-driven media (especially newspapers). The resultant film was appropriately entitled *Xin nüxing* (New Woman, 1934) starring Ruan Lingyu—the tragedy queen of the 1930s. The film climaxes with the female protagonist shouting repetitively into the camera (toward the audience), "I want to live!" This climax did not simply literally put words in Ai Xia's now-silent mouth (reinforced by the formal innovation of having the intertitles emerging from her mouth in the silent movie); more importantly, it ominously anticipated Ruan Lingyu's suicide, shortly after the film's release, on the eve of her court day when she was to face her first husband's accusation of bigamy. Ruan's suicide triggered another outburst of memorial writings. The by-now definitive mourning essay was penned by no other than Lu Xun, China's first Ibsen introducer, who scathingly criticized the dark society for encouraging scandalous gossiping, which led to Ruan's death.[34]

Kristine Harris also convincingly argues that the spectacle-obsessed public domain was responsible for disseminating and reproducing the chain of dead new woman incidents.[35] To push this further, I argue that gossip-mongering (in the form of spectacle production) demonstrated precisely the continued condemnation of the acting female body in the public sphere, especially when the female body was portrayed as vacillating between the old and the new, between the urbanite/bourgeois self-indulgence and the worker/activist's social concerns. This close parallel between Ai Xia, the female protagonist, and Ruan Lingyu was demonstrated in Tang Na's review of Ruan's *New Woman*, which used the identical vocabulary that he used a year previously in commenting on Ai Xia's suicide. Just as Ai Xia failed to transform from "Yesterday's I" to "today's I,"[36] Tang described the tragedy of the "new woman" as a "tragedy of the times," stemming from the Chinese Nora's failure to transform from

"Yesterday's I" to "today's I," or to cope with the contradictions between the self and society, between thinking and living.[37]

Tang Na's identical vocabulary in commenting on the two instances (one actual, the other fictional) underscored the reproducibility and mise-en-abyme structure of the "new woman" phenomenon on and off the screen. Importantly, the two reproducible elements were the figure of Nora and the result of death/suicide. The film *New Woman* continues and complicates the Nora figure by showing how the runaway woman ends up being abandoned, defamed, and forced into prostitution, and eventually has to commit suicide. The continued interest in the Nora phenomenon peaked in the year of 1935, known as the "Nora Year" due to multiple "Nora"-related headline news. The first was the controversies over the staging of Nora in Nanjing, the capital of the Nationalist government, which led to the firing of the high school woman teacher who played Nora. The same year also witnessed the contrasting news coverage of three events: a concubine of a dead president was condemned for remarrying, a former high official was congratulated for his remarriage, and a concubine of another official was applauded for killing herself upon her husband's death.[38] Ruan Lingyu's New Woman incident thus not only continued Ai Xia's suicide in 1934, but also resonated and coincided with a series of woman-related controversies in 1935.

One important reason for the reignited debate on Nora in 1935 was the conservative New Life Movement launched by the Nationalist Party in 1933. Amalgamating selected Confucian doctrines and modern state regimentation, the New Life Movement curtailed excessive commercialization and encouraged ideological conformity. Women were asked to cut down on (if not totally give up) their makeup and fashion expenses, and to refine themselves into a new type of good wives/wise mothers. The conservative effect of the government-sponsored regimentation of women's everyday practices in the public as well as private spheres becomes even more conspicuous once we relate it to the European campaign for women to go back home in emerging fascist countries like Italy.

Whereas this conservative regimentation had a very different historical imperative from that of the "talented women" phenomenon in late-imperial China, they shared the same somatophobia, which led to differential coding of writing women and acting women. Whereas writing anchored a woman at home, acting sent a woman out onto the public stage/screen. Furthermore, as the context of writing shifted with time, the ramifications of writing (and reading) also changed. Whereas writing for self-cultivation

251

and homemaking was approved, writing for personal fame or making a living was disparaged. The film *New Woman* shows that the female protagonist's fall into degeneration precisely coincides with her book entering into the public circulation system for monetary purposes. The money-oriented circulation of her book implicitly prefigures the prostitution of her body (the carnal form of material circulation and exchange). In that sense, the film suggests a cautionary tale, warning "new woman" against activities that might involve her in the commercial circulation system in which her body would be treated as the ultimate commodity. By this logic, the danger of acting consisted precisely in its being a conspicuous form of money-driven carnal circulation. Such danger could also be reconceptualized as its transgressive power that contributed to problematizing and undermining the gender-biased social regime.

To return to my initial inquiry regarding the ramifications of writing and acting practiced by the early twentieth-century writer-actresses, I conclude that writing did not necessarily endow the actress with more agency in the filmmaking processes; rather the social functions of women's reading, writing, and acting varied according to specific contexts. My analysis demonstrates that writing for self-cultivation was applauded; writing for money was considered suspicious; whereas flaunting and/or living off her body (as an actress or a prostitute) was punishable by (self-inflicted) death (hence the reproduction of the dead "new woman" incident). The honorable appellation of "writer-actress" or "writer star" may end up serving to contain the perceived threat posed by women's acting and the related somatic visibility in the public sphere. In other words, by privileging women's writing over acting unconditionally, one runs the risk of erasing modern girl/new woman's transgressive power, rather than encouraging female authorship.

NOTES

1. For Hansen's discussion of vernacular modernism in relation to early Chinese film actresses, see her, "Fallen Women, Rising Stars, New Horizons: Shanghai Silent Film and Vernacular Modernism," *Film Quarterly* 54, no. 1 (fall 2000), 10–22.

2. Michael G. Chang, "The Good, the Bad, and the Beautiful: Movie Actresses and Public Discourse in Shanghai, 1920s–1930s," in Yingjin Zhang ed., *Cinema and Urban Culture in Shanghai, 1922–1943* (Palo Alto, CA: Stanford University Press, 1999), 128–159.

3. She was reputedly the first Chinese woman who owned a car and who fixed her stocking garter in public.

4. "Bei wangji le de ren" (Forgotten Stars of Chinese Screen) in *Liangyou* (Young Companion), no. 105 (May, 1935).

5. Cheng Bugao, "Naimei nüshi xiaoshi" (A Sketch of Miss Naimei).

6. Zhang Shichuan, "Zi wo daoyan yilai" (Since I Started Directing), 10.

7. "Yang Naimei juantu chonglai" (Yang Naimei Made Her Comeback), n.p.

8. Ai Xia, "Xiandai yi nüxing" (Modernity), 3–4.

9. Ai Xia, "Wo de lian'ai guan" (My View on Love), 4.

10. Ai Xia, "Gei youzhi dianying de jiemei men" (To My Sisters Interested in Film Acting), 1–3.

11. Li Hen, "Kan! Ai Xia buda zizhao de kougong" (Look! Ai Xia's Voluntary Confession), 2.

12. Ai Xia, "1933 nian, wo de xiwang" (1933–My Hope).

13. *Xin qingnian* (New Youth) 4, no. 6 (June 15, 1918), Ibsen special issue.

14. Hu Shi, "Zhongsheng dashi" (The Greatest Event of My Life).

15. Lu Xun, "Shanghai wenyi zhi yipie" (A Glance at Shanghai Literature and Art), 170.

16. Hsu Hui-Chi, *Nuola zai zhongguo*, ("Nora" in China), 113.

17. Lin Xianzhi, "Nuola" (Nora), 133.

18. Kelly Oliver, *Witnessing, Beyond Recognition*, 24.

19. Hsu, *Nuola zai zhongguo*, 171.

253

20. See Michael Chang, "The Good, the Bad, and the Beautiful."

21. Granted, male writing and acting were also historically differentlated, with acting being coded as inferior, subservient, and morally suspicious. Nevertheless, relative to female acting, male acting had a publicly recognized tradition; top male actors easily became the center of public admiration, and even served as China's de facto cultural diplomat (as illustrated by Mei Lanfang's widely publicized tour in United States and the Soviet Union). This fostered a more receptive environment in early twentieth-century when male acting was required in modern spoken drama and cinema. Contrary to this, female acting was considered so problematic that early female roles on stage *and* screen were essayed by male actors.

22. Li, "Kan! Ai Xia buda zizhao de kougong," 2.

23. See works by Dorothy Ko, *Teachers of the Inner Chambers*; Susan Mann, *Precious Records*.

24. Shen Hao, trans., *Nüzi yu daoyanjia* (Women and Directors), 1–2. The author/translator claimed that the article was taken from an American film magazine, without, however, providing the reference.

25. See the special memorial issue published by *Dianying huabao* (The Screen Pictorial), no. 9 (March 1934).

26. "Shouwei zisha de nü mingxing Ai Xia" (Ai Xia—The First Female Star Who Committed Suicide), 203.

27. Li Sha, "Yi Aixia nüshi" (Remembering Miss Ai Xia), 4–5.

28. Ibid., 4–5.

29. Tang Na, "Ai Xia zhi zi" (The Death of Ai Xia), 5.

30. Yin Di, "The Death of Ai Xia," in *The Screen Pictorial* (Dianying huabao), no. 9 (March, 1934), 23.

31. Xia Yan, "Shui zhi Ai Xia yu si?" (Who Killed Ai Xia?), n.p.

32. Katherine Hui-ling Chou, *Biaoyan zhongguo* (Performing China), 88.

33. A contemporary journalist, Mao Fangmei, who worked for a major Shanghai newspaper, *Chen bao* (Morning Paper), obtained court permission to shoot a picture of Ai Xia lying in state. This picture was widely disseminated as Ai Xia's final image. See Chou, *Biaoyan zhongguo*, p. 88, note 49. Chou sees this as indicative of the public necrophilia for the female star. In my context, I suggest that the visual fixation complemented the discursive obsession with her suicide as yet another form of transfixing Ai Xia into an ultimate image of death.

34. Lu Xun (signed as Zhao Lingyi), "Lun 'Renyan kewei'" (On "Human Gossip Is Indeed Fearsome").

35. See Kristine Harris, "The *New Woman* Incident." Miriam Hansen also discusses this incident in her study of early Chinese actresses and their negotiation with vernacular modernity in "Fallen Women, Rising Stars, New Horizons."

36. Tang Na, "Ai Xia zhi zi," 5.

37. Tang Na, "Lun 'xin nüxing' de piping" (My Critique of *New Woman*), 352.

38. Hsu, *Nuola zai zhongguo*, 328–347.

11

Gender, Genre, and Performance in Eileen Chang's Films

EQUIVOCAL CONTRASTS ACROSS THE PRINT-SCREEN DIVIDE

YINGJIN ZHANG

"AN EXTRAORDINARY GENIUS" FROM WRITING TO REWRITING

Eileen Chang (Zhang Ailing, 1920–1995) envisioned a dismal world in 1947: "On the future wasteland, among ruined walls and debris, only a woman like *huadan* from the *bengbeng* theater can survive with resolution, for she alone feels at home everywhere, in any age and any society."[1] This vision contains threefold insight. First, as a recurring motif, *performance* is productive in Eileen Chang's entire writing career, from her overnight rise to fame in Japanese-occupied Shanghai to her solitary self-confinement in post–Cold War Los Angeles. Second, as a distinctive gender choice, Chang's preference for *female* performance is resilient and adaptable to her apocalyptic view of a collapsed civilization in literary works and to her fantastic reimagination of Hong Kong cosmopolitanism in screenwriting. Third, in terms of genre implication, *comedy* delivered by the female performer holds surreptitious attraction for the local audience despite the genre's alleged "lowly taste" or "junk" status, and with her characteristically desolate gesture, Chang presents the transgressive comic female as the only human representative capable of surviving the ruined world anywhere, any time.[2]

Gender, genre, and performance, therefore, constitute three key terms in Chang's creative career, not only her celebrated works of fiction and prose essays but also her much-neglected screenwriting.

This chapter investigates the imbrication of gender, genre, and performance in Chang's conscientious navigation across the print-screen divide. In sharp contrast to her overwhelmingly desolate and frequently sadomasochist literary stories, Chang developed a fresh entertaining style in her film comedies set in Shanghai and Hong Kong from the late 1940s to the early 1960s. In her screen world, genre issues take center stage while her signature gender critique has subsided considerably, and patriarchal values seem to rule her characters and leave little room for the kind of feminist subversion regularly attributed to her literary works. How to account for Chang's drastic change across the print-screen divide and how to appraise her contribution to Chinese cinema remain daunting challenges. This chapter demonstrates that the specificities of media and genre shaped Chang's film world, and crossing the print-screen divide expanded her artistic repertoire rather than diminishing her creative status. Through repetition and regeneration, female performance continued to mediate her genre choices and gender questions and illuminated her favorite strategy of "equivocal contrast" (a concept elaborated later) in and across literature and film.

For many critics, Eileen Chang's reputation rests squarely on her literary works. After publishing *A History of Modern Chinese Fiction* in 1961, C. T. Hsia continued to promote Chang as "an extraordinary genius," "the most excellent writer since May Fourth," "a must-read" Chinese author who ranks among the top Chinese writers of all time and who is comparable to a few first-rate modern Western authors.[3] Since the early 1990s, there has been a veritable boom of scholarship on Chang (or *Zhangxue*), but most scholars focus on her wartime literary writing, especially those from 1943 to 1945. This narrow focus raises a serious question regarding her postwar production. Although some have blamed the precarious postwar political circumstances for the "decline" in Chang's literary output, others cannot help but lament her sagging creativity, above all after she had decided to "leave her beloved city and country and become a permanent exile."[4] Her departure from Shanghai was followed reputedly by her "crisis of creativity caused by dislocation and exile from her familiar environment."[5]

However, Chang never stopped writing after she immigrated to Hong Kong in July 1952 and from there to the United States in the autumn of

256

1955. Indeed, she was even willing to publish "anti-Communist" novels in both Chinese and English, a kind of political venture she had avoided during the war but one she was compelled to accept during the Cold War. Furthermore, a significant part of her subsequent literary oeuvre consists of *rewriting* her own works—from short story to novel, from novel to novella, from novella to stage drama and screenplay, from screenplay to novella, from English to Chinese and vice versa, sometimes back and forth several times for decades. This constitutes an exceptional case in twentieth-century China whereby an established writer would go on rewriting her own stories repeatedly, often across linguistic and artistic media.

Admittedly, this chapter is not a study of Chang's lifelong obsession with rewriting. Nor does it concern a successive wave of rewritings spun off from her own writing and rewriting, such as adaptations of her works to film, stage, and radio by other artists, or various types of writing related to her, including a proliferation of Internet writings from countless Chang fans (or *Zhang mi*) around the world. Instead, this chapter is devoted to one special kind of Chang's writing that has largely escaped scholarly attention until the late 1990s: her neglected career in screenwriting.

257

A NEGLECTED CAREER IN SCREENWRITING: FROM SHANGHAI TO HONG KONG

Eileen Chang's fascination with film came in her childhood years, and she penned her first film article at the age of seventeen. Even at the height of her wartime literary career in 1943, she still found time to contribute film reviews to *The XXth Century*, an English monthly magazine edited by Kaus Mehnert and published in Shanghai from October 1941 to May 1945. For some scholars, Chang's film reviews reflect her insights into captivating human dramas, and they adequately prepared for her successful postwar screenwriting.[6]

In the context of Chinese film history, Chang's screenplays can be divided into two periods. First, in postwar Shanghai, she contributed the following titles to Wenhua Film Company, a private enterprise known for its quality films: *Buliao qing* (Love Without End, 1947), *Taitai wansui* (Long Live the Wife, 1947), *Aile zhongnian* (Sorrows and Joys at Middle Age, 1949), and *Jinsuo ji* (The Golden Cangue, not produced). The first three films were directed by Sang Hu and released to popular acclaim.

The screenplay of *Sorrows and Joys at Middle Age* is generally credited to Sang Hu alone, but Stephen Soong (Song Qi, a.k.a. Lin Yiliang) attributed it to Chang.[7] Citing Chang's letter dated January 2, 1990, Su Weizhen confirms Chang's authorship in *Sorrows and Joys at Middle Age*. Although Chang refused to accept the royalty payment from the screenplay's republication in Taiwan in October 1990 and claimed that her memory of the film was vague, she had been able to recall in an earlier letter to Su Weizhen such film details as the humorous performance by Shi Hui.[8] Finally, as the last screenplay from this postwar period, *The Golden Cangue* is based on Chang's novella of the same title, but the film was never produced, and the script is presumed lost.

Second, shortly after she emigrated to the United States, Chang started contributing screenplays to MP&GI (Motion Picture & General Investment, *Dianying maoye* or *Dianmao*) in Hong Kong from the late 1950s to the early 1960s and helped establish MP&GI as a rising Mandarin filmmaking powerhouse specializing in romantic youth and urban modernity. Chang's prolific screenplays in the MP&GI period include the following: *Qingchang ru zhangchang* (The Battle of Love, 1957), *Rencai liangde* (A Tale of Two Wives, 1957), *Taohua yun* (The Wayward Husband, 1958), *Liuyue xinniang* (June Bride, 1960), *Nanbei yijia qin* (The Greatest Wedding on Earth, 1964), *Xiao ernü* (Father Takes a Bride, 1963), *Nanbei xi xiangfeng* (The Greatest Love Affair on Earth, 1962), *Yiqu nanwang* (Please Remember Me, 1964), *Hungui lihen tian* (Sorrowful Separation, not produced), and *Hongloumeng* (Dream of the Red Chamber, in two parts, not produced).

The Battle of Love is based on *The Tender Trap* (1954), an American stage play by Max Shulman, while *The Greatest Love Affair on Earth* is based on *Charley's Aunt* (1892), a popular British play by Brandon Thomas. Both plays were adapted into Hollywood productions, *The Tender Trap* (1955) and *Charley's Aunt* (1941). Likewise, *Please Remember Me* is Chang's rewriting based on the Hollywood picture *Waterloo Bridge* (1940), and *Sorrowful Separation* is based on another Hollywood production, *Wuthering Heights* (1939), adapted from the 1846 novel by Emily Brontë. Neither *Sorrowful Separation* nor *Dream of the Red Chamber* was produced, and the latter is presumed lost.

With fourteen screenplays, Chang would have been "a heavyweight screenwriter," as Zhou Fenling suggests.[9] However, until recently, most scholars neglected her substantial contribution to Chinese cinema. One reason for such neglect is that the majority of scholars prefer Chang's literary works to her screenplays, and this preference derives from an entrenched prejudice against film, a dismissible form of entertainment, never quite comparable to literature that has enjoyed an elite status in Chinese culture for thousands of years. Another reason is that some scholars are quite uneasy with the financial motivation behind Chang's screen ventures in both periods. First, thanks to her legendary short-lived marriage to Hu Lancheng, a notorious pro-Japanese man of letters, Chang was accused of being a "female traitor" after the war, so screenwriting became an expedient source of income for her when most editors avoided publishing her literary works.[10] Second, in the United States, neither Chang nor her playwright husband, Ferdinand Reyher, had a regular income, and their situation turned worse when he suffered a stroke in 1961. William Tay thus justifies Chang's second crossing to the screen: "The writing of these screenplays had something to do with Reyher's poor health and their financial problems. By the mid-1960s, Reyher was partially paralyzed."[11] Fortunately, through Stephen Soong's arrangement, Chang was "paid $800-1,000 per screenplay, one of the highest fees paid any writer in Hong Kong" at the time.[12]

259

FILM COMEDIES IN CONTENTION: FROM ROMANTIC TO SLAPSTICK

The specter of financial motivation might have discouraged serious scholarly attention to Eileen Chang's screenwriting up to a decade ago. Two literary critics started to publish on Chang's film career in 1999, and they represent two substantially different views. On the positive side, William Tay contends that Chang's intention to problematize gender relations in Chinese societies continued through her Shanghai–Hong Kong film career. Tay is the first to suggest the connection between Chang's screenwriting and "romantic screwball comedy," a Hollywood genre popular in the 1930s and 1940s, and he is instrumental in arranging the republication of Chang's screenplays in the 1990s. Tay is impressed by Chang's accomplishment and speculates that, if she were to direct her screenplays, she would have fit Andrew Sarris's "auteur theory" perfectly.[13]

On the negative side, Leo Lee dismisses Chang's Hong Kong products: "these screenplays are not on a par with Chang's earlier work in Shanghai" because they are too much "driven by commercial intent" and their "comic flair . . . borders on the slapstick."[14] Lee complains,

"The well-guarded space of domestic comfort in *Long Live the Wife* is replaced by one of comic tension and conflict. Occasionally, as in *Father Takes a Bride*, such tensions erupt into near tragedy, and the happy ending seems rather forced."[15] Lee's disappointment goes further: "Whereas the screwball comedies still rely on 'talk,' on the clever repartee between the hero and heroine whose humor and sophistication are taken for granted, the slapstick situations in the Hong Kong films are sometimes intentionally vulgar (including scenes of a male character played by Leong Sing-por, dressed up in drag), as they are designed to generate laughter."[16] The vulgarity in question refers to *The Greatest Love Affair on Earth,* in which a middle-aged father appears in female drag, passing as a rich overseas Chinese woman and creating hilarious situations of courtship and pursuit. Nonetheless, such vulgarity is not Chang's invention, for the film's original source, *Charley's Aunt,* already features male drag as indispensable to a comedy of mistaken identities set in Oxford, England, in 1890.

Whatever "deficiency" one finds in Hong Kong comedies based on her screenplays, Chang might assume partial responsibility because she did not speak Cantonese and did not understand Cantonese custom well enough to create completely authentic local situations. For instance, as a MP&GI producer, Stephen Soong rewrote the Cantonese part of the dialogue for some of Chang's scripts. Director Wang Tianlin remembers Soong's warnings against altering any of Chang's Mandarin dialogue, although in reality Wang felt obliged to change a key scene in *Father Takes a Bride,* in which Hong Kong's custom of selling crabs in small bamboo cages is used instead of the Shanghai custom of merely wrapping crabs with strings. Indeed, Wang admitted to taking liberty with Cantonese dialogue while shooting Chang's comedies.[17]

Returning to Leo Lee's objection to Chang's Hong Kong comedies, one suspects that a conventional two-tiered media/genre value system might be at work: first, the primacy of literature over film; second, romantic comedy over slapstick comedy. Even more troubling may be the unstated two-tiered cultural-linguistic judgment: Mandarin over Cantonese. A third, three-tiered geocultural hierarchy is also visible: Hollywood over Shanghai over Hong Kong. To endorse Hollywood's authenticity and originality, Lee has furnished a list of eighteen Hollywood high or screwball comedies and domestic dramas from 1932 to 1950, which he believes Eileen Chang might have watched, and which at least "represents the essence of comedies and ethical dramas during Chang's era."[18]

Lee's negative assessment of Chang's Hong Kong comedies gives rise to a series of questions. What genre distinctions exist among a variety of film comedies? What gender implications are derived from genre choices? How does Eileen Chang negotiate such gender differences and genre implications in her venture across the print-screen divide? How do we evaluate the apparent contrast between her desolate gesture to a literary world plagued by decadence, depression, deformity, death, and destruction, on the one hand, and her spirited pursuit of a screen world of lighthearted humor, sensual pleasure, happy ending, and dream fulfillment on the other? Furthermore, how does her screen performance impact our perceptions of her literary works?

GENRE CHOICES: COMEDY, MELODRAMA, WOMAN'S FILM

As a genre, film comedy is assigned a negligible place in Chinese film history, but Chang's special relationship to film comedy deserves consideration. As early as 1943, she pointed out in a film review the incongruity between the general public's condescending attitude toward film comedy and our incontrollable tendency to laugh as part of human nature. For her, a good comedy should be "casual and spontaneous" and should "naturally flow with tears."[19] Sure enough, these qualities of performative improvisation and bittersweet sentiments would find their way into her screenplays.

We have encountered recent references to Chang's screenplays as "romantic screwball comedy" and "slapstick comedy," but "high comedy" was already suggested in 1947. Impressed by her newspaper article published ten days before the film's premiere in Shanghai, Hong Shen expressed his enthusiasm over *Long Live the Wife* and predicted that Chang "would become one of the most excellent writers of 'High Comedy' in our age."[20] With high comedy, romantic comedy, and slapstick comedy contending for the designation of Chang's films, a brief detour through Hollywood comedy genres is in order.

"High comedy, also known as comedy of manners, was invented by the British Restoration playwrights in the late seventeenth century" to showcase the aristocratic taste, especially through its "ingeniously sculpted, wittily curlicued language"; but thanks to a peculiarly American approach to class, in high comedy of American theater and movies, two otherwise conflicting "stances—traditional/conservative and American/

261

democratic—end up being compromised."[21] Steve Vineberg situates high comedy in a spectrum of comic genres familiar to American audiences (e.g., romantic comedy, situation comedy) and reminds us: "the boundaries that separate these comic genres are extremely fluid, and often movie comedy thrives on combinations of several different genres."[22] For instance, high comedy is often mixed with romantic comedy.

Most people consider romantic comedy and screwball comedy interchangeable, but Wes Gehring argues that they are two distinct genres. Originally a baseball term, "screwball" describes both an oddball player and "any pitched ball that moves in an unusual or unexpected way"; when carried over to film, "screwball comedy uses nutty behavior as a prism through which to view a topsy-turvy period in American history."[23] Whereas screwball comedy builds on farce and showcases physical comedy and ludicrous events, romantic comedy foregrounds love and is more reality-based, with little or no slapstick. Since love is treated "hardly more significant than a board game" by screwball comedy, its male character "must suffer through a ritualistic humiliation at the hands of the zany heroine and/or the plot itself," and its outcome is "essentially the same: an eccentrically comic battle of sexes, with the male generally losing."[24] With little modification, these words aptly describe gender implications in Chang's Hong Kong comedies, especially *The Battle of Love* and *June Bride*.

In addition to comedy, two other film genres are evoked to define Chang's screenwriting. First, Zhou Fenling foregrounds Chang's inclination for *melodrama,* and given melodrama's historical connection to the rise of middle classes in the West, Zhou portrays Chang as a "spokesperson" for Chinese middle classes.[25] Second, Poshek Fu points to *woman's film*—a popular Hollywood genre in the 1940s—as another source of inspiration for Chang, although he likewise recognizes that "movies about woman often take the form of romantic comedy—both genres provide woman a sympathetic space for resistance against prevalent gender hierarchy."[26] Mary Ann Doane's characterization of woman's film of the 1940s in Hollywood is instructive in this regard; they "deal with a female protagonist and often appear to allow her significant access to point of view structures and the enunciative level of the filmic discourse. They treat problems defined as 'female' (problems revolving around domestic life, the family, children, self-sacrifice . . .), and, most crucially, are directed toward a female audience."[27] Not surprisingly, many titles in Hollywood woman's film also fall in the category of melodrama, from maternal melodrama to romantic melodrama and love story, all of which are Chang's screen favorites as well.

Regardless of genre designations, a relatively strong female perspective and a sharp focus on gender differences distinguish the majority of Chang's screenplays. Although most of her comedies conclude with a happy ending in which patriarchal values are reinstated or at least reacknowledged, a careful reading of her narrative strategy reveals Chang's exposure of pervasive gender inequality in the Chinese patriarchal society. *Long Live the Wife* and *The Battle of Love* are among her critics' favorites. In the next two sections, we shall analyze these two films in terms of gender questions and performance acts, taking into consideration such topics as matriarchy/patriarchy and transgression/repression.

GENDER QUESTIONS: MATRIARCHY/PATRIARCHY IN *LONG LIVE THE WIFE*

263

As Peggy Chiao argues, in its "subversion and disintegration" of the age-old feudal patriarchy and its support of female independence, *Long Live the Wife* is more "progressive" and more realistic than many apparently revolutionary films in China. *Long Live the Wife* interrogates the traditional institution of marriage and rebels against repressive moral values.[28] The more Eileen Chang dwells on the sheer importance of being always virtuous in a fundamentally corrupt patriarchal world, the more effectively the film's subversive force is put to work. The dilemma of gender difference facing women protagonists in *Long Live the Wife* is exactly what Chang pinpoints as the ludicrous double standards for "female virtues" in a patriarchal society: "how to joyously uphold the principle of monogamy in front of a husband who believes in polygamy."[29]

Two male scholars also emphasize the subversive potential of *Long Live the Wife*. For William Tay, the film's narrative revolves around the imminent downfall of patriarchy under the assault of *femme fatales* like Shi Mimi, a socialite who specializes in seducing males with her charms. Meanwhile, as a resourceful "virtuous wife" who habitually tells lies to cover up family tensions, Chen Sizhen always comes at a critical moment to the rescue of her debauched husband and father. Tay's reading foregrounds the amazing abilities of the two principal women characters and suggests that the film may convey Chang's endorsement of the "replacement" of patriarchy by matriarchy in times of crisis.[30] Law

Kar concurs with Tay and states: "To the average audience, *Long Live the Wife* comes across as a light, even trivial family comedy with romantic overtones. To a more appreciative audience, the film describes the impending collapse of male, patriarchal authority, and woman's attempt to extricate herself from this social predicament (as the lead female character Chen Sizhen does) and forge her own way (as represented by the socialite Shi Mimi)."[31]

Nonetheless, not all recent readings of *Long Live the Wife* emphasize Chang's challenge to patriarchy. Poshek Fu considers this Shanghai comedy "less a feminist film and more a reflection of Chang's long-held views on the irony and multiplicity of the human condition."[32] Fu further reasons, "Comedy is thus a fitting genre for Chang because it requires a moral and emotional distance from life or individual fate so that one can laugh at it."[33] Like Fu, Leo Lee opines that Chang's "philosophy of life as comedy" engages "sorrows, joys, separations, and reunions" and her intention is rarely to privilege one aspect at the expense of the other but rather to work out compromises or complementarities between the otherwise opposing forces. Lee sees the primary function of Chang's comedy as that of "repair"—repairing a flawed relationship or a troubled marriage, as symbolized by Sizhen's failed effort to hide pieces of a broken bowl from her mother-in-law at the beginning of *Long Live the Wife*. Indeed, Lee asserts that, in Chinese society, such repair jobs belong to women rather than men, and the quintessential Chinese family ethics dictates that, in domestic life, a woman tries not so much to obtain her own happiness as to derive her satisfaction from the process of repairing her family members' blemishes so that the entire family obtains happiness. As Lee contends, by depicting Sizhen as constantly "supplementing" her father's and husband's insufficiencies, Chang has elevated her comedy to an ethical level higher than that of Western comedy.[34]

In a sense, Lee's argument on the self-sacrificing Chinese wife and her dutiful observance of ethical values sounds rather trite, but it underscores two important factors in our gender/genre consideration. First, as typical of comedy in general and romantic comedy in particular, *compromise* is deployed as the ultimate solution to conflicts arising from stark differences in gender, class, personality, and so on. The Hollywood romance of *It Happened One Night*, for example, can be read as a metaphor for "any kind of reconciliation—between the classes, the genders, the generations; between Depression anxiety and happy-go-lucky optimism."[35]

Hollywood romantic comedy, therefore, is a fundamentally conservative genre, privileging "social regeneration through coupling" to "self-actualization through uncoupling."[36] Given such genre constraint on gender choices, Shizhen's decision to seek reconciliation rather than divorce her husband matches the expectation of a romantic comedy. Second, the comedy's predilection for compromise dovetails Chang's vision of harmony. For her, it is "the placid and static aspects of life"—rather than heroic struggles—that captures "the numinous essence of humanity" or even "the essence of femininity."[37] Femininity, rather than matriarchy, was arguably a pressing gender issue that preoccupied Chang in the late 1940s. "In reality," she insisted, "people only engage in struggle in order to attain harmony."[38]

Unfortunately, neither harmony nor femininity helped the critical reception of Long Live the Wife in December 1947. After reading negative reviews of Love Without End in April 1947, which were punctuated with derogatory phrases such as "selfish," "weak," "pessimist," "empty," "vulgar," "erroneous," and "unpardonable," Chang intervened by publishing a newspaper article in which she dismisses anything extraordinary about her housewife protagonist in Long Live the Wife.[39] Nonetheless, Chang's preemptive effort failed, as the subsequent reviews proved negative again, dismissing the film as catering to "petty urbanites," censuring Chang for manufacturing cheap sympathy, ignoring human dignity, and winning the audience's tears with intelligent technique. Even Hong Shen expressed disappointment at Chang's failure to "discipline" the wayward husband and to take the educational function of cinema seriously.[40]

The historical irony remains that Chang's preference for harmony did not sit well in a field of cultural production preoccupied with war, revolution, and class struggle, a field in which gender questions were sidetracked and women writers marginalized. Given this irony, we may examine the ending of Long Live the Wife where Shizhen and her husband overhear Mimi seducing another middle-aged man. A close-up shot captures Mimi's alluring smile, her winking eye, and her sexy voice in which she retells her "secret" story in exactly the same way as she told it to Shizhen's husband not long ago: "I like movies but I am also afraid of watching them. A tragic movie would remind me of my unfortunate life." This ending is both conservative and potentially radical. It is conservative because Shizhen's threat of divorce is neutralized, and Mimi turns out to be a hooligan's wife, a victim of domestic violence. Yet, the ending is radical in that the domestic harmony in patriarchy is anything but stable or harmonious; worse still, Mimi's repetitive act signals another seduction to come, another performance of female transgression.

PERFORMANCE ACTS: TRANSGRESSION/REPRESSION IN *THE BATTLE OF LOVE*

A decade after *Long Live the Wife*, Chang would work out a much more radical scenario of female transgression in *The Battle of Love*—radical because her typical narrative of a married man between two (un)married women is replaced with a new narrative of an unmarried woman who simultaneously toys with three unmarried men. Set in Hong Kong, *The Battle of Love* plays directly to male fantasies and depicts the female protagonist Ye Weifang as a mischievous, yet sophisticated, *femme fatale*. On the one hand, she pretends to be satisfied as a "passive" object of male desire and invites voyeurism and fetishism through deliberate exhibitionist acts. On the other hand, she is self-confident and aggressive in that she knows how to manipulate male desires to her advantage, always returning the male gaze and eventually chasing after her own love interest.

As observed earlier, the screwball comedy male must suffer a ritualistic humiliation at the hands of the zany heroine, but Chang's scenario of transgression is so radical that Ye humiliates not just one male suitor but three. Her male cousin Shi Rongsheng warns He Qihua, a professor of archaeology, against the danger of pursuing Ye: "she is a flirt and loves lots of fun. . . . If anyone is serious about her, he is bound to be disappointed."[41] Yet, the fun of romantic comedy is such that we know Professor He—along with his perceived rival Tao Wenbing, a vainglorious office clerk—will suffer at Ye's hand. Only when He and Tao, after a slapstick fight, learn in utter disappointment that Ye has said the same words separately to each of them—"I am soft-hearted" and "can't bear to step on ants"—do they reluctantly admit that they have been "toyed with" all along and are "completely defeated" in the battle of love.

The turning point comes when three male characters confront Ye and force her to confess whom she loves. Ye descends a few steps down the stairways, and the camera assumes her point of view in a high-angle shot of her three dwarfed suitors. In a close-up shot, she declares that she loves her cousin Shi. According to the screenplay, Shi is frightened by Ye's declaration because he cannot provide her the luxury lifestyle she has enjoyed with her rich family. He cannot resist her sexual appeal, either, so he imagines that he must escape to Rangoon and become a monk. The next day, just as Shi tries to sneak out of the villa, Ye catches him, and the film ends with Ye triumphantly hugging Shi in his car.

Zhou Fenling argues that, from three males chasing a female in the first part of the film to a female chasing a male in the second part, Chang has subverted the conventional gender hierarchy by making Ye not only a dynamic agent but also a conqueror in the battle of love.[42] Nevertheless, Chang's vision of gender critique may have been compromised by male directors. In Chang's screenplay, Shi is terrified by Ye's aggressive sexuality and desperately seeks help from his male friends. Right before Ye's confession of love, Shi even joins He and Tao in raising arms to shout, "all men of the world unite, down with women!"[43] In the finished film, such insecure male emotions and outrageous male solidarity are gone. Instead, we are treated with at least three added sequences of patriarchal teaching, in which Shi instructs Ye not to seek pleasures in seducing every eligible bachelor she meets. For P. K. Leung, Chang's urban romance and youth culture "appeared to be too modern for the '50s" Hong Kong, so her written scenes of the lovers hugging and kissing each other were cut in the finished film, and her "sensitive discussion of the gender issue was given a discount."[44]

267

Discrepancies between Chang's screenplay and the finished film pinpoint male attempts at containing transgressive female sexuality. To cite another example: in Chang's screenplay, Tao suffers an initial humiliation when he brings Ye to her family's villa and shows it off as his own. Tao cannot find his way around and falls into an indoor swimming pool. When he runs into a bedroom to dry up, he is confronted with a family picture of Ye and her parents and sister. He escapes the villa in his car amidst Ye's laughter. When he stops by the roadside and takes out a picture of him and Ye, she suddenly opens her mouth and laughs at him sarcastically. Tao cannot tolerate it anymore and tears the picture to pieces—a symbolic gesture to disavow the castration threat.

Understandably, the scene of tearing the picture is absent in the finished film. However, the film still suggests the return of the repressed male phobia in its ending. Just as Shi drives his car out of the villa under the impression that he has safely evaded Ye, she pops her head up from the back seat and hugs him, and panic-stricken Shi almost loses control of his steering wheel and swerves desperately to avoid a head-on collision with an approaching car. Ye's unexpected reappearance proves that the transgressive female cannot be simply wished away, and the male strategy of containment no longer works effectively.

Indeed, Chang's enchantment with transgressive gender performance continued in *June Bride,* in which another unmarried woman simultaneously deals with three unmarried men. More radical than *The Battle of Love,* the woman is a bride who abruptly cancels the wedding in protest against the patriarchal marriage system in which woman is exchanged for money. While the groom scrambles to seek consent from a nightclub hostess to be his replacement bride, the runaway bride herself enjoys Hong Kong's tourist sites. This leads to a reversal of conventional gendered space: in contrast to the bride's frequent appearances in public spaces, the groom is confined to enclosed spaces such as a mansion and a nightclub.[45]

Yet, Chang's gender critique goes beyond a mere reversal of gendered spaces, for she presents the bride as a performer who refuses all three suitors the day before her wedding. She is inebriated after drinking. A tiny figure of her in full bridal apparatus is superimposed on a close-up of her intoxicated face, and when her face fades out, we are treated to three song-and-dance routines set in a misty forest. The first dance with the groom (a decent Hong Kong businessman) is a waltz coded as mutual attraction, but the bride sings of her suspicion of his financial deal with her money-crazy father. The second dance with the romantic musician from the Philippines is a cha-cha punctuated with her feeling of repulsion, as she sings of the musician's hybrid cultural manners. The third dance with the rude sailor from San Francisco is a tap dance of sorts marked by ambivalence, as she sings of his muscular physique and rough behavior. When the sailor carries her off her feet, she slaps him on the face and finds herself being dropped down . . . onto the sofa, where she wakes up shocked by her daydream.

Just as Ye's declaration of love for Shi is improbable given her indulgence in flirting with male suitors in *The Battle of Love,* in *June Bride* the bride's decision to marry the groom at the final moment is hardly convincing given her knowledge that he has secured a substitute bride. In both cases, the implausible happy endings are nothing but a genre/gender strategy of containment, whereby the threat of female transgression is disavowed and the comic female performer is brought under patriarchal surveillance. The ingenuity of Chang's comedy resides not so much in her invention of persuasive narratives or character motivations as in her ability to deliver triumphant female performance in transgressive acts while reducing male phobia by providing tricks of containment.

CONCLUSION: EQUIVOCAL CONTRAST AS PERFORMANCE

In aesthetic terms, the genre predilection for gender compromise in comedy seamlessly matches Eileen Chang's worldview. In "Writing of One's Own" (1944), Chang articulates her preference for the "equivocal contrast," a technique she believes is "appropriate" to depicting an era in which, contrary to war and revolution, "weak and ordinary people . . . cannot aspire to heroic feats of strength."[46] Rather than tragedy, Chang favors "prosaic, earth-bound" situations in which her typical "equivocal characters" appear "earnest about their lives" and share their feelings of "desolation."[47] Although Chang's screenplays are not as desolate as her print stories, her comedy world is still populated with equivocal characters, whose "placid and static" lives provide her with "a means of writing the truth beneath the hypocrisy . . . and the simplicity underneath the trivolity."[48] In hindsight, Chang's 1944 essay accomplished two things: first, it anticipated the charge of triviality against her Shanghai screenplays as well as the censure of vulgarity against her Hong Kong comedies; second, it articulated a balanced view of genders that finds perfect embodiment in romantic comedy, a genre she would choose as her all-time favorite in her screen career.

Committed to the equivocal contrast, Chang does not privilege the female perspective *alone* in her comedies. Patriarchal values appear prevalent in her screen world, and male points of view are foregrounded, albeit often as objects of humiliation. But the equivocal contrast between male-female perspectives does not reduce Chang's gender critique, and what Nicole Huang says of Chang's 1940s' essays also applies to Chang's films: "In transforming male fantasies into narrative devices and in employing male voices as a means to enhancing the theatricality of her work, Eileen Chang offers a brash and self-confident form of gender critique to both the literary sphere and the larger social world surrounding it."[49]

Nicole Huang's reference to the "theatricality" derived from Chang's play with male fantasies and male voices in her prose essays could be borrowed to illustrate her fiction and screenwriting as well. Indeed, we may reconceptualize Chang's film comedies as an artistic assemble of polyphony or polysemy, not so much structured in fixity as *conjunctural* between points. The conjunctural vision from performance studies directs our attention less to a stable structure of meaning and signification than to glaring cracks and fissures in literary and cinematic works. Perceived in this light, Chang's textual performance with equivocal contrasts, like performance in general, "isn't 'in' anything, but 'between.'"[50] This *be-tweenness* through performance explains why Chang is rarely committed to any single extreme position and why she tends to rewrite her stories repeatedly, shifting from one version, one language, or one medium to another but never completely satisfied with any single textual performance. In accordance to its conjunctural logic, performance insists on—and thrives on—repetition and improvisation, and each new act inevitably contributes new meaning and significance to both the performance text and its performative context.

As indicated in the introduction, the motif of performance runs through Chang's entire career. Because performance presupposes an audience, it is often in response to a certain preconceived audience that Chang's female performer improvises her acts, repeating prescripted lines with alterations, and producing surprises where they are least expected. For Su Weizhen, even private letter writing became a "back-stage performance" for Chang, and she would go so far as to evoke, in an autobiographic piece titled "Whispers," the scorching sun as a witness to her body and soul in an imaginary trial, caught in extreme mood swings between "self-elevation and self-debasement."[51] Self-elevation and self-debasement thus constitute dramatic tensions that would consume Chang's entire life and could be counterbalanced only through her incessant acts of writing and rewriting. In this sense, "Writing of One's Own" is one brilliant act of Chang's performance in front of her contemporary and future readers, a performance through which she justifies, among other things, her preference of harmony over extremity in times of extremities. After all, Chang is an ingenious female performer in and through writing.

Before concluding this chapter, I would address two more issues. First, in response to Leo Lee's criticism of the near tragic penultimate event in *Father Takes a Bride,* where two brothers are locked inside a public cemetery, we may be reminded that in modern high comedy, the viewer is often treated to "an aftertaste of melancholy," which derives in part from "the tone of characters who pretend to be gay and carefree and free-spirited but in truth care passionately and mourn their losses with heavy hearts," thus transmitting "the bitter taste of death" to the audience.[52] To quote Samuel Nathaniel Behrman, "The essence of the comic sense is awareness: awareness of the tragedy as well as of the fun of life, of the pity, the futility, the lost hopes, the striving for immortality, for permanence, for security, for love."[53] Again, the comedy's capacity for bringing extremes into coexistence—where comic characters take trivial matters seriously or conduct serious business in a lighthearted manner—finds a perfect fit with Chang's view of harmony and equivocal contrasts.

Second, I caution against promoting Eileen Chang as the inventor of woman's film in China. One such problematic example is Poshek Fu's assertion that *Long Live the Wife* "is the first film devoted to telling the women's story and thereby established a generic tradition of women's film in Chinese cinema."[54] Actually, woman's film has a long history in China. In 1924, Pu Shunqing wrote her first screenplay, *Aishen de wan'ou* (Cupid's Puppets, 1925), and she helped her husband Hou Yao direct "social problem dramas" and "family drama" focused on women's issues, including *Qifu* (The Abandoned Wife, 1924). As such, "Pu Shunqing may have been China's earliest female playwright to enter the world of cinema."[55] Wang Hanlun, one of the earliest female stars in China, went on to establish her company Hanlun Films in a male-dominated world of filmmaking in 1929 and produced *Nüling fuchouji* (Revenge of an Actress, 1929). Ai Xia, another famous actress, wrote a screenplay *Xiandai yi nüxing* (A Woman of Today, 1933) and starred in the film herself before committing suicide. In light of such evidence, Zhou Fenling's assessment that "Eileen Chang could be regarded as a pioneer in Chinese woman's film" also requires modification.[56]

Instead of "first" and "pioneer," I recommend "prolific" and "unique" as two accurate terms to describe Chang's film career. With fourteen screenplays, Chang surely is a prolific woman screenwriter. What makes her unique in modern China is her status as an extraordinary genius in literature whose career brought her across the print-screen divide and who left a significant corpus of screenplays. In conclusion, we may consider David Der-wei Wang's enumeration of three major areas where Eileen Chang's writing carries "epochal significance": first, from the epoch of literature to that of visuality; second, from the epoch of male voice to that of female polyphony; third, from the epoch of grand history to that of "trivial, variegated histories."[57] All three areas of significance are represented by Chang's film career, as this chapter has demonstrated, but I emphasize that inasmuch as her aesthetics is concerned, Chang cares very little about her epochal monumentality. "I am not capable of writing the kind of work that people usually refer to as a 'monument to an era' and I do not plan to try," she declared in 1944.[58] Rather than a monument fixed in time and aged with history, Eileen Chang prefers performance as an empowering, subversive, and self-rejuvenating trope that aspires to transcend all preconceived boundaries of space, time, genre, and gender.

NOTES

1. Zhang Ailing, *Zhang Ailing quanji* (Collected Works of Eileen Chang), 5: 8.
2. Ibid., 5: 6–7.
3. See Shui Jing, *Zhang Ailing de xiaoshuo yishu* (Eileen Chang's Art of Fiction), 6–7. See also C. T. Hsia, *A History of Modern Chinese Fiction*.
4. Leo Ou-fan Lee, *Shanghai Modern*, 269.
5. Leo Ou-fan Lee, "Eileen Chang and Cinema," 53.
6. Zhou Fenling, *Yanyi* (Gorgeous Differences), 340–347.
7. See Lu Hongshi, *Zhongguo dianying shi, 1905–1949* (Chinese Film History, 1905–1949), 189; Zheng Shusen, "Zhang Ailing yu Aile zhongnian" (Eileen Chang and *Sorrows and Joys at Middle Age*), 220.
8. Su Weizhen, "Zikua yu zibi" (Self-praise and Self-debasement), 27–39.
9. Zhou Fenling, *Yanyi*, 359.
10. See Chen Zishan, "1943–1949 nianjian de Zhang Ailing" (Eileen Chang during 1943–1949), 47–57.
11. Zheng Shusen, "Zhang Ailing, Laiya, Bulaixite" (Eileen Chang, Reyher, Bretch), 215.
12. Hong Kong International Film Festival (hereafter HKIFF), ed., *Transcending the Times: King Hu and Eileen Chang*, 178.
13. Zheng, "Zhang Ailing yu Aile zhongnian," 221.
14. Lee, "Eileen Chang and Cinema," 53.
15. Ibid., 53.
16. Ibid.
17. HKIFF, ed., *Transcending the Times*, 160.
18. Liee Oufan, "Zhang Ailing yu Haolaiwu dianying" (Eileen Chang and Hollywood films), 41–42.
19. Zhou, *Yanyi*, 346.
20. Quoted in Chen Zishan, ed., *Siyu Zhang Ailing* (Private Words on Eileen Chang), 268.
21. Steve Vineberg, *High Comedy in American Movies*, 1–2.
22. Ibid., 4.
23. Wes D. Gehring, *Romantic vs. Screwball Comedy*, 9.
24. Ibid., 2–4.
25. Zhou, *Yanyi*, 354, 369.
26. Poshek Fu, "Telling a Woman's Story," 131.
27. Mary Ann Doane, *The Desire to Desire*, 3.
28. Quoted in Zhou, *Yanyi*, 353.
29. Zhang, *Zhang Ailing quanji*, 3: 94.
30. Zheng, "Zhang Ailing de Taitai wansui" (Eileen Chang's *Long Live the Wife*), 219.
31. Kar Law, "The Cinematic Destiny of Eileen Chang," 142.
32. Fu, "Telling a Woman's Story," 131.
33. Poshek Fu, "Eileen Chang, Woman's Film, and Domestic Culture of Modern Shanghai," 23.
34. Li, "Zhang Ailing yu Haolaiwu dianying," 42–46.
35. Elizabeth Kendall, *The Runaway Bride*, 54.

36. See Mark Rubinfeld, *Bound to Bond*, 116.

37. Eileen Chang, *Written on Water*, 16.

38. Ibid., 16.

39. See Li Xiaohong, "1947 nian Shanghai baokan zhong de Zhang Ailing dianying" (Eileen Chang's Films Seen through Shanghai Newspapers and Magazines in 1947), 167–170.

40. See Chen, *Siyu Zhang Ailing*, 266–276.

41. This quotation is taken from the film's English subtitles. I am grateful to Wong Ain-ling for arranging a videotape screening of *The Battle of Love* at the Hong Kong Film Archive in July 2008.

42. See Zhou, *Yanyi*, 360–362.

43. Zhang, *Zhang Ailing quanji*, 12: 224.

44. P. K. Leung, "Eileen Chang and Hong Kong Urban Cinema," 151.

45. Ibid., 151–152.

46. Chang, *Written on Water*, 17–18.

47. Ibid., 17.

48. Ibid., 16–19.

49. Ibid., xviii.

50. Richard Schechner, Performance Studies, 24.

51. Su, "Zikua yu zibi," 27–28.

52. Vineberg, *High Comedy in American Movies*, 11.

53. Ibid.

54. Fu, "Telling a Woman's Story," 133.

55. Kristine Harris, "*The Romance of the Western Chamber* and the Classical Subject Film in 1920s Shanghai," 55.

56. Zhou, *Yanyi*, 355.

57. See Wang Dewei, *Luodi de maizi busi* (Wheat Dropped to the Ground is Not Dead), 64. For a discussion of the problematic binary logic in Wang's summary, see Zhang Yingjin, "Lu Xun . . . Zhang Ailing: Zhongguo xiandai wenxue yanjiu de liubian" (Lu Xun . . . Eileen Chang: Transformation of Modern Chinese Literature Studies), 2–9.

58. Chang, *Written on Water*, 18.

273

12

Chu T'ien-wen and the *Sotto Voce* of Gendered Expression in the Films of Hou Hsiao-Hsien

CHRISTOPHER LUPKE

THE ASSUMPTIONS OF AUTOBIOGRAPHY AND THE REFRACTION OF THE FEMALE VOICE

The auteur Taiwanese filmmaker Hou Hsiao-hsien (b. 1947) has emerged as one of the most sustained creative forces in (greater) contemporary Chinese cinema. That he continues to break new ground through unremitting exploration and experimentation is substantiated by the voluminous scholarship on him in Chinese, English, and Japanese. Two aspects of the Hou phenomenon receive somewhat less attention: one is his early work; the other is the nature of his collaboration with other intellectuals in the filmmaking process. Scholars and serious film aficionados alike know that there are profound elements of collaboration in the creation of his art from the initial conception of the story to the final touches of subtle dialogue, and everywhere in between. The most important and enduring of these collaborative relationships is that of Hou and the Taiwan-based author Chu T'ien-wen (b. 1956), often billed as his scriptwriter, or on some films as one of them along with Wu Nien-chen (b. 1952). In fact, she has been a partner in the way his films are conceived.

The influence of Chu in the film production is difficult to distill without resorting to detailed autobiographical and interview evidence about each and every film. For instance, we know from interviews of Hou and Chu, often conducted jointly, as well as various essays that Chu T'ien-wen has written, that there has been a synergistic energy at work in their artistic and professional relationship. Of course, in these interviews, Chu often adopts a self-deprecating persona vis-à-vis the director Hou, claiming it is his vision that she attempts to help realize. At the same time, Chu has a separate career of her own as an award-winning writer of fiction. Notwithstanding the fact that Hou is the driving cinematic force in the relationship, it is important to acknowledge, as the lengthy overview of Hou's oeuvre by Leo Chen observes, that the path that brought Hou to what we now consider to be the "Hou Hsiao-hsien aesthetic" was not traveled alone.[1]

In the early 1980s, Hou began generating films that caused a great stir among intellectuals in Taiwan, which by the end of the decade was resonating with the international film-viewing public. A key member of the "New Taiwan Cinema" movement, Hou and a few of his friends completely upended the film scene in Taiwan. He could not have done this without Chu. The subject matter of Hou's early independent films was somewhat varied, though "dynamic tension"[2] between the countryside and the city, the stresses of growing up, and moral conflicts between loyalty to one's cohort and a broader sense of criminal justice were all consistent refrains in his work. Three important early films—*Dongdong de jiaqi* (Summer at Grandpa's, 1984), *Tongnian wangshi* (A Time to Live, A Time to Die, 1985), and *Lianlian fengchen* (Dust in the Wind, 1986)— were said to each be loose autobiographies of the Hou team. *Summer at Grandpa's* was a reminiscence of Chu T'ien-wen's childhood experiences at the countryside home of her natal grandfather and grandmother. *A Time to Live, A Time to Die* depicted Hou's own experiences growing up in rural Taiwan. And *Dust in the Wind* highlighted the disaffection and disappointment of the young Wu Nien-chen as he grappled with the economic necessity of making a living in the ever-expanding metropolis of Taipei. Particularly vexing is *Summer at Grandpa's,* the first of these three auto-biopics, as it is the one of the three that must be most self-consciously and self-referentially gendered. Yet, paradoxically, despite its billing as loosely autobiographical, the film is centered on the young boy Dongdong, the eponymous character in the narrative, according to the Chinese title. What accounts for the fact that Chu's chance at autobiography on the screen is the only one of the three films rendered in which the protagonist could not be the one whose experience is highlighted? Does this paradox hold some of the keys for how the Hou/Chu collaboration works on the screen, and does it contain some information about the gender dynamics ongoing in their professional relationship? Are there deeper, more subtle, ways in which Chu is able to flex her discursive power in the cinematic enterprise? In contemplating these questions, I take a closer look at the film as well as bring in some facts about the relationship between Hou and Chu, and some mention of Chu's literary career, to suggest that Chu T'ien-wen is able to wield perhaps a hidden or subterranean voice over the film. This female voice is emblematic of a tenacious power that she subtly exercises in many of Hou's films, although I will restrict consideration to *Summer at Grandpa's*. The inquiry finds that the female voice in the film is not straightforwardly represented, but is doggedly present. However, the investigation also illustrates the way the female voice is suppressed in important ways and can only communicate its message through elliptical means. One could say that this somewhat muted way of articulating the female voice is carried out in the manner of *sotto voce*, originally a musical term indicating that the sound is lowered precisely for added dramatic effect. The overall narrative voice of *Summer at Grandpa's* appears to be male, but when the layers of narrative are peeled back, a contending voice emerges that is distinctly female. The female voice cannot totally overwhelm the dominant male voice, but it does succeed in disrupting it. The effect is a film with a multivocal tone, a much more complex and interesting representation of childhood adventure than if the film simply were a monological rendering of male initiation.[3]

HOU HSIAO-HSIEN'S EPISTEMOLOGICAL TURN

Hou was active in the film industry in a wide variety of roles for ten years before he co-directed the breakout omnibus film of New Taiwan Cinema *Erzi de da wan'ou* (The Sandwich Man, 1983), an adaptation of three of Huang Ch'un-ming's (b. 1935) short stories. Hou directed one portion of the tripartite project. The previous year, he had read a short story of Chu T'ien-wen's that appeared in a feature of the *Lianhe bao* (United Daily) on the topic of love stories. Intrigued, Hou contacted Chu to see if she would meet to talk about literature. Shortly thereafter, another of Chu's stories won the *Zhongguo shibao*'s (China Times) coveted short story prize.[4]

Along with Chu and Ch'en K'un-hou, Hou decided to adapt the story, entitled *Xiaobi de gushi* (The Story of Xiaobi), to the screen.[5] In the 1970s, Hou was steeped in the commercial aspects of film production, working almost every facet of the industry from scriptwriter to cinematographer, from assistant director to executive producer. He knew the business by heart, but his work to date was not remarkable. By the beginning of the 1980s, however, he was a restless spirit, equipped with a degree from the Taiwan Institute of the Arts and an overabundance of on-the-job training. He read widely in his leisure time, mainly popular works like the martial arts novels of Jin Yong and others, typical fare for a male growing up in post-war Taiwan. Aside from the fact that this was the germination of a lengthy professional collaboration, the encounter had two immediate and important effects that determined the course for all three luminaries. The first was the decision to make Chu's award-winning short story into a film. Ch'en was billed as director, while Hou and Chu worked on the adaptation of the short story into a film script. The second was that during these early interactions Chu recommended several literary works to Hou. The one he repeatedly mentions as the most influential was Shen Congwen's (1902–1988) autobiographical work *Congwen zizhuan* (The Autobiography of Shen Congwen, 1934).[6] The impact of Shen's limpid literary style on Hou, by his own admission, cannot be underestimated, as will become evident in the next section of this essay.[7] But Chu's work itself must have captured Hou's fancy in a powerful way too, because thenceforth all of Hou's cinematic productions involved Chu from the conception of the story through dialogue, often with revision occurring in the midst of the filming stage.

The Story of Xiaobi, subsequently made into a film of the same Chinese title but with the English name *Growing Up* (1983), featured a young boy raised in a "military family compound" *juancun* with a Taiwanese mother and a considerably older mainlander stepfather. It is told in the first person voice through the eyes of an observing neighbor girl recollecting her youth. She was captivated by the tortured boy Xiaobi who seemed always in trouble with authority and whose conflicts with his stepfather often deteriorated into public scenes. The stepfather was actually cast in a sympathetic light, a somewhat hapless retiree from the army who was completely stymied by the boy but devoted to Xiaobi's mother. The mother was caught in the middle and suffered for it. At a crucial point in the story, the mother committed suicide when her efforts to cultivate a sense of decorum and hard work in her son, in whom she had invested everything, seemed hopeless. The tragedy had the ironic effect of bringing the step-father to reconcile with Xiaobi. Profoundly remorseful, Xiaobi did indeed mend his ways and ended up a successful military man himself. There were no villains in the story. Chu took pains to develop the narrative im-partially. But what arose clearly out of the incident with Xiaobi's mother as the main theme of the story, and the film adaptation, was the traditional Chinese notion of *xiaoshun* (filiality)—respect for one's parents, elders, and ancestors, a recognition that one's actions in life were a reflection of those who raised oneself—and this must have struck a chord with Hou, because his films are fraught with examples of the conflict between filial-ity and the transgressive behavior of male youths.

Hou worked intensively with Chu and Ch'en on the film version of *Growing Up*. However, top billing as director was given to Ch'en. The first full-fledged collaboration with Chu on a Hou film was *Fenggui laide ren* (The Boys from Fenggui, 1983). With the refined literary sensibilities of Chu now influencing the work of this seasoned cinematic technician, and with Shen Congwen's autobiography in the back of Hou's mind—a work that describes in gritty detail Shen's youth in the Hunan hinterland but does so in a manner of "passionate detatchment"[8]—Hou embarked on his first film that pits the rural, pastoral vision of an idyllic Taiwan against the competitive, frenzied urban environment.[9] With this antagonism as his background canvas, Hou delves into the details of realistic depiction but simultaneously maintains an authorial distance as he depicts a small band of youthful hooligans who must flee their home in the Pescadores Islands for the anonymity of the port metropolis of Kaohsiung. *The Boys from Fenggui* employs many of Hou's pioneering techniques, such as the use of longer takes and longer shots than were customary at the time in commercial Taiwanese film. The absence of overwrought melodrama, a dominating love story, or a clearly defined ending that allowed emotional closure for the audience all became trademarks of Hou's work as he con-tinued to mature. His newly discovered ability to plumb the psychological depths of his protagonists was likely something that he inherited from the literary style of Chu T'ien-wen. The fastidiously observational style that eschewed judgments of the main characters and allowed the narrative to build on a series of cascading tableau, one after another, was likely some-thing that Hou incorporated into his cinematic technique as a result of the influence that Shen Congwen's dispassionate narrative voice exerted over him. But *The Boys from Fenggui* still retained several elements of more conventional filmmaking, such as the pervasive use of extradiegetic mood music (Vivaldi's *Four Seasons*). The power of the pastoral vision was something that Hou would develop further in his next film, *Summer at Grandpa's*, a film that Huang Chien-yeh suggests is a "mirror image" of *The Boys from Fenggui*.[10] More than any other film, this work from 1984 fully brought to the screen the epistemological, and in some cases the ethical, principles of Shen Congwen and a more complex, though deftly executed, narrative frame from Chu T'ien-wen.

Hou's homage to Shen is referenced by numerous film scholars in their discussions of him.[11] To comprehend the nature of this transference, we need to peruse Shen's work itself. In her discussion of Shen's autobiography, Janet Ng sees Shen as a mediating figure between the inaccessibility of the Chinese countryside in its most remote pockets and the voracious fascination of a rapidly growing urban middle class in places like Beijing. The interest of the urban intellectual class in the agrarian areas of China during the 1930s was fueled by a leftist tendency and manifested in such phenomena as the "going to the people" movement that sparked an ethnographic trend aimed at the elite and urban readership.[12] By converting experience so unimaginable to effete urban tastes into language that was readily consumed by them, Shen constructed a double identity for himself as the rural bumpkin part and parcel of the rustic culture in which he was raised and as an intellectual who could speak for the unwashed masses.[13] Shen's "double claim" of identity enabled him to provide a delicate, unobtrusive critique of his own against both sides: he condemned the violence and ruthlessness of the countryside but also cast a jaundiced eye on the decadence of modern city life.[14] The "position of in-betweenness" allowed him to be *both* critical and sympathetic at the same time. In hindsight, it is understandable that Hou Hsiao-hsien would be attracted by the "interstitial identity" that Shen manufactured for himself, as Hou often endeavored to communicate the ambivalences of a rapidly diminishing bucolic world in the face of the modernizing centers of Taipei and Gaoxiong.[15] In fact, cinema itself is a technology implicitly predicated on modernity and westernized society. For Hou all the accoutrements of the mise-en-scène are properties of the modern, urban world even when pressed into the service of portraying the vanishing countryside. Hou identifies with the young Shen of the autobiography who, when asked if he wishes to shield himself from the foment of the revolution and stay at home or if he would like to "see the action" in town, immediately responds, "see the action."[16] The young Shen's descriptions of "the action" are as devoid of judgment as those in *Summer*

279

at Grandpa's, a film in which several highly disturbing events take place. Admittedly, none of what happens in the small hamlet of Tongluo in Taiwan is quite as harrowing as the severed heads piled high from executions one reads of in Shen's autobiography. The impassive, matter-of-fact, tone with which Shen relates scenes of carnage anticipates the instances in *Summer at Grandpa's* when Dongdong or his sister Tingting witness near-death experiences. The children in both Shen's literary narrative and Hou's film lack the perspective to fully judge the experiences, and thus they do not register as being necessarily extraordinary. The effect on the reader/audience, by contrast, is one of bewilderment over the fact that what is considered quite extraordinary is represented to us as part of the "dispassionate" flow of life, the natural order where things happen without the assignment of moral value. In Hou's film, this was clearly a break from the recent past of melodramatic morality plays known as "healthy realism" that made up much of postwar Taiwan cinema.

CHU T'IEN-WEN AND THE LITERARY VOICE IN FILM

With the help of Chu T'ien-wen, Hou Hsiao-hsien was able to reconceptualize how he structured film narrative by using perspective as the starting point from which to shape the narrative form. Hou found in the work of Shen Congwen a voice for the subaltern characters that he sought to display on the screen for his own urban, well-educated audience, and increasingly for a global audience as well. But Chu T'ien-wen functioned, and indeed functions, as much more than a mere midwife for Hou. If we look at the writing style of her fiction we can see the imprint very clearly on the visual canvas of Hou's films. Of course, Chu herself has evolved dramatically from the teenage prodigy in a literatus family, whose works saw publication as early as high school. By her young mature period, she had become skilled in formulating interesting but short vignettes, such as the one that featured Xiaobi. In her most mature works, such as the award-winning novel *Huangren shouji* (Notes of a Desolate Man), Chu's work is able to explore human consciousness and a wide variety of social positions, and convey experiences quite foreign to her own.[17] Chu has become a highly versatile writer of literature and screenplays over the years, who excels at putting herself linguistically into the place of a wide variety of characters. Many of the characters, such as Xiaobi and the "I" narrator of *Notes of a Desolate Man,* are male. Chu is adept at getting inside the skin of the male psyche as few other female authors are. Turning our attention to Hou's films, we see that many of his most important protagonists are male, too. We cannot assume that just because the gender of the depicted character is male that the construction of such a character could not be conceived by a female author. Chu has demonstrated consistently that it can.

Although important female characters appear in Hou's films, the depiction of women in them is still a point of contention that has generated some debate. The criticism leveled against Hou was never more fierce than for that against arguably his best-known and most esteemed work, *Beiqing chengshi* (A City of Sadness, 1989). An entire book—*Xindianying-zhi si* (The Death of New Cinema) culled together all the negative critical pieces written on this film. One piece by coeditor Mi-tsou asks whether women can actually "enter history," implying that Hou has contrived a situation in which women are excluded from the central activities of major historical events, such as the February 28th Incident of 1947 in Taiwan and the protests of intellectuals against the Guomindang (GMD)-propped up government of Chen Yi. Mi-tsou argues that even though *A City of Sadness* contains ample scenes with women in them and even a large dose of voiceover by Hiromi, the wife of the Fourth Brother, in her exchanges with his niece, all their efforts are invested in "telling the story of men."[18] Mi-tsou further observes that the phenomenon of "men as agents" and "women as those who may narrate their stories" has occurred in previous Hou Hsiao-hsien films such as *Niluohe nü'er* (Daughter of the Nile, 1987), even though the female narrator Yang Lin is a central character in the film. When women are filmed together in dialogue in Hou's films, Mi-tsou continues, the subject matter of their discussions tends to comprise the affairs of men.[19] He concludes that Hou's films do little more than uphold the patriarchal order of traditional Chinese culture.[20] Rosemary Haddon sidesteps the critique to which Mi-tsou subjects Hou's films, whereas Yeh Yue-yü (Emilie Yeh) submits Mi-tsou's argument to a withering countercritique. Haddon believes that enlisting Hiromi as a narrator who contravenes both the official account of the GMD and its dicta at the time enables Hou to utilize the feminine voice to express sympathy with the viewpoint of the native Taiwanese, a more persuasive maneuver than had he, a "mainlander" (born in China and emigrating to Taiwan with his family at the age of one), assailed the government directly.[21] Many Taiwanese nativists distrust those who were born in China and came to Taiwan in the great GMD exodus even if they were children at the time. In fact, Taiwan-born Chu T'ien-wen is not fully accepted as "Taiwanese" by some because her father was a mainlander. According to Haddon, Hiromi's diary becomes "a testimony of resistance" that "records [her] gendered subjectivity."[22] It could be the case, if we raise the stakes of Haddon's argument, that this subversive exposure in language of the GMD's political repression and subsequent suppression of historical fact could only be enacted by an interrogating voice that by definition was different from that of the oppressive "whitewashing" of the GMD, in other words, by a *feminine* voice. Implicit in Yeh Yueh-yü's rejoinder to Mi-tsou is the necessity of a degree of "marginality" in Hou's interrogation of the GMD in order to counter the dominant, linear, and patriarchal ideology of the GMD historical account.[23]

What none of the readings of the feminine voice in *A City of Sadness* do is take a step backward and consider the other major female voice in the film, and that is the literary voice of Chu T'ien-wen. The script for *A City of Sadness* albeit was co-written by Chu and Wu Nien-chen, with Chu first drafting a scene-by-scene synopsis and Wu then carving out the dialogue. From these two texts, the screenwriters negotiated the details of the dialogue and the arc of the narrative with Hou during the making of the film.[24] This fact may temper the assertion that at the creative level *City* is imbued with a female voice. However, the screenwriter factor will prove vital when we return to the discussion of *Summer at Grandpa's*, Chu's ostensible autobiography in which Wu did not take part. The paradox of *Summer at Grandpa's* is that it is reminiscent of Chu's childhood and yet features a young boy in the starring role. We have learned from the above discussion of "The Story of Xiaobi" that Chu is fully capable of featuring male characters in her fiction. The most extensive example of this is *Notes of a Desolate Man* excavating the inner thoughts and ruminations of Xiao Shao, a gay man whose lover is dying of AIDS. The ultimate challenge for a writer of fiction, it could be said, is to become a literary chameleon, to fathom in language precisely that type of experience to which one has no access oneself. Chu accomplishes that in this meditation on male same-sex love, as she pursues the intricacies of androgynous subjectivity. In one revealing passage, Shao ponders over the cosmology of Japan's national religion and how it posits a female deity as its metaphysical origin.[25] Later, Shao opines on the odd case of the Japanese filmmaker Ozu Yasujiro (1903–1963) who, though a bachelor his whole life, was obsessed with the theme of marriage and the family, a theme that haunts practically all of his films.[26] How could one who had no empirical basis on which to conjure such stories contain such a rich reservoir for their exposition? This question strikes at the heart of Chu's own creative muse, an author for whom neither female nor male subjectivity, straight or gay, elderly or preadolescent, is forbidden territory.

Chu T'ien-wen's father, Chu Hsi-ning, was a first-generation mainlander who rose through the Republican military and wrote novels and short stories, many reminiscent of the countryside of his native Shandong youth. He escaped from mainland China in 1949, took up residence in Taiwan, and eventually married Liu Mu-sha, a native Taiwanese of Hakka ethnicity. The work of Eileen Chang (1920–1995) looms over the entire family, as it does over so many writers in Taiwan, for not only were the sisters deeply influenced by this important mainland author of the Republican era, but the father was as well. What is more, the Chu's befriended the Chinese intellectual Hu Lancheng (1906–1981, a former husband of Chang's), a figure with a checkered political past but a deep reverence for a Chinese identity associated with the "heartland" and a rich, carefully wrought writing style. Hu lived with the Chu family for a short period in the 1970s.[27] The work of Chang and the general literary milieu instill Chu with a reverence for language and the art of literary expression.

With Hou Hsiao-hsien's commercial training, scrappy youth experiences, and affection for popular fiction, and with Chu T'ien-wen's highbrow sensibility, her mixture of Christian, Confucian, and Sun Yat-sen values, and her devotion to a mythic vision of Chinese identity, the two were ripe for aesthetic breakthrough. Their collaboration forced each to examine their own stance, point of view, and creative preferences. In the end, they forged something much more rooted in the experience of Taiwan's recent history and more delicately fashioned for the screen.[28] Together, they expanded their horizons and explored new aesthetic territory, and were influenced by the works of recent Taiwan fiction such as Huang Ch'un-ming's and Ch'en Ying-chen's (b. 1936) short stories and Wang Wen-hsing's (b. 1939) novel *Jiabian* (Family Metamorphosis).

The combined efforts of the two have resulted in some of the most representative films of New Taiwan Cinema. For Hou's part, the theme of wayward youth stumbling through life is an issue that may never have struck Chu as worthy subject matter. For her part, Chu has honed and refined the way that Hou brings this material to the screen. That one is male and one is female is beneficial—each brings what is quintessentially masculine or feminine to their work. It would be a misperception

283

to credit Hou entirely with the form and content of his cinema, despite Chu's self-effacing comments that she is a mere interlocutor helping Hou achieve his vision.[29] Chu T'ien-wen works within the structure that Hou initially provides, but how she accomplishes that begs further understanding. There is a "gendered" aspect to Hou's films not just in the representation of women on the screen, addressed in important articles by Emilie Yeh and Rosemary Haddon, but in the very act of creation itself. Therefore, what remains to be done is to examine the film itself and discuss the ways in which Chu has moved back and forth through various characters, almost as a ventriloquist, to assume and tease out different, sometimes conflicting, voices, as the personalities of these characters are first outlined and then defined through the recording of their experiences. *Summer at Grandpa's* is an appropriate starting point for such an inquiry, because as an early film it is indicative of the founding ideas of their relationship and in it the issue of gender formation in young children is dealt with head on. Although ostensibly the story of a young boy during a summer adventure, the actions and events involving his younger sister play a critical role in the film.

284

THE PARADOX OF AUTOBIOGRAPHY IN *SUMMER AT GRANDPA'S*

Summer at Grandpa's is the first full manifestation of the Hou/Chu collaboration and the influence of Shen's idyllic imagery. It is primarily set in the countryside, a somewhat parallel locale to Shen's western Hunan. Though not far from Taipei, the verdant rice fields and pastures of Miaoli County were a world away from the congested urban environs of Taipei. The use of diegetic and extradiegetic sound in this film signals a substantial step beyond that of *The Boys from Fenggui*. *Summer at Grandpa's* was produced when the Hou team was consolidating a number of film techniques, such as the long take (time) and the long shot (distance), keyholing, the general avoidance of nondiegetic mood music overlay with some exceptions, the use of a stationary camera in which characters move in and out of the frame, ellipses in shot editing, the placement of hyper-situated objects,[30] voice-over, the mixture of the regional Hakka language with the dominant national language of Mandarin, and the foregrounding of diegetic sounds outside the visual film frame.[31] As Hou himself disclosed, *Summer at Grandpa's* represented a leap beyond his previous film

Boys from Fenggui, despite their difference in release dates of only about one year.[32] Many features of his mature style emerge in the latter film. Point of view is one dimension of the cinematic project that Hou completely transformed as a direct result of his encounter with Chu and his reading of Shen. Hou confesses he never contemplated it before he made the aesthetic turn. The conundrum involving point of view in this film is the ostensible fact that the film derives from Chu T'ien-wen's childhood experiences and yet primarily emphasizes the experience of the young boy, Dongdong. Dongdong, about ten years old, is sent with his approximately five-year-old sister Tingting to their grandparents' home in rural Taiwan while their mother is hospitalized, awaiting major, life-threatening surgery in Taipei.

There are two seemingly irreconcilable characteristics to confront: the first is the loose autobiographical nature of the film, focusing on the childhood experiences and recollections of Chu T'ien-wen; the second is that the film is presented as the experience and story not foremost of a young girl, but of a young boy. It could not be the case that she is assuming an observational narrative mode from the perspective of the young girl Tingting, because Chu had no brothers. From the film title to the initial scenes at school on the last day before summer break and the hospital scene in which the children say goodbye to their mother, the point of view is primarily channeled through Dongdong.[33] After all, while the English title—*Summer at Grandpa's*—seems neutral, the Chinese title—literally, *Dongdong's vacation*—makes clear that it *is* Dongdong's experience at the center of the film. Moreover, an essential element is inserted early in the film to ensure the sustained unity of this point of view—Dongdong's mother directs him to write her once a week about his experiences during vacation. These letters constitute an architectonic organizing device in the film that appears in the form of voice-over, a technique frequently deployed in subsequent films. On one level, the letters form a set of punctuation marks strategically inserted in the film that allow for assessment of the alien experiences Dongdong encounters. The letters show he does not fully grasp the import of these experiences or what his elders tell him about the various incidents that occur, but they do allow him to reflect verbally on the events. On another level, the letters also demonstrate Dongdong's effort to fulfill a filial responsibility to his ailing mother as he faithfully relays his experiences back to her. They help bring some nascent moral order to the random events through their recapitulation in language. In the hospital scene near the beginning of the film, the various characters are established, telegraphing how things may unfold with each of them. The mother is bedridden and her condition is questionable. The father is a marginal character whose only role in the film is to shuttle the children at the beginning and end.[34] Changming, Dongdong and Tingting's (maternal) uncle, lights a cigarette in the hospital room, apparently ignorant of the fact that smoking is against the rules. This illustrates his thoughtless and irresponsible side. Dongdong listens attentively to his mother and agrees both to write to her and to look after his little sister. The young girl stands by silently, unable at this tender age to process the gravity of the situation.

When Dongdong and Tingting are in transit to the village, they accidentally are separated from their uncle, in whose hands they have been entrusted. The ensuing shot sequence where the children disembark from the train demonstrates that Dongdong is resourceful enough to take charge of the situation, avoid panic, and wait calmly for their uncle to catch up, lest he be scolded for botching the job. This first unexpected turn of events in the film also allows for the dramatization of an urban versus rural encounter of the city boy, with his electric jeep, and the country kids, with their plaything, a turtle. Dongdong instructs Tingting to remain with him, and she silently obeys.

Tingting may largely be silent throughout the film, but she is not totally marginalized in it. Rather, her own encounters and observations form a subplot and provide a stark contrast to Dongdong's. The boy possesses the ability to express himself verbally, both to others and, through the letters, the spectator, while his younger sister is virtually devoid of the ability to render her experiences to language. She is a wide-eyed spectator, shadowing her older brother on his exploits with his newly found friends through creek and valley. The behavior of Dongdong is instinctually that of a young boy set loose to explore new friendships and adventures in Taiwan's northeastern countryside. The adults attend to other affairs, leaving the children to their own devices. Dongdong seamlessly blends in with the local network of young boys who are enthralled by competing in turtle races, catching bugs, lighting off firecrackers, splashing around naked, climbing trees, and engaging in other youthful exploits. Indications of early male bonding are embodied in the conscious attempt to exclude Tingting from their activities. This results in a near-tragic event where Tingting falls on the railroad tracks but is saved by a local "madwoman" named Hanzi. Tingting then forms her own special bond with this social outcast. Neither Tingting, because of her youth, nor Hanzi, because of her mental disability, engage in much dialogue. Their relationship is perpetuated through a series of events involving life and death: Tingting's accident on the tracks, Tingting finding a dead bird and bringing it to Hanzi, and Hanzi's fall from a tree that results in a miscarriage. The other children regard Hanzi as "Dinma" the crazy scourge, someone who hits and bites. But she is never represented doing that in the film. Their relationship becomes a subversive undercurrent built chiefly through silent action as a counterpoint to the main focus on Dongdong, his friends, his relationship with his uncle, and his interactions with his grandfather. Dongdong's experiences are replete with a range of linguistic modes of expression: hoots and hollers with his new friends; barely comprehensible (to the boy) discussions with his uncle about propriety, the motivations of his girlfriend's family, the uncle's fears of his father (Dongdong's grandfather); and his grandfather's paternal guidance in the memorization of classical Chinese poems, explanations of the family history, appreciation of good music, discussions of his mother's medical condition, and justifications of his discipline of Changming. Dongdong's experiences are bound to linguistic expression.

Two encounters in the final sequence provide an interesting contrast between the status of Dongdong and Tingting. In the first, as the children are getting into the car to return to Taipei with their father, Tingting catches sight of Hanzi walking down the lane near their grandparents' house, away from them. As Tingting calls out, presumably as a parting gesture, Hanzi does not turn to acknowledge her, and Tingting is quickly summoned back to the car. That the family members ignore her shout to Hanzi reinforces an implicit, taken for granted, understanding that Hanzi is a strange person with whom conventional human interaction is not possible, worthwhile, or even advisable. Hanzi's reaction is cryptic. She is never filmed interacting with adults in the film, except briefly with the young man who impregnates her. Perhaps she does not hear or does not have the capacity to acknowledge Tingting. Another possibility is that she deliberately walks away, because she cannot bare to face the child to whom she has grown attached, realizing Tingting is about to leave. Evidence to support this interpretation exists in the sequence when Tingting shows Hanzi the dead bird. Hanzi is overcome by melancholy at the bird's passing in a way that a normal adult would not be. The older (and male) Dongdong's callous reaction exaggerates how an adult might regard the incident with the bird.

In contrast to the unsatisfying way the two females part, Dongdong's departure from the boys receives considerably more validation. The

287

father makes a special point of stopping on the way out of town to give Dongdong the opportunity to bid farewell to his summer friends as they continue their daily ritual of swimming in the nearby creek. Dongdong calls to them and they return the gesture to him. This reinforces the notion in the spectator's mind that the vacation is Dongdong's and that his experiences comprise the central action of the film. It also serves as an important structural device that signals an end to the summer in the countryside. Chiao Hsiun-p'ing (Peggy Chiao) goes so far as to suggest it is Dongdong bidding farewell to his youth.[35] Even at the conclusion to the film, Tingting's relationships and her attempts at communication are not given full weight as Dongdong's are. This detail overshadows the experiences, growth, and transformations that have occurred to her in the film. However, it does not entirely occlude them. It realigns the film along the central path of patriarchal values displayed in nascent form by the young boys, in the form of transgression by the uncle, which I will mention below, and in the stoic countenance of the grandfather. Dr. Liu is a paragon of traditional Chinese masculinity adapting to the modern era. He is the family patriarch and a community leader as well. There is no distinction on the set between his home and his office. Implicit in his behavior is that social appearances must be upheld and fundamentals of ethical conduct must be maintained. He cannot tolerate his son Changming's irresponsible sexual behavior. He also disciplines Dongdong for making too much noise while he works and for losing his clothing when skinny-dipping in the creek. He also has no compunction against advising members of the community on personal and family issues, illustrating June Yip's point that in such an "organic community" extended familial relations and interpersonal ties among local denizens are viewed as part of the natural and social order.[36]

Their mother's medical condition is the impetus for the vacation. She has been left in Taipei for a risky operation. The film is interspersed at times with reports from Taipei about her precarious affliction. Dr. Liu interprets these developments and her prognosis for the rest of the family in a clinical tone. He is the voice of calm reason as others, such as his wife, react with fear, sorrow, a sense of helplessness, and a lack of complete understanding of either the medical condition or the facilities and personnel. Dr. Liu also advocates for Hanzi's sterilization and forgoes his own trip to Taipei to visit their daughter (family obligations) so that he may tend to the care of the injured Hanzi (community responsibility). Even when the two young children first meet him, he merely greets them with a demure nod of the head. His only smile in the film comes when Dongdong properly recites a Tang poem. By contrast, the grandmother is warm, welcoming, and friendly. She is the emotional barometer of the family and is usually situated in the kitchen. She cries on occasion, outwardly expresses worry, and displays anxiety for the friend of Dongdong who is temporarily lost. Together the patriarch and matriarch form an interesting example of heterosexual bonding that completes the array of emotions and values that should be exemplary to the youths, including those in their early twenties like Changming and his pregnant fiancée.

The film is a portrayal of childhood innocence exploring the world around itself in the summer months. But it noticeably plants several potentially life-shattering elements that force the children to reflect on the meaning of life. These include the precarious situation of their mother's health, the short-lived fear that one of the boys in the village may have washed out to sea, the truck-jacking, Tingting's near-fatal accident, Hanzi's fall, Changming's impregnating his girlfriend causing humiliation to the family, and his protection of the two thieves, childhood friends who engineered the truck-jacking. The combined force of these traumatic events is sufficient to give the children pause in their journey of self-discovery and discovery of the world around them. The film is artfully constructed from Dongdong's point of view so that the full implication of these events is shown to be digested by him with an almost matter-of-fact demeanor, indicating that at his age it would be impossible to entirely appreciate the mortal abyss he circumambulates throughout the film. Hou and Chu construct the narrative in the manner of Shen's autobiography. Dongdong lacks the perspective to assign different weights to various experiences, some quotidian and some monumental. More adventuresome and gregarious than his sister, he shows both the quintessential cruelty of an older brother in youth who attempts to ostracize his little sister and insouciance toward harrowing events. Although Cheshire overstates the case in professing that "Hou seems most interested in registering . . . fragments of the adult world that flicker around its edges" rather than "the child's consciousness" per se, he encapsulates the film quite eloquently in his conclusion that "moments of idyll are defined by the unraveling of a larger context."[37]

With the assistance of the observational eye of the omniscient camera, silent Tingting performs the fact that this story is also about her encounters with mortal danger, the meaning of life, and the value of human interaction. Hanzi is not viewed by Tingting as a crazy woman. By virtue of her disability, she is frozen in a childlike stage in which all life's creatures possess the same profound value. Her entrance on the screen presents her performing ritual incense-burning at the local god's altar. She is the only one who shows affection and pays attention to Tingting. She exhibits unfathomable loss in the face of her miscarriage. She shares with Tingting the inability to communicate verbally. This "lack" ironically opens up a different avenue for expression that can only be realized physically, as in the scene where the "dogged" Tingting insists on accompanying Hanzi while she convalesces. In the final shot of this sequence, the roles are reversed, and Tingting is viewed asleep while Hanzi comforts her.

The delineation of these contrasting characters offers a glimpse at the multivocal way in which Hou Hsiao-hsien and Chu T'ien-wen negotiate gender on the screen, highlighting Dongdong, who must shuttle between his wayward uncle and his strict grandfather on the one hand and who establishes his own male bonds through camaraderie with the local boys on the other; Tingting who silently but obdurately follows and observes; the uncle whose condition as a ne'er-do-well finds him in conflict with propriety; the grandfather whose laconic Confucianism is demonstrated by off-screen actions such as bailing out his son; the grandmother who expresses the sadness and fear that the grandfather only approaches clinically; and Hanzi, the mentally disabled woman who, despite efforts to control her behavior, is exploring her own sexuality and human relationships. This social web indicates that Chu T'ien-wen, moving back and forth between gendered experiences, personifies a capacity to lay an ostensible framework of patriarchal values while simultaneously undercutting it with the subversive *sotto voce* of a female voice.

NOTES

1. See Leo Chanjen Chen, "Cinema, Dream, Existence." Although Chu T'ien-wen dismisses the importance of her role, Chen argues "the relationship between the two has plainly been reciprocal," as it was Chu who brought to Hou's cinema an "écriture feminine" and a spirit of "desolation."

2. A concept elucidated by June Yip in her *Engendering Taiwan*, 67.

3. On the theme of male initiation in Hou's films from *The Boys from Fenggui* to *Daughter of the Nile*, see William Tay's "The Ideology of Initiation." Tay illustrates how the bildungsroman of Dongdong runs parallel to the "developmental history of Taiwan," which "constitutes a subtext" for this and other Hou films. Yip also discusses the theme of "initiation" in her treatment of this film. See Yip, *Engendering Taiwan*, 200–201.

4. See Chu Hsi-ning et al., *Xiaoshuo jiazu* (The Fiction Family), 291, for more details.

5. *The Story of Xiaobi* was subsequently published in a collection of short stories and prose pieces by Chu under the same title, *Xiaobi de gushi* (The Story of Xiaobi), 13–21.

6. Originally written in 1934, the version I used was published in 1969. It comprises eighteen pithy chapters on such topics as region and village life in remote western Hunan province where Shen grew up, vignettes of the 1911 Republican Revolution, images of brutal massacre, and depictions of the minority Miao people and their interactions with the majority Han ethnicity, all of interest to an urban-based, educated elite.

7. Hou was working on the film *The Boys from Fenggui* when Chu asked him about narrative perspective. Perplexed, Hou accepted Chu's suggestion to read Shen's autobiography. Hou was struck that Shen chooses a "perspective" from which to relate his experience of the countryside. He also cites Shen's "very cold, distanced approach" as an influence. See Michael Berry, "Hou Hsiao-hsien with Chu T'ien-wen," 247.

8. See Chen, "Cinema, Dream, Existence," 79. Huang Chien-yeh terms this Hou's "documentary" style. See his "Dongdong de Jiaqi" (Summer at Grandpa's), 71.

9. Hou's vision of the countryside is "not wholly idyllic." Many "complicated and difficult" problems emerge as a result of human interaction. See Yip, *Engendering Taiwan*, 199.

10. The former involves teens from the country coming to the city, whereas the latter describes the experiences of two city children coming to the country. See Huang, "Dongdong de Jiaqi" (Summer at Grandpa's), 71.

11. Emilie Yueh-yu Yeh and Darrell William Davis, for example, ascribe to Shen a near-Daoist quality, quoting Hou: "Like natural law, [Shen's point of view] has no joy and no sorrow. That I found to be very close to me. It doesn't matter if he's describing a brutal military crackdown or various kinds of death; life to him is a river, which flows and flows but is without sorrow or joy." See "Trisecting Taiwan Cinema with Hou Hsiao-hsien," 157.

12. See Janet Ng, "A Moral Landscape."

13. Janet Ng, *The Experience of Modernity*, 130.

14. Ibid., 132–133.

15. Ibid., 134–135.

16. Shen Congwen, *Congwen zizhuan* (The Autobiography of Shen Congwen), 28.

17. Chu T'ien-wen, *Notes of a Desolate Man*.

18. See Mi-tsou, "Nüren wufa jinru lishi?" (Can Women Not Enter History?), 136.

19. Ibid., 136.

20. Ibid., 140.

21. See Rosemary Haddon, "Hou Hsiao-hsien's *City of Sadness*," 56.

22. Ibid., 61.

23. Yeh offers a sophisticated rebuttal of Mi-tsou's argument. See her "Nüren zhende wufa jinru lishi ma?" (Do Women Really Have No Way to Enter History?), 76–79.

24. See the combined synopsis and draft screenplay in Wu Nien-chen and Chu T'ien-wen, *Beiqing chengshi* (A City of Sadness).

25. See Chu T'ien-wen, *Huangren shouji* (Notes of a Desolate Man), 118–119.

26. Chu, *Notes of a Desolate Man*, 192–193.

27. Chu relates in an interview how she and others founded *Sansan jikan* (Three Three Quarterly) in the late 1970s in part to provide Hu with a publishing venue. Chu notes

that Hu "shaped our reading habits and our ability to take in things around us so that we nurtured a very broad field of vision, where we could read about and observe all kinds of things rather than be trapped in a purely literary world." See Berry, "Hou Hsiao-hsien with Chu T'ien-wen," 241–242.

28. The other important catalyst for Hou's creative break was his meeting several other emerging filmmakers. See Berry, "Hou Hsiao-hsien with Chu T'ien-wen," 244–245.

29. Ibid., 246–247.

30. For a discussion of the concept of hypersituated object in film, see Kristin Thompson and David Bordwell, "Space and Narrative in the Films of Ozu," especially 64–66.

31. Peggy Hsiung-p'ing Chiao pinpoints this important feature of Hou's work. See her "Dongdong de Jiaqi" (Summer at Grandpa's), 138.

32. See Hou Hsiao-hsien. "Cong 'Fenggui' dao 'Dongdong,'" (From Boys of Fenggui to Summer at Grandpa's).

33. The point of view privileges Dongdong, but the young girl Tingting complicates that point of view. In addition, the film is permeated with Hou's own (third-person) POV with its understated tone, à la Shen Congwen. As Godfrey Cheshire observes, "the distinctive gaze comprises not only the subject's somewhat melancholy view of his situation but the filmmaker's more detached, critically observant perspective as well." See Cheshire, "Time Span," 61.

34. Tay argues that the "inconsequential" role of the father signifies the "absence of a powerful and dominating patriarchy." While true, the presence of the grandfather in *Summer* partially mitigates that absence and raises the countervailing point that traditional, extended families play a salutary role in the raising of children. See Tay, "The Ideology of Initiation," 157.

35. Chiao, "Dongdong de Jiaqi" (Summer at Grandpa's), 139.

36. Yip, *Engendering Taiwan*, 199.

37. Cheshire, "Time Span," 61.

13

To Become an Auteur

THE CINEMATIC MANEUVERINGS OF XU JINGLEI

JINGYUAN ZHANG

QUITE A few recent Chinese film directors share the ambition of becoming a recognized art film "auteur" (*zuozhe daoyan*), despite the fact that art films, in general, do not do well at the box office. For Fifth Generation film directors Zhang Yimou and Chen Kaige, success in art films has led to internationally funded and commercially successful blockbusters (*da pian*). Some successful Sixth Generation and later film directors, such as Jia Zhangke, Gu Changwei, and Jiang Wen, are still making art films, which normally have no government funding or affiliation with government studios. Of the few women feature film directors in China now, most work as independent art filmmakers, and Xu Jinglei is one of the most prominent of these.

Xu Jinglei has directed three films to date. While each of the three is a very impressive piece, each is also remarkably different from the others. The first, *Wo he Baba* (My Father and I, 2003), is a leisurely and fairly realistic urban drama in a plain style, covering the relationship between a young woman and her father over a period of many years. The second, *Yige mosheng nüren de laixin* (Letter from an Unknown Woman, 2004), is a visually lavish period piece, a fairytale tragedy covering two decades and two characters who rarely meet. The third, *Mengxiang zhaojin xianshi*

(Dreams May Come, 2006), is an experimental film consisting of a single conversation spanning a few hours in one hotel room. It is hard to find among these three films the kind of unity that auteur theory tends to look for. Nevertheless powerful unities are present even in this small early corpus, as we shall see.

Unity of directorial style has more than one function. It can help create a kind of film language or dialect special to the particular director, expanding the resources of each individual film to hold meaning. It can deepen the impact of each film by allowing the corpus to function as a literary whole. And it can function as a brand, increasing the popularity and impact of each particular film. To a large extent, these same functions can be played by a different kind of unity that unquestionably does characterize Xu Jinglei's films: the unity given to them by her own public persona, which itself is a kind of cultural and artistic product.

Xu Jinglei not only directed the three films, but also wrote the screenplays for the first two of them (the screenplay for the third was written by Wang Shuo). Yet Xu Jinglei's involvement unifies the three films in a far more conspicuous way. For she plays the female lead in each of her films, and even sings for the closing credits in the third.

By any measure, Xu Jinglei is a movie star and popular idol. She began as an actor in film and television, playing in several Sixth Generation films in addition to a number of big-budget Hong Kong films. In 2003, the year her first film appeared, she received high awards for her acting in three other films.[1] The following year she received a Best Actress award for her role in her own film.

Xu Jinglei has worked hard to cultivate and extend her public persona. For the year of 2006, her personal blog, mostly casual entries about her kittens, her travels, charity drives, and small thoughts, was the most linked-to blog in any language anywhere. She also runs, as owner and very visible general editor, two interactive on-line magazines, *Kaila* (Opening) and *Kaila jiepai* (Opening Street Scenes), which cover art, entertainment, fashion, current affairs, money management, and shopping advice.[2]

Star power is capital. It can help a director pull together the resources needed to make her own art. Film directing in China is a very competitive field, even as Hollywood, television, and the internet have been drawing Chinese audiences away from Chinese films. A director must win the confidence of investors and the necessary state approval, then lead and manage a large crew of creative professionals—actors, camera people, graphic artists, musical composers, recording technicians, and more—communicating her vision to the crew, resolving conflicts, and maintaining morale (a point Xu Jinglei has stressed).[3] The ultimate end is to lead and manage an audience. There is no reason to expect a woman to find it any easier than a man to accumulate and exercise that level of authority. Xu Jinglei was helped in this respect by the policy changes in the early 21st century. The Beijing government began to define the film industry as a "profit-making cultural enterprise," bringing it within the scope of the broad move toward free-market economic policies. Films could now be produced by private companies (as had previously been done only "underground"), and cinema houses could be owned by private entrepreneurs. For the first time, therefore, independent Chinese films could be widely distributed in China prior to gaining foreign recognition. Funding for government studios was significantly reduced, opening the field to real competition. There was henceforth no requirement to get state approval to submit a film to an international award competition, and state approval to shoot a film became much easier to obtain. In fact, Xu Jinglei's *My Father and I* was the very first film project to get a permit under the new policies. The new policies have made it much easier for independent films to make money, and have helped to blur the line between art films and commercial films.

But star power can also be a burden for an auteur. Not only can it bring unwelcome links between the artistic product and the director's personal life, it can also bring new political responsibilities to the director's work. For example, the persona of any female film star will be bound up with questions about how to conceive gender, especially if that star makes films about relationships between men and women.

MY FATHER AND I AND LETTER FROM AN UNKNOWN WOMAN

Xu Jinglei's first film, *My Father and I*, cost only two million yuan (about $240,000) to make. For this film, Xu Jinglei won the Best New Film Director award at the 23rd Chinese National Golden Rooster Award Competition in 2003, and the Best New Director and Best Screenplay awards at the fourth annual Chinese Film Media Awards in 2004.

At the beginning of the film, Xu's character Xiaoyu is a high school student whose mother dies in a traffic accident. Xiaoyu begins to live with her father, whom she did not previously know. The film charts their relationship through the father's arrest, Xiaoyu's marriage to a young man who despises her father, the problems faced by the daughter and father in caring for the child she bears after the divorce, and the father's illness and death. The film also glances briefly at Xiaoyu's life before and after her years with her father.

The focus throughout is narrowly on these two characters, and especially on the growth of Xiaoyu. Other characters appear only briefly (with the exception of an infant), and the two main characters rarely appear separately. Each loves and clings to the other; they depend on each other as the only family either of them recognizes. Xiaoyu seems to have shut down after the death of her mother. Her father struggles to help her open up and find her way in the world. He is gentle and motherly rather than fatherly with her; he is even more serious about cooking and cleaning than her mother ever was. He provides for her, he gives her very thoughtful advice, and when she steadfastly ignores her baby, he hires a nanny and tirelessly mothers the infant himself, never criticizing Xiaoyu. In these ways, he is the strong one. But he also lives on the edge of the underworld: drinking, gambling, running a bar, and managing prostitutes. Xiaoyu's worry that she cannot depend on him is confirmed when he is arrested and spends three years in prison. Later, to provide for her and the child, he sneaks off to gamble at night, leading to an accident that renders him unable to speak and virtually unable to move. Xiaoyu must now take care of him and the baby both, and in that way he teaches her the final lesson of responsibility and maturity (fig. 13.1).

Xu Jinglei's second film, *Letter from an Unknown Woman*, was more ambitious in that it aimed also at international recognition. *Letter* cost about twenty million yuan to make, ten times the cost of her first film, and involved international participation: camera work by award-winning Taiwan cameraman Pin Bing Lee, a musical score written in part by a Japanese composer, and final film editing done in Japan. This film won the Best Director award at the 52nd San Sebastian Film Festival in 2004 and the Best Cinematography award at the 25th Chinese National Golden Rooster Award Competition in Beijing in 2005.

Letter is an adaptation of a story written by Stefan Zweig in 1922, previously adapted to the screen in the 1948 film *Letter from an Unknown Woman*, directed by Max Ophüls.[4] Whereas the original story was a Freudian study of pathological female hysteria, Xu Jinglei's version suggests rather a classical tale of unrequited love, making no mention of mental illness. She at first intended to move the story from Austria

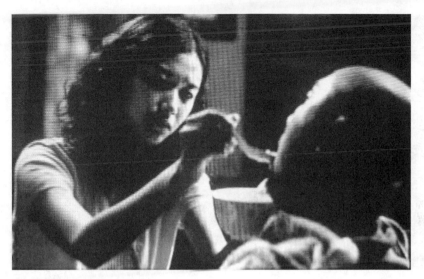

FIGURE 13.1 *My Father and I*, 2003

to contemporary Beijing, but in the end moved it to 1930s' and 1940s' Beijing and Chongqing.[5]

The film opens with a man, Mr. Xu, receiving a letter from a woman, Miss Jiang, whose name he does not recognize and who, the letter makes clear, has just died. The text of the letter serves as the voice-over narration for the entire film. It tells the story of Miss Jiang's life, which is also the story of her devoted love for Mr. Xu.[6] She has spoken with him on several occasions, and has even had two very brief sexual relationships with him, one of which produced a child; but every time he meets her he thinks he is meeting someone new. She spends her whole life waiting to be recognized. (In vivid contrast, late in the film, Mr. Xu's old manservant sees her face by accident one morning as she leaves the house after her only night there in many years. He immediately recognizes her and instantly perceives the course her life has taken. He stands devastated, trembling, unable to stop looking directly into her eyes.) When the child dies of an illness, Miss Jiang dies too, perhaps of despair, having left the letter (fig. 13.2).

These first two films, *Father* and *Letter*, have many story elements in common, despite their enormous stylistic differences. Each film focuses entirely on a single relationship between a woman and a man. The woman in each case is played by Xu Jinglei. Each relationship is asymmetrical in a

FIGURE 13.2 *Letter from an Unknown Woman,* 2004

way. For the man is significantly older than the woman, and in each film he counts as her superior in a second respect as well. In *Father,* he is her father, whom she comes to know only when she is an adolescent, because her mother had kicked him out of the home when Xiaoyu was an infant. In *Letter,* he has incomparably more wealth and education than she does. In fact, each film offers this second dimension of superiority as the explanation of the woman's love for the man. In *Letter,* Miss Jiang falls in love with Mr. Xu at the sight of his books and furniture.

Each film spans many years, tracing the entire history of the relationship. Each relationship and each film begins before the woman is an adult, when she is being raised only by her mother. Each film ends with the death of one of the parties to the relationship.

There are similarities, too, in the course each relationship takes. In *Father,* the great failing of the father is shown in two episodes of disappearance and concealment. In the first of these episodes, only when he is suddenly arrested does his daughter find out that he has been engaging in criminal activity. He must spend three years in prison, leaving her on her own. In the second episode, several years later, he is home from prison, but money is very tight, so he often disappears to gamble illegally, concealing what he is doing. On one of these gambling escapades he suffers a brain hemorrhage and loses most of his mental faculties permanently. *Letter*'s two episodes of culpable disappearance and concealment are even more overtly parallel to each other. In each episode, the man has been having sexual relations with the woman. In the first case, the affair lasts for perhaps a week; in the second case, it is a single night. In each case, the man ends the relationship, but he does not say he is doing so. Rather he says he must go out of town for a while, to a war zone, and promises to seek her out on his return. In each case, he breaks his promise.

In each film, the woman deals with the first disappearance by spending a few years in a relationship with a young man her own age. In *Father*, she marries a fellow college student; in *Letter*, she allows herself to be courted by a young military man who wishes to marry her. But in each film she returns to the older man before his second disappearance.

In each film, the way the man fails the woman is closely bound up with his use of prostitutes. In *Father*, the father's main criminal activity was the managing of prostitutes. In *Letter*, Mr. Xu is a womanizer and customer of prostitutes, which helps explain how he can meet a woman without remembering that he has been intimate with her in the past. In *Father*, the father in the course of his arrest is desperate to make sure that the police do not mistake his daughter for one of his prostitutes. In *Letter*, Mr. Xu once mistakes the woman for a prostitute and pays her for the night.

In each film, between the first and second disappearances, the woman has a child who both does and does not belong to the older man. In each case, the child is a story prop rather than a character in its own right. In *Father*, the woman has a child by the young man, born when she has returned to her father after the divorce. Her father is thrilled and absolutely devoted to the child, whom he considers simply as his own descendant, unrelated to the unpleasant ex-husband. In *Letter*, the woman conceives the man's child shortly before his first disappearance, and she raises the boy alone, never revealing his existence to the man until the letter itself.

In each film, despite the formal inequality within each relationship, the woman is strong or stubborn enough to maintain a kind of parity with the man. In *Father*, Xiaoyu and her father plainly have equal power in their relationship. She has the option of leaving him for an aunt or a husband, and she often complains successfully. In *Letter*, Miss Jiang maintains a kind of dignity throughout her life by never telling Mr. Xu of the true state of affairs, and by possessing and raising his child, in whom she feels she possesses Mr. Xu. In her view, her devotion is not slavish, but a free choice.

The narrative arc of each film reaches a peak in a reversal of the relationship. In *Father,* the overall story hinges on a reversal that comes in the final minutes of the film, when Xiaoyu's father has the brain hemorrhage. Up to this point, she has been unable to cope with her life, with the death of her mother and the abandonment and disgrace of her father's arrest. She has not participated in caring for her child. But her father's loss of his faculties simply forces her to pull herself together and take responsibility. She cares for him as though he is an infant; indeed, we see her feeding and cleaning him right next to the infant, who is clamoring for similar attention. She gives the infant a little more attention than before. Soon after, as the film ends, we glimpse her as a good mother. In *Letter,* too, the end of the film reveals a kind of reversal. The evening has gone dark around Mr. Xu's lamp as he reads the letter alone. When he has finished, we see several things we have not seen before: He seems genuinely moved, he is genuinely sad, and he is alone. He walks slowly to the door and gazes out at the house across the courtyard, where (as he now knows) the little girl used to live. Far into the darkness, he seems to see the little girl's face gazing at him through the window, a face he never noticed when it was really there. He has now become the one who gazes, who cannot forget but cannot communicate or be recognized.

In each film, Xu Jinglei attempts to portray the psychological depth of the female character by means of a double narrative line. In *Father,* as the story unfolds on the screen, we see Xiaoyu handling in silence the news of her mother's death and adjusting to the new style of household she finds with her father. But at the same time, the film offers an off-screen narrator's voice, the voice of Xiaoyu (Xu Jinglei), complementing the on-screen character's actions by narrating her emotions, providing factual background, and announcing lapses of time between scenes. In *Letter,* as in *Father,* the female lead played by Xu Jinglei is again the voice-over narrator. In this case, the device is pushed even farther, perhaps too far. By its nature, a letter such as this has an intimate tone, and the reading of the letter adds a psychological intensity to the scenes. When Miss Jiang encounters Mr. Xu for the second time, they are riding in a horse-drawn carriage. Without the voice of the narrator, we would not know how Miss Jiang is feeling; but the narration begins: "Your voice has a magical power that makes it impossible to resist. After years of changes, it was the same. As long as you were calling me, even if I were in my tomb, I would gather my strength to stand up and go with you."

Here, the carriage scene is injected with emotion in a way that suggests the excess not only of the woman's feelings, but also of the power of the narrative voice.

Despite their similarities, the two films feel very different. Xu Jinglei has said that in making *Father and I* her aim was "natural and smooth shooting, plain and realist design."[7] The camera is very often stationary. The musical score does not go far beyond a small repertoire of slow phrases on an electronic keyboard. The general effect is indeed one of a slightly gritty realism. *Father and I* is reminiscent of the melodrama tradition adopted especially by the great Fourth Generation women directors, such as Zhang Nuanxin and Huang Shuqin, featuring a strong story line presented in a slow and subdued lyrical manner by means of small details. *Letter from an Unknown Woman,* by contrast, is a wildly unrealistic story presented in a lavish way. The musical score is rich and beautiful, and at key moments melds hauntingly with the ethereal sound of whistles on the feet of homing pigeons. Musically and visually the film revels in lush signs of a romanticized old China. The key elements in the Chinese cinematic version of Zweig's story are the distinctively "Chinese" elements: the Beijing *siheyuan* (courtyard), flying kites, firecrackers, the Peking Opera, and so on. Such "autoethnographic" imagery characterizes many of the films recently exported from China, notably those by Zhang Yimou and Chen Kaige, and would seem to be aimed especially at an international audience; but it coincides also with the domestic cultural nostalgia for the good old days in prerevolutionary treaty-port Shanghai or ancient Beijing, common on Chinese silver screens in the early part of the twenty-first century. The cinematography is very richly communicative, as when Mr. Xu and Miss Jiang spend a night together toward the end. From the dark outside the room, we see only two elegant textured-glass windows, red in their centers but at a distance from each other, showing the occasional momentary shadow of a moving limb.

Xu Jinglei has said that her aim in *Letter from an Unknown Woman* was to be "purely aesthetic and poetic," setting the film in an earlier China in order to avoid social and political controversy.[8] The enchanting Chinese scenes and music, however, do not make up for the lack of clarity in the story itself. Even the off-screen narrator tells us less than we need to know. The aesthetic qualities seem to have come at the cost of neglecting basic storytelling elements, even defeating the purpose of avoiding controversy. For instance, Miss Jiang's obsession with Mr. Xu is almost entirely unexplained in the film, aside from the point that the little girl was impressed by the rich inviting quality of the man's furniture and books. True, both the plot and the cinematography alert us to look for things unsaid and unshown, in the abstract. But it is hard to imagine any motivation for her devotion, even a pathological motivation, consistent with Mr. Xu's personal shallowness and Miss Jiang's rock-hard strength, self-control, and pride.

The implausibility of Miss Jiang's character is a serious problem for the film. Many feminists, including myself, find Xu Jinglei's rendition of Zweig's story painful to watch, as she reproduces without any irony the logical extreme of the traditional value that a woman must live through her man as his selfless slave and still call it love.[9]

Many female college students in China saw something attractive in the independence of Miss Jiang, which they summed up in the slogan "I love you, but I have nothing to do with you" (*Wo ai ni, dan yü ni wu guan*). That is to say, loving a man does not give him a claim.[10] Xu Jinglei's own explanation, like Miss Jiang's, was quite different: that one who truly loves another wants nothing from that person. If one wants something in return, one becomes reactive; one's happiness comes to depend on what the other person chooses to give.[11] Miss Jiang says in the letter that her aim is to avoid being a burden to Mr. Xu in any way. But her obsessive love for Mr. Xu makes her very much dependent on him and desperate for contact with him; though her pride restrains her action, and to some extent she is able to regard his child as a substitute. Even the letter itself seems an attempt to reach him. Perhaps the aim is to punish him. Or perhaps it is to claim him from beyond the grave. In either case, she is in the end unable to maintain the selfless purpose that has motivated her life.

DREAMS MAY COME

Xu Jinglei's third film is *Dreams May Come* (2006). The official English title is a phrase from Hamlet's soliloquy about hesitating to act, but the Chinese title can be translated more literally as "Dreams shine into reality." The reference is partly to the imperfect border between oneself and the films one makes. In this low-budget experimental film, Xu Jinglei is once again the director and the female lead, though the screenplay is by her close friend Wang Shuo.

Wang Shuo himself was a cultural icon in the 1990s, though even for him this sort of story is unusual. He began writing for television dramas and films in the late 1980s, and most of his film scripts have strong story lines, for instance, *Wanzhu* (The Troubleshooters, 1988), *Yiban shi huoyan, yiban shi haishui* (Half Flame, Half Brine, 1989), and *Yangguang canlan de rizi* (In the Heat of the Sun, 1994; based on his story "Dongwu xiongmeng," Wild beast). Wang wrote the screenplay for *Dreams* after nearly seven years of silence, during which he experienced the death of his father and brother. The advertising for *Dreams* capitalized on his status as well as Xu Jinglei's, and on the rumors that these close friends were something closer. "One man. One woman. One night!" In fact no sexual or romantic sparks fly between the characters. Audiences are said to have been disappointed, as one might imagine.

While Xu Jinglei's second film was very different from her first, this third film is an even greater departure from the first two. Each of the first two films has a rich plot spanning many years, but *Dreams* is limited to one rather abstract conversation in one room. (It was shot in just 16 days.) Indeed, *Dreams* marks a sharp stylistic departure not only from Xu Jinglei's previous work, but from the broad trend of new Chinese art cinema in general. Beginning with Chen Kaige's landmark film *Huang tudi* (Yellow Earth, 1984), the Fifth Generation of filmmakers set a high standard of visual richness and excitement, exercising great care over what Aristotle called "spectacle." The pictures move the episodes forward. By contrast, *Dreams* is first and foremost a dialogue. One can follow the film well enough without looking at it at all. Though the film is visually interesting in its own way, the main interest is in the faces of the characters, and depends on the dialogue rather than vice versa. The conversation itself is highly self-referential and ironic, and complex enough to challenge any viewer. This avant-garde art film was not tailored to suit the taste of the masses, and did not fare well in Chinese cinema houses.

Which is not to say that it lost money. The film conspicuously features several brand names: of cell phones, a matchmaking website, and several beverages. (One of the characters alludes to this fact.) The film's opening night was financed by an electronics company of which Xu Jinglei was the spokesperson. The theme song she sang for the film became a popular single and was also sold as a cell phone ringtone.[12]

Despite the differences from Xu Jinglei's earlier work, there are intriguing similarities. Like her previous two films, this one focuses on the relationship between a woman, played by Xu Jinglei herself, and a man

303

who is not only older (the woman denies that they are of the same generation), but who counts as her superior in a second respect as well. For here,
the woman is an actor and the man is her employer and director. (In each
of her first two films, the part of the older man was played by a famous
director.) In the film, the Actor and Director are lifelong friends. No other
character appears for more than a few seconds. The Actor has come to
the Director's hotel room to report that she is desperately unhappy in her
current job. She does not want to continue acting in the low-grade television soap opera they have been shooting, which has the same title as the
film itself. She wants to break her contract. At the very least, she insists
on dropping the childbirth scene he wants to film the next morning. All
night, the Director tries with ingenious indirection to persuade her to
continue with the project, or talks sincerely with her about life and drama.
(It is often unclear which he is doing, and the interaction is quite busy
on this level.) Despite the man's formal superiority, the woman holds her
own in the exchange, and their positions sometimes seem to reverse:

> D: Suddenly I feel the script is lousy. I don't want to keep a single word. A
> couple of boring people talking meaningless nonsense. . . .
> A: Now you're being like me when I first came in, don't you think?
> D: How about you? Feeling better?
> A: I'm turning into you. . . . Just for the title, it's a pity if we stop making the
> series.

Unlike Xu Jinglei's first two films, this one does not begin and end
with a death. But it does climax near the end with a fantastic disquisition
on death and reincarnation. The film ends at daybreak with the immediate practical problem unresolved.

Dreams emphasizes many of the themes that *Father* and *Letter* have in
common: memory and forgetting, openness and secrecy, companionship
and loneliness, abandonment and concession of wrongdoing. In places
it may even be alluding to Xu Jinglei's earlier work, as in this speech
suggesting *Letter* and also suggesting in context that a filmmaker's work
tends to repeat:

> D: I'll go—[*The Director shouts the beginning of a vulgar curse, then catches
> himself.*]
> A: You'll go where?

D: [*Hardly concealing his invention*]—to mother's place. I haven't been there for weeks. There's a letter for me over there. From a childhood friend. He lives downstairs and saw me many times, but wasn't sure it was me; so he wrote to me at my Mom's address asking, 'Was it you I saw?' I've found in the past five years that there's no-one new in Beijing. You meet someone new at dinner, only to discover that you used to be friends. You cast your net and all you catch is fish you have caught before. Don't you feel that?

The Actor is certainly meant to suggest Xu Jinglei herself. In the soap opera, the Actor plays a character called Lao Xu, which is Xu Jinglei's name for herself on her blog. The Director's photos of the Actor are Xu Jinglei's own publicity shots. Hence, when we look at *Dreams* to find unities in Xu Jinglei's work, we should consider the film not only as one Xu Jinglei piece among others, but also perhaps as a kind of commentary on her artistic life, including her public persona.

Xu Jinglei has written in her blog that the film fits more than one moment of emptiness she herself has felt: first as an actor and then much later as a director, around the time of the making of this film. "I think that every person goes through this kind of experience at some time in life. One suddenly feels that one has lost one's way. Looking back or looking ahead, one can find no meaning in life. One holds all one's own precious things in suspicion, and one is unwilling to continue with what seems pointless."[13]

To explain her desire to quit, the Actor makes various complaints about the character of Lao Xu and about the screenplay. But the fundamental problem is that she is having trouble separating herself from her acting. She is finding it difficult to be real. "Maybe when we're drunk, that's the real us. . . . I'm always acting the character called myself. I thought no one knew, but everyone knows. They're all just watching a performance. Even when I'm drunk I'm acting." Accordingly, in at least one respect the film seems to aim to deflate Xu Jinglei's persona as a popular "idol" (a term used in the film). It attacks her visual image; for as the Actor says, she does not want to be seen as a "beautiful woman." And as the Director says to her, "We aren't a young girl anymore." There is hardly a moment when the film does not remind us of the imperfections of her teeth. She has a distinctly unflattering haircut. She talks while stuffing her mouth full of food. Soon after objecting that in a childbirth scene she would have to contort her face, she mistakenly tries to swallow a seltzer pill without water, contorting her face as she chokes and coughs.

The Director, played brilliantly by Han Tongsheng, stands in a way for Wang Shuo. The film's advertising played on that point, as mentioned above, and there is some physical resemblance. But the audience may be expected to notice from the opening credits that Wang Shuo is the film's screenwriter, not its director. Xu Jinglei is the director. Within the film, the Actor and Director often discuss the soap opera's Screenwriter, whom we never meet, and the changes the Director has made to the script without the Screenwriter's knowledge.[14] In some sense, the conflicts between the Actor and Director (or among all three characters) may represent the tensions among the different positions Xu Jinglei has occupied in making her films.[15]

The Director is a manipulator. The Actor knows this about him, but she is often fooled at the expense of her self-esteem. The Director is a great talker and persuader, a spinner of visions, avowing a new set of attitudes toward life and art at the drop of a hat whenever he thinks it will serve his purpose of finishing the project. The Actor does not believe that she herself is the kind of person who has ulterior motives (*xinyan*), and we have no reason to disagree. The Actor says the Director is a "big-head," whereas actors, we learn, are merely vain. But she has the strengths of stubbornness and a willingness to be confused. She is not attached to any account of her reasons, so she is not easily moved by ideas.

Dreams uses self-reference to play with the line between art and reality, suggesting that we write our parts not only individually but together. For example, agreed alterations to the eponymous soap opera are sometimes enacted in the film itself, as in the following two exchanges.

A: Can't you let Lao Xu talk less? It's annoying.

D: OK. Lao Xu will say less.

A: [*after a pause*] I wanted to say something. But you interrupted me. Now I won't tell you.

A: The one who treats me badly and deceives me: he shouldn't be made ridiculous either.

D: You really want to be good. I understand. We mustn't despise the bad guy. He's bad because he has problems, and had no other choice. . . .

A: He [*should be someone who*] thinks he's doing the right thing. . . . He should be relaxed and happy, smiling whatever happens. No matter what bad luck he has, he doesn't mind, it's just life. . . . [*The Director stares at her with a fixed grin.*] What are you thinking? Bad thoughts?

D: No. I'm not against you. I feel you're teaching me something. Life is just like this, and we have to go with the flow. [*pause*] I'm going for a smoke. [*pause*] Do you really think that?

A: No, I don't think like that, but I want to act like that so I will begin to think like that.

The Director and Actor do seem to agree both in ridiculing each other for supporting the tasteless illusions of popular programming and in challenging the value of keeping reality bare. Progress comes from pretending to be better. The conversation underlines at least two kinds of distinction between reality and dreams. One is a distinction between reality and acting or drama. The other is a distinction between reality and ideals. These two distinctions are not elided. Rather, while acting seems to be necessary to improve reality, drama that is too unrealistically good cannot hold people's attention. It is important not to direct too much of one's art to an audience too far beneath oneself. But the characters are of several minds about how to characterize their audience.

The climax of *Father* comes when the father loses his ability to speak. The conclusion of *Letter* shows Mr. Xu alone in the dark, unable to respond to the woman who has been speaking so deeply to him. In *Dreams,* the long dialogue ends by approaching a wordless portrayal of the very idea of an objective view of the matters at issue, or a view of bare reality. The Director's tales of his own possible reincarnations take standpoints so far removed from the petty concerns and illusions of daily life that they involve the forgetting of language. As the film crew begins to pound at the door, the Director turns off the light in the apartment. The warm artificial light of night becomes the bare cold blue of oncoming dawn. Sitting in silence on the floor, the Actor and the Director ignore the crew's interpellative shouts. The Actor's friends start sending text messages to her cell phone, but she types back that her keys are not working and she cannot chat. Actor and Director have ceased to talk. They now only make silly faces at each other in a way that strongly suggests the kind of outtake where the actors drop out of character.

Thus the film falls away, leaving the audience to check their own cell phones and decide when to get up and rejoin the world (fig. 13.3).

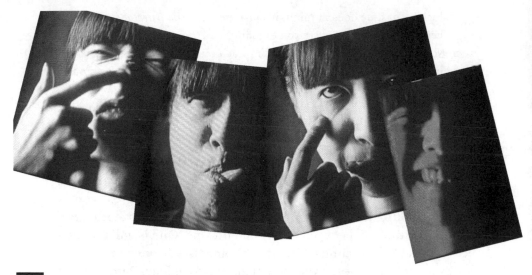

FIGURE 13.3 *Dreams May Come,* 2006

CONCLUSION

Partly because of the values shaping the social and intellectual life of the film academies, fresh graduates typically aim to make art films. (Xu Jinglei was trained as an actor rather than a director, in the Department of Performance at the Beijing Film Academy in the 1990s. She is now a professor there.) According to one estimate in 2005, 90 percent of Chinese feature film directors work on art films, and only 10 percent of directors produce commercial films.[16] In the face of so much competition for a tiny pool of domestic ticket sales, directors of art films must find sources of profit other than the domestic box office. Xu Jinglei has proved expert at doing so, becoming a multitalented cinematic force. She is a director, a screenwriter, an actor, and a magazine editor and writer. She owns a private media company, a cultural foundation, and a library for the blind. And she has been successful in each of these efforts. The fact that she is able to wear several hats in any one project, along with her savvy as a financial manager and networker, has allowed her to work more freely and independently than many other filmmakers can manage. She can afford to be true to her film-craft; she does not have to make a film she does not like.

There are three kinds of objective success at which a good art film director in China can realistically aim. The first is national recognition.

Xu Jinglei's first film gave her a national reputation as a first-rate director. The second kind of success is international recognition. Xu Jinglei's second film won prestigious international awards and established her as a name on the global stage. She now sometimes serves on juries for international film festivals. The third kind of success is to produce an experimental film that wins the admiration of a very select audience in the cultural world. Xu Jinglei's third film has achieved this success. For instance, the well-known artist Ai Weiwei praised this film as the bravest film exploration of the borderline state between reality and fantasy, between life and death.[17] Xu's work shows an astonishing combination of consistently high quality and diversity of style. That very diversity suggests that she has not yet found her voice. When she does so, she may become one of the great film directors of her generation.

NOTES

1. In 2003, Xu Jinglei won Best Actress for *Kaiwang chuntian de ditie* (Spring Subway, 2002) at the 26th annual Popular Cinema Hundred Flowers Film Awards, Best Actress for *Wo ai ni* (I Love You, 2003) at the 9th annual Huabiao Film Awards, and Best Supporting Actress for *Wo de meili xiangchou* (Far From Home, 2003) at the 23rd annual Chinese Golden Rooster Awards.

2. http://www.kaila.com.cn.

3. Xu Jinglei and Sun Ganlu, "Zhuanhuan yu yanyuan daoyan zhijian" (Between acting and directing), 302.

4. For details about this Hollywood classic, see Virginia Wright Wexman and Karen Hollinger, eds., *Letter from an Unknown Woman: Max Ophüls, Director*.

5. Zhang Huijun and Ma Yufeng, eds., *Suoyoude jinbu doushi zai chengdan zeren de guocheng zhong dedao de: yingpian 'Yige mosheng nüren de laixin' daoyan chuangzuo tan* (All Progress is Achieved through the Process of Taking Responsibility: A Conversation with the Film Director of *Letter from an Unknown Woman*), 52.

6. We see a playfulness in the choice of surnames for the two main characters in the film. Phonetically, the surname of each character is the same as that of the actor who plays the opposite character. Mr. Xu in the film is played by Jiang Wen, a well-known film director, and Miss Jiang is played by Xu Jinglei.

7. Xu Jinglei, interview in *Renmin luntan* (People's Forum), "Xu Jinglei: Qinqing dadong" (Xu Jinglei: Moved by Kinship), 57.

8. Zhang Huijun and Ma Yufeng, "Suoyoude jinbu," 52, 54.

9. Yu Hua has written a Chinese story mimicking and mocking Zweig's *A Letter from an Unknown Woman*, called "Zhanli" (Shudder). The story line is as follows: An aging poet at the end of his fame finds among his books a letter of admiration written by a girl twelve years ago. He has no memory of any encounters with the girl, but as he is a habitual

womanizer, he writes back to the girl. Very soon he receives a second letter from the woman, whom he had seduced and abandoned twelve years ago. Contrary both to Zweig's story and to Xu Jinglei's version, the woman in Yu Hua's story does not die alone in depression over her obsession with the poet. She has lived her own rugged life fully, and she chooses to confront the poet who is so forgetful of his past seductions. At the meeting, she plays a cat-and-mouse game with him, analyzing and satirizing his deplorable tricks. Near the end of the story the two have sex. As the woman has said that she would do, she looks straight into the man's face to observe his facial expression as he ejaculates—witnessing his final ugly convulsive shudder. Yu Hua's story is pungent and farcical. In many ways, it is a much more satisfactory contemporary Chinese rewriting of Zweig's story than Xu Jinglei's.

10. My conversations with college students in Nanjing in the summer of 2008.

11. Yi Lijing, "Xu Jinglei," 36.

12. Wen He, "Yibu chetouchewei de bagua dianying" (A Total Gossip Film), 69.

13. See Xu Jinglei's blog entry for October 11, 2006, http://blog.sina.com.cn/s/blog_46f37fb5010005hs.html.

14. Xu Jinglei has said that Wang Shuo gave her free rein to change the screenplay. Some changes were indeed made to the original text, but we do not know who made them or when. See her blog entry for October 11, 2006, http://blog.sina.com.cn/s/blog_46f37fb5010005hs.html.

15. In the film, the Director has serious trouble with his neck. In fact, Xu Jinglei had been having problems with her neck, learning only after the film was released that the problem was not with her cervical vertebrae. See her blog entry for September 30, 2006, http://blog.sina.com.cn/s/blog_46f37fb5010005do.html.

16. Li Lei, "Yishu dianying: jiannan de shangyehua" (Art films: A Difficult Commercialization), 15.

17. Ai Weiwei, "Ai Weiwei yanzhong de *Mengxiang zhaojin xianshi* he Wang Shuo" (*Dreams May Come* and Wang Shuo in the Eyes of Ai Weiwei).

Part V

<hr>

MIGRATION, DIASPORA, AND
TRANSCULTURAL PRACTICE
OF GENDER AND CINEMA

14

In Search of Esther Eng

BORDER-CROSSING PIONEER IN
CHINESE-LANGUAGE FILMMAKING

KAR LAW

TRANSLATED BY CHRIS TONG

THE FORGOTTEN MEMORIES OF ESTHER ENG

In an August 1995 issue of the American entertainment news magazine, *Variety,* Todd McCarthy published an article titled "Eng's Lost Pix, a Chinese Puzzle," mentioning Esther Eng for the first time in recent memory.[1] Despite the recent surge of scholarship on issues such as identity and gender in Asian cinema, film historians seem to have forgotten this pioneer in Chinese-language filmmaking. More unfortunately, her films seem to have eluded film archives altogether. If Eng had worked in the film industry today, she could have easily been seen as a champion of transnational filmmaking, feminist filmmaking, or antiwar filmmaking. In many ways, Eng was ahead of her time. As a Chinese-American woman filmmaker active from the 1930s to the 1950s, she put into practice many theories that later gained currency in academic scholarship.

I had just organized a retrospective called "Early Images of Hong Kong and China" for the Hong Kong International Film Festival in the autumn of 1995 when I first read McCarthy's article. Although I had come across information on Eng earlier in my archival research, his article particularly inspired me. When Frank Bren, an Australian friend of mine whom I had known for years through film festivals, approached me about coauthoring a book on Hong Kong cinema, it turned out that we both shared an interest in Eng.[2] It was then that we decided to retrieve her from oblivion.

Our initial research into Chinese and English sources was intermittent during the first two years. In 1998, we serendipitously made contact with Sally Ng (Ng Kam-ping), Esther Eng's youngest sibling. Sally Ng was more than seventy years old and was living in San Francisco. As someone who once managed her sister's film distribution business, she was able to provide us with valuable photographs, printed materials, and anecdotal information. Her contribution became an early foundation of our research into the film career of Esther Eng.

CHINESE-LANGUAGE FILMMAKING FROM SAN FRANCISCO TO HONG KONG

Esther Eng was born in San Francisco on September 24, 1914, to Chinese parents who emigrated from Taishan in mainland China's Guangdong province. Her father, Ng Yu-jat, was a merchant in San Francisco and father to ten children. Eng developed an early interest in the performing arts, working at the Mandarin Theatre where she could watch films for free. Cantonese opera was another popular form of entertainment at the time and has a long history in the United States. Cantonese opera troupes toured the West Coast as early as the mid-nineteenth century, when Chinese migrants arrived to work during the Gold Rush in California and on the transcontinental railroad. The transformation of San Francisco into a metropolis fueled the growth of Chinatown, and Cantonese opera subsequently flourished. However, the Chinese community suffered in the late nineteenth century because of the Chinese Exclusion Act. The devastating San Francisco earthquake of 1906 further destroyed the urban structures of Chinatown. It was only after Chinatown was reconstructed that the Chinese community expanded and recovered.

The 1920s was the golden age of Cantonese opera in North America. Troupes from Guangzhou and Hong Kong frequently toured the United States from coast to coast. San Francisco, as the main stop on the West Coast, was home to two venues, the Mandarin and Great China. There were occasionally performances of Beijing opera as well: Mei Lanfang, for example, performed at Great China in 1930 on his American tour. In the 1920s, troupes consisted of women only; men and women began to perform together in the 1930s. Male leads included Ma Sze-tsang, Sun Lan-chou, Tsang Sam-dor, and Lan Siu-gei; female leads included Wu Dip-ying, Tam Lam-hing, and Tam Yuk-jan. Starting in the 1930s, these stars often made appearances in San Francisco and New York.

Chinese filmmakers first employed sound technology in 1931, and Chinese sound films were shown in Shanghai and Guangzhou as early as 1932. Some filmmakers used equipment purchased overseas, while others improvised with their own equipment to achieve full or partial sound. Among the most successful sound films of that era was the remake of a Cantonese opera called *Baijinlong* (White Gold Dragon, 1933). Already popular among Cantonese speakers throughout Hong Kong, Guangdong province, and Southeast Asia, the opera was remade into a film by Shanghai's Tianyi Film Company in cooperation with the Cantonese opera star, Sit Kok-sin. The film premiered in 1933 to much acclaim and was so profitable that, according to legend, Tianyi subsequently opened a branch office in Hong Kong to produce Cantonese opera films for the markets in southern China and Southeast Asia.

In the same year, a Chinese-American from San Francisco named Chiu Shu-sun[3] made a Cantonese film called *Gelü qingchao* (Romance of the Songsters, 1933). Trained in mechanical engineering, Chiu adapted Hollywood film and sound technologies and planned to make the film with funds from his father and other Chinese merchants. Kwan Man-ching of Hong Kong's Lianhua Film Company became involved with the film when he met Chiu in San Francisco on a business trip. Kwan had studied in the United States earlier and apprenticed in Hollywood before returning to Hong Kong to work as a director for Lianhua. With the help of Kwan, Chiu recruited Kwan Tak-hing and Wu Dip-ying, who happened to be touring in San Francisco at the time, to be the male and female leads, respectively. *Romance of the Songsters* tells the stories of Cantonese opera singers from mainland China touring in the United States, combining romantic, comedic, and musical elements. Although the film was originally intended to be shown to Chinese-American communities in the United States, Kwan recommended the film to the head of Lianhua, Law Ming-yau, who distributed the film in Hong Kong, Guangdong province, and Southeast Asia to much box office success. Chiu and Kwan had plans to produce more Cantonese sound films for Lianhua, but the partnership never materialized. Consequently, they raised funds in the United States for their own company called Grandview Film Company. From 1935 onward, Grandview produced

Cantonese sound films in Hong Kong and showed them to Chinese-American audiences in the United States.

Chinese sound films emerged as a new phenomenon from 1933 to 1935, traveling from Shanghai to Guangzhou and Hong Kong and later to Southeast Asia and North America. Chiu Shu-sun and Kwan Man-ching were early pioneers experimenting with Cantonese sound film in San Francisco. They benefited from a creative environment nurtured by San Francisco's high concentration of Cantonese speakers, the geographic and cultural proximity to Hollywood, and the desire to experiment with film and sound technologies.

HEARTACHES: THE FIRST CANTONESE SOUND FILM MADE IN HOLLYWOOD

316

Eng's formative years were influenced by major artistic and historical developments. She was immersed in Cantonese opera as an adolescent in the 1920s and was particularly intrigued by the all-female troupes that played both male and female roles. Among the many performers whom she befriended was Wai Kim-fong. A childhood friend of Eng's, Wai began training for Cantonese opera at a young age and eventually achieved moderate fame touring the United States professionally. Her association with Wai, in addition to the burgeoning industry of Cantonese sound films in San Francisco, nurtured Eng's early interest in filmmaking. At the same time, the events in Asia in the 1930s fueled her artistic ambitions. Imperial Japan's militarist aggression in Shanghai during the January 28 Incident (1932) rallied the anti-Imperialist sentiments of people throughout China and beyond. *Shijiu lu jun kangzhan guangrong shi* (The Glorious Resistant History of the 19th Army, 1932), a Lianhua-produced film, was shown on the West Coast in the United States in 1934. In 1935, *Shengming xian* (Lifeline, 1935), an anti-Imperialist film directed by Grandview's Kwan Man-ching, created a sensation and was also shown in San Francisco. It was likely that, at this historical juncture, Eng committed herself to filmmaking, consolidating her artistic and antiwar passions. With the support of her father, Eng established the Kwong Ngai Talking Picture Company in 1935 at her family home, 1010 Washington Street.[4] One can read her patriotism in the emblematic address: "double 10" commemorates the date of the Chinese Revolution in 1911, while "Washington Street" honors George Washington, the first president of the United States. It was also at this time that she adopted the English name "Esther Eng" because "Ng" was difficult to pronounce and "N. G." stood for "No Good" in film parlance.

At the age of twenty-one, Eng had gone to university, but had no prior training or experience in filmmaking. Nonetheless, she and her friends managed to rent a studio on Sunset Boulevard in Hollywood and produced their first film, *Xinhen* (Heartaches, also known as Sum Hun, 1935), distributed by Cathay Pictures Ltd., California. Billed as "A Bruce Wong-Esther Eng Co-production," the film was directed by Frank Tong, starring Beal Wong as the male lead and Wai Kim-fong as the female lead. The film was shot partially in color by the noted Hollywood cinematographer, Paul Ivano, with James Wong Howe as consultant (fig. 14.1).

In the style of the classic "tearjerker," *Heartaches* tells the story of a tragic romance between a Cantonese opera singer (Wai) and a pilot training in the United States (Wong). The opera singer secretly finances the pilot's training and resolutely refuses his love in the wake of Imperial Japan's militarist aggression so as to force him to serve in the Chinese resistance. After the battle in Shanghai, her lover is married and returns

317

FIGURE 14.1 Esther Eng (sitting in the middle without hat) with crews of *Sum Hun*

to the United States with his wife. Despite having no regrets, the opera singer is so heartbroken that she falls seriously ill. The lovers eventually reunite, and she passes away in his arms. In addition to the conventional love story, however, the film contains a deeper commentary on wartime resistance. It shows how men and women can rise above interpersonal love to participate in the nation's defense and depicts true love as ultimately selfless and self-sacrificing.

Imperial Japan's aggression in China in the 1930s made international headlines, and the world watched China closely. Hollywood's Metro-Goldwyn-Mayer (MGM), for example, bought the rights to Pearl Buck's award-winning novel, *The Good Earth,* in 1933. MGM obtained permits to film on location in China and called for Chinese-American actors to audition in an attempt to avoid the offensive "yellow-face" acting by white actors. Eng was reportedly among the sixteen Chinese-American actors selected to star in the film. According to Eng, she was originally chosen for the role of Lotus, but there were so many delays and problems with preproduction that she began to focus on her own projects. Eventually, the male and female leads were given to white actors and the role of Lotus to someone else.

Heartaches premiered in February 1936 to Chinese communities in California to much applause. Encouraged by the success, Eng decided to break into the southern China and Southeast Asia markets. She and Wai Kim-fong boarded the passenger liner *President Hoover* in May 1936, arriving in Hong Kong a month later.

WARTIME FILMMAKING: ENG'S HONG KONG PERIOD

The Hong Kong film industry received Eng and Wai warmly upon their arrival because their reputation had preceded them: *Heartaches* was the first film produced by a Chinese filmmaker in Hollywood and was partially shot in color. *Heartaches* was scheduled to premiere under the Chinese title *Tiexue fanghun* at the Queen's Theatre, which usually showed Western films. According to the eleventh issue of *Rose,* See Ho Hotel organized a welcome party that boasted a guest list of representatives from more than fifty cinemas and companies, including publications such as *Ling Sing* and *Canton Magazine.*

Eng decided to stay in Hong Kong after the successful reception of *Heartaches,* and Wai would eventually perform in four of Eng's films. Eng produced and directed her next film, *Minzu nüyingxiong* (National

Heroine, 1937), using Yu Gai-ping's script. Wai plays a woman who enlists in the Chinese army to prove that women can also shoulder combat duties in the resistance. The film premiered in Hong Kong on March 13, 1937, and later in the mainland. To offset the serious subject matter in the film and to appeal to a wider audience, Eng added numerous musical numbers and comedic scenes. The film was billed as a contemporary tragicomedy—"a barrage of laughs and tears." At the young age of twenty-two, Eng was already a leading filmmaker of her generation.

Eng's early films reflected the historical situation of the late-1930s. Imperial Japan's militarist intentions were more than clear by 1936 and materialized in the Nanjing Massacre by the end of 1937. That women should carry out combat duties was no longer mentioned as theory, but became an actual practice. Lai Man-wai, known as "the Father of Hong Kong cinema," wrote on his New Year's Day greeting cards in 1936: "The frontline of defense is the air force, while the culture of resistance is film." In the spirit of Lai's statement, women prominently participated in the resistance effort. Actress-turned-pilot Li Xiaqing flew around the world to raise funds for the Chinese resistance, while League of Nations representative Hilda Yan trained as a pilot in solidarity with Chinese women and the Chinese Air Force. Eng's films reflected women's participation in the resistance and the concerted effort to boost Chinese morale during the war.

The concerns of Eng's next films shifted from wartime resistance to women in society. Her third film, *Shiwan qingren* (100,000 Lovers, 1938), premiered on International Women's Day on March 8, 1938, distributed by Grandview.[5] The romantic comedy tells the story of a man (Ng Chor-fan) who leaves behind his wife (Wai Kim-fong) in the countryside to find work in the city, where the daughter (Lam Mui-mui) of a tycoon falls in love with him. The love triangle is eventually resolved when the husband and wife reunite and return to the countryside. In the same year, Eng wrote and directed *Duhua fengyu* (Jealousy, 1938) and began filming *Sanshiliu nü tiangang* (36 Heavenly Ferocious Women, 1939), later renamed *Nüren shijie* (Woman's World, 1939). Premiered on February 1, 1939, *Woman's World* boasted an all-female cast. The thirty-six characters represented women from Hong Kong's different social strata: an old-fashioned teacher, a fashionably dressed secretary, a clever journalist, a conscientious lawyer, a compassionate doctor, a free-spirited nightclub hostess, a decadent socialite, an unlucky divorcee, and so on. The characters were played by various stars of the time, and the film was possibly Hong Kong's first film with an all-female cast (fig. 14.2).

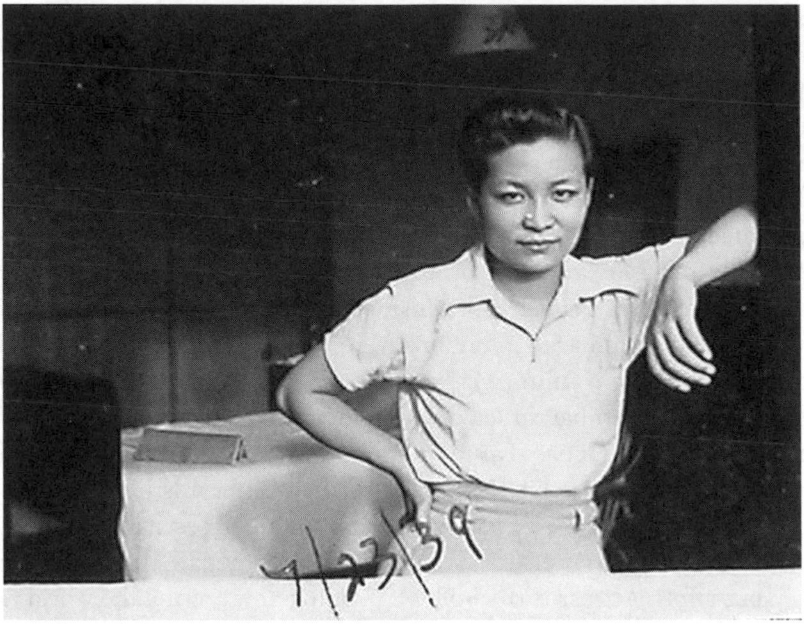

FIGURE 14.2 Esther Eng in Hong Kong, 1939

While Eng enjoyed professional success, her personal life suffered. She contracted malaria during the preproduction of her next film and was restricted to bed rest for three months. Furthermore, her relationship with Wai deteriorated because of the stress of collaboration. Eng and Wai had been childhood friends in San Francisco, and their relationship evolved into a romantic one by the time they settled in Hong Kong. By 1938, rumors suggested that a woman by the name of Lin had become involved with Eng. Eng and Wai separated, and Eng's affair with Lin lasted briefly.

The escalation of World War II eventually forced Eng and Wai to return to the United States in 1939. The United Kingdom had declared war on Nazi Germany, and Imperial Japan's forces had moved into southern China. The fall of Hong Kong seemed only imminent. After co-directing her last wartime film, *Yiye fuqi* (Husband and Wife for One Night, 1939), Eng returned to San Francisco in October at the plea of her family. Wai had already returned to the United States several months earlier. Nonetheless, Eng did not lose touch with the film industry in Hong Kong. In 1940, she wrote a letter to the editor of *Ling Sing*, reporting on her visits to various studios in Hollywood. She suggested that Hollywood's "B"-movie system would be a suitable framework for Hong Kong cinema, citing short production times, low budgets, and a flexible style that accommodated both creative and commercial concerns.

Upon her return to the United States, Eng teamed up with Grandview's Chiu Shu-sun and Kwan Man-ching on the film *Jinmen nü* (Golden Gate Girl, 1941). Eng and Kwan were credited as directors, and Chiu as cinematographer. Kwan also wrote the script and acted in a supporting role. The film tells the love story between a student fascinated with Cantonese opera (Cho Yee-man) and a Cantonese opera troupe member (Wong Hok-sing). Despite her father's objection, the student marries the troupe member and bears a daughter with him, dying in childbirth. The daughter grows up and eventually reconciles with her grandfather. An American film critic by the name of "Wern" wrote: "The story is easy to follow and is loaded with familiar scenes around Frisco, particularly Chinatown, but also the Waterfront, Golden Gate Park, etc."[6] It is worth noting that this is the only extant review of Eng's work by an American critic. Also noteworthy is that Bruce Lee's father—Lee Hoi-chun of Cantonese opera fame—was touring the United States at the time of filming, and Bruce Lee himself, then three months old, appeared in several scenes as a newborn girl.

The film was dubbed in English and Cantonese. The English version doubled as publicity for the "One Bowl of Rice Movement," an effort initiated in 1939 by Song Qingling and her friends around the world to raise funds for humanitarian efforts in China—to donate one bowl of rice at a time to the victims of war. Whether intended or not, the English version credited Eng as the director and Kwan as the scriptwriter, whereas the Cantonese version cited Kwan as the director with no mention of Eng. Nonetheless, Chinese communities in Hong Kong, San Francisco, and New York responded generously to the fundraising campaign. The prominent women pilots, Li Xiaqing and Hilda Yan, even flew to publicize the movement.

The escalation of World War II in the Pacific indirectly fueled Eng's career in the United States. While Eng was working with Grandview, she diverted her spare energy to a film distribution company that she had formed with her father. Golden Gate Silver Light Company had bought rights to numerous Cantonese films and begun distributing them to cinemas throughout North America and Latin America. By 1941, Eng's father had passed away, and the United States had declared war on Japan. Eng could not travel to Hong Kong, and film production had already stopped there in any case. With few opportunities to make films in Hollywood, she focused her energy on her distribution business. There was still a demand for Chinese-language films by diasporic Chinese communities in the Americas, and Eng, with the help of her sister, Sally, seized the opportunity.

The film industry in postwar Hong Kong proved to be disappointing for Eng. In September 1946, *Ling Sing* reported that Eng's company had distributed more than forty Cantonese films in the Americas. Eng, by then, had returned to Hong Kong to procure new films, on the one hand, and to look for directing opportunities, on the other. Postwar Hong Kong, however, lacked adequate equipment and film stock, and the production costs were too high, even compared to those of Hollywood "B" movies. Throughout September and October, local show-business articles suggested that Eng was disillusioned with the Hong Kong film industry. Eng herself spoke to a reporter in December of her negotiations with Nanyang Film Company about distributing its films in the Americas.[7]

322   Eng's last project in Hong Kong involved planning a film on guerilla fighters in the Chinese resistance against Imperial Japan. From mid-September 1946 to early 1947, she shuttled between Guangzhou and Hong Kong to secure funding and actors for the film. She had made the acquaintance of Ng Yim-ming, a Cantonese actor who claimed to have trained as a pilot in the United States before joining the Chinese Air Force. Ng was related to General Ng Fan, who led thousands of guerilla fighters during the resistance. On the condition that Eng cast Ng Fan in a leading role, Ng Yim-ming would persuade Ng Fan to fund the production and assemble a team of veterans to participate in the filming. Eng agreed and asked her friend Wu Peng—who would later be responsible for popularizing the martial arts hero, Wong Fei-hung, in his numerous films—to write the script. Preproduction continued to make progress, after Eng and Wu met with Ng Fan in Guangzhou on December 14 and later surveyed several battle sites in Zhongshan. The film was subsequently named *Youji yingxiong* (Guerilla Heroes), and it was reported that a popular Cantonese actor, Cheung Ying, had agreed to star in a leading role. Just as shooting was about to begin, the project took a downturn unexpectedly. *Sing Tao Evening Post* reported on January 12, 1947, that shooting was canceled because of financial and other complications.[8] Eng returned to the United States shortly thereafter. One could only speculate as to what differences of opinion existed between Eng, the director, and Ng Fan, the veteran.

Esther Eng never made films in Hong Kong and China again after 1947, but instead, continued to make films in the United States. Issues such as identity and gender became salient features in the early half of her filmmaking career. She challenged gender conventions, often wearing "masculine" clothes and hairstyles. She also openly courted women, expressing her sexual orientation. More significantly, she reversed the gender convention of wartime culture that "men should defend the country," as a popular saying goes. From her first film, *Heartaches,* Eng argued that women could also shoulder wartime responsibilities and participate in the resistance.

One could observe from her biography that her "identity politics" represented the margins of American, Hong Kong, and Chinese societies. Although she made films for Chinese-American communities in the United States, her work was not accepted by the mainstream film industry. Film literature in the United States hardly ever mentioned her name and work. In Hong Kong and China, she was welcomed and celebrated at a superficial level. Newspaper articles and entertainment magazines often reported the more "sensationalist" aspects of her career such as her "masculine" demeanor, romantic relationships, and professional setbacks, essentially casting her as the "other." In other words, as a Chinese-American lesbian filmmaker, she was doubly marginalized—a minority in the United States, as well as in Hong Kong and China.

Nonetheless, Eng was extremely productive in Hong Kong. Her most representative work was *National Heroine,* which she directed and distributed with her own company, Kwong Ngai. The other works were *100,000 Lovers, Woman's World, Husband and Wife for One Night,* and *Jealousy.* Although Eng had signed on to direct two additional films, *Niangzi jun* (The Amazons) and *Huangtang yuelao* (The Funniest God of Love), her desire to continue working in Hong Kong was waning.[9] On October 9, 1939, Eng returned to the United States.[10] Only several of her close friends received news of her departure and saw her off at the pier. According to the press, Eng was returning to the United States to raise funds for her own company in Hong Kong.

Eng visited Hong Kong twice during her lifetime. She completed five films during her stay of more than three years from June 1936 to October 1939. She left three additional film projects unfinished. Her second stay was merely six months from August 1946 to February 1947, since her project to make a film about the resistance against Imperial Japan failed to materialize. At the very least, she was able to acquire U.S. distribution rights to thirty films produced by the Nanyang Film Company.[11] Furthermore, she publicized plans to invite Hong Kong actors to make

Cantonese color films in the studios of Hollywood. Eng was merely in her early thirties and would continue her filmmaking career in the United States. Shortly after her return to San Francisco, she began to work with Grandview immediately.

LOVE AFTER WARTIME: ENG'S FILMMAKING IN THE UNITED STATES

By the fall of 1947, Eng had already directed a color film for Grandview in the United States. *Lanhu biyu* (Blue Jade, 1947) was produced by Chiu Shu-sun, starring the Cantonese opera performer Siu Fei-fei—originally named Li Fei-fei—as the female lead, with Liu Kei-wai and Tang Pui in the leading male roles. As in *Heartaches,* the plot revolves around a love triangle. A young teacher (Siu) falls in love with an engineer (Liu) who leaves for China. Upon returning to the United States, the engineer finds that the teacher has fallen in love with someone else. Scenic locations throughout California served as the backdrop for the film, which made its way to Hong Kong because of its romantic appeal.

324

In early 1948, after a tour of Latin America to distribute films for Nanyang, Eng began directing *Chilai chunyiwan* (Too Late for Spring, 1948). She wrote to her friend Cheung Jok-hong, publisher and chief editor of the Hong Kong journal *Ling Sing*:

> Ever since I finished *Blue Jade* for Grandview, I have been traveling in Latin America on film business. After that, I was planning to make another film, *Bixue du lanqiao* (Crossing the Blue Bridge), starring Wu Dip-lai. However, she could not make it to San Francisco for personal reasons. So I changed my schedule and began shooting another film, *Too Late for Spring,* starring Siu Fei-fei, Liu Kei-wai, and Suet Ying-hong; others such as Sek Yin-jee, Lee Chor-fun, and Shum Lit-fu; and newcomers Wong Chuk-fun and Lui Ming. Shooting has finished, and the film is being edited. Soon, it can be shown in Hong Kong.[12]

Shot on 16mm color stock, *Too Late for Spring* is a romantic comedy, released by Golden Gate Silver Light. Inspired by the Hollywood film *Back Street* (1941), the film tells the story of a Chinese-American woman (Siu) who falls in love with a Chinese-American GI (Liu). According to *Hei Man,* Eng was able to finance her production independently, supply

FIGURE 14.3 Esther Eng with actors on location of *Too Late for Spring*

her own camera and audio equipment, and make use of a large studio (fig. 14.3). Golden Gate Silver Light produced one more film, *Huangdao qingyan* (Mad Fire, Mad Love, 1949), which was shot on location in Hawaii. Unfortunately, the film has since been lost.

Eng staged a comeback in the two years since leaving Hong Kong. She began working with Siu Fei-fei, who not only starred in three of her films but also became a close friend in a relationship that lasted well into the 1950s. Eng's career was reported by English and Chinese newspapers in places such as Cuba, Hawaii, Seattle, New York, San Francisco, Hong Kong, Guangzhou, and Singapore.[13] She worked mainly on low-budget, independent productions, often shooting on location. The scripts usually focused on the romantic relationship between a young woman and a man with a worldly background. Unlike her earlier works, however, these films tended to highlight the love story and downplay historical trauma, perhaps speaking to the consolatory atmosphere of postwar Hong Kong.

After successfully establishing her film production and distribution company in the United States, Eng decided to stage a "glorious return" to Hong Kong. This time, Eng was accompanied by Siu Fei-fei and the Cantonese opera and film star, Wu Dip-ying. The three boarded the passenger liner *Gordon* on July 10, 1948, and were scheduled to arrive in Hong Kong on July 30.

A coincidence, however, changed the rest of her life. In her letter to Cheung Jok-hong dated July 26, 1948, Eng mentioned a change in her travel plans. Instead of sailing to Hong Kong with Siu Fei-fei as planned, they would stop over in Honolulu for several days and then fly to Hong Kong. During their brief stay, the local Chinese community warmly welcomed Eng and even invited her to make a film about life in Hawaii. Unable to refuse their sincere request, Eng went to work immediately, beginning with the script. She also telephoned San Francisco and invited Liu Kei-wai to Honolulu to perform with Siu Fei-fei and a local comedian, Lee Kok-sing. As it turned out, Eng and Siu stayed in Honolulu for three months and made *Mad Fire, Mad Love*.

Since Eng was the first person to produce a Chinese-language film in Honolulu, the local Chinese community was especially supportive. Several local Chinese newspapers frequently reported on Eng and her crew during their intense period of filming in August and September. Some even compared the occasion to turning a new page in the 50-year history of Chinese-Americans in Honolulu. The film tells the story of a Chinese sailor who has drifted to a small island in Hawaii. He meets a Hawaiian family of Chinese descent and is employed as a language tutor to the daughter (Siu). They soon fall in love, but the sailor must return to China to an arranged marriage; meanwhile, the young woman suffers discrimination by the locals for dating an outsider. Eventually, the sailor returns to the island and elopes with the young woman, sailing for China.

Copies of the film have been lost, and no historical documentation of the film can be found. Fortunately, Sally Ng was able to supply production stills and newspaper clippings to reconstruct a sense of the film. *Mad Fire, Mad Love* was an ambitious work, and it is unfortunate, if not perplexing, that the film seemed to have eluded the film history of Hawaii. The script, however, remains a rich source of material for analyzing the cultural politics, race relations, and gender conventions of the period.

RUNNING FROM THE CAMERA: ENG AS RESTAURANT OWNER IN NEW YORK CITY

At the height of her career, Eng suddenly retreated from the limelight and moved to New York City with Siu Fei-fei. In 1951, they opened a Chinese restaurant called BoBo in Manhattan, which was sold after some years, and opened a larger one next door called Han Palace, later renamed Esther Eng Restaurant. Another restaurant of hers called Eng's Corner on Mott Street was also notably successful. Friends from the Cantonese opera circle who visited the restaurants often called Eng "Brother Ha" out of respect.

Eng returned to filmmaking briefly for the last time in 1961. The film star Siu Yin-fei, who was on tour in the United States at the time, approached Eng about co-producing a Cantonese film. Siu Yin-fei would finance the film and star in it, while Eng would be the director. The plot would be loosely based on a murder in New York City's Chinatown in the 1930s. Although Eng had drafted and shot several scenes, directing and scriptwriting duties were transferred to Wu Peng, Eng's friend in Hong Kong, for unknown reasons. Wu then asked Chor Yuan to rewrite the script combining the scenes shot by Eng in New York with existing materials to be shot in Hong Kong.[14] The film eventually credited Wu Peng as director, Chor Yuan as scriptwriter, and Esther Eng as "location director."

The Hong Kong Film Archive currently has a copy of *Niuyue tangrenjie suishi an* (Murder in New York Chinatown, 1961), a black-and-white film shot on 35mm stock. The film stars Siu Yin-fei, Lo Hoi-tin, Kuang Chong-ping, and Chan Ching-wa. Despite the title, little of the film focuses on the murder. The film tells the story of a man (Lo) who emigrates to New York and works odd jobs at restaurants and laundromats. He befriends his employer (Siu), and the two fall in love and are eventually married. However, the man later finds a new love interest and decides to kill his wife. After the crime has been discovered, the man flees and is eventually caught. The film contains views of New York City and Niagara Falls in addition to a freeway car chase. Eng is believed to have shot these outdoor sequences on location.

The film industry never heard from Eng again until her death on January 25, 1970, at age 55. *The New York Times* obituary describes Eng as "theatrical director, producer, restaurateur, and a great lady."[15] According to Eng's obituary in *Variety:*

> She had also produced and directed motion pictures in Hong Kong and had brought Chinese opera companies to the U.S. She and some theatre associates opened the BoBo Restaurant on Pell Street when they were stranded in N.Y. Later she sold it and opened other restaurants. Survived by three brothers and four sisters.[16]

Unfortunately, most of Eng's films have been lost. Her extant oeuvre consists of *Murder in New York Chinatown* and partial footage of *Golden Gate Girl* on VHS tape, both housed at the Hong Kong Film Archive. Other materials include film scripts, story outlines, production stills, and set photos as well as numerous newspaper clippings and printed matter from Chinese and Western sources.

CONCLUSION: REMEMBERING ESTHER ENG

Esther Eng, or Ng Kam-ha, was active in Chinese-language filmmaking from 1935 to 1949, a period of nearly fifteen years. She could be placed in a line of Chinese women filmmakers who began working in the 1920s. In 1925, Xie Caijing directed *Guchu beisheng* (Cry of the Orphan, 1925) for Shanghai's Mingxing Film Company. Chinese-American woman filmmaker, Olive Young, visited Guangdong province in the mid-1920s to film documentaries. Tong Sing-to, who started out as an actress for Hong Kong's Lianhua Film Company in the early 1930s, eventually formed her own company and participated in film production and scriptwriting, as well as acting. Although Eng was not among the earliest Chinese women filmmakers, she was among the first to focus on feminist ideals and diasporic Chinese communities.

In the mid-1930s, Eng emerged as a pioneering figure in cross-border, cross-cultural filmmaking as well as Chinese-language filmmaking in the United States. The extant footage, film scripts, and story outlines allude to her support of the Chinese resistance, her attachment to the ideals of romantic love, and her concern for the place of women in society. She remained creative and active in adverse working conditions, pursuing her dreams and passions in the world of Cantonese opera and film. As a filmmaker who defied national, cultural, and gender boundaries working in a time of seismic political and historical movements, Eng deserves the in-depth research and analysis of more than one scholar. This essay remains a humble effort dedicated to the nearly lost memory of Esther Eng.

ACKNOWLEDGMENT

I would like to thank Sally Ng, Esther Eng's sister, for providing photographs and printed materials, and Frank Bren, my friend and collaborator, for additional photographs, newspaper sources in English, and his helpful correspondence.

328

NOTES

1. Todd McCarthy, "Eng's Lost Pix, a Chinese Puzzle."
2. See Kar Law and Frank Bren, *Hong Kong Cinema: A Cross-Cultural View*. The translator benefited from reading sections of this text.
3. Also known as Joseph Sunn and Joseph Chiu.
4. Kwong Ngai Talking Picture Company was later *renamed* Cathay Pictures.
5. See Mary Wong, ed., *Hong Kong Filmography, vol. 1, 1913–1941*.
6. Wern, review of *Golden Gate Girl*, directed by Esther Eng, *Variety*, May 28, 1941.
7. The Shaw Brothers reorganized their Tianyi Film Company under the new name Nanyang Film Company in 1937.
8. "Ng Kam Ha ji yu fan mei" (Ng Kam Ha Anxious to Return to U.S.), *Sing Tao Daily*, January 12, 1947.
9. "Ng Kam Ha jiuyue jiang hui mei" (Ng Kam Ha to Leave for U.S. in September), *Artland*, July 1, 1939.
10. "Ng Kam Ha fan mei zhaogu" (Ng Kam Ha Back to U.S. to Raise Capital), *Artland*, November 15, 1939.
11. "Ng Kam Ha chengfeng polang" (Ng Kam Ha Breaking Waves), *Ling Sing*, January 15, 1947.
12. "Ng Kam Ha zhi Zhang Zuokang de xin" (Letter to Cheung Jok Hong), *Ling Sing*, February 19, 1948.
13. For a sample of newspaper articles in English, see Betty Cornelius, "Esther Eng, Movie Maker, Visit Here"; and Frank Lynch, "An Interview with Woman Movie Director: Tragedy! They Love It." Samples of Chinese newspapers outside Hong Kong include: *Yule* and *Screen Voice* (Singapore); *New China Daily Press* and *The United Chinese News* (Honolulu); and *Dahua* (New York City).
14. Chor Yuan, *Oral History Archive*.
15. Obituary of Esther Eng, *New York Times*, January 27, 1970.
16. Obituary of Esther Eng, *Variety*, February 4, 1970.

Transpacific Waves in a Global Sea

MABEL CHEUNG YUEN-TING'S CINEMATIC ARCHIVE

STACI FORD

IN HER films, as in her life, Cheung Yuen-ting (Zhang Wan-ting in Mandarin, Mabel Cheung in English) moves deftly between continents, cultures, and pasts, triangulating between Hong Kong, the United States, and the Chinese Mainland. I argue here that her films merit more scholarly attention as an archive of the interconnectedness of national/transnational histories, of shifts in gender scripts, and of various issues surrounding Hong Kong and Chinese diasporic identities/experiences. Cheung's films offer a particular view of transpacific responses to and negotiations with globality in particularly salient moments. My assertion draws on and expands the notion of the archive as conceptualized in works by scholars such as Antoinette Burton and Geetanjali Singh Chanda. Films do myriad types of cultural work, and in many cases they can be read in context with other "archival" sources to explore heretofore marginalized histories.[1]

Cheung's films are representative of other types of Hong Kong cultural production (literature, music, cultural history) that draw from multiple aesthetic and technical traditions. Esther Yau characterizes Hong Kong films as both "provincial yet also Hollywood-like; they have become the cultural counterpart of the 'cosmopolitan capitalist' undertakings that many Asians, especially ethnic Chinese entrepreneurs, have launched since the nineteenth century." The films are, for the most part, "free from obligations of national self representation" and "apparently apolitical" in terms of Mainland China–Taiwan relations. Nonetheless, their "light doses of 'Chinese-ness' can be a panacea for those seeking alternatives to Hollywood fare and for homesick overseas Asian audiences."[2] I would add to Yau's appraisal of Hong Kong films their value as revealing transnational/global historical connections, as well as their ability to capture on screen the preoccupations of particular temporalities. Cheung's films address migration, gender, generation, and subethnic "Chinese-ness" in a rapidly globalizing world. As they do so, they contribute to a type of collective memory of diaspora/globality.

Another underappreciated aspect of Cheung's films is that they help increase the critical mass of women's stories (to be read alongside more male-stream histories, and literature) circulating in Hong Kong and East Asia. There is still a paucity of women's narratives in the body of work that constitutes Hong Kong historical archive, and those that exist are often filtered through western, usually male, narrators. Hong Kong has, for most of its recorded history, been a space where men outnumbered women as a percentage of the general population. (The balance began to shift more dramatically in the post–World War II period.) More significantly, the professional/academic enterprise of writing Hong Kong history has until quite recently been the preserve of scholars with very little interest in women's and/or gender history.[3] Compounding this imbalance is the plethora of orientalist popular histories, novels, and films that construct Hong Kong as an exotic playground for western men who have their pick of sexually available local women.

As a result of this imbalance and stereotyping in historical representation, many scholars who are interested in Hong Kong women's history are still engaged in the recuperative work of making women's stories visible even as the enterprise must reckon with postcolonial, postmodern, and transnational feminist critiques that caution against essentialism or universalism. From the perspective of transnational feminist inquiry, Cheung's films address a range of experiences, and they are an important counternarrative to wooden characterizations of Hong Kong and "Chinese" women circulating in western popular culture. They are also an important part of a larger conversation about Chinese women narrating their "journeys" across the Pacific. I am thinking here of the way Cheung's films might be read against written memoirs and autobiographies of women's lives in and "escape" from China during the late

331

twentieth century (such as Jung Chang's *Wild Swans*),[4] as well as the way the films speak to issues of sexual awakening and the commoditization of feminism as articulated in the "body writing" texts of a younger generation of Chinese women such as *Shanghai Baby* author Wei Hui.[5]

What follows is a brief discussion of Mabel Cheung's background, her work, and her place in a larger discussion of Hong Kong and Hollywood cinema traditions. Next, I will briefly discuss five of Cheung's films (*Qiutian de tonghua*, An Autumn's Tale, 1987; *Ba liangjin*, Eight Taels of Gold, 1989; *Songjia wangchao*, The Soong Sisters, 1997; *Boli zhi cheng*, City of Glass, 1998; and *Beijing yu lelu*, Beijing Rocks, 2001), focusing on the way they speak to the following historical themes: (1) The multiple legacies of the past, particularly Hong Kong's late-colonial era, for young generations of Hong Kong people; (2) The widespread impact of the "brain drain" migration from Hong Kong in the 1980s and early 1990s; (3) The significance of Hong Kong people's cultural and affective ties to the Chinese mainland in the years preceding and immediately following the handover period; (4) The simultaneous changes and continuities in women's lives, gender scripts, and attitudes as a result of migration and economic expansion. Following the discussion of individual films, I conclude by suggesting the ways in which Cheung's work informs the discussion of gender and feminism in a transnational frame. As Olivia Khoo has noted, while gender theory has begun to explore the dimensions of Chinese masculinity in diaspora, "the diasporic Chinese female remains a relatively neglected phenomenon." Cheung's films can be theorized to help redress this lack.[6]

CHEUNG AND THE HONG KONG SECOND WAVE

Cheung's films foreground the stories of East Asian "astronauts," particularly the generation of flexible citizens hedging their bets by moving between Hong Kong and "someplace else," pursuing education, second passports, and/or economic security in the face of the resumption of Chinese sovereignty in 1997.[7] Cheung and her partner/husband, Alex Law, belong to a cadre of filmmakers known as the "Second Wave" following on the heels of the better-known early-1980s' Hong Kong "New Wave" directors such as Ann Hui, Allen Fong, Tony Au, Yim Ho, Patrick Tam, and Tsui Hark. In addition to Cheung and Law, other well-known Second Wave auteurs include Wong Kar-Wai, Stanley Kwan, and John

Woo. These directors moved into their careers as Hong Kong's film industry contracted and became more dollar-driven in the wake of increased global competition with Hollywood. As such, film critics often dismiss their work as more commercial than the earlier New Wave offerings; yet they have a following among festival audiences and the Chinese diaspora internationally.

Second Wave filmmakers live as well as chronicle diaspora. They were/ are part of the mid-1980s/early-1990s "brain drain" exodus of Hong Kong people who sought to maximize their opportunities in light of anxieties about Hong Kong's reversion to PRC control. Cheung and Law, like many of their peers, studied and worked in the West, but also transited back and forth to Hong Kong. Second Wave directors have produced a formidable body of work often labeled "migration melodramas," many of which foreground women's experiences. Examples include Cheung's migration trilogy; *Feifa yimin*, The Illegal Immigrant, 1985; *An Autumn's Tale*; and *Eight Taels of Gold*; as well as Stanley Kwan's *Full Moon in New York*, 1989; Clara Law's *Ai zai ta xiang de ji jie*, Farewell China, 1990; Evans Chan's *Cuo ai*, Crossings, 1994, and *Zi jing*, Bauhinia, 2002; Allen Fong's *Mei guo xin*, Just Like Weather, 1986; and Peter Chan's *Tian mi mi*, Comrades: Almost a Love Story, 1996.

MABEL CHEUNG'S HISTORICAL TRAJECTORY

Cheung insists that being a woman is not a liability in the Hong Kong film industry.[8] However, she is one of a very small cadre of Hong Kong female directors (arguably the best known is First Wave director Ann Hui) to achieve commercial success and an international reputation. Born in 1950, Cheung spent her childhood in Hong Kong and earned a bachelor's degree in English from The University of Hong Kong. Following her graduation she studied drama and writing at the University of Bristol in England then returned to work as a producer at Radio/Television Hong Kong (RTHK) from 1978 to 1980. She was a graduate student in filmmaking at New York University from 1980 to 1983 where she met and married Alex Law. The two collaborate as filmmakers, alternating between directing/writing/producing depending on the project. (Although the couple was energized by the multicultural environment of New York, and the friends they made from Taiwan, the PRC, and American-born Chinese communities, at NYU they were two of only three ethnically Chinese students in their class.) The pair spent much of the 1980s working on films set in New York, and they acknowledge an intellectual/artistic debt to Woody Allen, Martin Scorsese, and Spike Lee (Spike Lee and Ang Lee were also at NYU during this period).

Cheung's years as a young director in New York dovetailed with what Roberta Garrett has called "The Return of the Woman's Film" in the 1980s and 1990s.[9] The most commercially successful of Cheung's films, the 1987 romance *An Autumn's Tale* is the story of a young woman from Hong Kong who survives the transition to Manhattan thanks to the support of the loveable Chinatown triad member, Figgy (Boathead) played by Chow Yun Fat. Cheung's films share plot and thematic elements with the "single girl in the city chick flicks" of Nora Ephron, as well as later Third Wave feminist films such as *Legally Blonde* (2001), *Miss Congeniality* (2000), and television series like *Sex in the City*. Cheung's film *The Soong Sisters* also fits nicely into Garrett's discussion of 1990s women's biopics, such as *A League of Their Own* and various costume dramas "based on female-oriented narratives."[10] Even Cheung's films that are based on fictional characters often interweave references to or actual news footage of "real" historical events, thus reaching out to Hong Kong people and to the Chinese diaspora across the globe. Comfortable within multiple film traditions and cohorts—Hollywood, art house, Hong Kong, and increasingly, the PRC—Cheung continues to turn to history—micro and macro—as a driving force in her work.

CHEUNG'S MIGRATION MELODRAMAS: *AN AUTUMN'S TALE* AND *EIGHT TAELS OF GOLD*

I have written elsewhere about Cheung's 1987 film, *An Autumn's Tale*, as an important transnational American studies text. Considered by many to be a Hong Kong classic, *An Autumn's Tale* claims the space of Manhattan for a twentieth-century, truly transnational cohort. Drawing on both Hollywood and Hong Kong cinematic convention, the film personalizes the impact of two intertwined migrations: the "brain drain" from Hong Kong, as well as the influx of immigrants from Asia and Central/South America in the post-1965 period. As the characters in the film selectively embrace and eschew certain trappings of "American-ness" and "Chinese-ness," they model how to manage in a new environment that presents a range of challenges. *An Autumn's Tale* combines pre-Tiananmen pan-Chinese solidarity and lighthearted romance; yet the film is also pointed in its critique of racism and the isolation of urban life in the U.S.

An Autumn's Tale, like all of Cheung's films, is a refreshing turnabout from Hollywood's orientalist portrayals of Chinese women as exotic and Chinese men as asexual or "inscrutable." The film subtly critiques white privilege and deploys humor to confront stereotype. It exposes intra- and cross-ethnic tensions within various communities of color in the United States, and uses humor to tackle sensitive topics (fig. 15.1). The film is also a lighthearted look at the way class intersects with gender to guarantee some individuals more success than others. Figgy (Chow) experiences a certain type of downward mobility in Reagan-era Manhattan, whereas Jenny (Chung)—who speaks perfect English and has a particular type of social capital as a result of her upbringing and education in Hong Kong— is able to assimilate more easily.

The film is loosely based on Cheung's own experiences as a graduate student at NYU. Cheung and Law (who wrote the screenplay) based the character of Figgy on a friend they knew in Manhattan. Unlike the final scene in the film, however, in reality, Figgy ended up in prison. Cheung says she deliberately rewrote history in *An Autumn's Tale* to "give our

335

FIGURE 15.1 *An Autumn's Tale,* 1987, released a decade before Hong Kong's reversion to Chinese sovereignty in 1997, is one of many "migration melodramas" engaging issues of gender in diaspora and contesting orientalist stereotypes in Hollywood film

friend a restaurant" (and a manufactured "happy ending") sending a sig-nal that outsiders can overcome marginal status in the United States.[11] Although Figgy's history is, literally, rewritten in *An Autumn's Tale,* the film also represents Cheung and Law's lived experience. While playful with personal history, it is, in a general sense, "true" to many of the circumstances and lived experiences of the "brain drain" generation.

Eight Taels of Gold reverses the path traveled in *An Autumn's Tale,* although it too captures a particular moment in history—China's rapid economic liberalization at the end of the twentieth century. The film begins in New York, but the action quickly moves to China. The contribution of this film to the archive is in the way the "New China" appears in the eyes of diasporic returnees. (It also reinforces certain Hong Kong stereotypes about their Mainland Chinese neighbors.) The film's protagonist, Slim (Sammo Hung), is a taxi driver who is barely scraping by in New York. After sixteen years, he is returning to his home village in China. Slim is anxious to convince family and friends that he has achieved economic success in America. In order to do so he borrows one friend's gold watch and another's gold chain because "A man is not a man without eight taels of gold." Slim is, in many ways, a reincarnation of Figgy from *An Autumn's Tale.* Unlike Figgy, Slim returns to China rather than staying in New York. Once again, as in *An Autumn's Tale, Eight Taels of Gold* weaves together the histories of the United States, Hong Kong, and Mainland China as characters make references to the legacies of the Cultural Revolution, the increased presence of American products and popular culture, and the rapid changes taking place in China. Slim's hometown has been transformed by capitalism, and when he tries to bargain with the cab driver to lower his fare, Slim is told that the first of Deng's "Four Modernizations" is to "Look out for Number One."

The most moving scenes in *Eight Taels of Gold,* are those that engage questions of belonging and home. Slim declares that he wants to be buried in China rather than in America because his "English is a three-legged horse. And I don't want to ride it in the afterlife." As in *An Autumn's Tale, Eight Taels of Gold* reflects on both the costs of uncoupling oneself from tradition and the desire to do so. Women and men struggle to balance new opportunities with older obligations in this changing world. Slim falls for his distant cousin, curiously named Odds and Ends (Sylvia Chang). She enjoys the financial independence that is hers thanks to her job as a waitress at a modern five-star hotel in Guangzhou. But she seeks for an even better life in America. Slim and Odds and Ends repeatedly debate the pros and cons of leaving China. But she faces different pressures than Slim. Not only does her future rely on her choice of husband, she feels the need to achieve a particular idealized standard of beauty as a modern woman. She tells Slim that she has heard it is possible to "change your face in America . . . even your skin. I'll change mine too, so I won't be so dark." When asked if such a rumor is true Slim replies, "Sure. They use the skin from your rear because it's soft and white." Slim issues a playful warning that if Odds and Ends undergoes surgery she'll be wearing her rear end on her face forever. The exchange is a critique of whiteness and hegemonic western standards of beauty, as well as a reminder of gender, national, ethnic, and cultural difference within the diaspora.

Both *An Autumn's Tale* and *Eight Taels of Gold* document the varied experiences and spaces of mobile lives. Cheung tells representative stories of the astronaut generation using autobiographical shards and mingling fictionalized characters with "real" events. Additionally, the settings themselves (usually filmed on location) are worth noting for their archival value. Cheung's films "freeze" various cities in particular temporal moments. Footage of places and spaces on both sides of the Pacific records the pace of urban development, changing landscapes, and, in the case of New York, a pre-September 11th skyline. Yet despite the fact that the films add to the collective memory of diaspora, in the migration melodramas, Cheung is more accidental than intentional historian. The historical stakes are higher when we consider Cheung's 1997 historical drama, *The Soong Sisters*.

337

THE SOONG SISTERS

Although none of the action takes place in Hong Kong, *The Soong Sisters* was dubbed Cheung's "handover film" because of the cultural work it does in terms of unifying Hong Kong film audiences with their newly reunified mainland compatriots. As Sheldon Lu writes:

> The integration of Hong Kong with China demands a new perspective in the self-representation of Hong Kong in cultural production and reception. For instance, the joint production of the epic film *The Soong Sisters* (Song jia huang chao) directed by Cheung Yuen-ting covers a time span of several decades and reflects on the political triangulation of the mainland, Taiwan, and Hong Kong as the three Soong sisters, originally from the same family, drift apart

and settle, by historical vicissitudes, in the three different parts of China after 1949. (The eldest sister Soong Ailing [Michelle Yeoh] and her husband live in Hong Kong, the second sister Soong Quingling [Maggie Cheung], widow of Dr. Sun Yat-sen, stays in the mainland, and the youngest daughter Soong Meiling (Vivian Wu/Wu Junmei), wife of Chiang Kai-shek, moves to Taiwan.)[12]

The 1997 epic biopic of the first women of China, Ai-ling, Ching-ling and Mei-ling Soong (and their relationships with their powerful husbands, H. H. Kung, Sun Yat-Sen, and Chiang Kai-Shek, respectively), was a lightning rod for historical disputes long before it opened to the public. Although the actual filming took less than four months to complete, the entire project dragged on for five years. Filmed in China, Cheung had to battle a range of logistical challenges and censorship authorities along the way. In the end, PRC censors cut 14 minutes from the film. Some critics dubbed Cheung's offering overtly pro-PRC in its perspective. Others took

issue with what they read to be a feminist snub of the Soong brothers who were excised from the story. Cheung claims she simply did not have enough time to include the brothers in the narrative.

The film succeeds in grafting women's history onto twentieth-century Chinese history. It is an aesthetic triumph featuring fine performances by internationally known stars Michelle Yeoh, Maggie Cheung, and Vivien Wu. *The Soong Sisters* stakes an important claim for the famous but often underappreciated trio of sisters as powerful actors on the international stage, as well as models of the Chinese Republic's "new women." In many ways, *The Soong Sisters* is an Asia-focused equivalent of the Euro/American costume dramas and historical "women's films" that became particularly popular at century's end. Cheung spent a significant amount of time and energy doing research for the film, although she does embellish some historical details and manufactures others.[13] The rich and detailed presentation of fashion, scenery, and architecture in the film facilitates a sort of mythologizing of the sisters, particularly Soong Ching-ling. The plot does, indeed, gloss over much of the violence perpetuated in the name of the Soong sisters' (and their husbands') interests and agendas. Cheung chooses to celebrate the triumph of sisterhood even as she foregrounds the genuine conflict that marked so much of the Soong/Sun/Chiang saga. However, the film does portray several "actual" events including the Xi'an incident, the creation of the Chinese Republic in 1911, and the revolutionary uprisings that marked so much of China's history prior to the establishment of the PRC in 1949.

Revolution and reconciliation are two key themes in the film and Cheung clearly believes there are lessons for today embedded in the Soong family narrative. In this film, as well as in the two films to be discussed hereafter, *City of Glass* and *Beijing Rocks,* frequent reference is made to revolution as historical reality and metaphor. But Cheung's films personalize revolution focusing on the micro-histories that rage within larger macro-revolutions. Additionally, Cheung's artistic touches enhance declarations about revolutionary (and related gender and generational) change. The bound feet of an elderly Chinese servant are juxtaposed against fleet-footed Ching-ling Soong as she flees her parents' home to return to Japan and marry Sun Yat-Sen, "The Lincoln of China." There is a clear connection between women's empowerment and the Chinese revolution. (Sounding a more contemporary preoccupation, the passages selected from Sun's speeches and personal utterances warn western countries of China's determination to associate with countries that will treat her as an equal.) *The Soong Sisters,* then, manages to do a significant amount of cultural, ideological, and historical work. It celebrates Chinese-ness, and the strength of Chinese women, but it also constructs the Soongs as exemplars of transnationality and vehicles through which we visualize the interconnection of American, British, Hong Kong, Taiwanese, and Mainland Chinese histories (fig. 15.2).

339

FIGURE 15.2 Cheung's 1997 film *The Soong Sisters* integrates micro and macro histories telescoping links between Greater China, Europe, Japan, and the United States.

CHILDREN OF THE HANDOVER: *CITY OF GLASS* AND *BEIJING ROCKS*

Cheung's second "handover" film does, in fact, reference Hong Kong's reversion to Chinese sovereignty on June 30, 1997. *City of Glass*, released in 1998, is one of many Hong Kong films examining the shift from British Colony to Special Administrative Region of the People's Republic of China. The dream-like camera work and highly sentimental style of the film signal a nostalgic tribute to the past rather than a critique of history. But the film, which celebrates youth and university life during two eras, the 1970s and the 1990s, explores how Hong Kong's history "between" China and Britain marks lives across generations and the globe. The plot begins on New Year's Eve of 1996, with the two main characters, Vivien (Shu Qi) and Raphael (Leon Lai), happily driving along London's streets towards Trafalgar Square. They are killed in a car crash as the clock strikes midnight. The remainder of the film alternates between flashbacks that reveal the deep connection between Vivien and Raphael over a twenty-year period, and the relationship that develops between Vivien's daughter, Susie (Nicola Cheung), and Raphael's son, David (Daniel Wu).

The film explores youth culture in cross-generational perspective, revealing the ways in which people and places are transformed as Hong Kong moves inexorably to its 1997 date with Beijing. However, there are important continuities as well. Both generations face uncertainty about their futures under PRC rule. Documentary-like footage of the 1970s student demonstrations is juxtaposed against scenes featuring 1990s Hong Kong youth swapping stories about their first sexual encounters. Both are rebellions of a sort. Parents and children negotiate change and define themselves in the wake of Hong Kong's shifting socioeconomic and political context. All four of the main characters are privileged Hong Kongers, yet each feels at sea. Vivien and Raphael try to reclaim the past but their attempt is, ultimately, futile. David and Susie struggle to understand their parents' affair, as well as their own growing attraction for each other. It is in the dialogue between the children of the dead lovers that we see the angst about identity, youth, and Chinese-ness—Hong Kong, Mainland, or overseas Chinese—as 1997 looms. When he first meets her, David dismisses both Susie and Hong Kong (the "city of glass" invoked in the film's title) as "a bunch of flashes and inside nothing." Susie brands David a "banana" and a "show-off" because he insists on speaking English, even though he was born in Hong Kong. But as the children come to better understand their parents and each other, their perspective on Hong Kong evolves as well. *City of Glass* is a Valentine to Hong Kong people who confront the quotidian challenges of life amidst the uncertainty ahead.

While it carries on with the theme of pan-Chinese youth identities in times of change, *Beijing Rocks* is, stylistically, a completely different film from *City of Glass*. The dreamy mise-en-scène has been replaced by fast-paced, handheld camera work, a vibrant soundtrack, and playful graphics deployed to mark transitions between the film's action and the actors' soliloquies. *Beijing Rocks* tells the story of a band of musicians struggling to break out of the underground rock scene into stardom. The film is also a sensitive exploration of the love triangle between Yang Yin (Shu Qi), Ping Lu/Road (Gong He), and Michael (Daniel Wu). Yang Yin, a young woman from Shanxi Province, is captivated by the temperamental rock-and-roll artist Ping Lu/Road, but she is also charmed by the wealthy (and ironically named) "Hong Kong Peasant" Michael (fig. 15.3).

Beijing Rocks explores various notions of Chinese manhood, as well as a more diffuse Chinese-ness. It telescopes the anxieties of Hong Kongers and Mainlanders (and their gradual dissolution on the road) and the exacerbation of generational difference thanks to the breakneck speed of economic liberalization in both China and Hong Kong. The characters

341

FIGURE 15.3 In the 2001 film *Beijing Rocks*, Cheung explores shifting notions of gender, consumerism, and youth culture in twenty-first-century China.

are complex, sexual beings opining on what it means to come of age at the dawn of a new century in China. Michael, who has come to Beijing to reenergize his music career, feels at sea in Beijing. He opines:

I was born in Hong Kong, and grew up in the US. Both my Chinese and English are a wreck. I'm a so-called struggling singer-songwriter. When I'm unhappy, my best trick is to sulk. My songs have never made the charts but last month I myself made the headlines. I screwed up—real bad—in a pool hall in Beijing. I hate coming to Mainland China. But my dad insisted that I come to learn Mandarin . . . He told me to lay low here for a while. Learn Mandarin, build up some connections, and get my mind straight. But my Mandarin is so bad I can't build up any connections in Mandarin, not to say think in Mandarin. What I can do now is to sulk in Mandarin.

But by the end of the film, Michael feels more at home in the Mainland, and he is on the road to reconciling with his father. The other protagonist, Road, is not so lucky. While Beijing is his home, real artistic success eludes. There is little room for his rebellious attitude in an industry (and a city?) that (in order to keep the peace) wants obedience packaged in a "hard rock" shell. He literally loses himself in despair and is killed in a motorcycle accident.

Men's struggles to come to terms with past histories and wounds are not the only preoccupation of the film. Yang Yin's autobiographical soliloquy recounts her history and hopes:

I was born three years after the Cultural Revolution and grew up in Anhui Province. My parents disappeared when I was a kid. I don't even have one photo of my childhood. On the eve of the new millennium I was alone in the village. It was totally dark. The 20th century was coming to an end . . . and there I was, all alone by myself . . . to face the arrival of the new century . . . with no relatives, no friends. I cried the whole night. The next day I decided to leave the village and see the world . . . I hope one day . . . I can sing a song . . . on the balcony on Tiananmen. And if I can do a striptease show there . . . So much frigging better.

Yang Yin talks like a rebel, but she is, actually, confined to stereotypically feminine duties, such as steadying Road and being a surrogate mother to the band. Yet she longs to be looked after as well. Of all of Cheung's heroines, Yang Yin seems the most tragic, albeit charming, with evident depth of character. She typifies the multiple burdens young women in twenty-first-century China bear. The film's conclusion illustrates this reality.

In the final scene, Yang Yin and Michael share a quiet moment following Road's memorial service. As Michael prepares to leave for Hong Kong, he gives Yang Yin a gift—Mexican jumping beans (a reminder of the name of his Hong Kong band)—and tells her they are magic. When one of the beans is crushed, Yang Yin realizes that the small insect inside is causing the movement. However, she decides not to shatter the "Hong Kong peasant's" illusion. She quietly disposes of the insect/bean and reassures Michael that she still believes in magic. There is symbolism in her "protecting" Michael (and all of the men in her life). Despite the bond that has formed between Beijingers and Hong Kong people in the film, secrets and asymmetries remain. While Michael returns to Hong Kong armed with greater self-knowledge and a trove of experiences from which to draw upon as he continues his music career, the future looks quite bleak for Yang Yin, who plans to "sleep a little" after the trauma of Road's death. Yang Yin bears a particular burden of representation. She seeks to move out of the "darkness" of rural China into the "light" of Beijing's bustling cultural scene. But she also feels (and is expected to assume) much of the work of "care" for the men in her life who seek a refuge from their own pasts, and who rely on her as a secure harbor from which to move out into their respective "new" worlds.

343

TRANSPACIFIC FEMINISM IN CHEUNG'S FILMS

Yang Yin's thoughtful pragmatism is evident in Cheung's other characters, and in many of the women of late-twentieth-century Hong Kong film—behind and in front of the camera. I am aware of and sympathetic to theoretical critiques of western women's "imperial designs" in larger conversations about transnational feminism. Nonetheless, I believe there is value in linking Cheung's films (and perhaps other Hong Kong women filmmakers' films) to a larger conversation about women, gender, empowerment, and cultural values on both sides of the Pacific. Cheung's films speak to discourses of western/neoliberal, Chinese/Asian values, and "wave" (particularly Third Wave) feminism(s).[14] To a certain extent, these films are representative of a particular Hong Kong feminist sensibility. While the storylines do not deal specifically with women's political activism, they do raise multiple issues about gender, national identity, and subethnic loyalties within the Chinese diaspora. Cheung's films promote small victories for women, but they also safeguard particular gender boundaries. Her cinematic worlds are spaces where empowerment and harmony coexist. Hong Kong people have, as a result of their unique history and geography, become experts in maintaining a certain tone of "harmony" (hexie), a very popular notion circulating in business, policy, educational, and even reform circles in Hong Kong. The notion of harmony coexists with protest and carefully calculated challenges to authority.

In a different type of "having it all" from that which is associated with Second Wave feminism in the West, women in Hong Kong claim multiple intellectual and corporeal legacies as Marie-Paule Ha has noted.[15] Hong Kong women (like Hong Kong men) have experienced the impact of tremendous demographic and economic change over the past several decades. The increase in numbers of dual-career households, declining birth rates, transnational mobility, and the shift from a manufacturing to a service economy has enhanced women's (particularly young and privileged women's) independence. But there is also a strong sense in Hong Kong civil society that women must uphold traditional values even as they embrace change. Eliza Lee and other scholars in gender studies in Hong Kong caution against easy generalizations about Hong Kong women or Hong Kong society, but they note that social reform is usually more successful in Hong Kong when it is perceived to support rather than undermine notions of social harmony.[16]

In this respect, Cheung models a Hong Kong–style feminism that resembles Third Wave feminism in the United States. (Here I use the term Third Wave to embrace both the feminism of younger women as well as the Third Wave critique of Second Wave feminism launched by women of color in the United States and beyond.) Cheung's cinematic Third Wave sensibility is not dissimilar to some of the "girl power" films that have been produced in recent decades. Her films portray women and men seeking harmony rather than confrontation as they navigate mobility, conflict, tragedy, or injustice in Hong Kong, New York, or Beijing. The films do not shrink from showing the very real inequalities that exist on both sides of the Pacific, but they refuse to pit women against men—even as they shine a particular light on individual or systemic sexism. While her plots focus mostly on Hong Kong's people of privilege, the preoccupations of middle-class youth become different in diaspora. This is something that separates the diaspora from expatriates. When Americans come to Hong Kong, many experience a status increase, whereas for the Hong Kong person who has grown up with a relative amount of privilege, a move to the United States is often accompanied by—at least initially— some status decline.

In terms of age, education, personal history, and intellectual viewpoint, Cheung straddles multiple generations of women's movements in the United States, Hong Kong, and Mainland China. Additionally, she has lived through multiple social, economic, and political changes in various places. That she collaborates with husband/partner Alex Law further complicates the question of authorship in her films and perhaps explains why she (like many Hong Kong people—women and men) continually returns to the theme of women in diaspora, but keeps men engaged in the conversation. In Hong Kong, harmony is prized for many reasons, one of which is that it helps to disarm those who are anxious about social change.

345

NOTES

1. Antoinette Burton, *Dwelling in the Archive;* and Geetanjali Singh Chanda, *Indian Women in the House of Fiction.*
2. Esther C. M. Yau, "Introduction: Hong Kong Cinema in a Borderless World," 2.
3. Currently, a number of scholars are researching Hong Kong women's/gender history. However, until recently, work of this type was seen as "outside" the purview of more mainstream Hong Kong history. Early pioneers in this field include Yip Hon Ming, Clara Ho, Irene Tong, Susanna Hoe, Maria Jashok, Janet Salaff, Vernoica Pearson, and Choi Po-King. The Gender Studies Program at The Chinese University of Hong Kong has devoted significant scholarly energy to women's history in a more multidisciplinary framework and the Women's Studies Research Centre at Hong Kong University has, over the past several years, conducted seminars and spring workshops in women's/ gender history. Additionally, scholars in legal studies, sociology/social work, history, English, fine arts, comparative literature and cultural studies at Hong Kong University have contributed significantly to the enterprise of women's history in Hong Kong. Gina Marchetti, Elaine Ho, and Esther Cheung have made important connections between Hong Kong women filmmakers and Hong Kong history. Marie-Paule Ha bridges the fields of history, film studies, and cultural studies and has theorized women's historical corporeal hybridity. See Marie-Paule Ha, "Double Trouble: Doing Gender in Hong Kong."
4. Jung Chang, *Wild Swans.*
5. Wei Hui, *Shanghai Baby.*
6. Olivia Khoo, *The Chinese Exotic,* 3.

7. The term "flexible citizenship" is Aihwa Ong's. See Ong, *Flexible Citizenship*.

8. Interview with Mabel Cheung Yuen-Ting and Alex Law in Stacilee Ford, *Mabel Cheung Yuen-Ting's* An Autumn's Tale.

9. See Roberta Garrett, *Postmodern Chick Flicks*.

10. Ibid., 51.

11. See Ford, *Mabel Cheung Yuen-Ting's* An Autumn's Tale, 93–94, for interview with Cheung Yuen-Ting and Alex Law.

12. Sheldon H. Lu, "Filming Diaspora and Identity," 274–275.

13. At a roundtable discussion of the film held at Hong Kong University in 2004, several of my colleagues in the Department of History commended the film as historically accurate in significant ways, but they also noted where liberties were taken. For example, the scene where Madame Kung (Ai-ling Soong) summons her friends and their automobiles in order to light the runway in order for the Chiangs to land is a fabrication.

14. Cheung is reluctant to label herself a feminist but is sympathetic to Third Wave feminisms, particularly those that seek consensus rather than conflict between men and women in the public sphere.

15. See Ha, "Double Trouble."

16. Eliza W. Y. Lee, ed., *Gender and Change in Hong Kong*.

Filming One's Way Home

CLARA LAW'S LETTERS TO OZ

SHIAO-YING SHEN

AUSTRALIA IS a young migrant nation.¹ A quick look into some of the classics of Australian cinema reveals the different waves of migrants. Australia's first color film *Jedda* (1955) deals with the tension between whites and aborigines, between the McManns and Jedda, in the country's Northern Territory.² Michael Powell's *They're a Weird Mob* (1966) portrays the arrival and assimilation of Nino Culotta, an Italian, into the Anglo-Celtic "mob" in Sydney.³ Clara Law's *Fu sheng* (Floating Life, 1996) might not be as yet considered a classic in the Australian cinema canon, but it does focus on the toil and pain of a Hong Kong family as it tries to accept and settle into their new Australian home.

This paper places Clara Law in the context of Australian cinema and concentrates on three of her works to examine a filmic working out of the psychic and emotional processes of migration. With *Yun tun tang* (Wonton Soup, 1994), I touch upon Ackbar Abbas's "love at last sight" notion to examine how Law relies on her Chinese-Australian female protagonist, the language of food and sex, and the use of visual colors and music to express the ache involved in a migrant's loss of home. Law's *Yu shang 1967 de nü shen* (The Goddess of 1967, 2000) is next placed in a comparative frame within Australian cinema to analyze how a filmmaker can be "lost"—at limbo—as she gropes for a film language that she can feel at home with to reflect upon her sentiments toward a new habitat. Then, my study of *Gei A Li de xin* (Letters to Ali, 2004) employs Michel de Certeau's concept of "walking rhetorics" to highlight the route through which Law traverses and then arrives at a film vocabulary that affirms and embraces a sense of home. In other words, this paper considers how a filmmaker's process of migration can be located not only in her migrating subjects, but also in her filmic language. That is, a filmmaker's sense of home can be sited in her act of filming.

Clara Law is a director known for her film style. Works that demonstrate Law's strong sense of style are various: *Qiu yue* (Autumn Moon, 1992) presents us with Hong Kong in clean lines and sedate cold colors; *You seng* (Temptations of a Monk, 1993) dazzles us with lustrous period costumes and exaggerated and paced acting; *The Goddess of 1967* transports us with high-contrast colors and a nearly surrealist tone. Clara Law has been seen as a filmmaker who is "developing into a virtuoso stylist,"[4] and that which she explores and communicates through her film style are the Chinese's tribulations in finding new places for home, the Chinese's compulsion towards migration. Her early *Wo ai tai kong ren* (The Other Half and the Other Half, 1988) treats Hong Kong's migrating fever and the phenomenon amongst Chinese of "serving time" for legal residency in North America during the 1980s. *Ai zai ta xiang de ji jie* (Farewell China, 1990) deals with a mainland couple's American dream and its tragic realization in New York City. *Autumn Moon* tells of a friendship between a Japanese tourist and a young Hong Kong girl who is about to leave her grandmother to move to Canada to join her already migrated family. *Wonton Soup* examines the sense of loss experienced by a Chinese-Australian woman as she revisits Hong Kong. *Floating Life,* a film made after Law herself moved to Australia, depicts the psychic toll involved in a Hong Kong family's move to Sydney. Looking at this lineup, Law's oeuvre can be said as supplying us with a rich, and often stylized, rendering of the varied faces and emotional shades of modern-day Chinese migration.

In 1999, I studied Clara Law as a Hong Kong filmmaker, seeing her as a female director producing films during Hong Kong's moment of transition.[5] This time I shall regard Law as an Australian filmmaker and examine the Australian story in her migration saga. The shift of the examining paradigm is not simply because of Law's relocation to Australia in the mid-1990s and the funding source of her pictures (AFC—Australian Film Commission, NSW Film and Television Office, SBS), but also because of the impulses detected from within her films—eradicating traces of Hong Kong, concentrating on the Australian landscape, attempting to excavate the darkness within the heartland of Law's antipodean new home. When I looked at Law as a Hong Kong filmmaker, I juxtaposed her with Ann Hui to see how these two female directors contemplated the Territory's historical transition, how they dealt with what Stephen Teo calls "Hong Kong's China Syndrome."[6] Reexamining Law as an Australian filmmaker gives us a chance to trace out the shape of a filmmaker's shift of identity, identification, and concerns. And, by juxtaposing other Australian films with her work, *The Goddess of 1967*, this study can also trace out the different strategies employed by filmmakers as they try to tell their distinctive Australian story. I shall end with a look into Law's 2004 documentary, *Letters to Ali*, and consider how her travels in the vast island-continent and her notion of home operate in her films.

My interest in Clara Law started with her *Farewell China:* I still remember my surprise when I saw her flagrant reference to June Fourth at the end of the film—its display of a figure of the goddess of democracy, a replica of the statue erected by the students at Tiananmen Square in 1989. But my desire to analyze her work began after viewing her *Wonton Soup*. This thirty-minute film occupies one segment of the four-part *Erotique*,[7] and is the film in which Australian elements first take presence in her work. Having its lead characters be Chinese-Australians, its editing done by Jill Bilcock,[8] and its post-production done Down Under, *Wonton Soup* brings to light the ineffable sense of melancholy as one breaks off from an old affiliation (Hong Kong) and settles into a new association (Australia). In this short, Law manages deftly to link female sexuality with the experience of migration. Before studying the filmed-in-Australia *The Goddess of 1967*, I shall first look into the set-in-Hong Kong *Wonton Soup*, and show the melancholia involved in the migrating process, the loss that comes as a migrant shifts identifications—Law's Hong Kong blues as she bids farewell to the Territory which nurtured her cinematic aspirations.

HONG KONG BLUES

My impression after first viewing *Wonton Soup* was the blueness of the film and the melancholic tune from the *er-hu* (Chinese two-stringed fiddle) and the accordion-like instrument. The film shows the interaction of an English-speaking Chinese-Australian couple; they meet up and stay in

Hong Kong because of the work situation of the female partner. Although quite devoted to each other, the woman every once in a while, especially after lovemaking, half-jokingly proposes breaking up. Every time the couple is intimate, the screen displays a bluish hue; in this blueness, in addition to the couple's bodies, Hong Kong's skies, architecture, and landmarks are also framed into shots.

This blue space is an intimate space; at the same time, it is a melancholic and perplexed space. After making love, the woman smilingly suggests separation, but fails to provide a reason for such a proposition. This blue space seems intimately related to the woman; it highlights a kind of psychic restlessness, a kind of state which is as yet difficult to name, to articulate. The woman's familiarity with Hong Kong is far more than that of her boyfriend's, and being the ex–Hong Kong native, so to speak, the woman drives her boyfriend in the rain, shows him Hong Kong landmarks through the wet car window, looking for the Shanghai tailor who used to be the boyfriend's parents' neighbor, looking for a long dispersed neighborhood. In contrast to the boyfriend, who migrated to Australia at a very young age, the woman, who moved to Australia as a teenager, can still find the apartment neighborhood where she experienced her first love, and reminisce about her first taste of romance. This Hong Kong tour, Hong Kong vanishing, Hong Kong nostalgia becomes like what Ackbar Abbas termed, a state of "deja disparu," a "love at last sight" sentiment. The woman experiences this state and sentiment, yet finds this elusive condition hard to express. When the boyfriend's notion of home is the taste of Vegemite,9 and feeling for Hong Kong is, "so many Chinese!" it becomes doubly hard for the woman to communicate her sense of restlessness and loss.

The film's blue world reappears in the end in the form of a montage sequence of Hong Kong landmarks and architecture. Before this, the woman has at last managed to utter the reason for wanting to part, and it is through the boyfriend's efforts that she has found the language for articulating the reason. The boyfriend could feel that the woman's mysterious desire for separation is related to some sense of Chineseness. When the woman is away on a business trip, he then diligently learns Chinese cooking, studies Chinese classic pornography to look into Chinese ways of lovemaking, and finds out how Chinese food affects the bodily flow of sexual energy. Returning from her trip, after enjoying her boyfriend's Chinese meal and Chinese way of lovemaking, the woman embraces the language of food to name her need for splitting: "maybe it's because you never take me to wonton soup." Greatly relieved, the Chinese-Australian boyfriend immediately offers to go for wonton soup. The woman then explains that in Hong Kong people do not have wonton soup; wontons are taken with noodles there. The boyfriend apologizes and admits, "This is not my City." The woman sadly acknowledges, "Nor mine." And bursts into tears.

Even amongst Chinese, not many would know the cultural import in the difference between wonton soup and wonton noodle soup. The film cleverly highlights this difference to bring forth the woman's sorrow and to illuminate its design of blue Hong Kong. The woman tells her boyfriend that wonton soup "does not exist" in Hong Kong, but clearly expressed her desire for wonton soup, not wonton noodle soup. The film's title is *Wonton Soup*, but the film never shows this Chinese snack; what the film does show repeatedly is Hong Kong in a sapphire hue— its Victoria Harbor, Bank of China —the past and future of Hong Kong. This crystalline Hong Kong accompanies the diasporic, migrated Hong Kongers (fig. 16.1). This Hong Kong resembles wonton soup: it does not exist, it has deja disparu. Intimate acts stir up the woman's bodily yearning, a longing for the lost Hong Kong. Her wish to part from the boyfriend embodies her frustration at not being able to communicate this deepest need.

351

FIGURE 16.1 The Chinese-Australian couple facing the Hong Kong skyscape (*Wonton Soup*, 1994)

However, when the boyfriend, through his Chinese food, provides her with the language to articulate her grief, and when the boyfriend utters the open sesame-like "This is not my City," they have then shared the loss of Hong Kong. It is only then that the woman can embrace the "Vegemite boyfriend" and smile. The point in presenting Hong Kong in such bluish splendor is to frame it into a surreal, idealized, and even a fetishized entity, a space to which the lovers cannot return, a city like wonton soup.

To convey a somber, and somewhat heavy, sentiment in thirty minutes, Law chooses not to employ dense dialogue or elaborate plot, but intricate visuals and sound. The use of sound/music in this Clara Law short is quite restrained. The opening sequence showing the reflective glass wall of an urban building is paired with a very slight guitar and accordion-like tune. It is not until the final sequence that the film releases its musical force. The five-minute final sequence comprises only six lines of dialogue; the rest is an audiovisual dance. This final sequence's musical theme is played out with the Chinese *er-hu*, with touches of piano and electronic accompaniment, and ends with the sound of rumbling thunder. Law's *Farewell China* says goodbye to China in 1990; the 1994 *Wonton Soup* follows as a work that has broken away from the China bond,[10] expressing the melancholia in parting, a final acceptance of the pain that comes with such separation, and a readiness to embrace a new relationship. The alluring and delicate blending of the *er-hu* and Western piano in the film's end, apart from conveying the sadness in separation, also suggests a consideration of a bastardized identity.

In 1996 with Australia as a base, Clara Law shot *Floating Life*, a film about a Hong Kong family whose members are dispersed in various parts of the globe (namely, Australia, Hong Kong, Germany). The film again tackles the psychic pains and adjustments of Chinese migrants of the 1990s; however, its fairytale-like structure sets a hopeful undertone for the depicted diasporic experiences. *Floating Life* employs drawings to distinguish its episodes, uses voice-overs to launch its different tales; it is like a series of bedtime stories told to a child, a story of family, a story of migration. In fact, there is a girl-child in *Floating Life*, and the film ends with a shot and the voice of the girl. The film closes with this beautiful Chinese-German girl playing in a fairytale-like setting of a house in the woods; this children's storybook-like setting highlights the hopeful stance *Floating Life* holds toward today's migrating Chinese. *Floating Life*'s optimism stems from Clara Law's evolved trust in the transportability and blendability of cultures. The Australian episodes in *Floating Life* are

352

more extended than its Hong Kong and German parts; the playful and promising blending of cultures also occurs in the Australian episodes.[11] In contrast to the aborted fetus in Hong Kong, and aside from the beautiful Eurasian girl in Germany, there is new life in the southern hemisphere—the migrated family is expecting the birth of a baby.

Parted from Hong Kong, Clara Law has eased her sense of loss, embraced new life Down Under, and at the turn of the century produced *The Goddess of 1967*. Totally erasing any trace of Hong Kong, Law, with an almost surreal style, traverses the Australian red land, exploring this southern hemisphere's "new gold mountain," looking for different cinematic ways of expression. However, starting anew, letting pass identity struggles, relinquishing the subject of migration, what is there then to express for a filmmaker who has made Chinese migration the core of her work?

LOST IN OZ[12]

As Clara Law's film narratives shifted Down Under, my interest in her work continued because of my attraction and disappointment towards *The Goddess of 1967*—attraction towards its fabulous visuals, and disappointment at how its images fail to base themselves on the historically particular, at how, abandoning her knowledge of Chineseness as a narrative tool, the film turns into more of a dazzling fable or parable. I will examine *The Goddess of 1967* in the context of other films made in Australia: in contrast to Nicolas Roeg's *Walkabout* (1971) and Sue Brook's *Japanese Story* (2003). These juxtapositions and comparisons will demonstrate a kind of in-betweenness in Law's first totally-shot-in-Australia feature film. And this in-betweenness suggests a move from a sense of loss (as conveyed by *Wonton Soup*) to a state of being lost as Law tries to locate a subject and form pertinent to her Australian film career.

The Goddess of 1967 is about a Japanese young man and a blind Aussie girl; it places them in the legendary Citroen DS (a 1967 vehicle of such beauty and technical perfection that car-buffs call it "the goddess"; pronounced the French way, DS is also a homophone for "déesse"—goddess) and sends them on a journey across the Australian inland. The young man from Tokyo visits Australia to purchase the Citroen from the blind girl who promises the sale only if the man drives them on a five-day journey to the west, to the opal-mining town of Lightning Ridge. On this journey, the backgrounds of the man and the girl gradually emerge, backgrounds that involve violence, murder, and incest. As they arrive at Lightning Ridge, it is revealed that the girl intends revenge on her incestuous opal-mining father/grandfather. The girl abandons her revenge at the last minute. And the film ends with the girl and the young man driving off to the vast unknown in the luminous pink Citroen.

Through the road trip in *Goddess,* Law fuses her cinematic sensibility to the Australian land, marrying graphics of automobile technology to computerized coloring and morphing of vast landscapes (bleach-bypass, high-contrast, and rear-projection are all employed). The Australian outback has rarely been seen in this fashion. It is no wonder then that the initial positive response to the film has identified it as a "moody spectacle," as "one of the most exciting and groundbreaking Australian movies of the year."[13] However, the film is spectacular and groundbreaking exactly because its stylistics have taken precedence, overwhelming, and in a way undermining, the pains and desires of the two leading characters. The Japanese young man and Australian young woman become ciphers of postmodern surface materiality/materialism and modern-day psychic interiority. It is as though without the subject of Chinese migration, Law shelters her film in dazzling visuals to compensate for the hollowness of her set-in-Australia story. This tendency to abstract in *Goddess* can be better explored when we see it together with an earlier film about a journey in the Australian desert—Nicolas Roeg's *Walkabout.*

The *Goddess of 1967* is in some ways like a thirty-years-after version of *Walkabout.* This Nicolas Roeg film staged the meeting of civilized and natural cultures on the Australian outback through the encounter of a white sister and brother pair with an aboriginal young man. Their journey together in the desert is launched by the violence and suicide of the father of the white siblings; their wandering ends with the suicide of the young aborigine. *Walkabout* is a modern-day parable, or some have said "a fairy story,"[14] of man's reflection on modernity and nature, of our alienation from nature. The British Roeg intended his film to be a parable, and so does not name his characters, recognizing them only as Girl, White Boy, and Black Boy in the credits,[15] and much of the film proceeds with little dialogue. At his time, Roeg's filming of Australian city, landscape, and nature presented a fresh modernistic way of examining the meeting of cultures (fig. 16.2). Thirty years later, Clara Law might have brought "groundbreaking" visuals to Australian filmic landscape; however, *Goddess* hesitates between really naming and abstracting the identity of her two leads (the Japanese man is named JM, the blind girl BG).

354

FIGURE 16.2 The boy, the aborigine, and the girl commencing their "walkabout" in the Australian Outback (*Walkabout*, 1971)

Whereas *Walkabout* is confident in keeping its narrative as a parable, not explaining the characters' background (for instance, the father's and the aboriginal boy's reasons for suicide are kept opaque), *Goddess,* with its various flashbacks, brings in sources of the malaise that inflicts its two leads. Whereas *Walkabout* is content to employ the spectacular Australian landscape as a dramatic and wondrous backdrop for its parable, at times bringing in images that push the tale into the realm of the mythological (the repeated emergence of a lone tree or tree figure, the eating of its fruit . . .),[16] *Goddess* adds Australian iconographies as it travels through the outback (cultural stereotypes, dingoes, child lost in the woods), rousing in the viewers a desire for more culturally specific details and emotions, yet confining us in a fable-like narrative design.

Walkabout begins with montages of urban life; *Goddess,* at the turn of the millennium, starts with images of the ultra-urban Japan, with shots of computer screens, bluish high-rises, tracks of bullet trains, and sounds of metal, and the Japanese man (JM) becomes the representative of such a culture. Modern man's desire for the material and nostalgia for the beautiful are embodied in JM's craving for the modern yet classic Citroen DS. Like *Walkabout,* much of *Goddess* takes place on a trip in the Australian outback, with JM driving BG in the DS (fig. 16.3). *Goddess* is not the first

FIGURE 16.3 JM and BG in the pink DS in the Australian bush (*The Goddess of 1967*, 2000)

time Law chooses a Japanese man to personify postmodern sensibility: In *Autumn Moon,* Law employed a Japanese male tourist (naming him Tokio) to help highlight the transitional state of pre-1997 Hong Kong. The insertion of such Japanese figures, whether into the Hong Kong or Australian context, brings out an intercultural zone; in Law's films, the Japanese male is possessor of modern machines (camcorder, satellite phone) with qualities seemingly in contrast to the fast-disappearing traditional Hong Kong elements in *Autumn Moon* or the ancient impervious arid land in *Goddess.* For the Anglo-British Roeg, white people in *Walkabout* represent city culture; for Law, it is the Japanese male who characterizes modernity, and the white blind girl in *Goddess* is more of the land, embodying a more instinctive culture. In other words, for the Chinese Clara Law, the Japanese male is not only a cipher of modernity but also a figure who witnesses, helps record, and communicates the experiences and transformations within an intercultural zone. Law discards her familiar Chinese elements, abandons the baggage of Chinese specificities, and relies on the more distant and metaphoric Japanese male figure to probe and travel into the Australian outback, the heartland of her new home. The Australia which Law's Japanese man witnesses emerge more clearly when we examine it with another film using a Japanese male—Sue Brooks's *Japanese Story*.

In 2003 another Australian film by a female director employed a Japanese man to examine that intercultural zone within Australia. Sue

Brooks's *Japanese Story* did not opt for the parable-narrative: Brooks names her Japanese man Hiromitsu Tachibana and her Australian female lead Sandy Edwards. Brooks's Hiromitsu is a combination of Law's Japanese males, both an introspective tourist and a potential shopper/buyer, going on a road trip to the exotic Australian outback, interested in what the iron-red land could yield. Brooks's story sends the geologist Sandy (played by Toni Collette) and the businessman Hiro (Gotaro Tsunashima) on a trek to the deserts of the Pilbara region in Western Australia (fig. 16.4). What Brooks stresses in her Japanese man is not so much his ultramodern quality but his capital, his potential powerful capacity to purchase. Still, Hiro, this foreigner, is again used to probe the psychic interiority of the Australian female. In both *Japanese Story* and *Goddess,* the Japanese man, the foreigner, exists to service the delineation of the Australian identity. JM in *Goddess* is given two flashbacks: one lasting only seconds as he recalls the Japanese city that is "like living in Mars," another as he recollects the incident that made him rich and able to buy the Citroen. BG in contrast is given various flashbacks and, therefore, more personal history. *Japanese Story* kills off its Japanese in an accident a little more than halfway into the film, and the rest of the film is immersed in the internal struggles of Sandy as she tries to comprehend this sudden loss. Brooks openly

357

FIGURE 16.4 Hiro and Sandy facing the Australian landscape (*Japanese Story,* 2003)

states that *Japanese Story* is "just her [Sandy] story, and from her point of view, it's as simple as that."[17] And in order to tell Sandy's Australian story, it needs the shock of an other, a foreigner; it needs a subdued Japanese story.

The Japanese story in both films involves a sensual, sexual connection between their leads. In these encounters, the Japanese male becomes the object of desire; we the audience or the film's female lead is the holder of the gaze. In other words, the Japanese male is feminized so as to bring out qualities in the Australian female. In *Japanese Story*, Sandy gazes at Hiro's lean and soft-lined body as he finishes a swim; in its sex scene, Sandy puts on Hiro's pants and gets on top of him while he remains still and naked. Felicity Collins, in her "*Japanese Story*: A Shift of Heart," considers Toni Collette as playing "a quintessential Australian role, a role honed into national recognition through a series of iconic performances of Australian masculinity by the likes of Chips Rafferty, Bill Hunter, Bryan Brown, Jack Thompson and Ray Barrett." If we consider a kind of "hard men," "mateship" as an essential part of Australian self-identity, then Toni Collette represents Australianess and conveys that masculine quality in female form; the Japanese man then needs to be, and is conveniently, feminized to highlight that. The Japanese male in *Goddess* (played by the model Rikiya Kurokawa) is not as feminized or inert as Hiro in *Japanese Story*; instead we are given to gaze upon his taut, muscular, and beautiful physique, to enjoy his gorgeous movements as he teaches BG to dance. And in the film's sex scene, he and BG are given equal exposure and sexual initiative. In contrast to JM's physical ease, the Australian BG (played by Rose Byrne) is portrayed with quirky but daring physical motions. While BG does not possess the gaze, she does possess a gun, dictates the direction of their drive into the outback, and is the initiator and the force behind the journey, behind the search in this Australian road movie. In other words, the sexual, gender, and cultural dynamics of these two films show *Japanese Story* to be highly interested in empowering Sandy, in stressing Sandy's experience, in telling an Australian story; while *Goddess*, although also privileging its Aussie girl, offers a more balanced narrative space to each of its protagonists. When compared to *Walkabout*, *Goddess* is not enough of a fable; when compared to *Japanese Story*, *Goddess* is not enough of an Australian story.

In 1971 the white girl and the aboriginal boy in *Walkabout* are sexually aware of each other, but their sexual impulses are not consummated.

In the end of the film, the already-adult white girl yearns, in her mind's eye, for that possible moment of connection. In year 2000, JM and BG sexually connect in *Goddess*, affirming the possibility of intercultural connection. And in 2003 sexual contact with the foreigner in *Japanese Story* becomes the triggering factor for the Australian Sandy to begin and accept a process of reflection and reconciliation. The non-consummation in *Walkabout* further communicates a sense of gloom that is often found in Roeg's work: exotic lands or specific locales help open a glimpse of an utopian moment (or a moment of dreaded clarity), an oasis within the harsh desert, to which one yearns but to which it is impossible to return.[18] The missed connection in *Walkabout* is the lesson and caution in Nicolas Roeg's modern-day fable. The connection with a foreigner in *Japanese Story* aids the very Australian and very female production team of Sue Brooks, Alison Tilson (writer), and Sue Maslin (producer) in bringing out a new element in the Australian identity. The roughness, the "undaintiness," in the image of the Australian female is not new in Australian cinema (e.g., the sheep-tending Aussie female is contrasted with the elegant English wife in Michael Blakemore's 1994 *Country Life*); what is added in *Japanese Story* is the incorporation of a struggling and softening reflectiveness in the Aussie Sandy after her encounter with, and the sudden loss of, the feminized Hiro. For Clara Law and her screenwriting partner Eddie Fong, the connection between JM and BG in *Goddess* is necessary. As they have parted from Hong Kong and decided on settling in their new antipodean home, it is critical to establish connection. The Asian male then becomes the vehicle for their journey of connecting. Through JM, Law and Fong share the Aussie BG's introspective journey, absorb the elemental vastness of the ochre land, and contribute a fresh filmic image of the ancient terrain to Australian cinema.

In many narratives, foreign eyes, or foreigners, are employed to help highlight their story's themes, concerns, or the situation of their protagonists. The British Roeg, in his parable-like Australian *Walkabout*, relied ironically on the aboriginal boy to bring out the malaise in modernity. Sue Brooks uses a Japanese man to obliquely touch upon an Australian issue. As one reads the articles on *Japanese Story*, one notices how the film is associated with works of desert journeys such as *Walkabout* and *Goddess*, but in the Australian writings, there are also observations of a political aspect in this intimate film. Lorena Cancela, in her preface to her interview with Sue Brooks, detects a political dimension in the film's mourning ritual. She sees Sandy's mourning of Hiro resonating with "events in contemporary Australian society," and "relating to the indigenous population, the Aborigines."[19] Felicity Collins detects a post-Mabo consciousness in *Japanese Story* (Mabo refers to the High Court case in 1993 that opened the way to selective restoration of native title to land in Australia). In Collins's reading of the film, she explicitly points out that *Japanese Story*'s "Sandy's inchoate struggle to meet her social obligations to show remorse and accept guilt resonates with the post-Mabo politics of reconciliation."[20] In other words, *Japanese Story* elicits in white Australians a process of facing the loss, of accepting the regret, of reconciling with the entangled and traumatic engagement of white Australia with the Aborigines. Cancela suggests that this process might be functioning "on an unconscious level,"[21] but actually the film makes conscious its social concerns in its insertion of the Yothu Yindi song "Treaty" at the beginning by way of having the foreigner Hiromitsu play the track in his hired car.[22] Yothu Yindi is an Australian multiracial band; their 1991 single, "Treaty," won a variety of awards.[23] The song signaled a high point when aboriginal culture gained access to the popular imagination; at the same time, the events surrounding the song also marked the ironic rejection of aboriginality by mainstream society. During the time of the award, the aboriginal leader of the band was refused service in a St. Kilda bar in Melbourne, allegedly on grounds of his color. By playing this song, which sings of, "Words are easy, words are cheap/Much cheaper than our priceless land . . . This land was never given up/This land was never bought and sold," at the beginning of the film—at Hiromitsu's arrival in the Australian desert—*Japanese Story* is calling on its Australian viewers' collective unconscious and nudging them towards a certain way of experiencing the film.

There is no reading of such resonant social and cultural details in the articles on Law's *Goddess*. While the language of Chinese food was compellingly employed to express diasporic loss in *Wonton Soup* and *Autumn Moon*, many Australian cultural signs and idioms are brought in but not really satisfactorily deployed or explored in *Goddess*. For instance, while the Australian landscape is walked through and imbued with mythical quality in *Walkabout*, while the iron-ore red Pilbara desert is driven through and radiates its economic potential and imperviousness in *Japanese Story*, the Australian outback constantly competes with the ultraslick Citroen and computerized imageries and becomes a lackluster dirt road in *Goddess*. Opal mining certainly qualifies as a quintessentially Australian activity, but Law seems only interested in using it to get underground, to use it as a way of bringing out the metaphor of "darkness within" or "darkness in the heartland," the Australian dead heart. When the setting and the cultural idioms are so obviously Australian, one wonders what is that "darkness"—that grandfather's incest—lying deep within the Australian heartland.

One possible way of reading that darkness is to identify it as a cross-generational suppression of the female. The grandmother's desire to dance in *Goddess,* her visits to the outback pub to satisfy her desire, is met with her own murder in the bush. The mother in *Goddess* is trapped in an incestuous relationship with BG's grandfather, seeks solace in religion, prays in an isolated church, but ultimately dies in the fire that burns away the abandoned church. BG's blindness seems to be a mark of past sins and her own suppressions; her acts of breaking away, as exemplified by the fabulous dance sequence midway in the film and final confrontation with the grandfather in Lightning Ridge, free her from her dark legacy and also help articulate the film's indictment of bush masculinity. Nonetheless, this "darkness within" or "darkness in the heartland" could be set in remote areas in the United States, Canada, or even China and still function as generational gender crimes. Law's tendency of touching on Australian cultural idioms and then shying away to clutch onto abstractions, parable-like constructions, and stylistics shows an inept hand at formulating an effective Australian story. But, it is with *Goddess,* through the red-haired BG, roaming in the southern hemisphere, in an elsewhere that is Oz, that Law manages to break away from her memory, mourning, and nostalgia of Chineseness, and ease away from her melancholic identification of being a Chinese migrant.

Whereas the sparse dialogue, the image, the music, and the use of food and sex were all so wonderfully mixed and so richly evocative in the thirty-minute *Wonton Soup,* cultural elements in *Goddess* can't seem to cohere; they become heavy-handed abstractions strung together, serving as road-stops for a surreal road trip. If we see *Goddess* as Law's first full-length Australian feature, she seems to be lost in Oz, resorting to universalities to tell her Australian story. *The Goddess of 1967*'s narrative could have taken the broadly fable-like strategy of *Walkabout* or the detailed socially and politically cognizant approach of *Japanese Story;* instead it oscillates between the two designs. In the end, the film's choice of the alien car as its third character, as its key image, with all its material and metallic luminosity, cruising through the endless outback, might well be *the* vehicle that helps Law travel into the vastness of her new home. Law's film is like

361

its blind girl, preoccupied with inner trauma, blind to the Australian landscape; it is also like its Japanese man, enamored with materiality, with the visuality of film, inarticulate about the source of its own incoherence.

The millennium *Goddess* is like the children from nineteenth-century Australian realist paintings—children lost in the immensity of the outback. It is no wonder then that Law sought to find another chance to articulate her sense of Oz, to try another filmic mode to get her out of her lost-in-Oz state. She found it in the story of Ali, through a 6000-kilometer trip crossing the dusty, dirt roads of Australia.

CLARA'S RUBY SLIPPERS

Four years after *The Goddess of 1967*, Clara Law released her documentary, *Letters to Ali*. The film records the 2003 road trip of the Kerbi family from

the southern Melbourne part of Australia to the northwestern town of Port Hedland. The aim of the trip was to visit a young Afghan asylum-seeker held at the Port Hedland detention center. The film, shot with digital cameras, reveals three aspects of the journey: the Trish family's desire to accommodate the Afghan teenager and extract him from the detention center; the sentiments of the young Afghan as expressed through his letters to Trish Kerbi; and Clara Law's own ruminations, in the form of word texts, about the road trip to Port Hedland, about her own migration, and about Australia.

"Ali" is the alias given to the Afghan boy in detention, and the face of Ali is never clearly shown in the film; one can say, Ali does not have much of a face or voice in the film. *Letters to Ali* is for the most part Trish Kerbi's family's response to Ali's situation, but it is very much framed and colored under Law's own somewhat detached and melancholic visual tone. The film comes through like Law's own letters to Australia. Her decision to voice her sentiments in the form of typed-on word texts corresponds to the epistolary format taken on by this documentary. Law abandons her past virtuosic stylistic displays, and allows the digital camera to record the trip, to capture the range of Australian light and terrain with the least filter mediation. With this documentary, Law travels far within the island continent, and comes closer to formulating her own picture of Australia. With *Wonton Soup*, there was only mentioning of Australia; with the three-continental *Floating Life*, about half of the film presents us with images of the antipodean Sydney suburbs; with the visually fabulous *The Goddess of*

1967, we traverse from Australian suburb, through the bush land, to the underground mines of Lightning Ridge. With *Letters to Ali,* a 6000-kilometer trip is documented. When interviewed for *Goddess,* Law expressed her sentiment toward the outback: "I found it really scary. The landscape seemed so vast and inhospitable; my first impression was that it was very hostile and primeval, without any feeling for the people that inhabited it."[24] Four years later, in *Letters to Ali'*s Web page, Law acknowledges, "to understand the vastness of Australia, one really has to physically travel through the land." Law admits that with Trish and Rob (Trish's husband) as her guides, the journey became "a great enjoyment," and she was able to "have the leisure to marvel at the beauty of nature, the boundless horizon, the intense light and changing colors of the sky, the immense primeval landscape." In a way, the documentary feels at times to be more about Law's marvel at Australia than a recording of Ali's ordeals. As a filmmaker known to be a "virtuoso stylist," Law seems to recognize the virtuosity of the Australian skyscape and landscape, and thus relegates her own voice to word-text, content with a digital camera, pleased to merely record, bowing to the land's awesome display of light and color.

Similar to her weak grasp of Australian cultural icons and idioms in *The Goddess,* key aspects of the political history behind mandatory detention in Australia are skipped over in her interview clips with Malcolm Fraser (former Prime Minister, 1975 to 1983) and Ian MacPhee (former Immigration Minister, 1979 to 1982). When asked about why *Letters to Ali* does not inform the viewers about the fact that it was the Labor government who introduced mandatory detention (in 1992 by the Keating Labor government), Law admits, "I didn't realize mandatory detention was introduced by Labor."[25] For Clara Law, a film stylist, it is surely not the historical or the political aspect of Australia that converts her into identifying with the country. Her arrival to Australia is similar to Ali's—to seek a form of asylum, a sanctuary from the uncertainties of what comes after Hong Kong's 1997 handover, to seek a haven where she can contemplate the evolution of her film style, and experiment on divorcing herself from representing Chineseness. Her conversion begins rather as she comes to sense how the country, with its unique light and color, melds well with her filmic palette. Law explores this in the fanciful computerized manipulations of the Australian landscape, mixing them with the technological design and beauty of the Citroen in *The Goddess.* Her conversion turns fuller in *Ali* as she travels from Australia's green-coastal south, through the dry inland with its sudden dust storms, through vast areas of red earth to the sunny north. This traversing becomes a process of appropriation; and as the Australian topography is being digitally recorded, Law enunciates her ruminations on migration, superimposes her word-text musings onto the images, and articulates her own "rhetoric of walking."

"Walking rhetorics" is a term introduced by Michel de Certeau in his article "Walking in the City." The article stresses how people or walkers, in contrast to administrative bodies or city designers, can produce their own space by their everyday walking, transgressing the constraints imposed by the established grids of the city. De Certeau then links this walking to speech-act, to the act of writing, thus, the "rhetoric of walking." Although the article is about the urban, de Certeau's formulation helps delineate the process of Law's approach to Australia. Australia begins as an idea of home in her *Wonton Soup* as she deals with and mourns the disappearing Hong Kong. Then images of suburban Sydney and flashing appearances of the iconic kangaroo come forth in *Floating Life*. Law then pictures a near-surrealistic road trip through the southeastern part of Australia vehicled by a fantastic pink Citroen. However, it is only when Law "walks" 6000 kilometers of land in a 4-WD that she can "appropriate" Australia. As Law gets down, dusty, and dirty in her journey to Port Hedland, at times even unable to see as dust storms attack, she tactilely feels the land and can then "poach" images of the landscape. It is also then that she can quietly articulate her "walk," her sense of the land, her practice of Australia. At long last, with the Trish family as her guide, Clara Law has been offered her "ruby slippers" in her filming of Ali's story: She walked through the red dusty road and somehow managed to identify Oz as home.

Clara Law, ever since she began filming about migration in *The Other Half and the Other Half,* has been practicing what Salman Rushdie states about the ever-favorite MGM classic, *The Wizard of Oz* (1939):

> the real secret of the ruby slippers is not that 'there's no place like home', but rather that there is no longer any such place *as* home: except, of course, for the home we make, or the homes that are made for us, in Oz: which is anywhere, and everywhere, except the place from which we began.[26]

Law has worn, and perhaps has been fixated on, her own ruby slippers and filmed about the desire for home for more than a decade. Her *Farewell China, Autumn Moon,* and *Floating Life* not only deal with migration and the desire for home, but also the desire for leaving. Law's ruby slippers embody an anxious sense of Chineseness,[27] and they also offer her a chance to escape from her "trouble," escape from the fear of displacement, an ambivalent sense of identity, and the difficult process of identification. As she, through *Letters to Ali*, walks the red earth of Oz and marvels at "the intense light and changing colours of the sky," Law has located an elsewhere from messy Chineseness, where filming becomes "a journey of capturing changing lights and colours," a filming journey which, she says with relish, "I could rely totally on my intuition." Documentary has never been Clara Law's genre; video has not been her favored material. Deciding on a story from the newspaper, filming without much pre-production work, Law's *Letters to Ali* breaks away from the sensibility of her previous work and emits a sense of settlement. *Letters to Ali* paradoxically leads Law away from and towards home: away from the grey and blue of the north to the light and color of the south, away from a troubling and struggling Chineseness to a settlement towards one's uprooted self. *Letters to Ali*, with its enabling video, allowed Law to find a renewed sense of the filmic, and manifested home as a form of film act. And so, filming *is* home, filming is escape, and Clara Law has filmed her way to an elsewhere that is Oz.

365

ACKNOWLEDGMENT

This essay was made possible with the support of an NSC research grant: NSC 92-2411-H-002-021.

NOTES

1. In *Australia in Brief*, an official booklet put out by the Australian Department of Foreign Affairs and Trade in 2003, Australia is described as a "multicultural society" with its "indigenous peoples and migrants from some 200 countries worldwide." Aside from the indigenous peoples which today make up 2.4 percent of Australia's population, most Australians are all descendants of settlers who migrated to the land since 1788. After the first wave of British and Irish migrants (there were also some Chinese migrant workers during the mid-nineteenth-century gold rush), another wave of Europeans (Italians, Greeks) came after the Second World War, then Asians (Vietnamese, Chinese) arrived after the White Australia policy was abolished in 1973.

2. *Jedda* touches upon the issue of assimilation and the predicament of the aboriginal people living under a dominant white culture. Barbara Creed, in her "Breeding out the

Black," studies the historical racial situation behind *Jedda* and highlights how its mother-daughter motif operates with racial issues in the film.

3. *They're a Weird Mob* ("mob" is also an Australian slang that refers to a herd of kangaroos) presents urban Australia in a comedic manner through the experience of a foreigner. The film not only depicts Sydney through the eyes of a fresh-off-the-boat Italian, but it is also filmed by the fresh-off-the-plane Englishman, Michael Powell. Jeanette Hoorn, in her "Michael Powell's *They're a Weird Mob*," does a close reading of the film's depiction of monoculturalism.

4. Stephen Teo, *Hong Kong Cinema*, 187.

5. See Shen Shiao-Ying, "Jiehe yu fenli de zhengzhi yu meixue" (Politics and Aesthetics of Connecting and Splitting). Also, an examination of the ending of *Farewell China* is included in Shen's "Obtuse Music and Nebulous Males."

6. Teo, *Hong Kong Cinema*, 207.

7. In *Erotique*, four international female filmmakers—Clara Law, Lizzie Borden from the U.S., German Monika Treut, and Brazilian Ana Maria Magalhaes—explore female sexuality in the form of thirty-minute dramatic shorts.

8. Jill Bilcox is the Australian editor who has edited films such as *Moulin Rouge* (2001) and *Japanese Story* (2003).

9. Vegemite™ is the trade name of an Australian vegetable extract used as a spread or flavoring.

10. Law's "China bond" has also been identified by critics (such as Louie Kam and Gina Marchetti) as nostalgia towards patriarchy, especially Confucian patriarchal order.

11. The father in *Floating Life* in the end decides to realize his long-dreamed lotus garden in the dry suburbs of Sydney; the father's penchant for tea turns out to also be part of Australian culture (but of course different teas).

12. "Oz" is an Australian slang for "Australia."

13. Excerpts of Adrian Martin's review as quoted in Palace Films Web site http://www.palace.net.au/goddess/goddess.htm.

14. Louis Nowra, *Walkabout*, 45.

15. The film's inclination toward the parable becomes obvious when one reads the novel on which the film is loosely based. In the book *Walkabout* by James Vance Marshall, more information is given about the characters: the white sister and brother are named Mary and Peter and are American children from Charleston. The screenplay for Nicolas Roeg's film was written by Edward Bond. For a comparison of the film and novel, see Anthony Boyles's "Two Images of the Aboriginal."

16. Articles, such as Leonard Held's "Myth and Archetype in Nicolas Roeg's *Walkabout*," have noted the mythological aspect of *Walkabout*.

17. Lorena Cancela, "Feminist Filmmaking without Vanity or Sentimentality: An Interview with Sue Brooks," 21.

18. Consider other Roeg films, such as *Don't Look Now* (1973) and *Bad Timing* (1986).

19. Cancela, "Feminist Filmmaking," 18.

20. Felicity Collins, *Australian Cinema after Mabo*, 182.

21. Cancela, "Feminist Filmmaking," 18.

22. In *Japanese Story*'s U.S. DVD release, Hiromitsu's playing of the Yothu Yindi track is cut from the film's opening and relegated to the DVD's special features. Also, Sandy's sustained struggle with moving Hiro's dead body is cut short in the American version.

23. Graeme Turner, in his "Redefining the Nation," begins with an examination of the hybridity of ethnicities in Australian films, and then concentrates on an analysis of the cultural significance and impact of the multiracial band Yothu Yindi and their 1991 song "Treaty."

24. From Palace Films's Web site http://www.palace.net.au/goddess/goddess.htm.

25. From World Socialist Web site, http://wsws.org/articles/2004/oct2004/law2-o11_prn.shtml.

26. Salman Rushdie, *The Wizard of Oz*, 57.

27. Rai Jones, in his "Framing Strategies," focuses on Law's *Floating Life*, and does a fine analysis of how the film performs the anxiety of Chineseness in the national, transnational, and diasporic condition, highlighting the strategy employed to manage it.

Filmography

Arzner, Dorothy	*Dance, girl, dance* (1940)
Bertolucci, Bernardo	*The last emperor* (1987)
Bi, Kenneth 毕国智	*Hainan jifan* 海南鸡饭 (Rice rhapsody, 2004)
Blakemore, Michael	*Country life* (1994)
Brooks, Sue	*Japanese story* (2003)
Bu Wancang 卜万苍	*Liangxin de fuhuo* 良心的复活 (Confession, 1926)
	Nüling fuchouji 女伶复仇记 (Revenge of an actress, 1929)
Cai Chusheng 蔡楚生	*Xin nüxing* 新女性 (New woman, 1934)
Chan, Evans 陈耀成	*Cuo ai* 错爱 (Crossings, 1994)
	Zi jing 紫荆 (Bauhinia, 2002)
Chan, Peter 陈可辛	*Tian mi mi* 甜蜜蜜 (Comrades: Almost a love story, 1996)
Chang, Eileen 张爱玲	*Hongloumeng* 红楼梦 (Dream of the red chamber, not produced)
	Hungui lihen tian 魂归离恨天 (Sorrowful separation, not produced)
	Jinsuo ji 金锁记 (The golden cangue, not produced)
Chang Mei-chün 张美君	*Jiazhuang yi niuche* 嫁妆一牛车 (An oxcart for a dowry, 1984)

Chang, Sylvia 张艾嘉   *Zui ai* 最爱 (Passion, 1986)

Shasha Jiajia zhanqilai 莎莎嘉嘉站起来 (Sisters of the world unite, 1991)

Mengxing shifen 梦醒时分 (Mary from Beijing, 1992)

Shaonü Xiao Yu 少女小渔 (Siao Yu, 1995)

Jintian bu huijia 今天不回家 (Tonight nobody goes home, 1996)

Xin dong 心动 (Tempting heart, 1999)

Xiang fei 想飞 (Princess D, 2002)

20 30 40 (2004)

Yige hao baba 一个好爸爸 (Run Papa run, 2008)

Chang, Sylvia 张艾嘉,   *Xin tongju shidai* 新同居时代 (In between, 1994)
    Samson Chiu 赵良骏,
    and Yonfan 杨凡

Chang, Sylvia 张艾嘉,   *Huangse gushi* 黄色故事 (The game they call sex,
    Wang Siao-di 王小棣,   1987)
    and Chin Kuo-chao 金国钊

Chang Yi 张毅   *Yuqing sao* 玉卿嫂 (Jade love, 1984)

Wo zheyang guole yisheng 我这样过了一生 (Kuei-mei, a woman, 1985)

Wo de ai 我的爱 (This love of mine, 1986)

Chauvel, Charles   *Jedda* (1955)

Chen Boer 陈波儿   *Bianqu laodong yingxiong* 边区劳动英雄 (Working hero in the communist base, 1946)

Chen Kaige 陈凯歌   *Huang tudi* 黄土地 (Yellow earth, 1984)

Bawang bieji 霸王别姬 (Farewell my concubine, 1993)

Chen Kunhou 陈坤厚   *Xiaobi de gushi* 小毕的故事 (Growing up, 1983)

Chen, Singing 陈芯宜   *Wo jiao A Ming la* 我叫阿铭啦 (Bundled, 2000)

Chen Ying-jung 陈映蓉   *Shiqi sui de tiankong* 十七岁的天空 (Formula 17, 2004)

Ch'en Wen-min 陈文敏   *Mangmang niao* 茫茫鸟 (The dazzling bird, 1957)

Ku lian 苦恋 (Bitter love, 1957)

Cheung, Mabel   *Feifa yimin* 非法移民 (The illegal immigrant, 1985)
    Yuen-Ting 张婉婷   *Qiutian de tonghua* 秋天的童话 (An autumn's tale, 1987)

Ba liangjin 八两金 (Eight taels of gold, 1989)

Songjia wangchao 宋家王朝 (The Song sisters, 1997)

Boli zhi cheng 玻璃之城 (City of glass, 1998)

Beijing yue yu lu 北京乐与路 (Beijing rocks, 2001)

Long de shenchu: shiluo de pintu 龙的深处: 失落的拼图 (Traces of a dragon: Jackie Chan and his lost family, 2003)

Chien Wei-ssu 简伟斯	*Dengdai yueshi de nüren* 等待月事的女人 (A woman waiting for her period, 1993)
	Hui shou lai shi lu 回首来时路 (Echoing with women's voices, 1997)
Chou, Zero 周美玲	*Shenti dianying* 身体电影 (A film about the body, 1996)
	Si jiaoluo 私角落 (Corner's, 2001)
	Yanguang sishe gewutuan 艳光四射歌舞团 (Splendid float, 2004)
	Ciqing 刺青 (Spider lilies, 2007)
	Piaolang qingchun 漂浪青春 (Drifting flowers, 2008)
Cukor, George	*The Women* (1939)
Dong Kena 董克娜	*Kunlunshan shang yikecao* 昆仑山上一棵草 (Small grass grows on the Kunlun mountain, 1962)
Duke, Daryl	*Tai-Pan* (1986)
Eng, Esther 伍锦霞	*Minzu nuyingxiong* 民族女英雄 (National heroine, 1937)
	Duhua fengyu 妒花风雨 (Jealousy, 1938)
	Shiwan qingren 十万情人 (100,000 lovers, 1938)
	Nüren shijie 女人世界 (Woman's world [previously named Sanshiliu nü tiangang 三十六女天罡, 36 heavenly ferocious women], 1939)
	Yiye fuqi 一夜夫妻 (Husband and wife for one night, 1939)
	Lanhu biyu 蓝湖碧玉 (Blue jade, 1947)
	Chilai chunyiwan 迟来春已晚 (Too late for spring, 1948)
	Huangdao qingyan 荒岛情焰 (Mad fire, mad love, 1949)
	Niuyue tangrenjie suishi an 纽约唐人街碎尸案 (Murder in New York Chinatown, 1961)
	Huangtang yuelao 荒唐月老 (The funniest god of love, not produced)
	Niangzi jun 娘子军 (The Amazons, not produced)
	Bixue du lanqiao 碧血渡蓝桥 (Crossing the blue bridge, not produced)
	Youji yingxiong 游击英雄 (Guerilla heroes, not produced)
Eng, Esther 伍锦霞 and Kwan Man-ching 关文清	*Jinmen nü* 金门女 (Golden Gate girl, 1941)
Fleming, Victor	*The Wizard of Oz* (1939)
Fong, Allen 方育平	*Fuzi qing* 父子情 (Father and son, 1981)
	Mei guo xin 美国心 (Just like weather, 1986)

371

Gao Laifu 高来福	*Nüxing de chouren* 女性的仇人 (The enemy of women, 1957)
Ho Chi-ming 何基明	*Xue Pinggui yu Wang Baochuan* 薛平贵与王宝钏 (Xue Pinggui and Wang Baochuan, 1956)
Hou Hsiao-hsien 侯孝贤	*Erzi de da wan'ou* 儿子的大玩偶 (The sandwich man, 1983)
	Fenggui laide ren 风柜来的人 (The boys from Fenggui, 1983).
	Dongdong de jiaqi 冬冬的假期 (Summer at Grandpa's, 1984)
	Tongnian wangshi 童年往事 (A time to live, a time to die, 1985)
	Lianlian fengchen 恋恋风尘 (Dust in the wind, 1986)
	Niluohe nü'er 尼罗河女儿 (Daughter of the Nile, 1987)
	Beiqing chengshi 悲情城市 (A city of sadness, 1989)
Hou Yao 侯曜	*Qifu* 弃妇 (The abandoned wife, 1924)
	Aishen de wanou 爱神的玩偶 (Cupid's puppets, 1925)
Hsiao Chü-chen 萧菊贞	*Bai ge jihua* 白鸽计划 (Our time our story: 20 years' new Taiwan cinema, 2002)
Hu, King 胡金铨	*Shanzhong chuanqi* 山中传奇 (Legend of the mountain, 1979)
Huang Shuqin 黄蜀芹	*Qingchun wansui* 青春万岁 (Forever young, 1983)
	Ren, gui, qing 人，鬼，情 (Woman, demon, human, 1987)
	Hua hun 画魂 (The soul of the painter, 1994)
	Cun ji 村妓 (The village whore [also known as *Zhangfu* 丈夫, Husband], 2000)
	Hei, Fulanke 嗨，弗兰克 (Hey, Frank, 2001)
Huang Yu-shan 黄玉珊	*Luoshan feng* 落山风 (Autumn tempest, 1988)
	Shuang zhuo 双镯 (Twin bracelets, 1990)
	Mudan niao 牡丹鸟 (Peony birds, 1991)
	Haiyan 海燕 (The petrel returns, 1997)
	Zhen qing kuang ai 真情狂爱 (Spring cactus, 1998)
	Nanfang jishi zhi fushi guangying 南方纪事之浮世光影 (The strait story, 2006)
	Chatianshan zhi ge 插天山之歌 (The song of Chatien Mountain, 2007)
Hu Mei 胡玫	*Nüer lou* 女儿楼 (Army Nurse, 1985)
Hu T'ai-li 胡台丽	*Chuanguo pojiacun* 穿过婆家村 (Passing through my mother-in-law's village, 1998)
Hui, Ann (Xu Anhua) 许鞍华	*Lai ke* 来客 (The boy from Vietnam, 1978)
	Feng jie 疯劫 (The secret, 1979)
	Hu Yue de gushi 胡越的故事 (The story of Woo Viet, 1981)

Touben nuhai 投奔怒海 (Boat people, 1982)

Ketu qiuhen 客途秋恨 (Song of the exile, 1990)

Yima de houxiandai shenghuo 姨妈的后现代生活
(The postmodern life of my aunt, 2006)

Jiang Huiling 江惠龄   Jinshui shen 金水婶 (Auntie Jinshui, 1987)

Jiang Wen 姜文   Yangguang canlan de rizi 阳光灿烂的日子 (In the
heat of the sun, 1994)

Keshishian, Alex   Truth or dare (1991)

Koster, Henry   Flower drum song (1961)

Kwan Man-ching 关文清   Shengming xian 生命线 (Lifeline, 1935)

Kwan, Stanley 关锦鹏   Ren zai Niuyue 人在纽约 (Full moon in New York,
1989)

Lai Man-wai 黎民伟   Shijiu lu jun kangzhan guangrong shi
十九路军抗战光荣史 (The glorious resistant
history of the 19th army, 1932)

Law, Alex Kai-Yui 罗启锐   Qi xiaofu 七小福 (Painted faces, 1988)

Wo ai Niu Wenchai 我爱扭纹柴 (Now you see love,
now you don't, 1992)

Law, Clara 罗卓瑶   Wo ai tai kong ren 我爱太空人 (The other half and
the other half, 1988)

Ai zai ta xiang de ji jie 爱在他乡的季节 (Farewell
China, 1990)

Qiu yue 秋月 (Autumn moon, 1992)

You seng 诱僧 (Temptations of a monk, 1993)

Yun tun tang 云吞汤 (Wonton soup, part of
Erotique, 1994)

Fu sheng 浮生 (Floating life, 1996)

Yu shang 1967 de nü shen 遇上 1967 的女神
(The goddess of 1967, 2000)

Gei A Li de xin 给阿里的信 (Letters to Ali, 2004)

Lee, Ang 李安   Tuishou 推手 (Pushing hands, 1991)

Xiyan 喜宴 (Wedding banquet, 1993)

Yinshi nannü 饮食男女 (Eat, drink, man and
woman, 1994)

LeRoy, Mervyn   Waterloo Bridge (1940)

Li Han-hsiang 李翰祥   Hong lou meng 红楼梦 (Dream of the red
chamber, 1977)

Li Hsing 李行   Bi yun tian 碧云天 (Posterity and perplexity, 1976)

Wangyang zhong de yi tiao chuan 汪洋中的一条船
(He never gives up, 1978)

Xiaocheng gushi 小城故事 (Story of a small town,
1979)

Zao'an Taibei 早安台北 (Good morning, Taipei,
1979)

Li Mei-Mi 李美弥   *Nüzi xuexiao* 女子学校 (Girl's school, 1982)

Li Pingqian 李萍倩   *Feng nian* 丰年 (Bumper harvest, 1933)

     Xiandai yi nüxing 现代一女性 (A woman of today, 1933)

Li Shaohong 李少红   *Hongfen* 红粉 (Blush, 1994)

Li Yu 李玉   *Jinnian xiatian* 今年夏天 (Fish and elephant, 2001)

     Hongyan 红颜 (Dam Street, 2005)

     Pingguo 苹果 (Lost in Beijing, 2007)

Lin Ch'ing-chieh 林清介   *Jinshui shen* 金水婶 (Auntie Jinshui, 1987)

Lin Nong 林农   *Dang de nüer* 党的女儿 (Daughter of the party, 1958)

Liu Jiayin 刘伽茵   *Niupi* 牛皮 (Oxhide, 2005)

Liu Li-Li 刘立立   *Yaner zai linshao* 雁儿在林梢 (Wild goose on the wing, 1979)

Liu Miaomiao 刘苗苗   *Mati sheng sui* 马蹄声碎 (Women on the Long March, 1987)

Lou Ye 娄烨   *Yihe yuan* 颐和园 (Summer palace, 2006)

Luhrmann, Baz   *Moulin Rouge* (2001)

Luo Shaohui 绍罗辉 and Ch'en Wen-min 陈文敏   *Xue Rengui zhengdong* 薛仁贵征东 (Xue Rengui's eastern campaign, 1957)

Mann, Daniel   *The mountain road* (1960)

Mayo, Archie   *Charley's aunt* (1941)

Mi Jiashan 米家山   *Wanzhu* 玩主 (The troubleshooters, 1988)

Ning Ying 宁瀛   *Zhao le* 找乐 (For run, 1993)

     Minjing gushi 民警故事 (On the beat, 1995)

     Xiari nuanyangyang 夏日暖洋洋 (I love Beijing, 2000)

     Wu qiong dong 无穷动 (Perpetual motion, 2005)

Ophüls, Max   *Letter from an unknown woman* (1948)

Peng Xiaolian 彭小莲   *Nüren de gushi* 女人的故事 (Women's story, 1989)

     Jiazhuang mei ganjue 假装没感觉 (Shanghai women, 2002)

Powell, Michael   *They're a weird mob* (1966)

Quine, Richard   *The world of Suzie Wong* (1960)

Ray, Satyajit   *Charulata* (1964)

Roeg, Nicolas   *Walkabout* (1971)

     Don't look now (1973)

     Bad timing (1986)

Sander, Helke   *The all-round reduced personality—Redupers* (1977)

Sang Hu 桑弧   *Buliao qing* 不了情 (Love without end, 1947)

     Taitai wansui 太太万岁 (Long live the wife, 1947)

     Aile zhongnian 哀乐中年 (Sorrows and joys at middle age, 1949)

Shao Luohui 绍罗辉   *Xue Rengui yu Liu Jinhua* 薛仁贵与柳金花 (Xue Rengui and Liu Jinhua, 1957)

Shi Dongshan 史东山   *Qi nüzi* 奇女子 (A wondrous woman, 1928)

Shui Hua 水华   *Geming jiating* 革命家庭 (A revolutionary family, 1960)

Sirk, Douglas   *All that heaven allows* (1956)

Steveson, Robert   *Back street* (1941)

Tang Huang 唐煌   *Liuyue xinniang* 六月新娘 (June bride, 1960)

Tang Shu Shuen 唐书璇   *Dong furen* 董夫人 (The arch, 1969)

    Bao fa hu 暴发户 (The Hong Kong tycoon, 1979)

Tang Xiaotan 汤晓丹   *Baijinlong* 白金龙 (White gold dragon, 1933)

Tian Zhuangzhuang 田壮壮   *Lan fengzheng* 蓝风筝 (Blue kite, 1993)

Tong, Frank 唐隶忠   *Xinhen* 心恨 (Heartaches; premiered in Hong Kong as Tiexue fanghun 铁血芳魂; also known as Sum Hun, 1935)

Tsai Ming-liang 蔡明亮   *Aiqing wansui* 爱情万岁 (Vive L'amour, 1994)

Tseng Chuang-hsiang 曾壮祥   *Sha fu* 杀夫 (The woman of wrath, 1986)

Tseng Wen-chen 曾文珍   *Dengdai feiyu* 等待飞鱼 (Fishing luck, 2005)

Tsui Hark 徐克   *Die bian* 蝶变 (The butterfly murders, 1979)

Walters, Charles   *The Tender Trap* (1955)

Wan Jen 万仁   *Youmai caizi* 油麻菜籽 (Ah Fei, 1983)

Wang Bin 王滨 and Shui Hua 水华   *Baimao nü* 白毛女 (The white haired girl, 1950)

Wang Ping 王苹   *Liubao de gushi* 柳堡的故事 (The story of Liubao village, 1957)

    Yongbu xiaoshi de dianbo 永不消失的电波 (The everlasting radio signals, 1958)

    Huaishu zhuang 槐树庄 (Locust tree village, 1961)

    Nihongdeng xia de shaobing 霓虹灯下的哨兵 (Sentinels under the neon lights, 1964)

Wang Qiming 王启民 and Sun Yu 孙羽   *Ren dao zhongnian* 人到中年 (At middle age, 1982)

Wang Tianlin 王天林   *Nanbei xi xiangfeng* 南北喜相逢 (The greatest love affair on earth, 1962)

    Xiao ernü 小儿女 (Father takes a bride, 1963)

    Nanbei yijia qin 南北一家亲 (The greatest wedding on earth, 1964)

Wang T'ung 王童   *Kan hai de rizi* 看海的日子 (A flower in the rainy night, 1983)

Wang Xiaoshuai 王小帅   *Dongtian de rizi* 冬天的日子 (The days, 1993)

    Jidu hanleng 极度寒冷 (Frozen, 1996)

Wang Ying 汪莹   *Nübing riji* 女兵日记 (Diaries of a female soldier, 1975)

Wong, Barbara Chun-Chun 黄真真   *Liulou houzuo* 六楼后座 (Truth or dare: 6th floor rear flat, 2003)

Wyler, William   *Wuthering Heights* (1939)

375

Xia Gang 夏钢	*Yiban shi huoyan, yiban shi haishui* 一半是火焰，一半是海水 (Half flame, half brine, 1989)
Xiao Jiang 小江	*Tongnian wangshi* 童年往事 (Electrical shadows, 2005)
Xie Caijing 谢采贞	*Guchu beisheng* 孤雏悲声 (An orphan's cry, 1925)
Xie Jin 谢晋	*Hongse niangzijun* 红色娘子军 (The red detachment of women, 1961)
Xu Jinglei 徐静蕾	*Wo he baba* 我和爸爸 (My father and I, 2003)
	Yige mosheng nüren de laixin 一个陌生女人的来信 (Letter from an unknown woman, 2004)
	Mengxiang zhaojin xianshi 梦想照进现实 (Dreams may come, 2006)
Yang Chia-yün 杨家云	*A Ma de mimi: Taiji "weianfu" de gushi* 阿妈的秘密：台籍"慰安妇"的故事 (A secret buried for 50 years: A story of Taiwanese "comfort women," 1995)
Yang, Edward 杨德昌	*Haitan de yitian* 海滩的一天 (That day on the beach, 1983)
	Yiyi 一一 (Yi Yi: A One and a Two, 2000)
Yang, Edward 杨德昌, Zhang Yi 张毅, Ke yizheng 柯一正 and Tao Dechen 陶德辰	*Guangyin de gushi* 光阴的故事 (In our time, 1982)
Yu Zhong 俞钟	*Wo de meili xiangchou* 我的美丽乡愁 (Far from home, 2003)
Yue Feng 岳枫	*Qingchang ru zhangchang* 情场如战场 (The battle of love, 1957)
	Rencai liangde 人财两得 (A tale of two wives, 1957)
	Taohua yun 桃花运 (The wayward husband, 1958)
Zen Zhuang Hsiang (Zeng Zhuangxiang) 曾壮祥	*Sha fu* 傻福 (The woman of wrath, 1985)
Zhang Junzhao 张军钊	*Yige he bage* 一个和八个 (One and eight, 1983)
Zhang Nuanxin 张暖忻	*Sha'ou* 沙鸥 (The drive to win, 1981)
Zhang Xian 张弦	*Chu chun* 初春 (Early spring, 1981)
Zhang Yibai 张一白	*Kaiwang chuntian de ditie* 开往春天的地铁 (Spring subway, 2002)
Zhang Yuan 张元	*Wo ai ni* 我爱你 (I love you, 2003)
Zhong Qiwen 钟启文	*Yiqu nanwang* 一曲难忘 (Please remember me, 1964)
Zweig, Stefan	*Brief Einer Unbekannten* (Letter from an unknown woman, 1938)

376

Glossary

Ai Xia	艾霞
Artland	《艺林》
Bengbeng	蹦蹦
Bing Xin	冰心
BoBo	宝宝
Brother Ha	霞哥
Buzhuo	捕捉
Cainü	才女
Cangliang	苍凉
Canton Magazine	《广州杂志》
Cathay Pictures Ltd.	国泰影片公司
Chan Ching-wa	陈清华
Chang Ai-ling	张爱玲
Chang Hsiao-hung	张小虹
Ch'ang-ming	昌明
Cheang, Shu Lea	(Cheng Shu-li) 郑淑丽
Chen Duxiu	陈独秀
Cheng Bugao	程步高
Ch'en I	陈仪
Ch'en Ying-chen	陈映真
Cheung, Maggie	张曼玉

Cheung Ying	张瑛
Chiang Ching-kuo	蒋经国
Chiang Fang-liang	蒋方良
Chiang Hsiu-ch'iung	姜秀琼
China Times	《中国时报》
Chinese Film Media Awards	华语电影传媒大奖
Chinese National Golden Rooster Award	中国电影金鸡奖
Chin Yung	金庸
Chor Yuan	楚原
Chow Hsuan	周萱
Cho Yee-man	曹绮文
Chuanju	川剧
Chu Hsi-ning	朱西宁
Chung Chao-cheng	钟肇政
Chu T'ien-hsin	朱天心
Chu T'ien-wen	朱天文
Congwen zizhuan	《从文自传》
Dai Jinhua	戴锦华
Dapian	大片
Dazhong yingxun	《大众影讯》
Deng Xiaoping	邓小平
Dianma	癫麻
Dianying huabao	《电影画报》
Dianying xin zuo	《电影新作》
Dianzi huache	电子花车
Ding, Fifi Naifei	(Ting Nai-fei) 丁乃非
Dongwu xiongmeng	《动物凶猛》
Duhui	都会
Erwa	二娃
Fen ling	分灵
Funü xin zhi	妇女新知
Gang of Four	四人帮
Gaozhigan wuzhi shenghuo	高质感物质生活
Golden Gate Silver Light Company	金门银光公司
Gonggong kongjian	公共空间
Gong Li	巩俐
Grandview Film Company	大观声片公司
Great China	大中华
Gu Changwei	顾长卫
Hakka	客家人
Han Palace	汉宫

Han Tongsheng	韩童生
Hanzi	寒子
Heartland	中原
Heian de dianying quan	黑暗的电影圈
Hei Man	《戏文》
Henyi	恨意
He Saifei	何赛飞
Hiromi	宽美
Ho P'ing	何平
Hou I-jen	侯宜人
Hsiao-shao	小韶
Hsieh Ts'ai-chün	谢材俊
Hsiu Tse-lan	修泽兰
Hsü Shih-hsien	许世贤
Huabiao Film Awards	中国电影华表奖
Huadan	花旦
Hua Mulan	花木兰
Huang Ch'ing-ch'eng	黄清埕 (黄清呈)
Huang Ch'un-ming	黄春明
Huangren shouji	《荒人手记》
Huanxiang	幻想
Hua wenhua	华文化
Hu Lan-ch'eng	胡兰成
Hu Mali	呼玛丽
Hung Huang	洪晃
Hu T'ai-li	胡台丽
Hutong	胡同
Iron girls/Tie guniang	铁姑娘
Jairen	佳人
Jia	家
Jiabian	家变
Jiang Qing	江青
Jiang Qitao	江奇涛
Jiankang xieshi zhuyi	健康写实主义
Jiaohua jiazhi/shiyong jiazhi	交换价值/使用价值
Jia Zhangke	贾樟柯
Jiti chuzou	集体出走
Juancun	眷村
Junzi	君子
Kaila	开啦
Kaila jiepai	开啦街拍
Kaneshiro Takeshi	金城武

379

Koa-a-hi	歌仔戏
Kua Ah-leh	(Kuei Ya-lei) 归亚蕾
Kuang Chong-ping	姜中平
Kuer yingxiang	酷儿影像
Kwan Tak-hing	关德兴
Kwong Ngai Talking Picture Company	光艺影片公司
Lai Hsien-tsung	赖贤宗
Lala shenfen	拉拉身份
Lam Mui-mui	林妹妹
Lang Hsiung	郎雄
Langman ai	浪漫爱
Lan Siu-gei	靓少佳
Lao Xu	老徐
Law Ming-yau	罗明佑
Lee, Ping Bing	李屏宾
Lee Chor-fun	李楚芬
Lee Hoi-chun	李海泉
Lee Kok-sing	李觉声
Lee Sin-je	李心洁
Leong, Isabella Lok-Sze	(Luisa Isabella Nolasco da Silva) 梁洛施
Leung, Gigi	梁咏琪
Leung, Tina	狄娜
Li Ang	李昂
Lianhua Film Company	联华影业公司
Liao Hui-ying	廖辉英
Li Fei-fei	李非非
Li Mei-mi	李美弥
Ling Sing	《伶星》
Lin Haiyin	林海音
Li Qinqin	李勤勤
Liu Haisu	刘海粟
Liu Hulan	刘胡兰
Liu Kei-wai	廖奇伟
Liu li dao ying	(Floating Islands) 流离岛影
Liu Li-li	刘立立
Liu Mu-sha	刘慕沙
Liu Ro-ying	(Liu, René) 刘若英
Liu Suola	刘索拉
Li Xiaqing	李霞卿
Li Xingyang	李兴阳
Li Yüan-chen	李元贞
Li Yün-ch'an	李芸婵

Lo Hoi-tin	卢海天
Love Stories	爱的故事
Lü, Hsiu-lien	(Annette Lu) 吕秀莲
Lui, Lisa	吕瑞容
Lui Ming	雷鸣
Lu, Lisa Yan	卢燕
Lu Xun	鲁迅
Maestro Zhang	张老师
Mao Zedong	毛泽东
Ma Sze-tsang	马师曾
Miaoli	苗栗
Mingding lishi	命定历史
Mingxing banyuekan	《明星半月刊》
Mingxing dianying gongsi/ Star Motion Pictures Company	明星电影公司
Mingxing Film Company	明星影片公司
Mingxing tekan	《明星特刊》
Mingxing yuebao	《明星月报》
Miss Jiang	江小姐
Mok, Karen	莫文蔚
Mr. Xu	徐先生
Munn dyad	母女二元对立论
Nanguo jushe	南国剧社
Nan ren po	男人婆
Nanyang Film Company	南洋影片公司
New China Daily Press	《新中国报》
New Taiwan Cinema	台湾新电影
Ng, Sally	(Ng Kam-ping) 伍锦屏
Ng Chor-fan	吴楚帆
Ng Fan	伍藩
Ng Yim-ming	伍冉明
Ng Yu-jat	伍于泽
Nongmin gong	农民工
Nüxing dianying	女性电影
Nüxing yishi	女性意识
Ozu Yasujiro	小津安二郎
Pan Mou	潘牟
Pan Yuliang	潘玉良
Pan Zanhua	潘赞化
Pei Yanling	裴艳玲
Phoenix Claws	鹰爪
Ping Yanni	平燕妮

Pi-yun	碧云
Po	婆
Qian Guomin	钱国民
Qian wanghun	牵亡魂
Qiong Yao	琼瑶
Qiu Yun	秋芸
Qujiangyu	去疆域
Rensheng ru xi	人生如戏
Rose	《玫瑰》
Ruan Lingyu	阮玲玉
Sange nüren yitaixi	三个女人一台戏
Sansan jikan	《三三季刊》
See Ho Hotel	思豪大酒店
Sek Yin-jee	石燕子
Shanghai Baby	上海宝贝
Shanghai Film Studio	上影厂 (上海电影制片厂)
Shao Mujun	邵牧君
Shen Congwen	沈从文
Shum Lit-fu	岑烈夫
Siheyuan	四合院
Siji zhijia	司机之家
Sing Tao Evening Post	《星岛晚报》
Sit Kok-sin	薛觉先
Siu Fei-fei	小非非
Siu Yin-fei	小燕飞
Song Qingling	宋庆龄
Suet Ying-hong	雪影红
Su Ning	苏宁
Sun Lan-chou	新靓就
Su Tong	苏童
Suzhi	素质
Tam Lam-hing	谭兰卿
Tam Yuk-jan	谭玉真
Tang Na	唐纳
Tang Pui	邓培
The Mandarin	大舞台
The United Chinese News	《中华公报》
Tian'anmen Square	天安门
Tian Han	田汉
Tianyi Film Company	天一影片公司
Tie T	铁T
T'ing-t'ing	婷婷
To, Alex	杜德伟

Tofu	豆腐
Tongluo	铜锣
Tong Sing-to	唐醒图
Tongxing/yixing kongjian, huayu	同性/异性空间，话语
Tongzhi	同志
Tongzhi ganxing	同志感性
Ts'ai Jui-yüeh	蔡瑞月
Tsai Ming-liang	蔡明亮
Tsang Sam-dor	曾三多
United Daily	《联合报》
Wai Kim-fong	韦剑芳
Wang, Alice	王毓雅
Wang Chen-ho	王祯和
Wang Ji	王姬
Wang Lingzhen	王玲珍
Wang Meng	王蒙
Wang P'ing	王苹
Wang Shouxin	王守信
Wang Shuo	王朔
Wang T'o	王拓
Wang Wen-hsing	王文兴
Wang Ying	王莹
Wanzhu	玩主
Wei Hui	卫慧
Wenyi pian	文艺片
Wo ai ni, dan yü ni wu guan	我爱你，但与你无关
Wong, Beal	黄悲路
Wong, James Howe	黄宗沾
Wong Chuk-fun	黄焯芬
Wong Hok-sing	黄鹤声
Wu, Daniel	吴彦祖
Wu Dip-lai	胡蝶丽
Wu Dip-ying	胡蝶影
Wu Ma-li	吴玛例
Wu Nien-chen	吴念真
Wu Peng	胡鹏
Wu Yigong	吴贻弓
Xiangtu wenxue zuojia	乡土文学作家
Xiao shimin	小市民
Xiaoshun	孝顺
Xiaoshuo jiazu	小说家族
Xiao youchanzhe	小有产者

Xiaoyu	小鱼
Xia Yan	夏衍
Xindianyingzhi si	新电影之死
Xin nüxing	新女性
Xin qingnian	《新青年》
Xinyan	心眼
Xiushen qijia zhiguo ping tianxia	修身齐家治国平天下
Xiuyang	修养
Xiyuzhongxin	洗浴中心
Yan, Hilda	颜雅清
Yang, Edward/ Yang The-ch'ang	杨德昌
Yang Hui-shan	杨惠珊
Yang Kuei-mei	杨贵媚
Yang Lin	杨林
Yang Naimei	杨耐梅
Yang Qiangyun	杨蔷云
Yen Ge-ling	严歌苓
Yen Ming-hui	严明惠
Ye wen ye wu	也文也武
Yingxi chunqiu	《影戏春秋》
Yishujia zazhi	《艺术家杂志》
Yoriumi Shimbun	《读卖新闻》
Yuan Xinzhi	袁新枝
Yu, Azed	游婷敬
Yu Gai-ping	余寄萍
Yu Hua	余华
Zhang Hanzhi	章含之
Zhang mi	张迷
Zhang Shichuan	张石川
Zhang Yimou	张艺谋
Zhang Yuliang	张玉良
Zhao Yun	赵云
Zheng Bo	郑波
Zhongjian renwu	中间人物
Zhong Kui	钟馗
Zhuangxue	张学
Zhuo Ya	卓娅
Zishu nü	自梳女
Zuojia mingxing	作家明星
Zuoyi juzuojia lianmeng	左翼剧作家联盟
Zuozhe daoyan	作者导演

Bibliography

Abbas, Ackbar. *Hong Kong: Culture and the Politics of Disappearance*. Minneapolis, MN: University of Minnesota Press, 1997.

Ai, Weiwei 艾未未. "Ai Weiwei yanzhong de Mengxiang zhaojin xianshi he Wang Shuo" 艾未未眼中的《梦想照进现实》和王朔 (*Dreams May Come* and Wang Shuo in the Eyes of Ai Weiwei). *Chengshi huabao* 城市画报 (Urban Pictorial), July 19, 2006. http://www.douban.com/group/topic/4160270. (accessed on December 1, 2010)

Ai, Xia 艾霞. "1933 nian, wo de xiwang" 1933 年, 我的希望 (1933—My Hope). *Mingxing yuebao* 明星月报 (Star Monthly) 1, no. 1 (1933).

——. "Gei youzhi dianying de jiemei men" 给有志电影的姐妹们 (To My Sisters Interested in Film Acting). *Dianying huabao* 电影画报 (The Screen Pictorial), no. 5 (1933): 1–3.

——. "Wo de lian'ai guan: bian 'xiandai yi nüxing' hou gan" 我的恋爱观: 编现代一女性后感 (My View on Love: Thoughts after Writing "Modernity"). *Mingxing tekan* 明星特刊 (Star special issue) 1, no. 2 (1933): 4.

——. "Xiandai yi nüxing" 现代一女性 (Modernity). *Mingxing tekan* 明星特刊 (Star special issue) 1, no. 2 (1933): 3–4.

Appadurai, Arjun. *Fear of Small Numbers*. Durham, NC: Duke University Press, 2004.

Australia Department of Foreign Affairs and Trade. *Australia in Brief*. Images of Australia Branch, DFAT, 2003.

Babuscio, Jack. "Camp and Gay Sensibility." In Richard Dyer, ed., *Gays and Film*, 40–57. New York: Zoetrope, 1984.

Bakhtin, Mikhail. *The Dialogic Imagination: Four Essays*. Ed. Michael Holquist, trans. Caryl Emerson and Michael Holquist. Austin, TX: University of Texas Press, 1981.

——. *Problems of Dostoevsky's Poetics*. Ed. and trans. Caryl Emerson. Minneapolis, MN: University of Minnesota Press, 1984.

——. *Tuosituoyefusiji shixue wenti* 陀思陀耶大斯基诗学问题 (Problems of Dostoevsky's Poetics). In *Bahejin quanji* 巴赫金全集 (The Complete Works of Bakhtin), vol. 5, 117. Shijiazhuang, China: Hebei jiaoyu chubanshe, 1998.

Barthes, Roland. "The Death of the Author." In *Image-Music-Text,* trans. Stephen Heath, 142–8. New York: Hill and Wang, 1977.

"Bei wangji le de ren" 被忘记了的人 (Forgotten Stars of Chinese Screen). *Liangyou* 良友 (Young Companion), no. 105 (1935).

Benjamin, Walter. "The Work of Art in the Age of Mechanical Reproduction." In *Illuminations,* trans. Harry Zohn, 217–51. New York: Schocken Books, 1968.

Berry, Chris. *Postsocialist Cinema in Post-Mao China: The Cultural Revolution after the Cultural Revolution*. New York: Routledge, 2004.

——. "Asian Values, Family Values: Film, Video, and Lesbian and Gay Identities." *Journal of Homosexuality* 40, no. 3–4 (2001): 211–31.

——. "China's New 'Women's Cinema.'" *Camera Obscura* 18 (September 1988): 8–19.

——. "Interview with Hu Mei." *Camera Obscura* 18 (1988): 32–42.

——. "Interview with Zhang Nuanxin." *Camera Obscura* 18 (1988): 20–5.

——. "Writing on Blank Paper: The Classical Cinema before 1976 as a Didactic Paradigm." In his *Postsocialist Cinema in Post-Mao China,* 27–36. New York: Routledge, 2004.

Berry, Chris and Feii Lu. *Island on the Edge: Taiwan New Cinema and After*. Hong Kong: Hong Kong University Press, 2005.

Berry, Chris and Mary Farquhar. *China on Screen: Cinema and Nation*. Hong Kong: Hong Kong University Press; New York: Columbia University Press, 2006.

Berry, Michael. "Hou Hsiao-hsien with Chu T'ien-wen: Words and Images." In his *Speaking in Images: Interviews with Contemporary Chinese Filmmakers,* 235–71. New York: Columbia University Press, 2005.

Bian, Shanji 边善基. "Shehui zhuyi de qingchun zhi ge—yingpian Qingchun wansui manping" 社会主义的青春之歌—影片《青春万岁》漫评 (A Song to the Socialism's Youth: Some Thoughts on *Forever Young*). *Dianying yishu* 电影艺术 (Film Art), no. 12 (1983): 26–9.

Blunt, Alison and Gillian Rose. "Introduction: Women's Colonial and Postcolonial Geographies." In Alison Blunt and Gillian Rose, eds., *Writing Women and Space: Colonial and Postcolonial Geographies,* 1–25. New York: Guilford Press, 1994.

Bordwell, David. *Narration in the Fiction Film*. Madison, WI: University of Wisconsin Press, 1985.

——. *Planet Hong Kong: Popular Cinema and the Art of Entertainment*. Cambridge, MA: Harvard University Press, 2000.

386

Boyles, Anthony. "Two Images of the Aboriginal: *Walkabout*, the Novel and Film." *Literature/Film Quarterly* 7, no. 1 (1979): 67–76.

Burton, Antoinette. *After the Imperial Turn: Thinking With and Through the Nation.* Durham, NC: Duke University Press, 2003.

——. *Dwelling in the Archive: Women Writing House, Home, and History in Late Colonial India.* Oxford: Oxford University Press, 2003.

——, ed. *Gender, Sexuality and Colonial Modernities.* London: Routledge, 1999.

Butler, Alison. *Women's Cinema: The Contested Screen.* London: Wallflower, 2002.

Butler, Judith. *Gender Trouble: Feminism and the Subversion of Identity.* New York: Routledge, 2006.

——. "Performative Acts and Gender Constitution: An Essay in Phenomenology and Feminist Theory." In Sue-Ellen Case, ed., *Performing Feminisms: Feminist Critical Theory and Theatre*, 270–82. Baltimore, MD: Johns Hopkins University Press, 1990.

Canby, Vincent. "Stylized China: *The Arch* Offers Tale of Virtue and Desire." *New York Times*, April 6, 1972.

Cancela, Lorena. "Feminist Filmmaking without Vanity or Sentimentality: An Interview with Sue Brooks." *Cineaste* 29, no. 2 (2004): 18–21.

Caughie, John, ed. *Theories of Authorship: A Reader.* London: Routledge & Kegan Paul, 1981.

Certeau, Michel de. "Walking in the City." In *The Practice of Everyday Life*, trans. Steven Rendall, 91–110. Berkeley, CA: University of California Press, 1984.

Chan, Anita Kit-wa and Wong Wai-ling, eds. *Gendering Hong Kong.* Oxford: Oxford University Press, 2004.

Chanda, Geetanjali Singh. *Indian Women in the House of Fiction.* New Delhi: Zubaan, 2008.

Chang, Eileen 张爱玲. *Liu yan* 流言 (Written on Water). Trans. Andrew Jones. New York: Columbia University Press, 2005.

Chang, Jung. *Wild Swans: Three Daughters of China.* London: Simon & Schuster, 1991.

Chang, Michael. "The Good, the Bad, and the Beautiful: Movie Actresses and Public Discourse in Shanghai, 1920s–1930s." In Yingjin Zhang, ed., *Cinema and Urban Culture in Shanghai 1922–1943*, 128–59. Palo Alto, CA: Stanford University Press, 1999.

Chen, Feibao 陈飞宝. *Taiwan dianying daoyan yishu* 台湾电影导演艺术 (The Art of Taiwan Directors). Taipei: Yatai, 1999.

Chen, Leo Chanjen. "Cinema, Dream, Existence: The Films of Hou Hsiao-hsien." *New Left Review* 39 (2006): 73–106.

Chen, Xiaomei. *Acting the Right Part: Political Theater and Popular Drama in Contemporary China.* Honolulu: University of Hawaii Press, 2002.

Chen, Yanru. "From Ideal Women to Women's Ideal: Evolution of the Female Image in Chinese Feature Films, 1949–2000." *Asian Journal of Women's Studies* 14, no. 3 (2008): 97–129.

Chen, Yansheng 陈炎生. *Taiwan de nüer: Taiwan diyiwei nüdaoyan Chen Wenmin de jiazu yikenfendoushi* 台湾的女儿: 台湾第一位女导演陈文敏的家族移垦奋斗史 (The Daughter of Taiwan: The Rural Migration and Struggles of the Family of Chen Wenmin—The First Taiwan Female Film Director). Taipei: Yushanshe, 2003.

Chen, Zishan 陈子善, ed. "1943–1949 nianjian de Zhang Ailing 1943–1949" 年间的张爱玲 (Eileen Chang during 1943–1949). In Lin Xingqian 林幸谦, ed., *Zhang Ailing* 张爱玲, 47–7. Hong Kong: Oxford University Press, 2007.

——. *Siyu Zhang Ailing* 私语张爱玲 (Private Words on Eileen Chang). Hangzhou: Zhejiang wenyi chubanshe, 1995.

Cheng, Bugao 程步高. "Naimei nüshi xiaoshi" 耐梅女士小史 (A Sketch of Miss Nai-mei). *Yingxi chunqiu* 影戏春秋 (Chronicle of Film and Theater), no. 11 (1925).

Cheshire, Godfrey. "Time Span: The Cinema of Hou Hsiao-hsien." *Film Comment* 29, no. 6 (1993): 56–63.

Chiao, Peggy Hsiung-p'ing 焦雄屏. "Dongdong de jiaqi: Tianye, tongnian, qinren guanxi" 冬冬的假期: 田野, 童年, 亲人关系 (*Summer at Grandpa's*: Wild fields, youth, and family relations). In Peggy Hsiung-p'ing Chiao 焦雄屏 ed., *Taiwan xin dianying* 台湾新电影 (New Taiwan Cinema), 137–9. Taipei: Shibao wenhua chuban, 1988.

Chor, Yuan 楚原. *Oral History Archive.* Hong Kong Film Archive, 2006.

Chou, Katherine Hui-ling 周慧玲. *Biaoyan zhongguo: nü mingxing, biaoyan wenhua, shijue zhenzhi, 1910–1945* 表演中国: 女明星, 表演文化, 视觉政治, 1910–1945 (Performing China: Actress, Performance Culture, Visual Politics, 1990–1945). Taipei: Rye Field Publications, 2004.

Chow, Rey. *Primitive Passions: Visuality, Sexuality, Ethnography, and Contemporary Chinese Cinema.* New York: Columbia University Press, 1995.

——. "Autumn Hearts: Filming Feminine 'Psychic Interiority' in *Song of the Exile*." In her *Sentimental Fabulations: Contemporary Chinese Films*, 85–104. New York: Columbia University Press, 2007.

——. "Loving Women: Masochism, Fantasy, and the Idealization of the Mother." In her *Women and Chinese Modernity: The Politics of Reading Between West and East*, 121–72. Minneapolis, MN: University of Minnesota Press, 1991.

Chow, Si-sum 周仕深 and Chang Ling-yan 郑宁恩, eds. *Yueju guoji yantaohui lunwen ji (shang)* 粤剧国际研讨会论文集(上) (International Conference on Cantonese opera, an anthology, vol. 1). Hong Kong: Xianggang zhongwen daxue yinyuexi yueju yanjiu jihua, 2008.

Chu, Hsi-ning 朱西宁, Liu Mu-sha 刘慕沙, Chu T'ien-wen 朱天文, Hsieh Ts'ai-chün 谢材俊, and Chu T'ien-hsin 朱天心. *Xiaoshuo jiazu* 小说家族 (The Fiction Family). Taipei: Xidai shuban youxian gongsi, 1985.

Chu, T'ien-wen 朱天文. *Huangren shouji* 荒人手记 (Notes of a Desolate Man). Taipei: Shibao wenhua chuban, 1994. Trans. Howard Goldblatt and Sylvia Li-chun Lin. New York: Columbia University Press, 1999.

——. *Xiaobi de gushi* 小毕的故事 (The Story of Xiaobi). Taipei: Yuanliu chuban gongsi, 1992.

Claiborne, Craig. *The New York Times Guide to Dining Out in New York*. New York: Atheneum, 1964.

Collins, Felicity. *Australian Cinema After Mabo*. Cambridge: Cambridge University Press, 2004.

——. "Japanese Story: A Shift of Heart." *Senses of Cinema* 29, no. 29. (2003). http://www.sensesofcinema.com/contents/03/29/japanese story.html (accessed on December 17, 2003).

Collins, Patricia Hill. "Gender, Black Feminism, and Black Political Economy." *Annals of the American Academy of Political and Social Science* 568 (2000): 41–53.

Colomina, Beatriz. *Privacy and Publicity: Modern Architecture as Mass Media*. Cambridge, MA: The MIT Press, 1996.

——, ed. *Sexuality and Space*. Princeton, NJ: Princeton Architectural Press, 1992.

Cornelius, Betty. "Esther Eng, Movie Maker, Visit Here." *The Seattle Times*, June 9, 1946.

Cowie, Elizabeth. "Fantasia" *m/f* 9 (1984): 71–104. Reprinted in Elizabeth Cowie, *Representing the Woman: Cinema and Psychoanalysis*. London: Macmillan, 1997.

Creed, Barbara. "Breeding Out the Black: Jedda and the Stolen Generations of Australia." In Barbara Creed and Jeanette Hoorn, eds., *Body Trade: Captivity, Cannibalism and Colonialism in the Pacific*, 208–30. New York: Routledge, 2001.

Crenshaw, Kimberlé. "Demarginalizing the Intersection of Race and Sex: A Black Feminist Critique of Antidiscrimination Doctrine, Feminist Theory and Antiracist Politics." *University of Chicago Legal Forum* (1989): 139–67.

——. "Mapping the Margins: Intersectionality, Identity Politics, and Violence Against Women of Color." *Stanford Law Review* 43, no. 6 (1991): 1241–99.

Cui, Shuqin. *Women through the Lens: Gender and Nation in a Century of Chinese Cinema*. Honolulu: University of Hawaii Press, 2003.

——. "Constructing and Consuming the Revolutionary Narratives." In her *Women through the Lens: Gender and Nation in a Century of Chinese Cinema*, 51–78. Honolulu: University of Hawaii Press, 2003.

——. "Desire in Difference: Female Voice and Point of View in Hu Mei's *Army Nurse*." In her *Women through the Lens: Gender and Nation in a Century of Chinese Cinema*, 200–218. Honolulu: University of Hawaii Press, 2003.

——. "Feminism with Chinese Characteristics?" In her *Women through the Lens: Gender and Nation in a Century of Chinese Cinema*, 171–99. Honolulu: University of Hawaii Press, 2003.

——. "Ning Ying's Beijing Trilogy: Cinematic Configurations of Age, Class, and Sexuality." In Zhang Zhen, ed., *The Urban Generation: Chinese Cinema and Society at the Turn of the Twenty First Century*, 241–63. Durham, NC: Duke University Press, 2007.

389

Cvetkovich, Ann. *An Archive of Feeling: Trauma, Sexuality and Lesbian Public Cultures*. Durham, NC: Duke University Press, 2003.

Dai, Jinhua 戴锦华. *Cinema and Desire: Feminist Marxism and Cultural Politics in the Work of Dai Jinhua*. London: Verso, 2002.

———. "Bu ke jian de nüxing: Dangdai Zhongguo dianying zhong de nüxing yu nüxing de dianying" 不可见的女性—当代中国电影中的女性与女性的电影. *Dangdai dianying* 当代电影 (Contemporary Cinema), no. 6 (1994). Trans. Mayfair Yang as "Invisible Women: Contemporary Chinese Cinema and Women's Film." *Positions* 3, no. 1 (1995): 255–80.

———. "Ren, gui, qing: yige nüren de kunjing" 《人 鬼 情》: 一个女人的困境. In Dai Jinhua 戴锦华, *Wu zhong fengjing* 雾中风景. Beijing: Beijing Daxue chubanshe, 2000. Trans. Kirk Denton as "*Woman, Demon, Human*: A Woman's Predicament." In Jing Wang and Tani E. Barlow, eds., *Cinema and Desire: Feminist Marxism and Cultural Politics in the Work of Dai Jinhua*, 151–71. London: Verso, 2002.

de Lauretis, Teresa. *Alice Doesn't: Feminism, Semiotics, Cinema*. Bloomington, IN: Indiana University Press, 1984.

———. *Technologies of Gender: Essays on Theory, Film, and Fiction*. Bloomington, IN: Indiana University Press, 1987.

———. "Cine-feminism and the Creation of Vision." In *The Global Cartographies of Cine-Feminisms*, 3–10. Seoul: The 10th International Women's Film Festival in Seoul, 2008.

———. "Rethinking Women's Cinema: Aesthetics and Feminist Theory." In her *Technologies of Gender: Essays on Theory, Film, and Fiction*, 127–48. Bloomington, IN: Indiana University Press, 1987.

———. "Sexual Indifference and Lesbian Representation." *Theatre Journal* 40, no. 2 (1988): 155–77.

Devadas, Vijay. "Rethinking Transnational Cinema: The Case of Tamil Cinema." *Senses of Cinema*, no. 41 (2006). http://archive.sensesofcinema.com/contents/06/41/transnational-tamil-cinema.html (accessed on May 5, 2010).

"Dianying dangan: Liu li dao ying" 电影档案: 《流离岛影》 (About *Floating Islands* by Zero Chou). *Taiwan dianying wang* 台湾电影网 (Taiwan Cinema). http://www.taiwancinema.com/ct.asp?xItem=12151&ctNode=252 (accessed on December 12, 2009).

"Dianying gongzuozhe: Zero Chou" 电影工作者: 周美玲 (About Zero Chou). *Taiwan dianying wang* 台湾电影网 (Taiwan Cinema). http://www.taiwancinema.com/ct.asp?xItem=12488&ctNode=39 (accessed on December 12, 2009).

Dianying huabao 电影画报 (The Screen Pictorial), no. 9 (1934). Special memorial issue on Ai Xia's death.

Ding, Xiaoqi 丁小琦. "Nü'er lou" 女儿楼 (*Army Nurse*). In her *Nü'er lou* 女儿楼 (Maiden House), 61–124. Beijing: Writer's Press, 1986.

Doane, Mary Ann. *The Desire to Desire: The Woman's Film of the 1940s*. Bloomington, IN: Indiana University Press; London: Macmillan Press, 1987.

——. *Femmes Fatales: Feminism, Film Theory, Psychoanalysis.* New York: Routledge, 1991.

——. "Film and the Masquerade: Theorizing the Female Spectator." In Patricia Erens, ed., *Issues in Feminist Film Criticism,* 41–57. Bloomington, IN: Indiana University Press, 1991.

——. "The Moving Image: Pathos and the Maternal." In her *The Desire to Desire: The Woman's Film of the 1940s,* 70–95. Bloomington, IN: Indiana University Press, 1987.

——. "The Voice in the Cinema: The Articulation of Body and Space." In Bill Nichols, ed., *Movies and Methods II,* 565–78. Berkeley, CA: University of California Press, 1985.

Donald, Stephanie Hemelryk. *Public Secrets, Public Spaces: Cinema and Civility in China.* Lanham, MD: Rowman & Littlefield, 2000.

Dong, Kena 董克娜. "Wo he dianying yishu" 我和电影艺术 (Film Art and Me). In Yang Yuanying, ed., *Tamen de shengyin: zhongguo nüdaoyan zishu* 她们的声音: 中国女电影导演自述 (Their Voices: Self-narration of Chinese Female Directors), 3–28. Beijing: Zhongguo shehui chubanshe, 1996.

Doyle, Jennifer and Amelia Jones. "New Feminist Theories of Visual Culture." *Signs: Journal of Women in Culture and Society* 31, no. 3 (2006): 607–615. Special issue.

Eagleton, Terry. *Literary Theory: An Introduction.* Oxford: Basil Blackwell, 1983. Trans. Wu Xiaoming 伍晓明 as *Ershi shiji Xifang wenxue lilun* 二十世纪西方文学理论. Xi'an: Shanxi shifan daxue chubanshe, 1988.

Edwards, Louise and Mina Roces, eds. *Women in Asia: Tradition, Modernity and Globalisation.* Ann Arbor, MI: University of Michigan Press, 2000.

Elley, Derek. "Berlin Film Festival Review: *Drifting Flowers.*" *Variety* (February 21, 2008). http://www.variety.com/index.asp?layout=festivals&jump=review&id=2 478&reviewid=VE1117936287&cs=1 (accessed on December 22, 2009).

Endacott, G. B. *A History of Hong Kong.* New York: Oxford University Press, 1973.

Ezra, Elizabeth and Terry Rowden. "General Introduction: What is Transnational Cinema?" In their *Transnational Cinema: The Film Reader,* 1–12. New York: Routledge, 2006.

Ferriss, Suzanne and Mallory Young, eds. *Chick Flicks: Contemporary Women at the Movies.* New York: Routledge, 2008.

Fischer, Lucy. *Shot/Countershot: Film Tradition and Women's Cinema.* Princeton, NJ: Princeton University Press, 1989.

Ford, Stacilee. *Mabel Cheung Yuen-ting's An Autumn's Tale.* Hong Kong: Hong Kong University Press, 2008.

——. "Claiming the Space: Fictionalising-Feminism in Xu Xi's 1990s Hong Kong Novels." *Lilith: A Feminist History Journal* 14 (2005): 52–64.

Foucault, Michel. *Discipline and Punish: The Birth of the Prison.* New York: Vintage Books, 1979.

——. "The Spectacle of the Scaffold." In his *Discipline and Punish: The Birth of the Prison,* 32–69. New York: Vintage Books, 1979.

——. "What is an Author." In Donald F. Bouchard, ed., *Language, Counter-memory, Practice: Selected Essays and Interviews*, 113–38. Trans. Donald F. Bouchard and Sherry Simon. Ithaca, NY: Cornell University Press, 1977.

Fu, Poshek. "Eileen Chang, Woman's Film, and Domestic Culture of Modern Shanghai." *Tamkang Review* 29, no. 4 (1999): 23.

——. "Telling a Woman's Story: Eileen Chang and the Invention of Woman's Film." In *Transcending the Times: King Hu and Eileen Chang* (The 22nd Hong Kong International Film Festival), 131–33. Hong Kong: Provisional Urban Council, 1998.

Fu, Poshek and David Desser. *The Cinema of Hong Kong: History, Arts, Identity*. Cambridge: Cambridge University Press, 2000.

Gaines, Jane. "White Privilege and Looking Relations: Race and Gender in Feminist Film Theory." In E. Ann Kaplan, ed., *Feminism and Film*, 336–55. Oxford: Oxford University, 2000.

Garrett, Roberta. *Postmodern Chick Flicks: The Return of the Woman's Film*. New York: Palgrave MacMillan, 2007.

Gehring, Wes D. *Romantic vs. Screwball Comedy: Charting the Difference*. Lanham, MD: Scarecrow Press, 2002.

Gledhill, Christine, ed. *Home Is Where the Heart Is: Studies in Melodrama and the Woman's Film*. London: BFI, 1987.

Goh, Robbie B.H. and Shawn Wong, eds. *Asian Diasporas: Cultures, Identities, Representations*. Hong Kong: Hong Kong University Press, 2004.

Gopinath, Gayatri. *Impossible Desire: Queer Diasporas and South Asian Public Culture*. Durham, NC: Duke University Press, 2005.

Grant, Catherine. "Secret Agents: Feminist Theories of Women's Film Authorship." *Feminist Theory* 2, no. 1 (2001): 113–30.

Grewal, Inderpal and Caren Kaplan. *Scattered Hegemonies: Postmodernity and Transnational Feminist Practices*. Minneapolis, MN: University of Minnesota Press, 1994.

——. "Postcolonial Studies and Transnational Feminist Practices." *Jouvert: A Journal of Postcolonial Studies* 5, no. 1 (2000). http://english.chass.ncsu.edu/jouvert/v5i1/grewal.htm (accessed on April 20, 2010).

Guess, Carol. "Que(e)rying Lesbian Identity." *The Journal of the Midwest Modern Language Association* 28, no. 1 (1995): 19–37.

Gully, Patti. *Sisters of Heaven*. San Francisco: Long River Press, 2008.

Guo, Shaohua. "Modern Woman in Conflict: Chinese Feminism and the Stardom of Xu Jinglei." Paper presented at Nanjing Conference on Gender and Chinese Cinema, June 2008. Printed in conference booklet, 83–101.

Ha, Marie-Paule. "Double Trouble: Doing Gender in Hong Kong." *Signs: Journal of Women and Culture in Society* 34, no. 2 (2009): 423–49.

Habermas, Jurgen. "Modernity—an Incomplete Project." In Hal Foster, ed., *The Anti-Aesthetic: Essays in Postmodern Culture*, 3–15. Port Townsend, WA: Bay Press, 1983.

Haddon, Rosemary. "Hou Hsiao-hsien's *City of Sadness:* History of the Dialogic Female Voice." In Chris Berry and Feii Lu, eds., *Island on the Edge: Taiwan New Cinema and After,* 55–65. Hong Kong: Hong Kong University Press, 2005.

Hall, Stuart. "Encoding/Decoding." In Stuart Hall et al., *Culture, Media, Language: Working Papers in Cultural Studies, 1972–79,* 128–38. London: Hutchinson, 1980.

Hansen, Miriam. "Fallen Women, Rising Stars, New Horizons: Shanghai Silent Film as Vernacular Modernism." *Film Quarterly* 54, no. 1 (2000): 10–22.

Haraway, Donna. "A Manifesto for Cyborgs: Science, Technology, and Socialist Feminism in the 1980s." *Socialist Review,* no. 80 (1985): 65–107.

Harris, Kristine. "The New Woman Incident: Cinema, Scandal, and Spectacle in 1935 Shanghai." In Sheldon Lu, ed., *Transnational Chinese Cinemas: Identity, Nationhood, Gender,* 277–302. Honolulu: University of Hawaii Press, 1997.

——. "The Romance of the Western Chamber and the Classical Subject Film in 1920s Shanghai." In Yingjin Zhang, ed., *Cinema and Urban Culture in Shanghai, 1922–1943,* 51–73. Stanford, CA: Stanford University Press, 1999.

Haskell, Molly. *From Reverence to Rape: The Treatment of Women in the Movies.* New York: Holt, Rinehart and Winston; New York: Penguin, 1973.

——. "The Woman's Film." In Sue Thornham, ed., *Feminist Film Theory: A Reader,* 31–40. New York: New York University Press, 1999.

Held, Leonard. "Myth and Archetype in Nicolas Roeg's *Walkabout.*" *Post Script* 5, no. 3 (1986): 21–46.

Heng, Geraldine and Janadas Devan. "State Fatherhood: The Politics of Nationalism, Sexuality and Race in Singapore." In Andrew Parker, Mary Russo, Doris Sommer, and Patricia Yaeger, eds., *Nationalism and Sexualities,* 343–64. New York: Routledge, 1991.

Hennessy, Rosemary. "Queer Theory: A Review of the *Differences Special Issue* and Wittig's *The Straight Mind.*" *Signs: Journal of Women in Culture and Society* 18, no. 4 (1993): 964–73.

Hong Kong International Film Festival, ed. *Transcending the Times: King Hu and Eileen Chang* (The 22nd Hong Kong International Film Festival), 150–52. Hong Kong: Provisional Urban Council, 1998.

"Hong Kong yinse xinwenwang" 香港银色新闻网 (Hong Kong Silver Screen News). *Dianying quan* 电影圈 (Screen Voice) 37 (January 16, 1939).

hooks, bell. *Yearning: Race, Gender, and Cultural Politics.* Boston: South End Press, 1990.

——. "The Oppositional Gaze." In Amelia Jones, ed., *The Feminism and Visual Culture Reader,* 99–100. New York: Routledge, 2003.

Hoorn, Jeanette. "Michael Powell's *They're a Weird Mob:* Dissolving the 'Undigested Fragments' in the Australian Body Politic." *Continuum: Journal of Media & Cultural Studies* 17, no. 2 (2003): 159–76.

Hou, Hsiao-hsien 侯孝贤. "Cong 'Fenggui' dao 'Dongdong'" 从《风柜 》到《冬冬》 (From *Boys of Fenggui* to *Summer at Grandpa's*). *Zhongguo shibao* 中国时报 (China Times), November 19, 1984.

Hsia, C. T. *A History of Modern Chinese Fiction*. New Haven, CT: Yale University Press, 1961.

Hsu, Hui-chi 许慧琦. *Nuola zai zhongguo: xin nuxing xingxiang de suzao ji qi yanbian 1900s–1930s* 娜拉在中国: 新女性形象的塑造及其演变 1900s–1930 ("Nora" in China: The Formation and Transformation of the New Woman Image 1900s-1930s). Taipei: National Politics University, 2003.

Huang, Chien-yeh 黄建业. "Dongdong de Jiaqi: Supu de xiangye shengmingguan" 《冬冬的假期: 素朴的乡野生命观》 (*Summer at Grandpa's*: A View of Life with the Simplicity of the Countryside). In his *Renwen dianying de zhuixun* 人文电影的追寻 (In Search of Literary Cinema), 69–74. Taipei: Yuanliu chubanshe, 1990.

"'Huangdao qingyan' jijiang faxing shangyin" 《荒岛情焰》即将发行上映 (Mad Fire, Mad Love, soon to release). *Xinguo ribao* 新中国报 (New China Daily Press), November 11, 1948.

Huang, Jianye 黄建业. *Renwen dianyingde zhuixun* 人文电影追寻 (In Search of a Humanist Cinema). Taipei: Yuanliu, 1990.

Huang, Shuqin 黄蜀芹. "Nüxing dianying—yige dute de shijiao" 女性电影——一个独特的视角 (Women's Film: A Unique Point of View). In Wang Renyin 王人殷, ed., *Dongbian guangying duhao: Huang Shuqin yanjiu wenji* 东边光影独好—黄蜀芹研究文集 (The View East is Special: Research Materials on Huang Shuqin), 151–160. Beijing: Zhongguo dianying chubanshe, 2002.

——. "Nüxing, zai dianyingye de nanren shijieli" 女性，在电影业的男人世界里 (Women, in the Male World of Film Production). *Dangdai dianying* 当代电影 (Contemporary Cinema), no. 5 (1995): 69–71.

——. "Nüxing—zai dianyingye de nanxing shijie li" 女性—在电影业的男性世界里 (Women in the Male World of Film Industry). In S. Louisa Wei and Yang Yuanying, eds., *Nüxing de dianying: duihua zhongri nüdaoyan* 女性的电影: 对话中日女导演 (Women's Films: Dialogues with Chinese and Japanese Female Directors), 55–59. Shanghai: Eastern China University Press, 2009.

——. "Xie zai Hua hun gongying zhi ji" 写在《画魂》公映之际 (On the occasion of the premiere of *The Soul of the Painter*). In Wang Renyin 王人殷, ed., *Dongbian guangying duhao: Huang Shuqin yanjiu wenji* 东边光影独好—黄蜀芹研究文集 (The View East is Special: Research materials on Huang Shuqin), 149. Beijing: Zhongguo dianying chubanshe, 2002.

——. "Zhenzhi de shenghuo/Zhencheng de fanying" 真挚的生活/真诚地反映 (Honest Lives/Faithful Record). *Dianying xinzuo* 电影新作 (New Films), no. 6 (1983): 77–81.

——. "Zhongguo ru jin yi meiyou nüxing dianying" 中国如今已没有女性电影 (To This Day China Still Has No Women's Film). *Shijie dianying zhi chuang* 世界电影之窗 (Window on World Cinema, also known as "Screen"), no. 11 (2007): 28–9.

Huang, Shuqin 黄蜀芹 and Gu Zhengnan 顾征南. "Fang Huang Shuqin tan Ren, gui, qing" 访黄蜀芹谈《人 鬼 情》 (An interview with Huang Shuqin about *Woman, Demon, Human*). *Dianying xinzuo* 电影新作 (New Films), no. 6 (1988): 63–6.

Huang, Shuqin 黄蜀芹 and Xu Feng 徐峰. "Liushi yu chenji: Huang Shuqin fang-tan lu" 流逝与沉积：黄蜀芹访谈录 (Time Passes, Much Remains: A Talk with Huang Shuqin). *Beijing Dianying Xueyuan xuebao* 北京电影学院学报 (Journal of the Beijing Film Academy), no. 2 (1997): 3–21.

Huang, Shuqin 黄蜀芹, Yang Meihui 杨美蕙 and Ge Hua 戈铧. "Zhuiwen ziwo" 追问自我 (Questioning the Self). In Wang Renyin 王人殷, ed., *Dongbian guan-gying duhao: Huang Shuqin yanjiu wenji* 东边光影独好—黄蜀芹研究文集 (The View East is Special: Research Materials on Huang Shuqin). Beijing: Zhongguo dianying chubanshe, 2002.

Hu, Shi 胡适. "Zhongsheng dashi" 终生大事 (The Greatest Event of My Life). *Xin qingnian* 新青年 (New Youth) 6, no. 3 (1919): 311–19.

Hwang Chun-ming 黄春明. "Kan hai de rizi" 看海的日子 (A Flower in the Rainy Night). In Hwang Chun-ming, *Shayounala, zaijian* 莎哟娜啦，再见 (Sayonara, Goodbye). Taipei: Yuanjing Chubanshe, 1976.

Ibsen Special Issue. In *Xin qingnian* 新青年(New Youth) 4, no. 6 (1918).

Irigaray, Luce. *This Sex Which is Not One*. Ithaca: Cornell University Press, 1985.

——. *Speculum of the Other Woman*. Trans. Gillian C. Gill. Ithaca, NY: Cornell University Press, 1985.

Jiang, Qitao 江奇涛. "Mati sheng sui" 马蹄声碎 (Horsehoof). In *Jiefangjun wenyi* 解放军文艺 (People's Liberation Army Art and Literature) 10 (1986): 34–57.

Jin, Fenglan 靳凤兰. *Yige nüdaoyan de dianying shengya* 一个女导演的电影生涯 (The Life and Career of a Female Film Director: A Critical Biography of Dong Kena). Beijing: Xueyuan chubanshe, 1994.

Johnston, Claire. "Dorothy Arzner: Critical Strategies." In her *The Work of Dorothy Arzner: Towards a Feminist Cinema*, 1–8. London: British Film Institute, 1975.

——. "Women's Cinema as Counter-Cinema." In Sue Thornham, ed., *Feminist Film Theory: A Reader*, 31–40. New York: New York University Press, 1999.

——. "Women's Cinema as Counter-Cinema." In her *Notes on Women's Cinema*. London: Society for Film and Television, 1973. Reprinted in Ann Kaplan, ed., *Feminism and Film*, 22–33. Oxford: Oxford University Press, 2000.

Jones, Rai. "Framing Strategies: *Floating Life* and the Limits of 'Australian Cine-ma.'" In Lisa French, ed., *Womenvision: Women and the Moving Image in Austra-lia*, 253–65. Melbourne: Damned Publishing, 2003.

Kam, Louie. "*Floating Life*: Nostalgia for the Confucian Way in Suburban Sydney." In Chris Berry, ed., *Chinese Films in Focus: 25 New Takes*, 97–103. London: BFI, 2003.

Kaplan, Caren, Norma Alarcon, and Minoo Moallem, eds. *Between Woman and Na-tion: Nationalisms, Transnational Feminisms, and the State*. Durham, NC: Duke University Press, 1999.

Kaplan, E. Ann. *Women and Film: Both Sides of the Camera*. London: Routledge, 1983.

——. *Looking for the Other: Feminism, Film and the Imperial Gaze*. New York: Rout-ledge, 1997.

——. "European Art Cinema, Affect and Postcolonialism: Herzog, Denis and the Dardenne Brothers." In Rosalind Galt and Karl Schoonover, eds., *Global Art Cinema*, 285–302. Oxford: Oxford University Press, 2010.

——. "Feminism, Aging and Changing Paradigms." In Devoney Looser and E. Ann Kaplan, eds., *Generations: Academic Feminists in Dialogue*, 13–30. Minneapolis, MN: University of Minnesota Press, 1997.

——. "Feminist Criticism of Claire Johnston and Pam Cook." *Jump Cut: A Review of Contemporary Media* 12, no. 13 (1976): 52–55.

——. "Melodrama/Subjectivity/Ideology: Western Melodrama Theories and Their Relevance to Recent Chinese Cinema." In *East-West Film Journal* 5, no. 1 (1991): 6–27.

——. "Problematizing Cross-Cultural Analysis: The Case of Women in the Recent Chinese Cinema." In Chris Berry, ed., *Perspectives on Chinese Cinema*, 141–154. London: BFI, 1991.

——. "Problematizing Cross-Cultural Analysis: The Case of Women in the Recent Chinese Cinema." *Wide Angle* 2, no. 11 (1989): 40–50.

——. "Trauma Future Tense: The Child in Cuarón's *The Children of Men*." Paper presented at the American Comparative Literature Association Conference, Harvard University, March 26, 2009.

Kendall, Elizabeth. *The Runaway Bride: Hollywood Romantic Comedy of the 1930s*. New York: Doubleday, 1991.

Khoo, Olivia. *The Chinese Exotic: Modern Diasporic Femininity*. Hong Kong: Hong Kong University Press, 2007.

Ko, Dorothy. *Teachers of the Inner Chambers: Women and Culture in Seventeenth-Century China*. Stanford, CA: Stanford University Press, 1994.

Ko, Dorothy, and Wang Zheng, eds. *Translating Feminisms in China*. Malden, MA: Blackwell Publishing, 2007.

——. "Introduction: Translating Feminisms in China." *Gender & History* 18, no. 3 (2006): 463–71.

Kraicer, Shelly. "Film Review: *Fish and Elephant*." *The Inside Out Toronto Lesbian & Gay Film & Video Festival* (2002): 1–3.

Kristéva, Julia. "Women's Time." Trans. Alice Jardine and Harry Blake. *Signs: Journal of Women in Culture and Society* 7, no. 1 (1981): 13–35.

Kwan, Man-ching 关文清. *Zhongguo yintan waishi* 中国银坛外史 (Unofficial History of Chinese Cinema). Hong Kong: Xianggang guangjiaojing chubanshe, 1976.

Lai Hsien-tsung 赖贤宗. "Chaoyue fushi de yishu guanghua: Huang Yushan dianying Nanfang jishi fushi guangying" 超越浮世的艺术光华: 黄玉珊电影《南方纪事浮世光影》 (The Glory of Transcendent Art: Huang Yu-shan's film *The Strait Story*). *Ziyou shibao* 自由时报 (The Liberty Times), November 3, 2005. http://www.libertytimes.com.tw/2005/new/nov/3/life/article-1.htm (accessed on November 27, 2009).

Laing, Heather. *The Gendered Score: Music in 1940s Melodrama and the Woman's Film*. Hampshire, UK: Ashgate, 2007.

Lanser, Susan Sniader. *Fictions of Authority: Women Writers and Narrative Voice.* Ithaca: Cornell University Press, 1992. Trans. Huang Bikang 黄必康 as *Xugou de quanwei—nüxing zuojia yu xushu shengyin* 虚构的权威—女性作家与叙述声音. Beijing: Beijing daxue chubanshe, 2002.

Lao Zi. *Dao De Jing.* Trans. Derek Bryce. Amerystwyth, UK: Cambrian News, 1984.

Lau, Shing-hon 刘成汉. "Tang Shu Shuen—qishi niandai xianggang dianying de duxingzhe" 唐书璇—七十年代香港电影的独行者 (Tang Shu Shuen: The lone rider in Hong Kong cinema in the 1970s). In *Dianying fu bi xing ji* 电影赋比兴集 (A Collection of Films Fu, Bi, Xing), 360–66. Taipei: Yuan Liu, 1992.

Law, Kar. "The Cinematic Destiny of Eileen Chang." In *Transcending the Times: King Hu and Eileen Chang* (The 22nd Hong Kong International Film Festival), 143–46. Hong Kong: Provisional Urban Council, 1998.

——. "The Significance of *The Arch.*" In *A Comparative Study of Post-War Mandarin and Cantonese Cinema–The Films of Zhu Shilin, Qin Jian and Other Directors* (The 7th Hong Kong International Film Festival Publication), 163–64. Hong Kong: Urban Council, 1983.

Law, Kar and Frank Bren. *Hong Kong Cinema: A Cross-Cultural View.* Lanham, MD: Scarecrow Press, 2004.

Lee, Eliza W. Y., ed. *Gender and Change in Hong Kong: Globalization, Postcolonialism, and Chinese Patriarchy.* Hong Kong: Hong Kong University Press, 2003.

Lee, Leo Ou-fan. *Shanghai Modern: The Flowering of a New Urban Culture in China, 1930–1945.* Cambridge, MA: Harvard University Press, 1999.

——. "Eileen Chang and Cinema." *Journal of Modern Literature in Chinese* 2, no. 2 (1999): 37–60.

Lee, Ngo 李我. *Liwo jianggu (yi)* 李我讲古(一) (Lee Ngo Remembers I). Comp. Chow Shu-guy. Hong Kong: Cosmo Books, 2003.

Lee, Sang Wha. "Conceptualizing 'the Asian' and Asian Women's Studies." *Asian Journal of Women's Studies* 14, no. 4 (2008): 28–53.

Letters to Ali. http://www.letterstoali.com (accessed on August 23, 2004).

Leung, Helen Hok-sze. "Queerscapes in Contemporary Hong Kong Cinema." *Positions* 9, no. 2 (2001): 423–47.

Leung, P. K. "Eileen Chang and Hong Kong Urban Cinema." In *Transcending the Times: King Hu and Eileen Chang* (The 22nd Hong Kong International Film Festival), 150–52. Hong Kong: Provisional Urban Council, 1998.

Levine, Philippa. *Gender and Empire.* Oxford: Oxford University Press, 2004.

Li Ang 李昂. *Sha fu* 杀夫 (The Woman of Wrath). In Li Ang 李昂, *Sha fu: Lucheng gushi* 杀夫：鹿城故事 (The Woman of Wrath: Stories of Lu City). Taipei: Lianjing chuban shiye gongsi, 1983.

Liao, Hui-ying 廖辉英. "Youma caizi" 油麻菜籽 (Ah Fei). In Liao Hui-ying 廖辉英, *Youma caizi.* 油麻菜籽 (Ah Fei). Taipei: Huangguan zazhishe, 1983.

Li, Cheuk-to. "The Return of the Father: Hong Kong New Wave and Its Chinese Context." In Nick Browne, et al., eds., *New Chinese Cinemas: Forms, Identities, Politics.* Cambridge: Cambridge University Press, 1994, 160–79.

Li Chih-Ch'iang 李志薔. "Yi ze chuzou de yuyan—Wo jiao A Ming la" 一则出走的 寓言—《我叫阿铭啦》(A Parable about Flight: *Bundled*). *Ziyou shibao* 自由时报 (Liberty Times), August 7, 2001. http://www.libertytimes.com.tw/2001/new/ aug/7/life/article-1.htm (accessed January 5, 2010).

Li Hen 梨痕. "Kan! Ai Xia buda zizhao de kougong" 看!不打自招的口供 (Look! Ai Xia's Voluntary Confession). *Mingxing tekun* 明星特刊 (Star Special Issue) 1, no. 3 (1933): 2.

Li, Lei 李磊. "Yishu dianying: jiannan de shangyehua" 艺术电影: 艰难的商业化 (Art Films: A Difficult Commercialization). In *Zhongwai wenhua jiaoliu* 中外文 化交流 (China and the World Cultural Exchanges), no. 12 (2005): 14–17.

Lim, Song Hwee. *Celluloid Comrades: Representations of Male Homosexuality in Contemporary Chinese Cinemas*. Honolulu: University of Hawaii Press, 2006.

Lin, Fangmei 林芳玫. *Jiedu Qiong Yao aiqing wangguo* 解读琼瑶爱情王国 (Interpreting Qiong Yao's Kingdom of Love). Taipei: Commercial Press, 2006.

Lin, Vita H.S. 林杏鸿. "Jiaohan 'Kaimaila' de nüxing: Taiwan shangyepian daoyan ji qi zuoping yanjiüyanjiu" 叫喊 '开麦拉'的女性: 台湾商业片导演及其作品研究 (Women Who Shout "Action": A Study of Women Directors of Commercial Films in Taiwan). Master's thesis, Institute of Art Studies, National Cheng Kung University, 1999.

Lin, Xianzhi 林贤治. "Nuola: chuzou huo guilai" 娜拉: 出走或归来 (Nora: Leaving or Return). In Hui-chi Hsu 许慧琦, *Nuola zai zhongguo: xin nuxing xingxiang de suzao ji qi yanbian 1900s–1930s* 娜拉在中国: 新女性形象的塑造及其演 变 1900s–1930 ("Nora" in China: The Formation and Transformation of the New Woman Image 1900s–1930s), 133. Taipei: National Politics University, 2003.

Lin, Yutang 林语堂. *Zhongguo chuanqi* 中国传奇 (Chinese Legends) Trans. Chang Jin Yu. Changsa, China: Hillslope Publishing, 1989.

Li, Oufan 李欧梵. "Zhang Ailing yu Haolaiwu dianying" 张爱玲与好莱坞电影 (Eileen Chang and Hollywood Films). In Lin Xingqian 林幸谦, ed., *Zhang Ailing* 张爱玲, 41–42. Hong Kong: Oxford University Press, 2007.

Li Sha 丽莎. "Yi Aixia nushi" 忆艾霞女士 (Remembering Miss Ai Xia). *Dianying huabao* 电影画报 (The Screen Pictorial), no. 9 (1934).

Li, Shaohong 李少红. "Wo de nüxing juewu" 我的女性意识 (My Feminine Consciousness). In Wei Shiyu 魏时煜 and Yang Yuanying, 杨远婴, eds., *Nüxing de dianying: duihua zhongri nüdaoyan* 女性的电影: 对话中日女导演 (Women's Films: Dialogues with Chinese and Japanese Female Directors), 155–63. Shanghai: Eastern China University Press, 2009.

Liu, Shouhua 刘守华. "Zhanhuofengyanzhong de yan'an dianying shiye" 战火烽 烟中的延安电影业 (Yan'an Film Industry during the War). *Bainian chao* 百年潮 (Hundred Year Tide) 1 (2006): 63–67.

Li, Xiaohong 李小红. "1947 nian Shanghai baokan zhong de Zhang Ailing dianying" 1949 年上海报刊中的张爱玲电影 (Eileen Chang's Films Seen through Shanghai

Newspapers and Magazines in 1947). In Lin Xingqian 林幸谦, ed., *Zhang Ailing* 张爱玲, 167–70. Hong Kong: Oxford University Press, 2007.

Li, Yu-ning, ed. *Chinese Women through Chinese Eyes*. New York: M.E. Sharpe, 1992.

Lo, Kwai-Cheung. *Chinese Face/Off: The Transnational Popular Culture of Hong Kong*. Urbana, IL: University of Illinois Press, 2005.

Lu, Annette 吕秀莲. *Xin nüxing zhuyi* 新女性主义 (New Feminism). Taipei: youshi wenhua (Youth Cultural), 1974.

Lu, Hongshi 陆弘石. *Zhongguo dianying shi, 1905–1949: Zaoqi Zhongguo dianying de xushu yu jiyi* 中国电影史, 1905–1949: 早期中国电影的叙述与记忆 (Chinese Film History, 1905–1949: Narratives and Memories in Early Chinese Cinema). Beijing: Wenhua yishu chubanshe, 2005.

Lui, Yi Tin 雷怡天. "Chow Hsuan Talks about the Love Script" 周萱大谈念爱经. *International Screen* 国际影画 143 (1967): 26–27.

Lu, Li 陆离. "Tang Shuxuan fangwen ji" 唐书璇访问记 (Interview with Tang Shu Shuen, 1970). *Zhongguo xuesheng zhoubao* 中国学生报 (Chinese Students' Weekly), 1970.

Lu, Sheldon H. "Filming Diaspora and Identity: Hong Kong and 1997" In Poshek Fu and David Desser, eds., *The Cinema of Hong Kong: History, Arts, Identity*, 274–75. Cambridge: Cambridge University Press, 2000.

Lu, Xiaoning. "Performing, Embodying and Constructing Socialist Subjectivity." PhD dissertation, Stony Brook University, 2007.

Lu, Xun 鲁迅. (signed as Zhao Lingyi). "Lun 'Renyan kewei" 论人言可畏 (On "Human Gossip is Indeed Fearsome"). In *Tai Bai Biweekly*《太白》半月刊 2, no. 5 (1935). Reprinted in Liu Siping 刘思平 and Xing Zuwen 邢祖文, eds., *Lu Xun yu dianying* 鲁迅与电影 (Lu Xun and Cinema), 34–8. Beijing: Zhongguo dianying chubanshe, 1981.

——. "Shanghai wenyi zhi yipie" 上海文艺界之一瞥 (A Glance at Shanghai literature and Art). In Hui-chi Hsu 许慧琦, *Nuola zai zhongguo: xin nuxing xingxiang de suzao ji qi yanbian 1900s–1930s* 娜拉在中国: 新女性形象的塑造及其演变 ("Nora" in China: The Formation and Transformation of the New Woman Image 1900s–1930s), 170. Taipei: National Politics University, 2003.

Lynch, Frank. "An Interview with Woman Movie Director: Tragedy! They Love It." *Seattle Post*, June 2, 1948.

Manalansan IV, Martin F. *Global Divas: Filipino Gay Men in the Diaspora*. Durham, NC: Duke University Press, 2003.

Mann, Susan. *Precious Records: Women in China's Long Eighteenth Century*. Stanford, CA: Stanford University Press, 1997.

Marchetti, Gina. *From Tian'anmen to Times Square: Transnational China and the Chinese Diaspora on Global Screens*. Philadelphia: Temple University Press, 2006.

——. "Gender Politics and Neoliberalism in China: Ann Hui's *The Postmodern Life of My Aunt*." *Visual Anthropology* 22, no. 2–3 (2009): 123–40.

Marchiniak, Katarzyna, Anikó Imre, and Áine O'Healy, eds. *Transnational Feminism in Film and Media: Visibility, Representation, and Sexual Differences*. New York: Palgrave Macmillan, 2007.

——. "Introduction: Mapping Transnational Feminist Media Studies." In their *Transnational Feminism in Film and Media: Visibility, Representation, and Sexual Differences*, 1–18. New York: Palgrave Macmillan, 2007.

Martin, Fran. *Situating Sexualities: Queer Representations in Taiwanese Fiction, Film and Public Culture*. Hong Kong: University of Hong Kong Press, 2003.

Massumi, Brian. "The Autonomy of Affect." In his *Parables for the Virtual: Movement, Affect, Sensation*, 23–45. Durham, NC: Duke University Press, 2002.

Mayne, Judith. *The Woman at the Keyhole: Feminist and Women's Cinema*. Bloomington and Indianapolis: Indiana University Press, 1990.

——. "Female Authorship Reconsidered." In her *The Woman at the Keyhole: Feminist and Women's Cinema*, 89–123. Bloomington, IN: Indiana University Press, 1990.

——. "Female Narration, Women's Cinema: Helke Sander's *The All-Round Reduced Personality/Redupers*." In Patricia Erens, ed., *Issues in Feminist Film Criticism*, 380–94. Bloomington, IN: Indiana University Press, 1990.

——. "Lesbian Looks: Dorothy Arzner and Female Authorship." In Bad Object-Choices, ed., *How Do I Look: Queer Film and Video*, 103–134. Seattle: Bay Press, 1991.

McCabe, Janet. "Conceiving Subjectivity, Sexual Difference and Fantasy Differently: Psychoanalysis Revisited and Queering Theory." In her *Feminist Film Studies: Writing the Woman into Cinema*, 88–111. London: Wallflower, 2004.

McCarthy, Todd. "Eng's Lost Pix, a Chinese Puzzle." *Variety*, August 21–27, 1995.

McLaren, Margaret A. *Feminism, Foucault, and Embodied Subjectivity*. Albany, NY: State University of New York Press, 2002.

McRobbie, Angela. "Chantal Akerman and Feminist Film-making." In Pam Cook and Philip Dodd, eds., *Women and Film: A Sight and Sound Reader*, 198–203. Philadelphia: Temple University Press, 1993.

Mendoza, Breny. "Transnational Feminisms in Question." *Feminist Theory* 3, no. 3 (2002): 295–314.

Meng, Yue 孟悦 and Dai Jinhua 戴锦华. *Fuchu lishi dibiao* 浮出历史地表 (Emerging from the Historical Horizon). Zhengzhou: Henan renmin chubanshe, 1989.

Mercer, John and Martin Schingler. *Melodrama, Genre, Style, Sensibility*. London: Wallflower, 2004.

Minsky, Rosalind. "Commentary on 'The Signification of the Phallus.'" In her *Psychoanalysis and Gender*, 137–77. New York: Routledge, 1996.

Mi-tsou 迷走. "Nüren wufa jinru lishi? Tan Beiqing chengshi zhong de nüxing juese" 女人无法进入历史? 谈《悲情城市》中的女性角色 (Can Women Not Enter History? On Female Characters in *A City of Sadness*). In Mi-tsou 迷走 and Liang Xinhua 梁新华 eds., *Xindianying zhi si: Cong Yiqie Wei Mingtian dao Beiqing Chengshi* 新电影之死: 从《一切为明天》到《悲情城市》(The Death of New Cinema:

From *All for Tomorrow* to *A City of Sadness*), 135–40. Taipei: Tangshan chubanshe, 1991.

Modleski, Tania. "Time and Desire in the Woman's Film." *Cinema Journal* 23, no. 3 (1984): 326–38.

Mohanty, Chandra Talpade. "Cartographies of Struggle—Third World Women and the Politics of Feminism." In Chandra Talpade Mohanty, Ann Russo, and Lourdes Torres, eds., *Third World Women and the Politics of Feminism*, 1–50. Indianapolis: Indiana University Press, 1991.

——. "Under Western Eyes: Feminist Scholarship and Colonial Discourses." In Chandra Talpade Mohanty, Ann Russo, and Lourdes Torres, eds., *Third World Women and the Politics of Feminism*, 1–80. Indianapolis: Indiana University Press, 1991.

Mulvey, Laura. "Film, Feminism and the Avant-Garde." *Framework* 10 (1979): 3–10.

——. "Visual Pleasure and Narrative Cinema." *Screen* 16, no. 3 (1975): 6–18.

Naficy, Hamid. *An Accented Cinema: Exilic and Diasporic Filmmaking*. Princeton, NJ: Princeton University Press, 2001.

Nancy, Jean-luc. *Being Singular Plural*. Trans. Robert D. Richardson and Anne E. O'Byrne. Stanford, CA: Stanford University Press, 2000.

Ng, Janet. *The Experience of Modernity: Chinese Autobiography of the Early Twentieth Century*. Ann Arbor, MI: University of Michigan Press, 2003.

——. "A Moral Landscape: Reading Shen Congwen's Autobiography and Travelogues." In her *The Experience of Modernity: Chinese Autobiography of the Early Twentieth Century*, 119–43. Ann Arbor, MI: University of Michigan Press, 2003.

"Ng Kam Ha chengfeng polang" 伍锦霞乘风破浪 (Ng Kam Ha Breaking Waves). *Ling Sing* 伶星 (Ling Sing) 138 (January 15, 1947), bi-daily edition.

"Ng Kam Ha fan mei zhaogu" 伍锦霞返美招股 (Ng Kam Ha Back to US to Raise Capital). *Yilin* 艺林 (Artland) 62 (November 15, 1939).

"Ng Kam Ha goude ershi bu nanyang yingpian banquan" 伍锦霞购得二十部南洋影片版权 (Ng Kam Ha Acquired Rights of Twenty Nanyang Movies). *Cheng bao* 成报 (Sing Pao), December 28, 1946.

"Ng Kam Ha huaxia huiguan pai yejing" 伍锦霞华夏会馆拍夜景 (Ng Kam Ha Filming Night Scenes in Wah Ha Association). *Zhonghua gongbao* 中华公报 (The United Chinese News), October 4, 1948.

"Ng Kam Ha jiuyue jiang hui mei" 伍锦霞九月将回美 (Ng Kam Ha to Leave for US in September). *Yilin* 艺林 (Artland) 57 (July 1, 1939).

"Ng Kam Ha ji yu fan mei" 伍锦霞急于返美 (Ng Kam Ha Anxious to Return to US). *Xingdao ribao* 星岛日报 (Sing Tao Daily), January 12, 1947.

"Ng Kam Ha paipian zuo kaijing daji" 伍锦霞拍片昨开镜大吉 (Ng Kam Ha Started Shooting Yesterday). *Xinguo ribao* 新中国报 (New China Daily Press), August 19, 1948.

"Ng Kam Ha sumiao" 伍锦霞素描 (A Sketch of Ng Kam Ha). *Dahua* 大华 (Da Hua), October 10, 1947.

"Ng Kam Ha xiayue guiqu" 伍锦霞下月归去 (Ng Kam Ha to Go Home Next Month). *Ling Sing* 伶星 (Ling Sing), September 9, 1946, bi-daily edition.

"Ng Kam Ha xiongxin wanzhang" 伍锦霞雄心万丈 (Ng Kam Ha Full of Ambition). *Cheng bao* 成报 (Sing Pao), December 22, 1946.

"Ng Kam Ha yanqi fanmei" 伍锦霞延期返美 (Ng Kam Ha Postpones Her Home Trip) *Wah Kiu Man Po* 华侨晚报 (Overseas Chinese Daily), September 29, 1946.

"Ng Kam Ha zai tandao paishe qicaipian 'Huangdao liuhen'" 伍锦霞在檀岛拍摄七彩片 "荒岛留痕" (Ng Kam Ha Shooting in Honolulu a Color Film "Traces in a Desert Island") *Yule* 娱乐 (Amusement) 285 (September 8, 1948).

"Ng Kam Ha zhi Zhang Zuokang de xin" 伍锦霞致张作康的信 (Letter to Cheung Jok Hong). *Ling Sing* 伶星 (Ling Sing) 334 (February 19, 1948), bi-daily edition.

Ni, Zhen 倪震. "Yige wanmei de ren shi gudu de" 一个完美的人是孤独的 (A Person Complete in Herself is Lonely). In Wang Renyin 王人殷, ed., *Dongbian guangying duhao: Huang Shuqin yanjiu wenji* 东边光影独好—黄蜀芹研究文集 (The View East is Special: Research Materials on Huang Shuqin), 39–51. Beijing: Zhongguo dianying chubanshe, 2002.

Niu, Hongbao 牛宏宝. *Xifang xiandai meixue* 西方现代美学 (Modern Western Aesthetics). Shanghai: Shanghai renmin chubanshe, 2002.

Nowra, Louis. *Walkabout* (Australian Screen Classics). Sydney: Currency Press & ScreenSound Australia, 2003.

Obituary of Esther Eng. *New York Times*, January 25, 1970.

Obituary of Esther Eng. *New York Times*, January 27, 1970.

Obituary of Esther Eng. *Variety*, February 4, 1970.

Oliver, Kelly. *Witnessing, Beyond Recognition*. Minneapolis, MN: University of Minneapolis Press, 2001.

Ong, Aihwa. *Flexible Citizenship: The Cultural Logics of Transnationality*. Durham, NC: Duke University Press, 1999.

Pang, Laikwan and Day Wong, eds. *Masculinities and Hong Kong Cinema*. Hong Kong: Hong Kong University Press, 2005.

Pickowicz, Paul and Yingjin Zhang. *From Underground to Independent: Alternative Film Culture in Contemporary China*. Lanham, MD: Rowman & Littlefield, 2006.

Price, Vivian. "Nütongzhi zhuti zai zhongwen Zhongwen dianying zhong de jüeqijueqi" 女同志主体在中文电影中的崛起 (Emerging Lesbian Subjectivities in Chinese Films). *Dianying xinshang* 电影欣赏 (Film Appreciation) 118 (2004): 11–19.

Ramanathan, Geetha. *Feminist Auteurs: Reading Women's Films*. London: Wallflower, 2006.

Report on Mad Fire, Mad Love. *Hawaii Chinese Journal*, November 11, 1948.

Report on Mad Fire, Mad Love. *Hawaii Chinese Journal*, November 18, 1948.

Rich, Ruby B. *Chick Flicks: Theories and Memories of the Feminist Film Movement*. Durham, NC: Duke University Press, 1998.

——. "New Queer Cinema." *Sight & Sound* 2, no. 5 (1992): 30–5.

Rofel, Lisa. *Desiring China: Experiments in Neoliberalism, Sexuality, and Public Culture.* Durham, NC: Duke University Press, 2007.

Rubinfeld, Mark. *Bound to Bond: Gender, Genre, and the Hollywood Romantic Comedy.* Westport, CT: Praeger, 2001.

Rushdie, Salman. *The Wizard of Oz.* London: BFI, 1992.

Sang, Tze-Lan D. *The Emerging Lesbian: Female Same-Sex Desire in Modern China.* Chicago: University of Chicago Press, 2003.

Schechner, Richard. *Performance Studies: An Introduction.* London: Routledge, 2002.

Schoene, Berthold. "Queer Politics, Queer Theory, and the Future of 'Identity': Spiraling out of Culture." In Ellen Rooney, ed., *Feminist Literary Theory*, 283–302. Cambridge, MA: Cambridge University Press, 2006.

Scott, Joan Wallach, ed. *Feminism and History.* Oxford: Oxford University Press, 1997.

Sek Kei 石琪. "Dong furen"《董夫人》(*The Arch*). *Zhongguo xuesheng zhoubao* 中国学生周报 (Chinese Students' Weekly) 897 (September 26, 1969).

Shao, Mujun 邵牧君. "Yayi nüxing benwo de tongku—dui Ren, gui, qing de yidian dujie" 压抑女性本我的痛苦—对《人 鬼 情》的一点读解 (The Suffering of the Oppressed Female Self: A Reading of *Woman, Demon, Human*). *Dianying yishu* 电影艺术 (Film Art), no. 8 (1988): 39–42.

Shen, Congwen 沈从文. *Congwen zizhuan* 从文自传 (The Autobiography of Shen Congwen). Taipei: Shiyue chubanshe, 1969.

Shen, Hao 沈诰, trans. "Nuzi yu daoyanjia" 女子与导演家 (Women and Directors). *Mingxing Tekan* 明星特刊 (Star Special Issue), no. 6 (1925): 1–2.

Shen, Shiao-Ying 沈晓茵. "Jiehe yu fenli de zhengzhi yu meixue: Xu Anhua yu Luo Zhuoyao duei Xianggang de yongbao yu shiluo" 结合与分离的政治与美学: 许鞍华与罗卓瑶对香港的拥抱与失落 (Politics and Aesthetics of Connecting and Splitting: Ann Hui and Clara Law's Love and Loss of Hong Kong). *Zhongwai wenxue* 中外文学 (Chung-Wai Literary Monthly) 29, no. 10 (2001): 35–50.

——. "Locating Feminine Writing in Taiwan Cinema: A Study of Yang Hui-shan's *Body* and Sylvia Chang's *Siao Yu*." In Sheldon H. Lu and Emilie Yueh-yu Yeh, eds., *Chinese Language Film: Historiography, Poetics, Politics*, 266–79. Honolulu: University of Hawaii Press, 2005.

——. "Obtuse Music and Nebulous Males: The Haunting Presence of Taiwan in Hong Kong Films of the 1990s." In Laikwan Pang and Day Wong, eds., *Masculinities and Hong Kong Cinema*, 119–36. Hong Kong: Hong Kong University Press, 2005.

Shih, Shu-mei. *Visuality and Identity: Sinophone Articulations across the Pacific.* University of California Press, 2007.

Shing, Kofeng 成可风. *Interviews with Friends of Esther Eng.* New York City, 1999–2000.

Shi Ying 时影. "Shouwei zisha de nu mingxing Ai Xia" 首位自杀的女明星艾霞 (Ai Xia—The First Female Star Who Committed Suicide). In Shi Ying 时影, ed.,

Minguo dianying 民国电影 (Republican Cinema), 203. Beijing: Tuanjie chuban-she, 2004.

Shohat, Ella. Introduction to her ed., *Talking Visions: Multicultural Feminism in a Transnational Age*, 1–64. New York: New Museum of Contemporary Art; Cambridge, MA: The MIT Press, 1998.

——. "Area Studies, Gender Studies, and the Cartographies of Knowledge." *Social Text*, 20, no. 3 (2002): 67–8.

——. "Post-Third-Worldist Culture: Gender, Nation, and the Cinema." In Elizabeth Ezra and Terry Rowden, eds., *Transnational Cinema: The Film Reader*, 39–56. New York: Routledge, 2006.

Shui, Jing 水晶. *Zhang Ailing de xiaoshuo yishu* 张爱玲的小说艺术 (Eileen Chang's Art of Fiction). 3rd ed. Taipei: Dadi chubanshe, 2000.

Silverman, Kaja. *The Acoustic Mirror: The Female Voice in Psychoanalysis and Cinema*. Bloomington, IN: Indiana University Press, 1988.

——. *Threshold of the Visible World*. New York: Routledge, 1996.

——. "Dis-embodying the Female Voice." In Patricia Erens, ed., *Issues in Feminist Film Criticism*, 309–27. Bloomington, IN: Indiana University Press, 1990.

——. "The Female Authorial Voice." In her *The Acoustic Mirror: The Female Voice in Psychoanalysis and Cinema*, 187–234. Bloomington, IN: Indiana University Press, 1988.

——. "Fragments of a Fashionable Discourse." In Tania Modleski, ed., *Studies in Entertainment*, 139–52. Bloomington, IN: Indiana University Press, 1986.

Sing, Wah 盛华. "Yu Tang Shuxuan tan dianying" 与唐书璇谈电影 (Talking about Film with Tang Shu Shuen). *Tupou* 突破 (Breakthrough Magazine), (October 15, 1969): 28–30.

Smelik, Anneke. *And the Mirror Cracked: Feminist Cinema and Film Theory*. New York: St. Martin's Press, 1998.

Song, Zhao 宋昭. *Mama de yisheng: Wang Ping zhuan* 妈妈的一生：王苹传 (The Life of My Mother: Biography of Wang Ping). Beijing: Zhongguo dianying chuban-she, 2007.

Stokes, Lisa Odham and Michael Hoover. *City on Fire: Hong Kong Cinema*. London: Verso, 1999.

Su, Tong 苏童. "Hongfen" 红粉 (Blush). In *Su Tong zuopin ji* 苏童作品集 (Selected Works of Su Tong), 193–234. Taiyuan: Beiyue Art and Literature Press, 1999.

Su, Weizhen 苏伟贞. "Zikua yu zibi: Zhang Ailing de shuxin yanchu" 自夸与自闭：张爱玲的书信演出 (Self-praise and Self-debasement: Eileen Chang's Performance via Letter Writing). In Lin Xingqian 林幸谦, ed., *Zhang Ailing: Wenxue, dianying, wutai* 张爱玲：文学，电影，舞台 (Eileen Chang: Literature, Film, Stage), 27–39. Hong Kong: Oxford University Press, 2007.

Sugg, Katherine. *Gender and Allegory*. London: Palgrave, 2008.

Suleiman, Susan. *Authoritarian Fictions: The Ideological Novel as a Literary Genre*. New York: Columbia University Press, 1983.

Szeman, Imre. "Who's Afraid of National Allegory? Jameson, Literary Criticism, Globalization." *South Atlantic Quarterly* 100, no. 3 (2001): 803–27.

Tan, E. K. "Desire, Repetition, Subjectivity: Unknown Woman as Phallic Signifier." Paper written for Nanjing Conference on Gender and Chinese Cinema, 2008. Printed in conference papers booklet, 115–19.

Tang, Na 唐纳. "Ai Xia zhi zi" 艾霞之死 (The Death of Ai Xia). *Dianying huabao* 电影画报 (The Screen Pictorial), no. 9 (1934): 5.

——. "Lun 'xin nüxing' de piping" 论新女性的批评 (My Critique of New Woman). *Ming Bao* 明报 (Ming Newspaper), February 26, 1935.

Tang, Shu Shuen. "Director's Notes" and "Production Notes." Publicity pamphlet of *The Arch*, 1969.

Tay, William. "The Ideology of Initiation: The Films of Hou Hsiao-hsien." In Nick Browne, Paul G. Pickowicz, Vivian Sobchack, and Esther Yau, eds., *New Chinese Cinemas: Forms, Identities, Politics*, 151–59. Cambridge: Cambridge University Press, 1994.

Teo, Stephen. *Hong Kong Cinema: The Extra Dimensions*. London: British Film Institute, 1997.

——. "Chinese Melodrama: The Wenyi Genre." In Linda Badley, et al., eds., *Traditions in World Cinema*, 203–13. New Brunswick, NJ: Rutgers University Press, 2006.

——. "Reverence and Fear: Hong Kong's China Syndrome." In his *Hong Kong Cinema: The Extra Dimensions*, 207–18. London: BFI, 1997.

Thompson, Kristin and David Bordwell. "Space and Narrative in the Films of Ozu." *Screen* 17, no. 2 (1976): 41–73.

Tsai, Eva. "Kaneshiro Takeshi: Transnational Stardom and the Media and Culture Industries in Asia's Global/Postcolonial Age." *Modern Chinese Literature and Culture* 17, no. 1 (2005): 100–32.

Turim, Maureen. *Flashbacks in Film: Memory and History*. New York: Routledge, 1989.

Turner, Graeme. *Making It National: Nationalism and Australian Popular Culture*. Sydney: Allen & Unwin, 1994.

Turner, Matthew. "Hong Kong Design and the Roots of the Sino-American Trade Disputes." *Annals of the American Academy of Political and Social Science* 547 (1996): 37–53.

Vineberg, Steve. *High Comedy in American Movies: Class and Humor from the 1920s to the Present*. Lanham, MD: Rowman & Littlefield, 2005.

von Moltke, Johannes. *No Place Like Home: Locations of Heimat in German Cinema*. Durham, NC: Duke University Press, 2005.

Wai, Chi Chuk 尉迟速. "Liangwei guopian qingnian daoyan: Tang Shuxuan, Tu Zhongxun" 两位国片青年导演: 唐书璇、屠忠训 (Two Young Chinese Directors: Tang Shu Shuen and To Chung Fun). *Xianggang shibao* 香港时报 (Hong Kong Times), October 15, 1970.

405

Wang, Ban. *The Sublime Figure of History: Aesthetics and Politics in Twentieth-Century China*. Stanford, CA: Stanford University Press, 1997.

——. "The Cold War, Imperial Aesthetics, and Area Studies." *Social Text* 20, no. 3 (2002): 45–65.

Wang, Chen-ho (Wang Zhenhe) 王祯和. *Jiazhuang yi niuche* 嫁妆一牛车 (An Oxcart for a Dowry). Taipei: Jinzita chubanshe, 1969.

Wang, Dewei 王德威. *Luodi de maizi busi: Zhang Ailing yu "Zhangpai" chuanren* 落地的麦子不死: 张爱玲与 "张派"传人 (Wheat Dropped to the Ground Is Not Dead: Eileen Chang and the Inheritors of the "Chang School"). Jinan: Shandong huabao chubanshe, 2004.

Wang, Lingzhen 王玲珍. "Chinese Women's Cinema." In Yingjin Zhang, ed., *A Companion to Chinese Cinema*. Oxford: Blackwell Publishing, forthcoming.

——. "Hua Mulan xushi de beihou: zai kan Huang Shuqin de Ren, gui, qing" 花木兰叙事的背后: 再看黄蜀芹的《人 鬼 情》(The Other Side of the Hua Mulan Story: A Critical Re-viewing of Huang Shuqin's Film *Woman, Demon, Human*). In Zhang Hongsheng 张宏生 and Qian Nanxiu 钱南秀, eds., *Zhongguo wenxue: chuantong yu xiandai de duihua* 中国文学—传统与现代的对话 (Chinese Literature: A Dialogue between Tradition and Modernity), 652–673. Shanghai: Shanghai guji chubanshe, 2007.

——. "Nüxing de jingjie: lishi, xingbie he zhutijiangou—jianlun Ma Xiaoying de Shijieshang zui tengwo de ren qule" 女性的境界: 历史, 性别, 和主体建构: 兼论马晓颖的《世界上最疼我的那个人去了》(Female Cinematic Imaginary: History, Gendered Subjectivity, and Ma Xiaoying's *Gone Is the One Who Held Me Dearest in the World*). *Chung-Wai Literary Monthly* 34, no. 11 (2006): 27–52.

Wang, Shuo 王朔. *Dongwu xiongmeng* 动物凶猛 (The Animal Is Ferocious). Beijing: Zhongguo wenlian chubanshe, 2009.

Wang, T'o (Wang Tuo) 王拓. *Jinshui Shen* 金水婶 (Auntie Jinshui). Taipei: Xiangcaoshan, 1976.

Wang, Wen-hsing 王文兴. *Jiabian* 家变 (Family Metamorphosis). Taipei: Hongfan Chubanshe, 1973

Wang, Zongyuan 王宗元. "Hui Sao—gushi lide gushi" 惠嫂—故事里的故事 (Hui's Wife—the Story within the Story). *Renmin ribao* 人民日报 (People's Daily), 1961.

Watson, Scott and Shengtian Zheng. *Art of the Great Proletarian Cultural Revolution: 1966–1976*. Catalogue for the Morris and Helen Belkin Art Gallery, Vancouver, 2002.

Wei, Hui 卫慧. *Shanghai Baby* 上海宝贝. Trans. Bruce Humes. New York: Washington Square Press, 1999; New York: Simon & Schuster, 2001.

Wei, S. Louisa (Wei, Shiyu) 魏时煜. "Bainian yinmu nüxing he nüxing dianying chuantong de shanbian" 百年银幕女性和女性电影传统的嬗变 (Transformations of Women's Screen Images and Women's Cinema in the Last One-hundred Years). In Yang Yuanyin 杨远婴, ed., *Zhongguo dianying zhuanyeshi yanjiu: dianying wenhua juan* 中国电影专业史研究：电影文化卷 (Study of Chinese Film History: Volume on Cinematic Culture), 439–503. Beijing: Zhongguo dianying chubanshe, 2006.

——."Women's Trajectories in Chinese and Japanese Cinemas: A Chronological Overview." In Kate E. Taylor, ed., *Dekalog 4: On East Asian Filmmakers*. London: Wallflower Press, forthcoming.

Wei, Shiyu 魏时煜 and Yang Yuanying 杨远婴. *Nüxing de dianying: duihua zhongri nüdaoyan* 女性的电影：对话中日女导演 (Women's Films: Dialogues with Chinese and Japanese Female Directors). Shanghai: Eastern China University Press, 2009.

Wen, He 文河. "Yibu chetouchewei de bagua dianying" 一部彻头彻尾的八卦电影 (A Total Gossip Film). In *Zhongguo xinwen zhoukan* 中国新闻周刊 (China News Weekly), July 10, 2006, 68–69.

Wern. "Review of *Golden Gate Girl*," directed by Esther Eng. *Variety*, May 28, 1941.

Wexman, Virginia W., ed. *Introduction to Film and Authorship*, 1–20. New Brunswick, NJ: Rutgers University Press, 2003.

Wexman, Virginia W. and Karen Hollinger, eds. *Letter from an Unknown Woman*. New Brunswick, NJ: Rutgers University Press, 1986.

Widmer, Ellen and Kang-i Sun, eds. *Writing Women in Late Imperial China*. Stanford, CA: Stanford University Press, 1997.

Wong, Mary, ed. *Hong Kong Filmography, vol. 1, 1913–1941*. Hong Kong: Hong Kong Film Archive, 1997.

Wray, B. J. "Performing Clits and Other Lesbian Tricks." In Amelia Jones and Andrew Strephenson, eds., *Performing the Body Performing the Text*, 186–98. New York: Routledge, 1999.

"Wu Dip Ying yefang Ng Kam Ha" 胡蝶影夜访伍锦霞 (Wu Dip Ying Paid Ng Kam Ha a Night Visit). *Cheng bao* 成报 (Sing Pao), January 15, 1947.

Wu, Nien-chen 吴念真 and Chu T'ien-wen 朱天文. *Beiqing Chengshi* 《悲情城市》 (*A City of Sadness*). Taipei: Sansan shufang, 1989.

Wu, Peng 胡鹏. *Wo yu huangfeihung: wushinian dianying daoyan shengya huiyilu* 我与黄飞鸿：五十年电影导演生涯回忆录 (Me and Wong Fai-hung: My 50 Years in Film). Hong Kong: Sanhe maoyi gongsi, 1995.

Xia, Yan 夏衍. "Shui zhi Ai Xia yu si?" 谁致艾霞于死? (Who killed Ai Xia?). In Cheng Jihua, ed., *Xia Yan dianying wenji* 夏衍电影文集 (Collection of Xia Yan's Writings on Film), 44–45. Beijing: Zhongguo dianying chubanshe, 2000.

Xu, Gary. *Sinascape: Contemporary Chinese Cinema*. Lanham, MD: Rowman & Littlefield, 2007.

Xu, Jian. "*Blush* from Novella to Film: The Possibility of Critical Art in Commodity Culture." In *Modern Chinese Literature and Culture* 12, no. 1 (2000): 115–63.

Xu, Jinglei 徐静蕾. "Xu Jinglei: qinqing dadong" 徐静蕾：亲情打动 (Xu Jinglei: Moved by Kinship). Interview in *Renmin luntan* 人民论坛 (People's Forum), no. 2 (2004): 56–58.

407

———. "Xu Jinglei: Wo de mubiao shi dang ge zajia" 我的目标是当个杂家 (My Aim Is to Become a Dilettante). Interview in *Dazhong dianying* 大众电影 (Popular Cinema), no. 6 (2007): 34–37.

Xu, Jinglei 徐静蕾 and Sun Ganlu 孙甘露. "Zhuanhuan yu yanyuan daoyan zhijian" 转换于演员导演之间 (Between Acting and Directing). In Ge Fei, Jia Zhangke, et al., *Yigeren de dianying* 一个人的电影 (One Person's Film), 295–309. Beijing: China Citic Press, 2008.

"Yang Naimei juantu chonglai" 杨耐梅卷土重来 (Yang Naimei Made Her Comeback). *Dazhong yingxun* 大众影讯 (Popular Movie News) 2, no. 49 (1942).

Xu, Minxia 徐敏霞. "Zhan zai shijisui de weiba shang 站在十几岁的尾巴上" (Before Turning Twenty). In Zhao Changtian, ed., *Shaonian Wenzhang Jing Tianxia* 少年文章惊天下 (Young Writings that Startled the World), 152–162. Hong Kong: Cosmo Books, 2001.

Yau, Ching 游静. *Filming Margins: Tang Shu Shuen, A Forgotten Hong Kong Woman Director.* Hong Kong: Hong Kong University Press, 2004.

———. *Xing/bie guangying: Xianggang dianying zhong de xingbie wenhua yanjiu* 性/别光影: 香港电影中的性别文化研究 (Sexing Shadows: Genders and Sexualities in Hong Kong Cinema). Hong Kong: Hong Kong Film Critics' Society, 2005.

Yau, Esther. "Border Crossing: Mainland China's Presence in Hong Kong Cinema." In Nick Browne, et al., eds., *New Chinese Cinemas: Forms, Identities, Politics*, 180–201. Cambridge: Cambridge University Press, 1994.

———, ed. "Introduction: Hong Kong Cinema in a Borderless World." In her *At Full Speed: Hong Kong Cinema in a Borderless World*, 1–31. Minneapolis, MN: University of Minnesota Press, 2001.

Yeh, Emilie Yueh-yu 叶月瑜. "Nüren zhende wufa jinru lishi ma? Zai du Beiqing chengshi" 女人真的无法进入历史吗? 再读《悲情城市》(Do Women Really Have No Way to Enter History? A Re-examination of *A City of Sadness*). *Dangdai* 当代 (Contemporary) 101 (1994): 64–83.

———. "*A Summer at Grandpa's*." In Yingjin Zhang and Zhiwei Xiao, eds., *Encyclopedia of Chinese Film*, 323. New York: Routledge, 1998.

Yeh, Emilie Yueh-yu 叶月瑜 and Darrell William Davis. *Taiwan Film Directors: A Treasure Island.* New York: Columbia University Press, 2005.

———. "Trisecting Taiwan Cinema with Hou Hsiao-hsien." In their *Taiwan Film Directors: A Treasure Island*, 133–76. New York: Columbia University Press, 2005.

Yi, Lijing 易立静. "Xu Jinglei." In *Renwu zhoukan* 人物周刊 (Southern People Weekly), April 21, 2006, 34–36.

Ying, Di 英娣. "The Death of Ai Xia." *Dianying huabao* 电影画报 (The Screen Pictorial), no. 9 (1934): 23.

"Ying fang hui" 迎芳会 (Reception Party for Wai Kim Fong). *Meigui*《玫瑰》(Rose) 11 (1936).

Yip, June. *Envisioning Taiwan: Fiction, Cinema, and the Nation in the Cultural Imaginary.* Durham, NC: Duke University Press, 2004.

Young, Helen Praeger. *Choosing Revolution: Chinese Women Soldiers on the Long March*. Chicago: University of Chicago Press, 2001.

Yu, Azed 游婷敬. "Wenxue bichu xia de nüxing shenying: Qiantan Huang Yushan de dianying" 文学笔触下的女性身影—浅谈黄玉珊的电影 (Literary Images of Women: Some Thoughts on the Films of Huang Yu-shan). *Taiwan dianying biji* 台湾电影笔记 (Taiwan Film Notes), May 8, 2004. http://movie.cca.gov.tw/files/15-1000-753,c138-1.php (accessed on October 15 2009).

Yu, Hua 余华. "Zhanli" 战栗 (Shudder). In his *Yu Hua zuopin ji* 余华作品集 (Selected Works of Yu Hua) 2: 239–74. Beijing: Zhongguo shehui kexue chubanshe, 1994.

Zhang, Ailing 张爱玲. *Zhang Ailing quanji* 张爱玲全集 (Collected Works of Eileen Chang). Multiple vols. Taipei: Huangguan, 1991.

Zhang, Huijun 张会军 and Ma Yufeng 马玉峰, eds. "Suoyou de jinbu doushi zai chengdan zeren de guocheng zhong dedao de: yingpian Yige mosheng nüren de laixin daoyan chuangzuo tan" 所有的进步都是在承担责任的过程中得到的：影片《一个陌生女人的来信》导演创作谈 (All Progress is Achieved Through the Process of Taking Responsibility: A Conversation with the Film Director of *Letter from an Unknown Woman*). In *Beijing dianying xueyuan bao* 北京电影学院学报 (Journal of the Beijing Film Academy), no. 3 (2005): 52–60.

Zhang, Junxiang 张骏祥, Xu Sangchu 徐桑楚, Ye Ming 叶明, et al. "Zhizhe de yishu zhuiqiu—Shangying xin pian Ren, gui, qing zuotan" 执着的艺术追求—上影新片《人 鬼 情》座谈 (A Steadfast Artistic Ambition: A Symposium on *Woman, Demon, Human*, the new film from the Shanghai Film Studio). *Dianying xinzuo* 电影新作 (New Films), no. 2 (1998): 54–62.

Zhang, Nuanxin 张暖忻 and Li Tuo 李陀. "Tan dianying yuyan de xiandai hua" 谈电影语言的现代化 (On the Modernization of Film Language). *Dianying wenyi* 电影文艺 (Film Art), no. 3 (1979): 79–80.

Zhang, Shichuan 张石川. "Zi wo daoyan yilai" 自我导演以来 (Since I Started Directing). *Mingxing banyuekan* 明星半月刊 (Star Biweekly) 1, no. 5 (1935): 9–11.

Zhang, Xian 张弦. "Guanyu Qingchun wansui gaibian de yi feng xin" 关于《青春万岁》改编的一封信 (A Letter about the Screen Adaptation of *Forever Young*). *Dianying xinzuo* 电影新作 (New Films), no. 1 (1983): 77–79.

Zhang, Yingjin 张英进. *Chinese National Cinema*. New York: Routledge, 2004.

——. *Screening China: Critical Interventions, Cinematic Reconfigurations, and the Transnational Imaginary in Contemporary Chinese Cinema*. Ann Arbor, MI: Center for Chinese Studies, 2002.

——. "Lu Xun . . . Zhang Ailing: Zhongguo xiandai wenxue yanjiu de liubian" 鲁迅 . . . 张爱玲：中国现代文学研究的流变 (Lu Xun . . . Eileen Chang: Transformation of Modern Chinese Literature Studies). *Zuojia* 作家 (Writer Magazine) 7 (2009): 2–9.

Zhang, Zhen, ed. *The Urban Generation: Chinese Cinema and Society at the Turn of the 21st Century*. Durham, NC: Duke University Press, 2007.

Zheng, Shusen 郑树森. "Zhang Ailing de Taitai wansui" 张爱玲的《太太万岁》(Eileen Chang's *Long Live the Wife*). In Chen Zishan, ed., *Siyu Zhang Ailing* 私语张爱玲 (Private Words on Eileen Chang), 219. Hangzhou: Zhejiang wenyi chubanshe, 1995.

——. "Zhang Ailing, Laiya, Bulaixite" (Eileen Chang, Reyher, Bretch). In Chen Zishan, ed., *Siyu Zhang Ailing* 私语张爱玲 (Private Words on Eileen Chang), 215. Hangzhou: Zhejiang wenyi chubanshe, 1995.

——. "Zhang Ailing yu Aile zhongnian" 张爱玲与哀乐中年 (Eileen Chang and Sorrows and Joys at Middle Age). In Chen Zishan 陈子善, ed., *Siyu Zhang Ailing* 私语张爱玲 (Private Words on Eileen Chang), 221. Hangzhou: Zhejiang wenyi chubanshe, 1995.

Zhou, Fenling 周芬玲. *Yanyi: Zhang Ailing yu Zhongguo wenxue* 艳异: 张爱玲与中国文学 (Gorgeous Differences: Eileen Chang and Chinese Literature). Taipei: Yuanzun, 1999.

Index

FILM AND CULTURE A SERIES OF COLUMBIA UNIVERSITY PRESS

EDITED BY **John Belton**

Intelligence Work: The Politics of American Documentary
JONATHAN KAHANA

Eye of the Century: Film, Experience, Modernity
FRANCESCO CASETTI

Shivers Down Your Spine: Cinema, Museums, and the Immersive View
ALISON GRIFFITHS

Weimar Cinema: An Essential Guide to Classic Films of the Era
NOAH ISENBERG

African Film and Literature: Adapting Violence to the Screen
LINDIWE DOVEY

Film, A Sound Art
MICHEL CHION

Film Studies: An Introduction
ED SIKOV

Hollywood Lighting from the Silent Era to Film Noir
PATRICK KEATING

Levinas and the Cinema of Redemption: Time, Ethics, and the Feminine
SAM B. GIRGUS

Counter-Archive: Film, the Everyday, and Albert Kahn's Archives de la Planète
PAULA AMAD

Indie: An American Film Culture
MICHAEL Z. NEWMAN

Pretty: Film and the Decorative Image
ROSALIND GALT

Film and Stereotype: A Challenge for Cinema and Theory
JÖRG SCHWEINITZ

Hideous Progeny: Disability, Eugenics, and Classic Horror Cinema
ANGELA M. SMITH